COMPARATIVE MASS MEDIA SYSTEMS

COMPARATIVI

LONGMAN SERIES IN
PUBLIC COMMUNICATION

SERIES EDITOR: RAY ELDON HIEBERT

MASS MEDIA SYSTEMS

L. JOHN MARTIN
ANJU GROVER CHAUDHARY

Comparative Mass Media Systems

Longman Inc., 1560 Broadway,
New York, N.Y. 10036
Associated companies, branches, and
representatives throughout the world.

Developmental Editor: Gordon T. R. Anderson
Editorial and Design Supervisor: Diane Perlmuth
Interior Designer: Antler & Baldwin, Inc.
Production Supervisor: Ferne Y. Kawahara
Manufacturing Supervisor: Marion Hess

Library of Congress Cataloging in Publication Data
Main entry under title:

Comparative mass media systems.

   (Longman series in public communication)
   Includes index.
   1. Mass media—Social aspects.   2. Underdeveloped
areas—Mass media.   3. Mass media—Communist
countries.   I. Martin, L. John (Leslie John),
1921–   . II. Chaudhary, Anju Grover, 1945–
III. Series.
HM258.C58916   1983   302.2′34   82-14908
ISBN 0-582-28328-0
ISBN 0-582-28327-2 (pbk.)

Manufactured in the United States of America

CONTENTS

v

PREFACE

Metacommunication, or the study of the workings of communication systems, mass media, and journalism in general, is a field that has fascinated many people for at least three hundred years. Numerous books and articles have been and continue to be written about the press of individual countries, of regions of the world, and of the entire world. They discuss mass media descriptively, analytically, and anecdotally.

This is not another book on the press, radio, television, and film in individual countries, regions, or the world as a whole. Rather, it considers some important concepts and functions of mass communication, and it does so comparatively.

In addition to an overview of world mass media systems, six key concepts or functions of the media are analyzed in the book.

1. The concept of news. What do we mean when we speak of news? Is news the same thing everywhere? Would an editor or reporter in Cairo, Egypt, use the same criteria for selecting a news item as would his counterpart in Cairo, Illinois?

2. The concept of the role of mass media. Do they play the same social, political, and economic roles in Moscow, Idaho, as they play in the Moscow of the Soviet Union? What differences are there in the roles media are assigned and in their spontaneous functions in various parts of the world?

3. The educational, persuasive, and opinion-making function of the media. Are they exercised in the same way and by the same groups and individuals in Santiago, Chile, as they are in Santiago, Spain?

4. The entertainment function of mass media. Do mass media have an entertainment role universally, and if not, how does the concept of this role differ in various parts of the world?

5. The concept of press freedom. Do we consider this concept to be the same everywhere, and if not, what are the differences?
6. The concept of media economics. Someone has to pay for media operations, but how and by whom should the costs be defrayed?

We could have made the comparisons country by country, but this would have been an endless task. Besides, many countries approach mass media in the same way. A continental approach also seemed unnecessarily complicated and duplicative. We finally decided to generalize about the First, Second, and Third Worlds, by which we mean the West, the Communist countries, and those developing countries lumped together as the Third World. This approach poses problems, as will become apparent, because often there are almost as many differences within a system as there are between systems. But there are differences within a single country too. The breakdown seemed to lend itself best to rough generalizations.

We had some important help with the essays on the Third World from John C. Merrill, who selected and worked with contributors on that part of the world. Similarly, John J. Karch served as our adviser and editor for the Communist world. We are grateful to them for their counsel and assistance. It would have been difficult to put a book of this nature together without their help.

The contributors to this volume were carefully selected for their expertise in the topic on which they write and the system they cover. Many are nationals of countries within that system. All are authors of other important works in the field of comparative mass communication, although they may not have focused on a single concept or function of mass media as they were asked to do for this book. For that reason they found this approach both novel and intriguing. We are grateful to them for trying to live within the tight deadlines we imposed on them.

We also wish to thank the series editor, Ray E. Hiebert, for his encouragement and his many suggestions, and Gordon T. R. Anderson, executive editor at Longman, our publisher, for his patience, support, and wisdom when things seemed to be going contrary to plan.

Finally, we want to thank our families for their willingness to put up with our long and erratic hours during the preparation of this book.

L. John Martin
Anju Grover Chaudhary

College Park, Maryland

COMPARATIVE MASS MEDIA SYSTEMS

PART 1

WORLD MASS MEDIA SYSTEMS

---

1. GOALS AND ROLES OF MEDIA SYSTEMS

L. JOHN MARTIN
ANJU GROVER CHAUDHARY

NEWS MEDIA

On his return to Venice from China, Tibet, and India in 1330, a saintly and ascetic Franciscan friar, Odoric, brought news of the binding of women's feet in China and the training of cormorants to fish. No one in Venice had ever heard of such things, and so his report was a newsy feature story. He also reported on a land of dog-faced people and on a species of fowl with two heads. This, too, was of great interest to the people of Venice, who had only recently heard similar news stories from Asia by another Venetian "foreign correspondent," Marco Polo.

What is news? Is it anything people want to hear or read about, whether or not it is true? If it has to be true, how do we distinguish between news and non-news in any day's newspaper? Note that our early reporter, Friar Odoric, had some factual reports and some of questionable accuracy—you take your pick.

1

All people are intrigued by curious stories such as the ones that Friar Odoric told after his years of travels in Asia. Not all such news gets into the press in certain areas of the world. But the stories are told in coffeehouses or at the well by travelers and gossips worldwide.

Obviously, one must distinguish between what is news and what is considered appropriate content for mass media. Journalists and scholars have a hard time defining news. There are dozens of definitions in textbooks and professional journals. One reason for this difficulty is that most authors fail to recognize an important distinction. News per se can be defined pretty broadly in terms of the teller and the audience. Certain events are news to one audience but not to another. Different criteria must be used, however, when speaking of what is appropriate for publication in a newspaper or for broadcasting on radio or television. Many more factors must be taken into account, such as the preferences of the reporter and the editor, what reporters and editors think the majority (or a specific minority) of the audience wants to know about, the nature of the medium (i.e., what the publisher or owner considers the mission of the medium to be), cultural and ideological constraints (e.g., what people customarily expect of media).

In comparing Western, Communist, and Third World views of what is news, we are concerned mainly with the latter kind of definition. We have found no evidence that human curiosity differs from one culture to another. Curiosity is a universal human trait, and one that we share with lower mammals and even insects. It is related to the instinct of self-preservation, although it has been known to result in capture or even death. News in the first sense is anything that satisfies or feeds one's curiosity—anyone's curiosity, whether he or she belongs to the First, Second, or Third World. Given this meaning, news is a universal.

When we examine what is appropriate content for mass media, news acquires totally different definitions in the three ideological systems into which we have divided the world. In the Western world, news is looked on as a commercial commodity by mass media. It is bought and sold like all other commodities. The raw materials from which the news is fashioned are events that may or may not be readily accessible to all. Naturally, Western countries that trade in news would like to have free access to all events with commercial value. These might include the acts of governments, elite groups, and individuals.

The acts in themselves are not news. They become news when they have been processed by a reporter and editor, much as air and water are not commodities that can be traded commercially until they have been bottled and marketed. Copyright inheres in the manner of presentation—the packaging—rather than in the event itself. Among the trillions of events that clutter the earth each instant of time, the reporter selects a few, just as a jeweler may select a few uncut stones to polish. In the West, emphasis is placed on this selection process, on what is singled out for attention, on the specific facts and the specific angle.

Definitions

Western textbooks define news in terms of interest, proximity, importance, size, novelty, and timeliness. Only in a buyer's market is the interest of a news item of major significance. In such a system, the wishes of readers, listeners, and viewers are paramount because they shop around for the news they want; they are not forced to accept what a publisher or broadcaster wishes to provide.

Interest is a major criterion of news value in the Western world. The gatekeeper is generally the final arbiter of what should be published in this system, and he is guided primarily by what he thinks his audience wants to know about. In most Third World countries and in the Communist world, reporters and editors are not the final arbiters of the appropriateness of a news item. In Communist countries, censors and political commissars interpret Marxist-Leninist doctrine and thus determine what the people *need* to know. What they *want* to know is irrelevant. In the Third World, national development and certain educational goals are usually set by the government in power. Through direct control (i.e., ownership), indirect control (i.e., censorship), or both, decisions are made by the powers that be as to what is appropriate.

In all three systems, proximity is a criterion for news selection. Galtung and Ruge (in Tunstall 1970) found it to be true in Western media. Others (Ume-Nwagbo, forthcoming) suggest similar editorial preferences in Third World countries, to the extent that the editor has a choice. Thus, African editors prefer news of their immediate region over news of more distant African countries. Whether there is parallel reader preference for local and regional news has not been determined throughout the Second and Third Worlds, but in the United States, studies such as that of Hero (1959) show that foreign news does not get the reader interest that is given to local and national news. "Proximity" is used here in the geographical sense, but it applies equally in the psychological sense of feeling close to something or someone, for whatever reason.

News of the elite (i.e., of important people), generally is given preference by all editors. In the West, such selection is based on the assumption that the elite are known to larger segments of the audience, hence news about them is of more general interest. In the Third World, elite news *must* be played up in the press. Thus, in many Asian and African countries, a picture of and news about the head of state must appear on the front page of the newspaper every day. As for the Communist world, intelligence analysts in the West have long followed the rise and decline of Communist leaders by measuring the amount of news published about them in their press.

In Communist countries, however, it is not the personality but the position of a leader that counts. The chief figures in media are impersonal. It is the Revolution, the Party, or the coming election that plays a major role in media because it is these social or political processes that make news. Individuals are merely social symbols. In the Western world and in most Third World countries, there is an explicit concern with people and their activities, although it is true that concern rises with the prominence of the individual. In the Communist world, concern does not focus on the individual but on the group or society at large. Outstanding workers, model teachers, national heroes, and inspiring artists are singled out by media because in the Communist philosophy group effort counts, and by focusing on especially successful individuals, the group as a whole may be uplifted.

In many Western countries the personal as well as the public lives of prominent individuals are kept in the limelight because it is felt that people have a right to know all about their leaders. In the Communist world very little information appears in media about the personal affairs of the powerful because their personal lives are considered a private matter. In the United States the political news coverage preceding an election frequently focuses on the personal characteristics of the candidates; in most other Western countries, the Communist World, and the Third World, when there is a choice of candidates, the emphasis is on issues and candidates' or their party's stand on them.

Size, too, is a measure of the importance of a news event in all three systems, although in the Second and Third Worlds, the decision to publish is based primarily on ideological and political criteria rather than on the size of an event or the number of persons or things involved. Size may be played down or exaggerated to fit ideological or political guidelines.

Novelty is of great importance only in the Western world. If a newspaper or broadcast program is to be sold, it must provide something that other media have not provided. Hence, "scoops"—being first with the news—are of the essence. In the Communist world and in many Third World countries, media do not compete, and making a profit is not crucial. Novelty is subordinated to usefulness, to making a point or advancing a cause.

Timeliness is closely tied to novelty. Because news of events in the West are generally accessible to all, the only way one reporter can scoop another is by being first with the story. The more competitive a country, the more refined the measures of timeliness are. News is reported up to the minute in the United States and frequently up to the second in Japan. Timeliness is emphasized more in economically advanced societies because they have the economic means to utilize the technology of rapid communication. The need for fast information varies according to a country's political system as well. In a democratic system, for example, the public's views are valued; hence quick distribution of information is necessary so that the government can have feedback from the public before it makes important policy decisions. As Ben Bagdikian (1971) put it: "As fast communications accelerate social reaction times, all parties in the process need faster information. Leaders need it because they must make policy decisions to meet the challenge of their constituents who have the same information and react spontaneously to it" (p. 266).

Time is measured in much larger chunks in developing countries; and because Communist media do not compete with one another for reader attention, time is a relatively unimportant factor in news values. Moreover, in a controlled system the media are often late in reporting news events because they must go through government clearance. Cost is another factor that influences standards of timing in developing countries. News media often receive their copy by mail rather than by electronic channels, which are expensive to install and operate.

News Content

In the West, negative news is thought to be of greater interest than positive news. Klaus Schoenbach (see Chap. 2) attributes the greater interest in negative news to the fact that the West expects progress; hence failure is newsworthy because it is an aberration, an unusual situation. Socialist societies, on the other hand, expect failure and find progress to be more newsworthy. They select their news functionally, according to whether it tends to stabilize the system. Negative news is upsetting. It leads to rising frustrations and a desire for change. Any system opposed to change is going to downplay negative news.

Even the West recognizes the unsettling nature of negative news. President Reagan protested strongly when mass media singled out unemployed individuals and families in reports on the U.S. economy because such reports are bad for the party in power. But Western ideologues, who have nothing to lose from negative news because they can pontificate regardless of who is in power, believe that negative news is good for the system, that it keeps people interested in change and, they hope, in progress. The press is interested in negative news because it promotes dissatisfaction and therefore interest in more news (i.e., reports of change) in the hope that there will be a change for the better. Obviously, authoritarian states that desire no change, or at least no intervention on the part of the public in the kind of change that occurs, want as little dissatisfaction as possible; they report as little negative news as they can get by with.

In the Communist world, negative news may be used to provide an object lesson. In a handbook on the preparation of radio newscasts, journalists are told that news is

> not the impartial photographing of that which occurs in our enterprises and construction sites, in scientific and higher educational institutions. It is a question of the purposeful, directed selection of those facts and events which represent the broadest social interest, which graphically and convincingly propagandize the policy of our Party, mobilize the people for the successful construction of the Communist society. (Boglovskiy and L'vov 1963)

"Events," says Inkeles (1958) of the Communist world, "are regarded as being news only insofar as they can be meaningfully related to" the process of creating the Communist society (p. 140).

In the Third World, negative news is avoided because of the fragile political structure of most Third World governments. "If we follow the Western norm," writes Indian journalist Mukerjee (*Illustrated Weekly of India* 1976), "we will be playing up only these dark spots and thus helping unwittingly to erode the faith and confidence without which growth and development are impossible."

Most newspapers of the world print a fair amount of foreign news. This is especially true in the Third World and Europe, and it is true to some extent in the Communist world. In the Soviet Union, *Pravda*, the official Communist party organ, normally has less foreign news than *Izvestia*, the organ of the Soviet parliament. However, Communist world media carry more foreign news commentary than hard news. U.S. editors assume—and there is some evidence to bear them out—that Americans are not as interested in foreign news as they are in domestic news.

There are other reasons for the paucity of foreign news in the American press. For one thing, foreign news is more expensive to cover than domestic news, and profit considerations are an important criterion of news selection. Foreign news is also more difficult to cover because it is less accessible than news in the United States, where the law facilitates access. In 1978, for example, the International Press Institute reported that eleven Third World countries refused entry to or expelled foreign correspondents. Third World and Communist countries not only make it difficult for foreign journalists—who may or may not be impartial observers—to visit the country but, once admitted, they often forbid direct observation of the news. Much news is filtered through some government source. Wire services manage to gather a fair amount of news all over the world in spite of technical and logistical factors that also inhibit news gathering abroad. But one must recognize that news in and about many countries is the news that these countries are willing to let the outside world have about them. This means that governments in some countries have the power to set an initial agenda of news.

Wolfe (1964) and others suggest that the United States is more self-sufficient than most countries and thus does not have to be as concerned about what is going on outside its borders. This is obviously not true in Third World countries, which are prone to devote a great amount of their news space to foreign news—as much as 30 to 50 percent, as a study by Abu Lughod (1962) showed. Foreign news may be cheaper for Third World countries than domestic news because foreign news is covered by wire services. It is less expensive to subscribe to these services than to hire local reporters. Nevertheless, this forces Third World countries to carry news stories selected by foreign rather than domestic newsmen. News can, it is true, be edited to suit local biases. Moreover, an agenda of sorts has been set by governments in those countries that control access to and exportation of news. But the final agenda is set by foreign news agencies.

In the past, it was mainly expatriates who read newspapers in the colonies, and they wanted to keep in touch with the mother country (Lent 1976). This is no longer a strong factor. Far more relevant is the argument that foreign news is less likely to arouse dissatisfaction than is domestic news. In fact, foreign news may rally people to the government by appealing to their nationalism and team spirit; domestic news may accentuate the shortcomings of the government. Much foreign news is negative. Gans (1979) says that U.S. mass media are especially interested in exposing the political and social deficiencies of socialism and communism and in calling critical attention to the brutalities of dictators. Media in Second and Third World countries treat the West in the same way. Otherwise, "the Soviet point of view, which dominates the TASS World Service," writes Kruglak (1962, p. 146), "is that the U.S. is worth mentioning only when its acts coincide with those of the U.S.S.R."

News Presentation

Objectivity used to be an important criterion of news presentation in the United States and, to a lesser extent, other English-speaking countries. It was a convention of news reporting that separated fact from value (Schiller 1981). It called for reporting unadorned by value-laden adjectives and adverbs. In recent years, American journalists have gained more license to set the tone in their reporting through the injection of subjective description. Objectivity, recognized as an impossible and unattainable ideal in that all news is written from a reporter's viewpoint, is rapidly being replaced by concepts of fairness, accuracy, and lack of bias. Efforts to include other viewpoints are still made, but the very selection of other views to be included is a subjective intrusion. Moreover, a balance must be struck between getting other viewpoints and meeting deadlines. Being too scrupulous about getting all viewpoints may mean that a story is not published or that a reporter is scooped by less scrupulous competitors.

Objectivity, which is a Western invention, more specifically, an invention of the English-speaking countries—and truth are defined in terms of the beliefs and values of one's own culture. They are enhanced and abetted by the natural tendency in a free society to approach an issue from a competitively unique angle so as to make the product more salable. Presenting all viewpoints makes news objective. It is also good business, since it is hard to sell a viewpoint that has already been presented before. Besides, truth emerges, as John Milton averred in the seventeenth century, through a "self-righting process" in the "open market place of ideas," i.e., through the presentation of a large number of facts from a large variety of angles.

The Second and Third World see news in an altogether different light. Their emphasis is on what news does rather than on what news is. Its purpose is to manipulate not titillate people. Since they are not trying to sell news but to use it for a particular end, objectivity—i.e., presenting all viewpoints—is not only unnecessary, it is counterproductive. In the Communist World, the purpose of news is to shape public opinion along Socialist lines. In the Third World it serves to educate the public and helps in nation building. Hence, journalists in the three ideological systems focus on totally different types of events as grist for their mass media mills, and when they write their reports, they use different criteria in their presentation of the facts. Journalists in Second and Third World countries have been less hampered by considerations of objectivity. But neither have these reporters been constrained by the need to be interesting, since their primary goal is not to sell news but to use it for specified ends. News presentation in the Communist and Third World, therefore, often is in the form of communiqués that are variations of "The following statement was issued by...."

Attempting to be objective is in the nature of a criminal act in the eyes of some writers on Communism. "The Communist journalist must always ask himself why he is selecting a particular news item or theme for his article, feature, essay or satirical sketch," according to Buzek (1964, pp. 56–57). The journalist must be concerned about the position he is taking and the purpose he is serving. "To deviate from these principles is to commit the crimes of objectivism and escapism" (ibid.). From the Chinese viewpoint, Liu (1971) writes that "to both Mao Tse-tung and Lenin, a journalist is primarily an action-oriented political commissar whose sole duty is to help the Communist party carry out revolution" (p. 44).

In the Third World, objective, truthful, and comprehensive coverage of news is difficult to achieve because the journalistic profession is regarded mainly as a governmental function. A journalist's efforts to write accurate and independent accounts of events would come into direct conflict with the government leadership, and media are supported by the government. One must therefore consciously slant news stories to agree with the opinions of the government. Arab editors, says McFadden (1953), believe that opinion, not news, sells their papers.

Objective reporting in the American and British sense are not found in all Western countries. German journalists prefer to give their stories "perspective" by providing interpretive background and writing subjectively. Swedish journalists give a lively twist even to straight news stories for fear of boring their readers. Australian journalists, especially political reporters, "play up" or "play down" stories to support their particular political slant.

With such differences in guidelines, it is no wonder that member nations of UNESCO have difficulty agreeing on a New World Information Order, which calls for regulation of the right of access to information, more balance in news coverage, the licensing of journalists, and the right of reply to false news reports. Naturally, the West insists on free access to information for everyone; it does not want to be cut off from the raw materials it needs for its news industry. The Second and Third Worlds could care less about providing commercial wire services and news media with free resources. They are interested in how these resources will be used, and they are not at all certain that commercial news organizations will use them in the best interests of Second and Third World countries. So they ask for balance, not in the cause of objectivity, but because they know that the overwhelming weight of news coverage favors the Western world.

THE MASS MEDIA ROLE—INFORMATION, PERSUASION, ENTERTAINMENT

Mass media may be classified as autonomous or ancillary. Autonomous media make their own rules of operation, set their own goals, and decide on their own content. Publishing or broadcasting—for profit, self-aggrandizement, or out of altruism—is the principal activity of owners of autonomous media. Most print media in the Western world and some print media in the Third World are autonomous. Very few countries have autonomous broadcast media, although the United States is one that does. In such countries, broadcast media are either privately owned or are controlled by a public corporation.

Ancillary media are owned or directly controlled by a government, a political party, or an organization like a labor union or a religious system. The primary purpose of ancillary media is to advance the goals of or serve as mouthpiece for their owners, whose principal activity must be something other than the purveying of news. Such media are in the nature of house organs. In the Communist world and in many Third World countries, mass media are ancillary.

Naturally, the role of mass media differs according to whether they are autonomous or ancillary. But certain consequences of exposure to mass media result not because of an imposed role but because of the nature of communication. In this sense, media are passive rather than active. Such spontaneous outcomes occur whether media are autonomous or ancillary. One might, therefore, speak of a spontaneous role as opposed to a defined, or assigned, role of mass media.

Spontaneous Role

A major spontaneous role of mass media is to develop community consensus. Through exposure to the same information and the same interpretations of events, people learn to think along the same lines. They do not necessarily arrive at the same conclusions, although that may happen; but they focus on the same elements of an issue. This has been referred to as the agenda-setting function of the press (McCombs and Shaw 1972) or, more appropriately in the present context, the agenda-building role of mass media (Lang and Lang 1982). The Langs conceptualized mass media as interacting with the public and with leaders on an issue, and in the process developing a consensus about that issue. This consensus does not mean that everyone agrees about the issue. The Langs were writing about the series of events lumped under the heading Watergate, and sides were taken on that issue. What mass media contributed was to define the issue and delimit its parameters.

Primitive societies develop consensus through face-to-face communication. As a community grows, face-to-face communication becomes less feasible, although consensus is still needed. In developed societies, there are many more areas of concern and therefore more possibilities of differences of opinion or nonconformity. Society can tolerate only a certain amount of randomness in behavior or environment, after which anarchy sets in. Predictability (e.g., how traffic will operate or how much things will cost at the store) is essential. And this predictability emerges from the consensus engendered by mass media.

2. Another important spontaneous role of mass media is to pass along a society's social heritage. In primitive societies, one's heritage and traditions were first passed along by word of mouth. Later, the church carried on this socializing role. Today, mass media are the purveyors as well as the molders of a community's social heritage. In the process they both reflect and challenge the existing system, contributing to the general education of the public.

Mass media also expand our life space. In primitive societies most people are born, grow up, and die within a narrowly circumscribed area both in a psychological and a physical sense. Mass media
3. expand people's horizons, permitting them to experience things vicariously that it would be impossible for them to envision in a face-to-face society. This represents another dimension of public education.

4. But while our experiences are multiplied by them, mass media also help simplify our lives by laying out and discussing alternatives, just as lawyers for the defense and the prosecution argue a case before a judge. That leaves the public with the task of marking its X on the ballot, indicating how it stands on the issue. Mass media audiences do not have to research each issue for themselves.

5 Mass media also help create wealth by helping to create a demand for things. Thus mass media facilitate a rise in the standard of living. They describe how others live, create an expectation, and inspire human ingenuity to make it possible for people to share in the better life. They make mass production feasible, which in turn creates jobs and provides money for the purchase of products.

There probably are other spontaneous roles of mass media. But in all systems, the above consequences of the introduction and use of mass media are the most visible and inevitable. As societies march from primitive to transitional and finally to modern status, they make ever increasing use of mass media, which in turn speeds their march to modernization.

Defined Role

Textbooks often define the threefold role of mass media as informing, persuading, and entertaining. From the point of view of the audience, this is what is thought of in speaking of the role of mass media. People buy newspapers and magazines, listen to radio and television, or go to the movies because they want to be informed, persuaded, and entertained.

The public wants to be informed about what is happening in its immediate vicinity and in distant areas. Asked why they want to know, most people will answer that they want to make informed decisions about their lives (Martin 1980, Porter 1982). An important reason for gathering and storing information is to create a bond with fellow members of the community by possessing a common fund of knowledge. This, like shared experiences, draws people together and makes them feel secure.

The desire for information is universal, and while some people may want information unavailable to their friends, such information would have to be on a matter of common concern. Thus, if people are focusing on an incipient war between Britain and Argentina, exclusive information on a secret British landing on the Falkland Islands may be desirable. If no one is paying particular attention to a conflict between Algeria and Morocco, inside information on that topic may be ignored. In other words, too much diversity in media coverage within a society is superfluous. People normally have little desire for uncommon information. So much for the bonding role of information.

Information that is useful for decision making must also be pertinent to the system. The information content of mass media in all three systems generally fulfills this need, and while certain additional isolated items of information might enable people to cope with their environment more efficiently or effectively, much of the information carried in the media of other systems would probably be useless, if not unsettling.

The entertainment role of mass media is similar in all three systems, except that Second and Third World media tend to assign the greatest proportion of this role to audiovisual media. Music, dancing, and drama are the main forms of entertainment; and in all three systems, but especially in the Third World, there is a strong emphasis on projecting and perpetuating a community's cultural heritage through these arts. Western print media, which have different economic constraints from those in the Communist world and much of the Third World, find it necessary to include entertainment so as to make their print media attractive and salable. This is an economic necessity. This does not mean that Second and Third World print media are devoid of entertainment. Nevertheless, a large proportion of media content, especially in the Third World, plays a dual education and entertainment role. It takes affluence, such as is found mainly in the West, to devote major chunks of time and money to entertainment.

The Telecommunication Code of Brazil, for example, explicitly states that the goals of broadcasting are educational and cultural, "even in their aspects of information and entertainment" (Katz 1977, p. 111). In many African countries, folk art is used to transmit cultural values, traditions, beliefs, and languages. It is not surprising to find many Third World countries concerned about the content of imported television programs, which, in the words of the Brazilian Minister of Communication, imposes on young people a climate that is alien to Brazilian culture and imports a foreign culture (ibid., p. 115). Whether they want it or not, Third World countries are finding that with increasing modernization, the emphasis in programming is shifting from culture and tradition to light entertainment.

The Soviet Union presents cultural education programs selectively, including those that reflect favorably on the Communist way of life and withholding anything considered harmful or degrading for the people (e.g., crime, violence, and sex). Thus *Pravda* is full of features on leading Russian literary figures.

In the persuasive role of mass media the three systems differ most. The Western audience recognizes the right of its autonomous media to present ideas in an attempt to persuade readers, listeners, and viewers. Some persuasive messages are welcomed as useful in decision making, some are tolerated, and some are resented. In the Communist world persuasive content is taken for granted; propaganda and agitation are considered major roles of mass media. In the Third World the principal role of mass media is developmental one of nation building. Persuasion is the main instrumentality. People expect and accept persuasive communication from mass media and do not necessarily prefer information separated from opinion, as Americans have come to expect.

Does the presentation of an opinion imply advocacy? In the United States journalism scholars distinguish between interpretation and editorializing. Interpretation, or news analysis, it is said, merely explains a situation without advocating a line of action or even suggesting that a particular way of looking at the situation is the correct one. An editorial, on the other hand, recommends a viewpoint or proposes action on the part of the individual or government. But it is not too far-fetched to suggest that advocacy inheres in the very selection of interpretive facts, and many believe that the line between interpretation and advocacy is very thin (Hulteng and Nelson 1971).

Partly because of the historical association of newspapers with political parties, some Western newspapers do not separate news and opinion. Luchsinger of the *Neue Zuercher Zeitung* says that "to observe the realities as precisely and soberly as possible by no means makes it impossible to have one's own standpoint and opinion" (1977, p. 5). He adds that one can "objectively and correctly analyze and comment" on international affairs without losing one's perspective. *Le Monde* director Fauvet says that this elite Paris newspaper "makes judgments, often severe, sometimes categorical; but it also believes it has that right because, at the same time, it gives its readers all the elements of information possible for them to make their own judgments as well" (Viorst 1974, p. 46).

But other Western countries—for example, the United States, Canada, and Germany—attempt to distinguish between news and opinion. Swedish newspapers also try to separate the two, but they tend to pep up their news writing to avoid dullness (Pers 1954). Some Third World newspapers patterned after the Western press, for example, those in India, also attempt to make the distinction; but the majority do not.

Western media actively seek the opinions of their readers, listeners, and viewers as countervailing but, more desirably, reinforcing inputs. "Letters to the editor" columns in newspapers and the "mail bag" solicited by broadcast media are popular with both audiences and editors, who look for feedback from their publics. Letters also serve as a safety valve against frustration, as social psychiatrist Bryant Wedge (1969) showed in his study of students in Brazil and the Dominican Republic. Violence erupted in the latter country, where letters to the editor were suppressed, but not in Brazil, where they were permitted.

American newspapers, like those of most Western countries, invite opposing views. In the Communist world letters are encouraged, but only those letters are published that "bring light to abuses, deal with moral matters, suggest improvements, and contribute in some way to national progress" (Merrill and Fisher 1980, p. 175). A *Pravda* editor told an American reporter that "it is not convenient to publish" letters complaining about the behavior of local policemen. He also admitted that some letters were written by the newspaper's own correspondents (Kaiser 1976), a practice not unknown elsewhere, even in the United States. Until recently, China published very few letters to the editor. African editors discourage readers from commenting on the shortcomings of government leaders (Wilcox 1974).

We have referred to the spontaneous role of mass media to pass along a nation's social heritage. This also, in a sense, is the function of education. Mass media educate the public, consciously or unconsciously, in a number of ways. One defined role of mass media, for instance, is political education. And mass media in all systems have long felt it to be their responsibility to contribute to the education of the public. In fact, the UN General Assembly in 1962 specifically emphasized the important part that information media had to play in education. The new techniques of communication, the UN pointed out, "offer special opportunities for acceleration of the education process" (quoted in Schramm 1964, p. vii). In 1964, UNESCO stressed the priority educational role of television in Africa. Educational television has since been widely used in African schools and has been a boon to them in view of the shortage of trained teachers on that continent.

Many African networks have purchased the BBC series on learning English. Adult education through group listening to radio began in Britain in 1928 (Hiniker 1968). In 1955, the BBC started regular broadcasting to schools, and in 1971, it inaugurated the Open University, which offers a complete university curriculum through a combination of radio, television, correspondence study, and tutorials. France started an educational service, Television scolaire, even earlier than Britain, and Italy's Telescuola has been functioning since 1958. Most other Western countries have similar programs (see Schramm 1977, Lee 1981).

Communist countries have been providing formal educational courses on television for some time. The Soviet Union offers science and languages at the high school level, plus vocational subjects. Actually all programs in Communist countries have a teaching objective. Poland's Television Technical College has taught mathematics and applied technology since 1966, and East Germany's Television Academy offers a variety of adult education courses.

Outside Africa, too, the Third World has been very much aware of the educational potential of radio and television. India has been using radio for instructional purposes since 1950. In 1956, it began rural forums via radio, and more recently these have been broadcast on television as well. Iran mounted a family planning campaign on television in 1970. In Latin America, El Salvador was first to use educational television on a large scale, but other Latin American countries soon followed suit.

Looking at roles from the point of view of the press, autonomous media, to the extent that they are permitted to do so, arrogate to themselves the role of watchdog over both government and community. This is an adversary role; they watch what the government or the community is doing and blow the whistle when they feel that some segment of society might object to what is being done. Naturally, not all mass media in a given country take the same stand on an issue.

But the theory is that in countries where autonomous media exist—mainly in the First World—all relevant sides will be exposed and the "self-righting process" will set in.

By definition, ancillary media do not play an adversary role unless they are ancillary to some organization other than the government and the government permits an adversary posture, which is highly unusual. Military governments, for example, are careful not to let the press challenge their power. But countries in which media are mainly of the ancillary type frequently have an adversary underground press. This is especially true in the Communist world. In the Third World, in the days when many countries were colonial dependencies of major powers, underground newspapers frequently sprang up. Native newsmen often made their reputations as opposition journalists and ended up as leaders of their countries after independence. This, too, is the genesis of Communist journalism. Once these anti-establishment journalists come to power, their role changes, as does that of their newspapers. In communities where journalists are part of a small, educated elite, it is difficult to be critical of one's intimates. Native journalists did not have this problem under colonialism, for they found themselves in an adversary role vis-à-vis the colonial government.

Media also play three active maintenance roles in all countries. In varying degrees and by different methods they help maintain their social, political, and economic systems. In primitive, face-to-face societies, the town crier kept people informed about general social functions in the community. Announcements were made from the pulpit in churches. Banns were "published" to inform the community that a new family was to be founded. Social interaction remains essential even in mass society, and mass media today serve as bulletin boards in all systems. Community newspapers serve this purpose universally; in addition, society pages contribute to social maintenance especially in the Western world. Factory and collective farm publications generally do this in Communist countries, and radio bulletin board announcements commonly provide social links in many Third World countries.

No modern political system could function without the catalytic help of mass media. Even in authoritarian states, government regulations must be brought to the attention of the public; and in democratic states, candidates for public office and issues are publicized and their merits debated in the press. In all systems, large segments of mass media space and time are devoted to problems of government. Since the activities of government are of common interest to all members of the public, mass media find they can reach more readers, listeners, and viewers with government and political news than with almost any other category of news.

The third maintenance function—that of keeping people informed about their economic interdependence—is another role that mass media have either accepted or assumed, depending on whether the media are ancillary or autonomous. Once again, this is a function that came with the rise of mass society, since in primitive societies it is taken care of on a person-to-person basis. All countries use media to maintain and move goods and services. In the Western world, much of this is done through paid advertising. Communist countries use media to exhort the citizenry to greater production and to provide progress reports on commerce and industry. In the Third World, mass media are used according to the kind of political system that prevails in the country, some adopting Western and other Communist practices.

ECONOMIC FACTORS

Mass media play necessary roles in modern society. Without them, the social, political, and economic interaction that creates a society could not exist on a modern scale. Primitive communities can manage necessary interrelationships among members of the community through interpersonal communication. But as the community grows, the intervention of mass media becomes essential. Who organizes, controls, and pays for media? Who benefits from their services, and how? These questions are central to mass media operations, roles, influence, content, and rights and privileges.

Insights into the role that economics plays in mass media systems may be gained by looking at the evolution of so-called developing countries. Some, but by no means all of them, have been moving in the past quarter century from tribal societies to highly centralized national systems. One of the first things these countries did to achieve nationhood was to organize radio networks that could reach all segments of the nascent nation. Radio is the cheapest form of mass communication. Capital investment and upkeep are shared with the audience, who buy their own receiving sets. When even the cheap transistor receivers available in all parts of the world today are beyond the means of the individual, the community can buy sets that can be installed in public places. The problem of literacy does not arise, and programs can be tailored to the needs and interests of all community segments at the times of day that are best for reaching them.

Most radio systems and practically all television systems (because

of the greater capital investment required for television) were sponsored or built by the national governments. These governments therefore control the day-to-day content of programs, as well as their long-
range goals. And because they hire and pay the staffs, governments
also influence the tone of broadcasts. Electronic media are typically
under government control in all three systems. The United States is
one of a very few countries where broadcasting is mostly commercially organized and controlled.

In the Third World and in Communist countries, governments
pounced on radio as an ideal instrument for rallying, educating, and
guiding their publics along predetermined and approved lines. In
Communist Russia the Bolshevik government had to cover vast dis-
tances and reach a number of cultural and linguistic groups with unifying and centrally orchestrated messages. This was far more easily
accomplished by radio than through the dissemination of printed materials. The Third World frequently had the added problems of low
literacy and the fact that many languages had no written form.

Government need for the unifying force of communication inspired the installation of radio systems. In the Communist world, the
greatest need was political; in the Third World, the need was both
political and social. The Western world's need was largely economic; it
was a need satisfied most readily through print media, except in the
United States, where broadcast networks more easily spanned the
vast territory that had to be covered. Here was a free enterprise system that depended on competitive appeals to the public for patronage.
What was essential was a mass media system that would even-
handedly provide time to all competitors. The competitors paid for
this time on the air and passed along their costs to customers.
Government's role was limited to serving as an arbiter to make sure
that all competitors had equitable access to the public (in the economic and political realms) and that the social needs of the community
were not ignored. This required a regulatory agency like the Federal
Communications Commission (FCC) in the United States, rather
than outright ownership and control of broadcasting, as in the Second
and Third Worlds.

Economic control of media, whether electronic or print, is completely in the hands of the government in all Communist countries.
Profit making is not a concern. Media budgets are part of the state
budget (see Hopkins, Chap. 16), and although media attempt to be
self-sufficient, that is not a primary consideration. Newspaper and
magazine revenues, apart from subsidies from the state and from factories, farms, or other sponsoring organizations, derive mainly from
circulation. Broadcast media similarly are state supported. Their major source of revenue in practically all Communist countries other

than the Soviet Union is from receiving-set license fees, which vary according to the kind of set. In most countries there is a family radio license fee; in some there is an additional car radio license fee and a smaller fee for wired receivers. Annual television fees cover radio reception as well. In the Soviet Union annual license fees were abolished in 1962 because of the resistance of the population to paying them. (They are difficult to collect in most countries.) Instead, the Soviet Union imposed an excise tax on the sale of all radio and television receivers.

Advertising as a source of revenue for electronic media is minimal in almost all Communist countries. The Soviets were skeptical about advertising in the early days and believed it was a means of swindling the people. But by the 1960s they began to see advertising as an important element in commerce and a promoter of production (Paulu 1974). As in many Western European countries, advertisers do not sponsor programs. Instead, blocks of time—mostly between five and fifteen minutes—are set aside for commercials during prime time. The emphasis is on information rather than on a hard sell. Of course, income from such commercials is merely a bookkeeping transfer from one state account to another, as one Czech broadcasting official put it (ibid.). Advertisements also appear in small local newspapers offering services, such as tutoring, or the sale of used merchandise. This cannot account for major sources of income, however. Special advertising supplements in major newspapers report on the arrival of consignments of consumer goods in state-owned stores, which again may provide bookkeeping transfers of funds to the newspapers concerned. Revenue from advertising is highest in Yugoslavia where, in the early 1970s, broadcasting was supported 19 percent by commercials (as against 74 percent by license fees), and is next highest in the German Democratic Republic (ibid.).

Clearly, the state is the major beneficiary of mass communication in the Communist world in that it is able to orchestrate the content, goals, and tone of mass media. Nevertheless, as Hopkins points out in Chapter 16, just as there are commercial sponsors of broadcasting in the West, in Communist countries there are political sponsors of mass media, such as divisions of the Communist party's Central Committee. Other sponsors of media may be the military, youth groups, and cooperatives.

In the West, print media are generally under the economic control of individuals or organizations other than the government. Revenue derives mainly from circulation and advertising. But indirect government subsidies, such as cheaper mailing privileges, are generally accepted. Scandinavian countries are also experimenting with direct subsidies to party newspapers. Since Western countries all have competitive commercial systems, advertising is a natural source of revenue and also covers a large proportion of broadcasting costs. Most of the countries, in addition, levy a license fee on set ownership to pay for the government or publicly run broadcasting systems.

Economic controls of mass media in the Third World range all the way from outright ownership of media and the means of dissemination, as in Communist countries, to complete economic independence. Unlike in the West, however, economic control by an individual or organization does not carry with it assurance of noninterference with the news and editorial judgment of editors and reporters. The latter are directly or indirectly controlled by the government through official mandatory training programs, licensing, and pre- or post-publication censorship in many cases.

Depending on the kind of economy prevailing in a country, revenue derives from advertising and circulation in print media, and from advertising and license fees in broadcast media. There also are direct and indirect government subsidies. When publications are privately owned—that is, unless the government is a co-owner—the publisher is permitted to keep all profits. Frequently, however, free space in print media must be provided for government communiqués and announcements; occasionally, the government pays for this space. The major cost of broadcasting is programming. The production of local programs is relatively cheap, but is often of low quality. Moreover, the broadcast industry requires a tremendous amount of program material, and first-class entertainment programs are very expensive to produce. Most countries, even those in the West, are forced to import some of their entertainment, which is looked upon as a form of cultural invasion by many, especially in the Third World but even in First World countries such as Canada. Yet, as Vasquez points out in Chapter 15, the cost of excluding such foreign influence is often beyond the means of developing countries.

THE CONCEPT OF PRESS FREEDOM

In today's world, not only does every country have a press, but almost all countries give constitutional recognition to the concept of press freedom and freedom of expression (Martin 1969). Such negative provisions as Article 8 of the Vatican's Constitutional Laws of 1929 are rare, if not unique. It says: "The public exercise of printing, lithography, photography and other mechanical or chemical reproduction of characters, designs, or figures is forbidden without the authorization of the Governor. It is forbidden to affix or offer to the public even gratuitously, announcements, writings, printed matter, books, engravings, lithographs, photographs, statues, of any kind without the authorization of the Governor." The laws of most states both provide for free speech and publication and specify restrictions on this freedom.

Most frequently, the constraint makes freedom of the press subject to law, public order, and morality, or permits suppression if offenses are committed in the exercise of press freedom. Constitutions of Communist countries and a few others limit freedom of expression when it advocates overthrow of the country's system of government or preaches racial, national, or religious hatred or chauvinism. And some Third World constitutions prohibit the use of mass media in ways that may endanger peace. Several countries in all three systems guarantee press freedom only to their own citizens. In short, all organized states prescribe the conditions under which press freedom operates within their boundaries, whether through their constitutions or through their municipal (i.e., statutory) laws or decrees. Even if the only law of the land respecting the press says that the state may make no law and may pass no decree affecting the press, freedom of expression is constrained, since it may be the public's desire to limit the press.

To understand how press constraints work, one must analyze the meaning of press freedom. The English-speaking world has for three hundred years worshiped at the shrine of freedom of the press. "The press" has been anthropomorphized and sanctified. Collectively it has been referred to as the "fourth estate," the "fourth branch of government," or the "fourth power." Freedoms have been granted to and withheld from the press as an institution, and they have often been different from the freedoms granted to individual citizens or the constraints placed upon the latter.

Very soon after printing was brought to Europe in the fifteenth century, the licensing and censorship of printers was instituted because their potential for interactive defamation and sedition was recognized right away. By "interactive defamation" and "interactive sedition" is meant the phenomenon in which people not only think defamatory or seditious thoughts and possibly pass them on to another individual but where, through multiple sharing of a thought, that thought is reinforced, expanded, and perpetuated. The need to control the mushrooming potential of published ideas is a realization that comes rapidly—often instinctively rather than from experience—to rulers and governors. True, only sedition is aimed directly at the ruler or government, possibly leading to a joint public effort to overthrow the regime. But defamation can lead to disruptions that, in the long run, may adversely affect the ability of those in power to control the population. Defamation and sedition are therefore kept in check either through pre- or post-publication legal restraints. Pre-publication controls, such as censorship, licensing, subsidies, and outright government ownership of the means of mass communication, are most common in the Second and Third Worlds. Post-publication controls, which include criminal and civil prosecution, confiscation, fines, denial of subsidies, and the revocation of licenses, are common in the First and Second Worlds. Several Western and Third World countries also use the right of reply as a means of defusing hurt feelings.

It is apparent when one analyzes press freedom and repression that what makes the press as an institution potentially dangerous— everyone recognizes its positive and beneficial roles—is not that it is a cooperative venture produced through the collaborative efforts of a large number of people. It would be just as dangerous if it were the product of a single journalist. It acquires its threatening character through its interactive audience. Laws that govern the press, therefore, focus on the size of the audience or potential audience. If the audience is relatively small, approaching a limit of zero (i.e., no audience at all for a given message, which therefore remains in the mind or in the personal diary of the author), the threat is reduced, and legislation to control the message is superfluous. This means that the real target of control is the audience and that what is being protected is society and, ultimately, the power structure.

Furthermore, the concern of states is not over giving the press freedom to disseminate ideas but with the ideas themselves. Most states would pay no attention to the mass media if it were not for two things: the ideas that they can potentially disseminate and the fact that the state has some ideas of its own that it would like to bring to the attention of the public. Some states are more permissive than others in the range of ideas that may be publicly (i.e., interactively) discussed or advocated by individuals or their institutions. To illustrate the difference between freedom of the press and freedom of ideas, consider that no state would object to someone, at his own expense, printing the alphabet, even a million times, and disseminating it to the population. Many states would object to the publication of ideas about a better way to run the government. Some states might not object even to that, but they would ban publication of the idea that everyone in the power structure is a crook and that the people ought to let the power structure in some other country take over the government. In other words, our concern is more with the freedom of ideas than with the freedom of the press. The amount of freedom in a country may be measured by the point on this continuum from alphabet to advocating revolution at which the courts, the police, or the army may step in and call a halt to mass media activity.

States have not always been neutral about printing. From the fifteenth to the eighteenth century, even in what are today among the freest countries in terms of permissiveness (e.g., Britain), printing was done only under special dispensation from the government, which granted licenses selectively (see Siebert 1952). To the present day, in the most repressive countries from the point of view of individual freedoms (e.g., the Soviet Union), even typewriters and duplicating machines must be registered (see Hopkins, Chap. 16).

As each new mass medium made its appearance, people felt that it represented "the end of civilization as we know it" and that tight controls needed to be exercised over the medium's use. This was the reaction to the invention of motion pictures (Cooke 1982), and judging by the almost universal governmental control of broadcasting, it is a feeling still prevalent about electronic media. At the start at least, the distrust of a medium is due more to the new behavior pattern it imposes on people than to its content. It is felt, for example, that people should not spend so much time with their eyes glued to the television set. Because of religious injunctions against graven images, motion pictures and television were at first outlawed in Moslem countries. The focus in all this is on the medium rather than on the message; for all intents and purposes, the medium is the message. But as the medium becomes a part of the culture and is accepted as a necessary institution, the focus switches to the content, which then is closely scrutinized.

The Western World

If one had to characterize the differences in the concept of press freedom in the three major systems being evaluated here by making a generalization, one would have to do it in terms of the primary interests served. In the Western world, in spite of legal hedging and qualifications, press freedom belongs primarily to the individual and secondarily to private groups—whether social, political, or economic— formed by individuals. In the Communist world, press freedom is delegated primarily to the party in power (i.e., the Communist party) as the presumptive representative of the people. Press freedom is a collective rather than an individual right. Secondarily, press freedom belongs to the state, since the role of media is an active, guiding one in Communist countries rather than a passive one of mirroring the people, and guidance is the responsibility of the government. In the Third World, where the primary role of the press is educational, and where the government both sets the sights and leads the way, press freedom is principally a government prerogative. Secondarily, and this is a gross generalization about a highly disparate group of countries, press freedom belongs to various vested interests, whether economic, political, ethnic (tribal), or power-based (e.g., military).

Of all Western countries, the United States probably offers the most consistent, individually oriented press freedom. This is so mainly because it has a powerful judiciary whose decisions cannot be executively countermanded and whose traditions and inclinations lean in the direction of the right of the individual to reveal whatever he knows or believes to be a fact, and to comment on whatever he likes whether it deals with a political, economic, or social issue. Britain has a similar philosophy of press freedom, and like the United States, it permits prepublication censorship only in wartime. Even then, it is voluntary and is controlled by press-selected individuals. Britain, however, is more protective of its courts and public officials in its laws than is the United States. Judges and public officials take precedence over private individuals in Britain, where privilege has long been an accepted fact, even when it comes to press freedom.

Since World War II, Germany and Austria have given individuals a measure of press freedom similar to that found in the United States. Austria grants the legal right of professional secrecy to journalists, whereas Britain denies this right and the United States has been ambivalent in protecting newsmen's sources. In another sense, Austrian law protects individual privacy more strongly than English-speaking countries do, but at the expense of press freedom. Newspapers and magazines may be seized or banned to protect the privacy of the individual (Merrill, Bryan, and Alisky 1970). The German police have been known to arrest and jail editors for publishing information considered to be secret. Like several other Western countries, German news media police themselves through a press council, which, however, also serves as a lobby with the government in matters affecting the press.

While French courts protect the press against illegal seizure, both the state and private individuals may initiate the confiscation of French newspapers and magazines for derogatory comments or for material (e.g., a cartoon) insulting to the French president. Censorship of the press and the confiscation or banning of periodicals is permissible in times of crisis under a nineteenth-century law, which was reinforced by a 1959 constitutional provision giving the head of state the right to take any necessary action regarding the press.

The Third World

Government intervention in mass media is a universal phenomenon. Governments, either directly or through their courts, step in to protect themselves, their citizens, or foreign governments and leaders. Most governments are more likely to intervene in their own behalf than in behalf of others. In the Western world, or more generally, in large and wealthy countries, the protection of citizens is given more attention than the protection of foreign leaders and their governments. The smaller, poorer, and hence more vulnerable states are more assiduous in monitoring press defamation of foreign powers, especially friendly ones. Generally, governments or their courts do not intrude in behalf of their citizens or of foreign leaders and governments unless asked to do so by the injured party.

The degree of press freedom in a country may be measured in two important ways, and the three major systems differ significantly in terms of these two indices. One criterion is whether governments take direct action against the press through their police or military for the commission of certain undesirable acts, or whether the government must sue through the courts. In most Western and in some Third World countries, direct police or military action is not a normal or even a viable procedure. In the majority of Third World countries and in the Communist world, it is a frequent occurrence. Moreover, in countries that require a judicial mandate prior to police intervention, a judicial review of government action, or both, it is highly unlikely that an arrest, confiscation, or suspension will occur for unspecified crimes. This does occur from time to time in the Third World. The second criterion is whether the media may be constrained or punished for what they do *not* say (i.e., errors of omission). This is not common in the Western world but is widespread in the Third World and standard practice in the Communist world.

One must not be so naive as to think that police or military action is the only way mass media can be constrained or restrained. The Third World, especially, has devised every conceivable means of keeping the press in line. Most Third World countries require permits for the publication of a newspaper or magazine, and in some countries these permits must be renewed annually. (Broadcasting is universally controlled, even in those few countries that have commercial broadcasting systems, because of the limited number of available channels or airwaves.) Many Third World countries license journalists, and in some countries citizenship is a requirement for ownership of news media. Newsprint, presses, ink, and other necessary supplies and equipment for a news operation are government supervised or rationed in many Third World countries; even electricity has been cut off when a newspaper has failed to support the government.

A most common restriction on press freedom in the Third World is to deny access to government news. This is often achieved by refusing to accredit or license certain journalists, by making government news available only through official communiqués rather than direct access to the source of the news, and most frequently through pre-publication censorship of all news published or broadcast. Another increasingly common control over the foreign news content of mass media in the Third World is achieved by creating a domestic wire service as a funnel for all foreign and even local news. This wire service subscribes to or acquires in some other way (e.g., free from a major country, or by pirating it off the air) the daily news file of international wire services and supplies its selected and edited version of the news to its media. Subsidies, both direct and through payment for government advertising and even news placements, are common in the Third World, although they are also to be found in the Western world, especially in the form of lower postal rates for newspapers and magazines.

The Communist World

Communism defines press freedom differently from the Western world, but lays claim to having true freedom of the press, which, it says, does not exist under capitalism. Communists say that press freedom cannot exist in a system where only the monied classes have access to mass media. If one has to be wealthy to reach a mass public with a message—as one must in a country where presses, paper, and ink have to be purchased on the open market—one cannot speak of press freedom. This is tantamount to Hobson's choice, since the only choice available is letting the wealthy speak for you. Since the poor —the masses—are in the majority, the truly democratic thing to do is for the government to give the masses the wherewithal for mass communication. This the Soviet Union guarantees in Article 125 of its 1936 ("Stalin") Constitution:

> In conformity with the interests of the working people, and
> in order to strengthen the socialist system, the citizens of the
> USSR are guaranteed by law: (a) freedom of speech; (b)
> freedom of the press; (c) freedom of assembly, including the
> holding of mass meetings; (d) freedom of street processions
> and demonstrations. These civil rights are ensured by
> placing at the disposal of the working people and their
> organizations printing presses, stocks of paper, public
> buildings and streets, communications facilities and other
> material requisites for the exercise of these rights.

Lenin believed that it would lead to utter chaos and anarchy if every Tom, Dick, and Harry could enter a building at will and run off hundreds of pamphlets whenever the spirit moved him. To keep things under true democratic control, only the party and the government and their assignees have the right to express the views of the masses. No one may speak for the masses except their duly elected and appointed representatives (i.e., the Communist party). This, for Communist countries, represents true, democratic freedom that avoids plutocracy at one end of the spectrum and anarchy at the other.

To achieve such freedom—and obviously this conceptualization of press freedom is totally different from that found in Western philosophy—Communist countries find it essential for their media to speak with a single voice. Anti-Soviet propaganda and agitation are forbidden, as are unfettered criticism of the government or the party in the Soviet Union. Criticism must be constructive and controlled (through censorship, for example). As Lenin put it:

> The capitalist (and with them, wittingly or unwittingly, many Socialist Revolutionaries and Mensheviks) define as "freedom of the press" a state of affairs under which censorship is abolished and all parties freely publish all kinds of newspapers. In reality, this is not freedom of the press, but freedom to deceive the oppressed and exploited masses of the people by the rich, by the bourgeoisie. (Quoted in Markham 1967, p. 103)

Even criticism of the enemies of the people (e.g., the United States) must be properly orchestrated and have a purpose. Random criticism can lead only to unpredictable and undesired results. Similarly, in domestic affairs, sensationalism, crime news, and other emotion-rousing reportage are frowned upon unless there is a lesson to be learned from them. In short, nothing is left to chance. While in the Western world facts are often permitted to speak for themselves, in the Communist world they are carefully weighed lest they deliver the wrong message.

Press controls are exercised in four ways: (1) Printing and broadcasting equipment and supplies are parceled out only to approved organizations and groups; (2) journalists are selected and trained by the state in Communist ideology to exercise self-censorship; only they may work for news media; (3) news sources are carefully controlled and news agencies are state owned; and, just to double-check on the first three controls, (4) a department of censorship has existed in the USSR since czarist days (called Glavlit at that time) to approve all copy before publication. Other Communist countries have similar controls.

Prospects

Is the world heading in the direction of more or less press freedom? Do the experiences of the past shed any light on this question?
It took three hundred years for printing to be freed from the fetters of
government control in the West. But by the nineteenth century, the
ownership of a printing press and the dissemination of reading materials had become accepted in the West as not in themselves subversive acts.

Radio and television, however, are still under close government
control in all countries. There is a limited number of channels and
airwaves, and a free-for-all approach to broadcasting is untenable.
Government must control allocations so that all people are equitably
served. If, however, government decides who gets access to the airwaves, rules must be devised as to who gets a license to broadcast.
There are many ways in which this can be done. A first-come, first-
served basis may mean that younger people, who enter the competition later, may never get a chance. Clearly one must have criteria for
terminating a license. One may offer licenses to the highest bidder,
but that goes against the grain in most democratic societies. Ultimately, a merit system suggests itself. How well does the licensee
perform? This inevitably leads to government control because some
public or government body must set the rules and evaluate the performance. Most governments skirt the issue by holding the broadcasting franchise themselves.

In deciding whether media should be introduced into a given society, certain values must be taken into account. Motion pictures and
television found some resistance in Islamic countries because of the
injunction against graven images in the Koran. Even printing was resisted by the Islamic clergy on the pretext of the sanctity of paper,
since the name of God could be written on it (Lerner 1958). But what
the ulema feared was a loss of power.

It is reasonable to assume that governments will hang on to their
control of a medium as long as it is feasible but, as is true of all legal
sanctions, when they become impossible to enforce, government will
bow to the inevitable. While the reception of broadcasting is becoming more and more difficult to control, its transmission is still relatively easy to monitor. Governments will therefore soon have to free
up the reception of both radio and television programs by collecting
their revenue in some way other than by annual license fees, which
are too costly to collect and almost impossible to enforce. The Soviet
Union has resorted to excise taxes on receiving sets, and other countries have placed a surtax on electricity. Whatever the method, it represents a relaxation of government control of reception.

In the realm of publication and transmission, most countries in the Second and Third Worlds still have difficulty entrusting this activity to citizens. Over the past half century Communist countries have broadened the definition of organizations that may publish, but party and government control remain strict. The Third World has gone in both directions. Most Latin American and Asian countries have given more groups and individuals licenses to address the public. But other countries, notably in Africa and the Middle East, have gone for tighter controls. Relaxation of such controls depends on trust. If governments can trust the public not to use the mass media to try to overthrow them, or if they feel secure enough not to fear such efforts, or if they are not so wedded to their power but are willing to give it up if the public is dissatisfied with their performance, there will be no need to control mass media. But these are unlikely eventualities. One must therefore expect governments to continue to attempt to control publication and transmission.

How about the freedom of ideas? Ideas, after all, are what cause the greatest concerns. There certainly will be greater freedom in the ideas that may be presented. In the United States, we have witnessed in the past couple of decades a great relaxation in obscenity laws. We can, in this century, refer to "legs" in print without calling them "limbs," and we can be far more explicit in writing about sex and in pictorial nudity. Radio and television are becoming increasingly bold in what they can talk about and show.

These are just some areas in which mass media have become more free. Similar relaxations may be witnessed in other parts of the world. Criticism of certain groups of people (e.g., public officials other than top leaders) is becoming acceptable in Second and Third World countries. Gradually it may become permissible to discuss economic or social problems in countries that have banned such matters from the press and broadcast media. In most cases, relaxation alternates with a tightening of controls when there is a negative reaction by people who feel things are moving too fast or in the wrong direction. But as populations become better educated, opportunities for diversity increase, and with every change in the cycle, the freedom of ideas becomes a little greater. History has shown this to be the case.

REFERENCES

Abu Lughod, Ibrahim. "International News in the Arabic Press: A Comparative Content Analysis." *Public Opinion Quarterly* 26 (1962): 600–611.

Bagdikian, Ben H. *The Information Machines: Their Impact on Men and the Media.* New York: Harper & Row, 1971.

Boglovskiy, T., and Z. L'vov. "Posledniye Izvestiya po Radio" ("The Latest

News on Radio"). In *Developments in Soviet Radio*. Moscow: State Committee of the Council of Ministers, USSR, on Radio and Television—Scientific-Methodological Department, 1963.

Buzek, Anthony. *How the Communist Press Works*. New York: Praeger, 1964.

Cooke, Alistair. Introduction to Masterpiece Theatre series "Flickers," May 22, 1982.

Gans, Herbert J. *Deciding What's News: A Study of CBS Evening News, NBC Nightly News, Newsweek and Time*. New York: Vintage Books, 1979.

Hero, Alfred O. *Mass Media and World Affairs*. Boston: World Peace Foundation, 1959.

Hiniker, Paul J. "The Mass Media and Study Groups in Communist China." In International Communication Institute, *Mass Communication and the Development of Nations*. East Lansing: Michigan State University Press, 1968.

Hopkins, Mark. "Media Economics in the Communist World." In L. J. Martin and A. G. Chaudhary, eds., *Comparative Mass Media Systems*. New York: Longman, 1983.

Hulteng, John L., and Roy Paul Nelson. *The Fourth Estate: An Informal Appraisal of the News and Opinion Media*. New York: Harper & Row, 1971.

Illustrated Weekly of India, October 10, 1967.

Inkeles, Alexander. *Public Opinion in Soviet Russia: A Study in Mass Persuasion*. Cambridge: Harvard University Press, 1958.

IPI Report, no. 1 (January 1979): 3–15.

Kaiser, Robert G. *Russia: The People and the Power*. New York: Pocket Books, 1976.

Katz, Elihu. "Cultural Continuity and Change: The Role of Mass Media." In Majid Teheranian, Farhad Hakimzadeh, and Marcello L. Vidale, eds., *Communications Policy for National Development*. London: Routledge & Kegan Paul, 1977.

Kruglak, Theodore E. *The Two Faces of TASS*. Minneapolis: University of Minnesota Press, 1962.

Lang, Kurt, and Gladys Engel-Lang. *The Battle for Public Opinion: The President, the Press and the Polls During Watergate*. New York: Columbia University Press, 1982.

Lent, John A. "Foreign News Content of U.S. and Asian Print Media: A Literature Review and Problem Analysis." *Gazette* 22 (1976): 169–82.

Lerner, Daniel. *The Passing of Traditional Society: Modernizing the Middle East*. Glencoe, Ill.: Free Press, 1958.

Liu, Alan P. L. *Communications and National Integration in Communist China*. Berkeley: University of California Press, 1971.

Luchsinger, Fred. "A Modern Newspaper—Nearly 200 Years Old," In *The Neue Zürcher Zeitung Speaks for Itself*. Zurich: Neue Zürcher Zeitung, 1977.

McCombs, Maxwell E., and Donald L. Shaw. "The Agenda-Setting Function of Mass Media." *Public Opinion Quarterly* 36 (Summer 1972): 176–87.

McFadden, Tom J. *Daily Journalism in the Arab States*. Columbus: Ohio State University Press, 1953.

Markham, James W. *Voices of the Red Giants.* Ames: Iowa State University Press, 1967.

Martin, Linda H. "Correlates of Print Media Exposure." Master's thesis, University of Maryland, 1980.

Martin, L. John. *International Propaganda: Its Legal and Diplomatic Control.* Gloucester, Mass.: Peter Smith, 1969.

Merrill, John C.; Carter R. Bryan; and Marvin Alisky. *The Foreign Press: A Survey of the World's Journalism.* Baton Rouge: Louisiana State University Press, 1970.

———, and Harold A. Fisher. *The World's Great Dailies: Profiles of Fifty Newspapers.* New York: Hastings House, 1980.

Paulu, Burton. *Radio and Television Broadcasting in Eastern Europe.* Minneapolis: University of Minnesota Press, 1974.

Pers, Anders Yngve. *Newspapers in Sweden.* Stockholm: Swedish Institute, 1954.

Porter, Gail Lupton. "Why They Read and Who Reads What: Information Utility, Market Segmentation, and the Government Magazine Editor." Master's thesis, University of Maryland, 1982.

Schiller, Dan. *Objectivity and the News.* Philadelphia: University of Pennsylvania Press, 1981.

Schramm, Wilbur. *Big Media Little Media: Tools and Technologies for Instruction.* Beverly Hills: Sage, 1977.

Siebert, Frederick. *Freedom of the Press in England, 1476–1776.* Urbana: University of Illinois Press, 1952.

Tunstall, Jeremy. *Media Sociology: A Reader.* Urbana: University of Illinois Press, 1970.

Ume-Nwagbo, Ebele N. "Foreign News Flow in Africa: A Content Analytical Study on a Regional Basis." *Journalism Quarterly,* forthcoming.

Vasquez, Francisco J. "Media Economics in the Third World." In L. J. Martin and A. G. Chaudhary, eds., *Comparative Mass Media Systems.* New York: Longman, 1983.

Viorst, Milton. "*Le Monde*: Very Serious, Very Successful." *Columbia Journalism Review,* September/October 1974.

Wedge, Bryant. "The Case Study of Student Political Violence." *World Politics* 21 (January 1969): 183–206.

Wilcox, Dennis. "The Black Press in Africa: Philosophy and Control." Ph.D. dissertation, University of Missouri, 1974.

Wolfe, Wayne. "Images of the U.S. in the Latin American Press." *Journalism Quarterly* 41 (1964): 79–86.

PART 2

THE NATURE AND TREATMENT OF NEWS

---

2. NEWS IN THE WESTERN WORLD

KLAUS SCHOENBACH

According to journalism texts, "news" can be defined as "an account of something real" (Campbell and Wolseley 1961, p. 6), something that "has 'actually happened'" (Harriss, Leiter, and Johnson 1981, p. 27), "truthful and complete accounts of the social world" (Altheide 1976, p. 196), or "a report of an event, containing timely ... information which has been accurately gathered and written by trained reporters for the purpose of serving the reader, listener, or viewer" (Ault and Emery 1965, p. 16). Whereas in the first three quotes the criterion for news is its accordance with reality, the last definition is more cautious: News is not necessarily true, but newsmakers should select and present it as truthfully as possible.

These definitions of news are typical not only of definitions in American textbooks but also of those in Western European discourses on journalism. So, for instance, Dovifat (1967) argues in Germany that news need not be defined as "true" accounts of reality. Crucial for its quality, however, is that newsmakers are truthful, responsible people, trying hard.

Tuchman (1978) summarizes this view as follows: News is supposed to be "factual and hard-nosed, a veridical account of events in the world" (p. 5). This certainly is a definition with which many members of Western industrialized and capitalist societies would agree. Moreover, it provides an important distinctive feature for a comparison with news in Eastern European countries. Their news, according to Tuchman, is "propaganda"—it is not accounts of reality but distorted pictures of the world, determined by the will of a few rulers. Newsmakers there do not even try to be accurate, she maintains. During the last fifteen years, however, in addition to this simple and popular distinction between Western and Eastern news, a less evaluative and more descriptive one has gradually developed.

Traditional Western news definitions are normative: They enable us to evaluate news. So the quality of news can be assessed in terms of its "truth" or "accuracy." Inaccurate news, then, mainly results from the weaknesses of journalists, who may not be trained properly to serve their audience or may not try hard enough. Help in this case is provided by freedom of the press and by making sure that there are as many "dealers" as possible in the libertarian "marketplace of ideas." What one journalist may neglect or distort can be balanced, neutralized, by another.

The notion that a single person was capable of reporting the complete truth was abandoned as early as in the eighteenth century (Davis and Baran 1981). To get an accurate picture of what was going on took more than one observer and reporter. Pluralistic views of reality, taken together, were expected to provide a representative mosaic of the truth. In this perspective, newsmaking was conceived of as a system of checks and balances. Early research about the process of gathering and selecting news seemed to prove this idea.

Over thirty years ago, David M. White asked a wire editor why he dismissed specific news items. Most often, he was told: "not interesting" and "no space" (White 1950). What was regarded as interesting and deserving of space more or less seemed to be up to the autonomous "gatekeeper." But some doubts about this autonomy arose even in the early stages of news research. It was clear, for instance, that journalists were highly dependent on news agencies and other sources of news, on events that were prefabricated, narrowed down before they reached the media. Still, much remained to be decided upon. In 1949, the news editor whom White observed used only a tenth of all the news items he had to choose from.

Even more important for the defense of the journalistic autonomy perspective was the notion that journalists obviously are not mere gatekeepers, regulating the flow of news. Very often they actively create news. They invite politicians to interviews; they try to find out what is wrong with the economy; they uncover corruption.

News in the West—is it a kaleidoscopic, manifold, exciting picture of what is going on? Three decades of research have shown that these seemingly autonomous and idiosyncratic criteria for the selection of news to a great extent are rationalizations of organizational, professional, and cultural constraints.

Organizational research provided the first findings that endangered the assumption of the autonomous journalist, responsible only to his (or her) audience and his conscience. Each news organization—a newspaper, a TV station, a radio station—tries to make sure that its members follow the organization's rules (Ruehl 1969). An important subset of rules, often rigidly enforced, determines what is news. Several steps are needed to make sure that every member of the news organization knows what to do about its norms (Schoenbach 1977), and to those steps we now turn.

SELF-SELECTION

Since the editorial policies of many news media are well known, there is at least one criterion for selecting an employer: Potential media employees can decide whether they are willing to obey the organization's rules. But owing to media concentration and the attempt to save on personnel costs, this is often an ideal situation. Freedom to choose the medium one wants to work for is restricted. Moreover, editorial stances provide only superficial information about the conventions governing the creation, selection, and presentation of news. Since news has to be made, selected, and presented under severe time constraints, no news organization is able to establish formal rules for each and every event, each and every topic. Rules cannot be exhaustive. "Bureaucratic routine" (Rock 1973, p. 73), comprising quickly and easily applicable conventions, has to replace formal decisions (Gans 1979). The organization cannot assume that these conventions are known by a new journalist. A second step becomes increasingly important.

SELECTION OF MEMBERS BY THE MEDIUM

By further clarifying news conventions to applicants, and by finding out whether they are willing to obey them, the organization tries to make sure that new members can be relied on to keep the rules. But since job interviews are too short to explain the nuances of news rules, a third step is indispensable.

SOCIALIZATION

Usually, a new member of an organization is not allowed to solve important tasks immediately. Experienced journalists work with newcomers, showing them how to perform membership roles and only gradually allowing them to work alone. The objective of this phase is to make new journalists familiar with the more or less implicit conventions. But as newsmaking is complex, an organization can never be sure that there will not be situations in the future that are hard to resolve (1) because a self-selective, selected, and trained member will not know what to do in terms of what the organizational rules demand; or (2) because definite rules just do not exist. In the first case, organizations have measures for securing compliance.

SOCIAL CONTROL

Social control includes all kinds of behavior by organization members that show individuals whether they are right or wrong. These behaviors, sanctions, may range from a step up in the hierarchy (a positive sanction) to the firing of the noncompliant member (a negative sanction). In between are many less dramatic measures, such as frowning, a smile, a friendly word, a slap on the back (Breed 1955). But these measures assume definite routines that can be enforced. In some situations it may be necessary to develop new, ad hoc guidelines for the selection and presentation of news.

SOCIAL CREATION OF NEWS CONVENTIONS

The process of formulating new norms incorporates the interpretation and elaboration of existing news rules or the construction of new ones (Lester 1982). This process can consist of a series of transactions among the organization members rather than of the exercise of power and the enforcement of obedience.

If news is not shaped by many responsible journalists whose different perspectives create a mosaic of the truth, the libertarian notion of the marketplace of ideas is seriously endangered. But there is still hope that the great number of distinct news organizations in Western society may secure a pluralistic picture of reality (Epstein 1973; Davison, Boylan, and Yu 1982). For this reason, it is important to fight against the disappearance of news organizations—for instance, in the process of press concentration.

News in the West has become somewhat restricted, but is it still a manifold picture of the world? In the 1960s two important studies showed that even this limited expectation may not be met. Thomas H. Guback (1968) found that a 1960 campaign speech by John F. Kennedy was treated identically by fifteen New York broadcasting stations. Although the main topic of the speech was the Cuban policies of the United States and what should be changed about them, one short attack on Kennedy's campaign opponent, Richard M. Nixon, was all the stations reported. Guback assumed there was a common frame into which the broadcasters placed Kennedy's speech. In this case the frame was the "election campaign," and Kennedy, whatever he said, was treated as a candidate trying to put his opponent down.

In a second study, three British researchers, James D. Halloran, Phillip Elliott, and Graham Murdock (1970), found that despite both ideological and qualitative differences of the media, the coverage of a 1968 anti-Vietnam demonstration in London was amazingly similar. Tabloids, prestige papers, commercial and public TV stations, leftist and ultraconservative media had been focusing on the same limited aspect of the upcoming event: It was reported as necessarily violent. After the demonstration was over and only a handful of the 60,000 marchers had had a short scuffle with the police, the media nevertheless maintained the violent image they had constructed of the march by putting the rare violent scenes at the center of their reporting. The British researchers verified some of the hypotheses two Norwegian social scientists had formulated in 1965: Johan Galtung and Mari Holmboe Ruge (1970) suggested that some criteria of news selection and presentation are common to all media of a specific culture, in fact, to all media of the world.

Galtung and Ruge suggested that their "perception theory of news" in their variety of reportable occurrences is comparable to the variety of sounds to be heard when one turns the tuning knob of a shortwave radio receiver. Using this analogy, Galtung and Ruge hypothesized a number of conventions for news media all over the world in selecting and creating events worth reporting. Some of these criteria are cultural proximity of the event; relevance of one's own group or country; consonance with what had been expected (but also a certain amount of surprise within this consonance); duration of the event, which must be no longer than the time period between two consecutive issues of the medium or program; the simplicity of an event (is it easy to report and to understand?); and the fact that the event had been in the news before.[1] In addition, the two Norwegian authors assumed that four specific news values apply to the "Northwestern corner of the world" better than to other regions: "The more the event concerns elite nations,... the more the event concerns elite people,... the more the event can be seen in personal terms, as due to the action of specific individuals,... the more negative the event is in its con-

sequences, the more probable that it will become a news item"
(p. 265).

The ideal-typical news for Western capitalist societies, therefore,
is supposed to be elite centered; to focus on powerful and prominent people, powerful and highly developed nations; and to be negative
and personalized.[2] Galtung and Ruge speculate about the commonali-
ties and differences between this news and that in Communist
societies. News in the Soviet Union or East Germany, they argue,
should be elite centered as well. Indeed, Gerbner and Marvanyi
(1977) show a strikingly similar concentration on highly industrialized countries of U.S., Western European, Eastern European, and
Soviet newspaper coverage. On the other hand, Communist media
should differ from Western media in focusing on positive events and
on structures instead of persons. News, therefore, is an ideological
product; basic philosophical differences are represented in it. Person-
alization, for instance, is the consequence of cultural idealism. Human
beings are regarded as masters of their destinies (Galtung and Ruge
1970). A culture with a materialistic philosophy, however, necessarily
emphasizes structural factors. People are replaceable instruments of
history. Negative news is worth reporting in societies that take for
granted inevitable positive change—that is, "progress." In cultures
in which progress is something to fight for, success is news, failure is
"old". It is a basic notion of Augustinian—a "Western"—philosophy
to assume a linear and persistent movement toward an ultimate and
positive goal. Thus in Western societies "diambiguous"—literally,
"straightforward"—occurrences have a better chance to become news
than "slow-moving historical circles" or "indeterminate or fluid"
situations. "Process may be forced on occurrences whose direction is
indecisive" (Rock 1973, p. 77). This perspective of culturally defined
news converges with the notion that news is a product of one specific
group in society—for instance, the white middle class in the United
States (Tuchman 1978, Gans 1979)—if we assume that the norms for
the culture as a whole in fact are defined by the white middle class.

What is typical news in the West in the view of Galtung and
Ruge? Anyone accustomed to the traditional idea of Western news as
an account of reality will be struck by their avoidance of such expressions as "objectivity." In their theory, there is no such thing as
"untruthful" news. News is not an account but a socially accepted
"metaphor" of reality (Lee 1976). News shows how a culture "officially" perceives and defines reality.[3]

To structure reality is one of the major tasks of every culture.
Niklas Luhmann (1971), one of Europe's leading system theorists,
suggests that one ought even to define culture as the ultimate frame
of how to structure reality, how to reduce its complexity. Journalists,

then, to a great extent, know what to present as news simply because they have been socialized in and by their cultures. It does not necessarily take an explicit construction of a "news consensus," as Epstein (1973) assumes. Journalists do not always have to look at one another's products to find out what events are agreed upon to be news.* Graber's content analysis (1971) of twenty American newspapers, for instance, revealed an amazing uniformity of the news coverage of "professional" journalists, regardless of which paper they worked for. Even the "unprofessional" readers' letters to the editor did not differ in substance from the press in general. Thus, there still is typically Western news because cultures in the "northwestern corner of the world" share philosophical conceptions of reality. But Galtung and Ruge abandon the old notion that the unifying feature of Western news is its truthfulness, as opposed to the "propagandist" nature of communist media.

Winfried Schulz (1976), a West German mass communication researcher, speculated about the reasons why Western cultures maintain the guidelines for the news that Galtung and Ruge hypothesized. In what has so far been the most comprehensive and extensive study of their assumptions, Schulz found that Galtung and Ruge basically were right as far as the news of ten different West German media was concerned. Based on a content analysis of almost 6,000 news items, Schulz confirmed that news heavily concentrates on elite persons, elite nations, negative events, and actions of people. Differences among observed media were small—their consonance was strong.

Schulz uses the system-functional perspective in evaluating his results. He does not discuss the quality of news in terms of its closeness to reality but in terms of its usefulness for society. Herbert Gans (1979) shares this viewpoint when he defines news as "information which is transmitted from sources to audiences, with journalists... summarizing, refining, and altering what becomes available to them in order to make the information *suitable* [italics added] for their audiences" (p. 80).[4]

To be highly selective in newsmaking, Schulz argues, is functional in a system that tries to make sure its members are able to take common action by sharing perceptions of what is at stake. Not only may the narrow scope of the news selection rules be functional for a system but also the news substance. Since society can pay only a limited amount of attention to events, negative occurrences threatening the order of a system must be dealt with more frequently and extensively.

---

* If they do, however (Crouse 1973), their incentive is not so much to define news as such, but to make sure that competitors do not happen to cover a detail they might have missed.

Political conflicts have to be settled, disasters have to make every-body aware that their causes must be corrected. "Functional" in this case is everything that stabilizes the system. Concentration on elite actions, for instance, assures members of society that there is suf-ficient continuity in political and social life. The same people make news all the time. News is the "eternal recurrence" of a ritual, con-veying the impression of an "endlessly repeated drama whose terms are familiar and well understood" (Rock 1973, p. 77; see also Roshco 1975).

But what, asks Schulz, if we think it functional to allow or even enhance social change? Then, showing that important actions are taken only by a small elite and that only some elite nations are worth covering, makes news dysfunctional. So if news is a "social insti-tution," (Tuchman, 1978, p. 4), and as such necessarily controlled by cultural norms, it no longer makes sense to talk about "biased" news. What we have to talk about, then, are "biased" cultural norms. That news "limits knowledge" (ibid., p. 210) is nothing to worry about. The question is: How does it limit knowledge? Does it provide us with the appropriate pictures of the world? Do we, for instance, get "the in-formation we require if we are to act as informed and intelligent decision-makers in a democratic society?" (Halloran, Elliott, and Murdock, 1970, p. 313).

Several studies have shown that news in the West tends to be uniform and system stabilizing. In Graber's content analysis (1971) of the presidential campaign coverage in 1968, it becomes clear that American newspaper news is highly personalized, dealing with the personal characteristics of the candidates to a much greater extent than with the issues for which they stand. Patterson and McClure (1976) show that TV network news in the 1972 election campaign pre-sented the candidates as though they were sports heroes surrounded by cheering crowds, instead of depicting the political dimensions of the election. Gans (1979) found that "altogether, a very small number of knowns, probably less than fifty and most of them high federal of-ficials, are repeatedly in the news" (p. 12). Only 30 percent of all the news items in West German TV news do not mention at least one distinct person, and only 1 percent do not mention people at all. These findings are based on an extensive content analysis of about three hundred news programs in spring 1977 (Schatz 1980). News editors in the United States, asked to rank-order news items accord-ing to their newsworthiness, unanimously attributed top priority to negative events (Clyde and Buckalew 1969). Schoenbach (1978) was able to show that negativism and elite action are common criteria even for the selection of local news in newspapers.

Does news in the West present a somewhat greater variety of events than news does in totalitarian countries? Or do only the general perspectives of the two systems differ from each other and the ways these perspectives are enforced? What basically distinguishes a free press from a tightly controlled one obviously is not the abundant diversity of the former and the uniformity of the latter. Their differences are gradual. Both evidently tend to be consonant; but in Western societies there is some pluralism possible, at least *within* the system. The media may be elite centered, but they are allowed to report about different elites. They may be negativistic, but they can choose between murders and bankruptcies. Hopple's analysis (1982), for instance, reveals a significant similarity in the international coverage of the British *Guardian* and the *New York Times*, both in the amount of conflictual events they portray and in terms of the countries they present as actors in conflicts. But evidently, there is at least some temporal diversity in their reporting. They do not cover the same conflicts at the same time.

Western news values are not necessarily made for eternity. As a result of recent economic and political crises, a continuous movement toward the better is not as self-evident as it used to be. One consequence of this new cultural definition of reality could be a less linear, one-dimensional perspective of news reporting, an extended interest in long-term developments. The more it becomes clear that the mere fact of voting presidents out of office does not automatically change persistent structures, the less attention Western media might pay to persons instead of structures.[5] One might ask whether future news in the West will provide more "knowledge about," more understanding of our environment (Park 1940) instead of mere "acquaintance with it".

NOTES

1. Somewhat similar ideas, phrased in a more impressionistic and less systematic way, can be found in the seminal book by Lippmann (1922).

2. News criteria can always compensate for each other: A strongly negative event—a plane crash, for instance—is news, although one of the other factors, such as "prominent persons involved," may be lacking (Galtung and Ruge, 1970).

3. This is what De Fleur and Dennis (1981) probably have in mind when they define news as "a report that presents a contemporary view of reality" (p. 422).

4. Molotch and Lester (1974) focus on the functions of news not for the audience as a whole but for individuals. They define news as "events" and state: "Occurrences become events according to their usefulness to an indi-

vidual who is attempting on a particular occasion to order her or his experience" (p. 102). Most often, then, defining news is a question of power.

5. Discussions with my colleague Dr. Richard Perloff, Department of Communication, Cleveland State University, were very helpful in developing these ideas.

REFERENCES

Altheide, David L. *Creating Reality: How TV News Distorts Events.* Beverly Hills: Sage, 1976.

Ault, Phillip H. and Edwin Emery. *Reporting the News.* New York: Dodd, Mead & Co., 1965.

Breed, Warren, "Social Control in the Newsroom." *Social Forces,* 1955, pp. 326–35.

Campbell, Lawrence R., and Roland E. Wolseley. *How to Report and Write the News.* Englewood Cliffs, N. J.: Prentice-Hall, 1961.

Clyde, Robert W., and James K. Buckalew. "Inter Media Standardization: A Q-Analysis of News Editors." *Journalism Quarterly* 46 (1969): 349–51.

Crouse, Timothy. *The Boys on the Bus.* New York: Random House, 1973.

Davis, Dennis K., and Stanley J. Baran. *Mass Communication and Everyday Life.* Belmont, Calif.: Wadsworth, 1981.

Davison, W. Phillips, James Boylan, and Frederick T. C. Yu. *Mass Media: Systems and Effects.* 2nd ed. New York: Holt, Rinehart and Winston, 1982.

DeFleur, Melvin L., and Everette E. Dennis. *Understanding Mass Communication.* Boston: Houghton Mifflin, 1981.

Dovifat, Emil. *Zeitungslehre.* I. *Band.* 5th ed. Berlin: DeGruyter, 1967.

Epstein, Edward Jay. *News From Nowhere.* New York: Random House, 1973.

Galtung, Johan, and Mari Holmboe Ruge. "The Structure of Foreign News." In Jeremy Tunstall, ed., *Media Sociology.* London: Constable, 1970.

Gans, Herbert J. *Deciding What's News.* New York: Vintage Books, 1979.

Gerbner, George, and George Marvanyi. "The Many Worlds of the World's Press." *Journal of Communication* 27, no. 1 (1977): 52–66.

Graber, Doris A. "Press Coverage Patterns of Campaign News: The 1968 Presidential Race." *Journalism Quaterly* 48 (1971): 502–12.

Guback, Thomas H. "Reporting or Distorting?" In Harry Jay Skornia and Jack William Kitson, eds., *Problems and Controversies in Television and Radio.* Palo Alto, Calif.: Pacific Books, 1968.

Halloran, James D., Phillip Elliot, and Graham Murdock. *Demonstrations and Communication: A Case Study.* Harmondsworth, England: Penguin, 1970.

Harriss, Julian, Kelly Leiter, and Stanley Johnson. *The Complete Reporter.* 4th ed. New York: Macmillan, 1981.

Hopple, Gerald W. "International News Coverage in Two Elite Newspapers." *Journal of Communication* 32, no. 1 (1982): 61–74.

Lee, Jae-Won. "Reality, Metaphor, and Reporter's Role." *Journal of Communication Inquiry,* Spring 1976, pp. 124–36.

Lester, Marilyn. "Generating Newsworthiness: The Interpretive Construction of Public Events." *American Sociological Review*, 45 (1980): 984–94.

Lippmann, Walter. *Public Opinion*. New York: Macmillan, 1922.

Luhmann, Niklas. "Oeffentliche Meinung." In Niklas Luhmann, ed., *Planung*, pp. 9–34. Opladen, West Germany: Westdeutscher Verlag, 1971.

Molotch, Harvey, and Marilyn Lester. "News as Purposive Behavior." *American Sociological Review* 39 (1974): 101–12.

Park, Robert E. "News as a Form of Knowledge." *American Journal of Sociology* 45 (1940): 669–86.

Patterson, Thomas E., and Robert D. McClure. *The Unseeing Eye*. New York: Putnam, 1976.

Rock, Paul, "News as Eternal Recurrence." In Stanley Cohen and Jack Young, eds., *The Manufacture of News*, pp. 73–84. Beverly Hills: Sage, 1973.

Roshco, Bernard. *Newsmaking*. Urbana: University of Illinois Press, 1975.

Ruehl, Manfred. *Die Zeitungsredaktion als organisiertes soziales System*. Duesseldorf (West Germany): Berltesmann, 1969.

Schatz, Heribert. *Fernsehnachrichten in Demokratietheoretischer Sicht*. Duisburg, West Germany: Duisburger Materialien zur Innenpolitik und Verwaltungswissenschaft, 1980.

Schoenback, Klaus. *Trennung von Nachricht und Meinung*. Freiburg, West Germany: Karl Alber, 1977.

———. "Die isolierte Welt des Lokalen." *Rundfunk und Fernsehen* 25 (1978): 260–77.

Schulz, Winfried. *Die Konstruktion von Realitaet in den Nachrichtenmedien*. Freiburg, West Germany: Karl Alber, 1976.

Tuchman, Gaye. *Making News*. New York: Free Press, 1978.

White, David M. "The 'Gate Keeper': A Case Study in the Selection of News." *Journalism Quarterly* 27 (1950): 383–90.

3. NEWS VALUES VERSUS IDEOLOGY: A THIRD WORLD PERSPECTIVE

MUNIR K. NASSER

In the final days of 1981 three major international events made headlines across front pages and television screens in the West:

- The Polish Government Imposes Martial Law and Cracks Down on Solidarity Labor Movement
- The U.S. Government Charges Libya's President Qaddafi Sends "Hit Teams" to Assassinate Top U.S. Officials
- Israel Annexes the Golan Heights

Most probably, these same headlines flashed across mass media in Third World countries, but with a political slant. Media audiences in the majority of Third World nations probably were presented with different versions of these stories, depending on the gatekeepers' ideologies, professionalism, concepts of news values and, most important, instructions from the Ministry of Information. The way these stories were treated and presented to the public in Third World countries would also have depended on the diplomatic relations between the country of the story's origin and the country where it was received. Moreover, the emphasis or deemphasis given these stories in the Third World would have depended on the country's political orientation and its declared position vis-à-vis superpower politics and regional conflicts.

The mass media in a socialist country with leanings toward Moscow, for example, would probably have presented martial law in Poland as "a legitimate move by the Polish government against the disruptive Solidarity labor movement." The same media would have featured the news of Israel's annexation of the Golan "as an outright aggression against friendly Syria." The Libyan "hit team" story would have been presented as "an alleged plot by the U.S. to discredit Qaddafi and justify military action against Libya."

The media of a Third World country friendly to the United States would probably have used a different yardstick to judge these stories. Martial law in Poland would have been described as "a repressive move by the Communist government to crush the legitimate right of the Polish people to organize in labor unions." Israel's move to annex the Golan would have been described as "an act of self-defense against the aggressive Syrians." Using the same standard of judgment, the media would have described Qaddafi as an "erratic, irrational ruler who is messing things up for a superpower."

These contrasting examples of news slant underscore the close interdependence between mass media and politics in the Third World. In a developing country, where media are used for mobilization and national development, Western criteria of news evaluation and selection take a back seat. The criteria applied by Third World gatekeepers in screening information and judging the newsworthiness of events are indicators of the interrelationships between the domestic media system and the political and cultural environment in a given country. World mass media systems are made unique by the interaction of certain cultural traits, economic conditions, political philosophies, and levels of professionalism. These factors combine to make media perform specific tasks that are essential to society. Such tasks include surveillance of the environment to alert the public to threats or problems developing in the world. Media also provide an agenda-setting and interpretation function to help the public coordinate and categorize the various elements of society. In addition, media provide their consumers with entertainment of various kinds.

In Third World countries today, the most important function of media may be the dissemination and interpretation of news and information. Gatekeepers of these media, whether publishers, editors, reporters, or government officials, make judgments about what is newsworthy and what is not. From the thousands of events that occur in the world, gatekeepers select and evaluate facts, ideas, and events that make up the news for their audiences. In this selection process, they use certain yardsticks to help them measure the newsworthiness of events. Like their counterparts in the First and Second Worlds, they have specific news values that they use as criteria to judge and treat the news.

The purpose of this chapter is to examine the nature and treatment of news in the Third World and to investigate the dominant news values and concepts that guide media gatekeepers in their evaluation and selection of news. The focus is on news values, news sources, and news content, which are discussed and contrasted with Western concepts. The discussion attempts to shed light on these and other questions: What is news in Third World countries? What kind of news content should one expect to find in the press and broadcasting of the developing nations of Africa, Asia, and Latin America? How is this content different from or similar to the news one finds in other parts of the world?

WESTERN AND THIRD WORLD NEWS CONCEPTS

The concepts of objectivity and speedy dissemination in a free marketplace of ideas where journalists act as "watchdogs" over the government are essential to an open and democratic society in the West.

To understand how Third World news concepts differ from or are similar to those in the West, we must consider the Western news model first. There is no universally accepted definition of news in the West, but a common definition found in many newswriting textbooks in the United States and taught to beginning students of journalism is that news is an accurate, fair, balanced, and objective report that must have certain news values based on such criteria as impact, prominence, proximity, timeliness, human interest, conflict, and oddity. These criteria are supposed to help reporters and editors judge the value of the news and whether a story should be prominently displayed, played down, or neglected altogether. The news story normally follows a journalistic formula known as the "inverted pyramid" in which information is arranged in descending order of importance with the most important feature in the "lead" paragraph. This formula was popularized and standardized by the American news services Associated Press (AP) and United Press International (UPI), which relied on telegraphic style for speedy delivery of news. Accurate, objective, balanced, and rapid news became vital ingredients in the Western news formula.

The Western concept of a *free press* is also basic to the dissemination of news and information. This concept is based on the premise that a freely informed public is essential for an open and democratic society to function effectively. The press is expected to report conflicting opinions and facts on matters of public concern in a "free marketplace of ideas" until the "truth" is discovered by the public. The people have a "right to know" what their government is doing, and news must provide essential facts for them to form sound opinions on public issues. Also, mass media are expected to monitor government policies and actions in their role as "watchdogs" over government and as guardians of people's rights. This role often leads to an adversary relationship between media and government.

Perhaps the most dominant principle in the Western press is "objectivity." News should be presented as factual reports of events without the bias of the reporter. "Both sides" of an issue should be fairly presented without making any one view more dominant than another. But objectivity as a journalistic standard has been difficult to attain in the West. Many journalists argue against it because they feel they can never completely divorce themselves from the issues and events they are covering. This has led to the emergence of the "new journalism" school of thought, which holds that journalists should be more than messengers and should get involved in the message and openly admit their biases.

Western criteria for news evaluation and selection are also influenced by the tastes and preferences of media audiences. In competitive media markets dominated by commercial interests and advertising pressures, the gatekeepers' main concern is to give the public what it wants in order to achieve the largest audience possible. In the news area, however, gatekeepers use traditional criteria of news values to determine what the public should get as news. There have, however, been some attempts by the Western news media to study the preferences of audiences in news and information.

One such study, a survey made in 1973 by the American Newspaper Publishers Association, found more than forty general categories of news in American daily newspapers. The survey found more space devoted to sports than to international news and more space given to crime than to cultural events. The most widely read topics in the press, according to this survey, were accidents, disasters, natural phenomena, government affairs, taxes, and crime (ANPA 1973). More recent surveys reveal a shift in audience preferences and reading habits. Today's newspapers are characterized by content more directly relevant to the lives of readers. The American press is expanding traditional definitions of news to include consumer reporting, personal concerns, alternative life styles, social trends, and entertainment news. This "marketing approach" to news focuses on topics with high readership, such as consumer affairs, people, adventure, crime, and sex news. This change was brought about by changing values in society and, most important, by feverish attempts of the media to expand their audiences in the face of vigorous competition between and among news organizations, particularly television news (Dennis and Ismach 1981).

Many Third World nations reject the Western news model because it does not suit their needs.

Many of the Western news values and techniques have been assailed in the Third World on the grounds that developing societies have totally different requirements of their news media from the more economically advanced societies of the West. Third World critics argue that many developing countries have fragile political structures that cannot withstand media scrutiny of the failures of government economic and social programs. They charge that Western media are preoccupied with the negative side of life when covering their own societies. Also, they accuse the major Western news agencies of being obsessed with so-called action or spot news such as disasters, wars, corruption, political intrigues, and civil disorders (Ng'weno 1978, Aggarwala 1979). Other critics argue that it is unfair or impossible for Third World nations to use a yardstick of newsworthiness that is not related to the problems of developing nations. They only ask that news be presented in its context and judged by news values that are relevant to local situations. As one Indian journalist has written, "In our environment there will be for a long time to come, much that is ugly and distasteful. If we follow the Western norm we will be playing up only these dark spots and thus helping unwittingly to erode the faith and confidence without which growth and development are impossible" (Illustrated Weekly of India 1976).

Third World countries often assign journalists the roles of educators and nation builders. This is seen as an extension of the political philosophy of the government to forge a new society. Journalist's roles may vary from one society to another, depending on the tradition of journalism in the country and the standard of professionalism inherited from colonial times. Some African journalists, for example, have played a major part in the struggle for their countries' independence. Others consider their work a patriotic duty and a national service. The model role expected of journalists in the Third World was vividly articulated by Zambia's President Kenneth Kaunda in a speech to newsmen in his country. After instructing them on how they should handle certain news, Kaunda said:

Our news media must reflect the nature of our society,
project and defend our philosophy, our values and our

interests as a sovereign state. If you do not, you are not with us as a nation. I know some of you have always wanted to project an image of disunity in the party and the nation. The facts you have been gathering, the preparation of facts in a distorted manner, the expressions of terminology used in all news media, the choice of items for the front page stories, the choice of headlines and the emphasis given to the Party and Government and life in Zambia in general all indicate the intentions of some of our newsmen. Some of you have been the instruments of our enemies bent on the destruction of Zambia. Some of you have been preoccupied with the failures of some of our development programs. You must stop it before other measures are taken. (Barton 1979)

The burden of this speech is probably echoed year after year in Third World countries. Similar political and economic overtones were heard from other Third World leaders at the UNESCO Latin American Intergovernmental Conference in San Jose, Costa Rica, in 1976. Venezuelan President Andres Perez sharply criticized Western media and news agencies for subjecting developing nations to alien values that threaten their national identity. "I firmly believe," he told the conference, "that international regulation of communication is required to ensure the sacred right to information by guaranteeing that only the truth will be reported and to safeguard the unrestricted right to express opinion. The communication industry cannot have priority over public and social order" (Tatarian 1978).

The rationale of Third World governments for restricting Western-style investigative reporting is that their societies are too fragile to stand much probing into the failures of government. They argue that in societies where the state lacks established institutions and the majority of the people are illiterate and more loyal to racial, religious, or tribal groups, the concepts of a free press and investigative reporting are not suitable. Instead, journalists are expected to commit themselves to a new concept of reporting known as "development journalism." Over the last two decades, Third World nations have been giving high priority to national development programs to better their social well-being through economic programs. Because mass media and news are considered vital in promoting such programs, journalists are increasingly regarded as active partners fostering their nation's growth. There has been no clear-cut definition of "development news," but Aggarwala (1979) provided a definition that represents the kind of journalism practiced in many Third World countries. "Development news," he said, "is not different from regular news or investigative reporting.... In covering the developing news beat, a journalist should critically examine, evaluate and report the relevance of a development project to national and local needs, the difference between a planned scheme and its actual implementation, and the difference between its impact on people as claimed by government officials and as it actually is."

This kind of development journalism is generally welcomed by Third World reporters as an outlet for serious reporting in areas not related to sensitive political news, which is often the target of government censorship. They expect this form of reporting to ultimately lead to the growth of democratic debate in the press. But in many instances, development journalism backfires because its successes alert governments to the importance of economic and social reporting and its potential usefulness to mobilizing mass support behind government policies. Governments eventually extend the concept to cover all mass media and integrate them into their official information policies (Righter 1978). A distinction must be made between development journalism and "development support communication," which is designed to support and promote the cause of economic development. In countries where the media are controlled by the government, a certain overlap occurs, and the two concepts are often confused (Smith 1980).

THIRD WORLD CRITERIA FOR NEWS SELECTION

Most often ideological, political, cultural, and socioeconomic realities in a Third World nation determine the type of news that nation reads, hears, or views.

Any attempt to assess criteria of news evaluation and selection in Third World nations requires a consideration of such factors as the ideological, political, socioeconomic, demographic, and cultural realities in these nations. No formula exists in the Third World that could be applied universally to news selection in the developing countries of Africa, Asia, the Middle East, and Latin America. Yet some factors are common to most of these countries.

The majority of Third World governments use one technique or another for controlling the content of news media in their countries. Some of them exert prior control over content by notifying editors as to "sensitive" topics, which they must leave aside. Other governments pass laws specifying which information must not be published or broadcast. Still other governments resort to direct official censorship to stop any news "harmful to the state" from being disseminated.

But more important and subtle forms of news control are practiced by Third World governments. By far the most dominant considerations in the selection of news are political and ideological. In his study of the African news media, Alcino Louise da Costa, director of the weekly *Afrique Nouvelle*, identified several criteria used by African editors to evaluate international news for their national audiences. It should be noted here that these African criteria are also commonly employed in other parts of the Third World.

1. "The psycho-political security" criterion gives prominence to reassuring news coming from countries with which particularly close relations are maintained. Any news items considered to be politically pernicious are not included in the press or broadcasting. This applies in particular to the state-controlled media, where the regime will not allow any news that may discredit its national policies or disturb public opinion.

2. "The community of interests" criterion gives priority to the dissemination of good news about countries with the same political, economic, cultural, or ideological interests. The media take into account the interests of other countries belonging to the same organizations as their own governments. In this regard, close relations with a country are more decisive in the selection of news items than geographic proximity.

3. "The imperatives of national policy" criterion must contribute to legitimizing or strengthening governmental positions. According to this criterion, the media should disseminate news about other countries only if it is compatible with policies set by their own government. News items dealing with national liberation movements and with fighting against apartheid and racism are selected and emphasized if they coincide with the government's declared positions (da Costa 1980).

At the local level, criteria for domestic news may vary from one country to another. But certain rules of thumb are basic to news selection in many developing nations. As with international news criteria, domestic news criteria select reassuring information that strengthens confidence in governmental actions and projects a good image of the country and the head of state. Most often, the activities of the president or head of state and the party in power are given full coverage. In some countries the head of state's speeches, which sometimes last over two hours, are covered in their entirety by radio and television and the full text is printed in the press. The same amount of coverage is accorded high-ranking government officials in their activities and speeches. Many governments issue directions forbidding journalists to summarize speeches delivered by the head of state or cabinet ministers. In the very few developing countries with opposition parties, however, the opposition press usually focuses on the negative aspects of the government. Their criterion is to defend their party's position and publish news that discredits the government in power (da Costa 1980).

Other internal factors also play an important part in influencing decisions about domestic news. The minister in charge of information and the heads of departments under him usually decide the editorial criteria for the daily budget of news. These criteria depend largely on the degree of loyalty to the regime, commitment to the party, and level of professionalism. During wars, crises, and national tensions, many ministers of information insist on screening radio and television news programs before they are put on the air. In some cases, they dictate to editors the content and headlines for certain news stories.

In some parts of the Third World, news values are often decided on regional political and cultural considerations. In the Middle East, for example, Arab mass media have their own set of news values that make them distinctive from media in other areas. In deciding what is news, Arab gatekeepers consider the cultural and sociopolitical background of their audiences to be of paramount importance. Once gatekeepers determine the ideological, social, or religious profile of the audience, it becomes easier for them to select the news that meets their needs. Traditional values, religious beliefs, and political ideologies are often so strong in a country that gatekeepers have to take them into consideration when selecting the news. A gatekeeper in Saudi Arabia, for example, will consider the strict Islamic laws and the dominant Arab culture as part of his news criteria. In a more open society, such as Lebanon, a gatekeeper does not have to deal with the same cultural or religious pressures as his Saudi counterpart. Sometimes the selection of news is influenced by the cultural bias of editors. This usually happens when editors unconsciously conform to accepted norms in society and make choices different from editors elsewhere because of their different cultural perspectives (Rugh 1979). By the same token, the flow of news between and within Arab countries is most often guided by political and ideological concerns. This flow is impeded by censorship policies designed to control subversive propaganda. But probably the most important political factor, unique to the Middle East, that influences decisions in Arab newsrooms is the Arab-Israeli conflict, which has been the major preoccupation of the region for the last three decades. The value of the news is often measured against the background of the Arab-Israeli conflict and the position of the state toward the conflict (Aboubakr 1980).

Another Third World area that has its own distinctiveness is Asia. Pran Chopra (1980) of the Press Foundation of Asia pointed to some cultural aspects of Asian journalism that make it distinctive. He found that Asians receive and read their news in English more than any other people whose mother tongue is not English. He also found that more Asian journalists have been brought up in a Western educational and cultural background. The news criteria employed by Asian journalists therefore are largely determined by the interplay of foreign influences and Asian cultural and sociopolitical influences. At the local level, the selection of domestic news in the Asian media is strongly colored by the demographic background of the Asian media and journalists, and reflects Western news values. Emphasis is placed on political news rather than on economic or agricultural news, and rural areas figure very little in the news content. The reason for this bias is the strong city background of the Asian press, which makes it city-oriented in its concerns and reflects the biases of the urban middle classes. This is true in other Third World countries, but in Asia it is particularly significant because the urban middle classes have a higher proportion of people who have been educated in the West. Asian media, therefore, reflect the interests of these people and their preoccupation with Western problems and issues.

In Latin America, too, news values have to be considered in the framework of political and cultural realities. Although many of the influences discussed above apply to Latin America, the continent still has a distinctiveness of its own. The mass media in Latin America have been established on American commercial models and are heavily influenced by Western styles of journalism. Most of the news media in Latin America adhere to a principle of news evaluation based on competition for information in a free enterprise system that maximizes market profits (Tunstall 1977). Some critics of the Latin American news media, such as Fernando Reyes Matta of Mexico, point to the fact that such Western influences most often distort realities of current events in Latin America. They charge that the application of Western news formulas to Latin American facts will result in their being seen from foreign journalistic perspectives. These perspectives often emphasize the superficial, the anecdotal, and the unrelated elements of events, and neglect the news of more important social and economic developments in society. A great number of facts appear and disappear from the news flow without any indication of their background or impact. The selection of news is often determined by the drama of events, sensationalism, and rapid dissemination with no attempt at interpretation or to place events in a social context. As a result, the predominance of negative over positive facts became a basic part of the professional news yardstick (Matta 1980).

Another distinctive feature of Latin American news is the practice of treating government announcements as news. In many capitals of Latin America, journalists look for news in presidential palaces, ministerial offices, and government agencies. There they wait for the spokesman of the system to speak, and they record his pronouncements verbatim. The description and interpretation of events have been left to the rhetoric of government officials, and the journalists' role has been reduced to one of mere recorders. The trivial details of ceremony and the traffic in and out of officials' offices are judged important by this formula. This situation is attributed to the low professional standards of journalists, who often do not have a university degree or professional training in journalism. Their salaries are generally low, and most of them have little respect or prestige in society. According to Robert Pierce of the University of Florida, these practices are common throughout the world, but in Latin America they are more acute. He thinks there is much less tendency for Latin American reporters to place things in context or interpret them to the readers. Pierce believes, however, that Latin American editors and reporters are becoming aware of the interpretive and investigative reporting which has been developing rapidly in some Latin American countries (Pierce 1979).

SOURCES OF NEWS FOR THIRD WORLD MEDIA

Major Western news agencies tend to set the agenda and define news values, styles, and formats in the Third World.

The four major Western news agencies, AP, UPI, AFP, and Reuters, have largely shaped the presentation of news in Third World countries and defined the news values for their mass media. Almost all newspapers and radio and television stations in the non-Communist countries have little choice but to rely directly on these agencies as their main source of world news. Few news media in the world can claim independence in gathering foreign news. The extent of Third World media dependence on Western agencies has been documented in several quantitative studies. A recent study by Schramm dealing with news coverage of fourteen Asian newspapers found that over 75 percent of the nonlocal news content came from the four Western news agencies (Schramm et al. 1978). Another study, of Nigerian broadcast media, found that 85 percent of the news content came from Reuters, AP, AFP, and Visnews (Golding and Elliott 1979).

The agencies have also influenced the concept of news in Third World countries by playing an agenda-setting function and promoting the idea of speed and impartiality. The "inverted pyramid" formula has standardized news reporting and has introduced a uniform journalistic practice throughout the world. The news values of Third World editors have been influenced by the agencies' news format and style and by the relative weight they place on certain kinds of news. Most often the agencies have influenced their client practices through the force of example and constant exposure of editors to the Western style of reporting. Also, the agencies have shaped Third World news values through their involvement in training programs for national news agencies. In Africa, for example, Reuters helped establish news agencies for many newly independent countries and trained many of their staffs. Later, Reuters became dependent on these agencies for almost all its news from some African countries (Boyd-Barrett 1980). The same can be said of Agence France Presse and the Francophone African countries.

In addition to their dependence on Western news agencies for foreign news, Third World news media have been influenced by the style and format of Western journalism. Many newspapers and magazines in the developing countries have been closely modeled upon the *New York Times*, the *Times* of London, *Time*, and *Newsweek*. In broadcasting, too, American and British radio news formats have served as models for nearly every country in the world. The specialized radio news services developed by AP and UPI for their local American clients have been adapted for other countries.

In television news, two major news-film agencies dominate the Third World. Visnews, which is largely owned by Reuters and the BBC, sells to the world the entire news-film resources of the NBC television network in the United States, the BBC network in Britain, and the NHK network in Japan. The second major news-film agency is UPITN, which is owned and operated by UPI and the British ITN television network. Each day, Visnews sends out its video stories to 193 customers in 98 countries in the world. Each client station receives from 12 to 15 minutes of video news of which it uses an average of 4 to 5 minutes on its newscasts. Television stations with limited resources use all the news-film they receive. The reason for this heavy dependency on foreign canned news is its high technical quality, its more visually dramatic material, and its cheap price compared to local production (Tunstall 1977).

The criteria employed by Western news agencies in judging and treating the news have been flexible enough for adaptation by local journalists. The concept of neutrality and the "two-sides style" of Western journalism have been easily manipulated for political purposes in some Third World countries. Local editors have selectively edited a two-sided story into a one-sided story merely by leaving out what one side said, depending on their political orientation or criteria. For the government-controlled media, the Western formula has enabled them to disseminate good news about friendly countries and bad news about adversaries. For the privately owned media, publishers have given priority to their commercial interests and have selected controversial and "soft" news that attracts more readers and more advertising revenue (da Costa 1980).

The overall dependence of Third World nations on Western agencies has been slightly reduced by the development of alternative sources of news. In recent years the growth of national and regional news services in the Third World has started to provide an alternative supply of news through exchange arrangements and cooperation between national agencies. The national agency has often served an important purpose by helping the government control and influence incoming foreign news. In some countries the national agency has existed for no other purpose than to receive, translate, and edit the copy of major world news agencies before passing it to the local media. The editors of such agencies have become powerful gatekeepers, who select news only to suit the government's political purposes. The dual role of the national agency as distributor and censor has served as a guidance channel for the local press and broadcasting and has given clues to the editors as to how the regime would like them to treat certain stories. Many Third World governments have justified such practices on the ground that control of the foreign news at the source is necessary to protect against the bias of the Western news agencies. Critics of such measures have charged that the concentration of flow of news in the hands of the national agency is a form of political censorship (Boyd-Barrett 1980).

The leading example of cooperation among Third World nations is the Non-Aligned News Agency (NANA), which was brought into existence in 1976 by a decision of the Fifth Non-Aligned Summit Conference in Colombo. The eighty-five-nation members decided to share information from their national agencies and provide objective and authentic information relating to nonaligned countries and the rest of the world. The political declaration of the conference said that the purpose of the news pool was to overcome "the situation of dependence and domination in which the majority of countries are reduced to being passive recipients of biased, inadequate and distorted information."

The Yugoslav news agency Tanjug, which coordinates the news pool, receives a daily limit of 500 words of news items from each of the 41 participant agencies, then translates and transmits the pool offerings in English, French, and Spanish. In 1977, over 60 percent of the content of the pool was provided by just 7 countries, led by Yugoslavia and Egypt (Pinch 1978). Very little of the material is critical of the participants' political positions, but most of it is colored by ideological rhetoric. At first, some of the agencies sent to the pool summaries of speeches of their heads of states and some public relations

material; but in recent years they have been sending more meaningful information about their societies. Some critics of the pool believe
that it is limited by its intergovernmental character. They charge
that the decision to establish the pool was more an act of political solidarity than a pragmatic decision. The flow of news passes to governments rather than the press, and keeps politicians aware of what is
happening in other parts of the world (Smith 1980, Boyd-Barrett
1980).

A collaborating supplement to NANA, and an important source
of news for many developing countries, is Inter Press Service (IPS).
This news agency, which was started by a group of individuals in
Latin America in 1964, is dedicated to the presentation and interpretation of news dealing with the problems of the Third World. It
emphasizes such issues as development, liberation movements, cooperation among developing nations, and major powers' policies toward
the Third World. IPS has rejected Western journalistic styles and
adopted a specific political cause. It does not place as much emphasis
on the "spot news" style of Western journalism as on interpretation
and analysis. Its aim is to provide Third World readers with educative
information that will help them place social and political problems of
the world in proper perspective (Smith 1980).

Bilateral news-exchange agreements between national news
agencies have increased in recent years and have allowed for more
alternative sources of news. The expansion of regional news agencies
has also been significant. In Africa, for example, a Pan-African agency has been developed by the Organization of African Unity to organize regional pools of news. In the Middle East, Egypt's news agency
MENA has placed correspondents in seven Arab states and has provided an Arabic service to the whole Arab world. Also, MENA has
maintained cordial relations with Western agencies and has translated AFP's service into Arabic. Besides its close cooperation with
NANA, MENA has been instrumental in creating several regional
news organizations, such as the Arab News Agencies Federation, the
African News Agencies Federation, and the Islamic News Agencies
Federation. The main function of these federations has been to review
policy objectives, training programs, and news exchange.

In Latin America, the regional news agency LATIN was created
by Reuters and some prestigious newspapers in Latin America.
LATIN is often criticized for its close association with Reuters and
some conservative Latin American publishers and for not paying
much attention to national developmental projects (Boyd-Barrett
1980). Also, the dominance of Western news values in the continent is
assailed on the grounds that any effort to create a major Latin American news agency only duplicates the services of Western news agen-

cies and that the availability of news agency material only discourages daily newspapers from having overseas correspondents (Smith 1980).

A different source of news is sometimes available from Communist countries to Third World countries with socialist forms of government or close ties with Moscow. The Soviet news agency TASS, for example, is distributed free of charge in several Third World countries. Although TASS has news values in line with the Communist political ideology, some newspapers in the Third World take advantage of its services because it is free. Others refuse to take it because they are aware of its ideological bias to serve the interests of the Soviet state and influence world public opinion through propaganda and agitation. In the Middle East, for example, most Arab editors depend heavily on Western news agencies for non-Arab news. Exceptions are Iraq and Syria, which use TASS heavily. By the mid-1970s, TASS had outlets in every Arab country except Saudi Arabia, but its material was not used regularly by Arab editors because they regarded it as "pure propaganda" (Rugh 1979). The influence of TASS around the world also declined during the 1970s as a result of competition from the Chinese news agency Hsin Hua (NCNA) and the poor quality and reliability of the TASS service (Smith 1980).

NEWS CONTENT OF THIRD WORLD MEDIA

In most Third World countries, the news media give the public what the public "needs," not what the public "wants."

In their surveillance function, news media in the West, and especially in the United States, tend to emphasize what people want rather than what they need. Western gatekeepers are guided by feedback data obtained by readership surveys and audience ratings to determine the likes and dislikes of the public. This information tells broadcasters that people watch lively, entertaining, and dramatic television newscasts with plenty of action, sex, crime, and tragedy and that they avoid the serious and complex issues of the world. This "happy talk" formula is widely used in local stations throughout the United States in order to increase audiences and maximize profits. Critics point to the danger of this formula in view of public opinion surveys that show increasing dependence of the American public on television as their major source of news. In print journalism, a few editors and publishers follow television's formula. These are the popular newspapers that emphasize trivia and sensationalism, such as the *New York Post* and the *National Enquirer*. But there is evidence that this trend is moving to some serious dailies, which may subordinate news of public affairs in favor of sensation and gossip. Many news-papers in the United States have remodeled their news pages to in-clude more television-type entertainment material, such as features, pictures, interviews, and human interest news. Some critics compare this trend to the old era of yellow journalism in the United States dur-ing which publishers tried to outdo one another in reporting trivial and sensational news (Hulteng 1979).

Although such practices can be found in the news media of some developing nations, the majority of Third World countries do not appreciate them. Their main concern is to guide their media toward reporting positive governmental goals that will help in the develop-ment of the nation. Their emphasis, therefore, is on information they think the public needs. The tastes and wants of the public count very little in the gatekeepers' criteria of news selection. The news content of the media in the Third World may be similar in some respects to the content of Western media because of the similarities in their news sources. But most of the news content of Third World media differs in scope, focus, and treatment. This is best illustrated in the way the Third World press handles foreign news.

Several studies show that Third World news media print a lar-ger amount of foreign news than some of their Western counterparts. A multinational study of foreign coverage in sixty dailies around the world found that the Third World nations included in the study (Gha-na, India, and the Philippines) devoted more news space to foreign news than did American and Soviet newspapers, which reflects the low priority of editorial attention to the outside world. This study also found an inverse relationship between commercial sponsorship and foreign news coverage. The publicly owned press tended to give high-er priority to foreign news than did the commercial press (Gerbner and Marvanyi 1977).

Other studies of foreign news in the Arab media show the impor-tance of international affairs to the Arab gatekeeper. In 1971, Dajani and Donohue conducted a content analysis of six Arab dailies and compared the results with a similar study done ten years earlier (Abu Lughod 1962). The comparison found changes in attitudes and in ties to the various foreign powers competing for influence in the Middle East. While Abu Lughod found that the volume of foreign news in the Arab press was affected by the Arab's dependence on outside powers and Arab concern for internal development, the Dajani and Donohue study showed that such a hypothesis did not hold for the 1970s, be-cause of basic changes that had occurred in the Arab world. These changes included the following political developments: Algeria win-ning independence from France; a socialist party taking power in Syria and Iraq; Arab Socialism becoming an accepted slogan in the

Arab world; the defeat of Egypt, Syria, and Jordan in the 1967 war with Israel; the prominence of the Soviet Union as a close friend of the Arabs; the rise of the Palestine Liberation Organization as an important force in Middle Eastern politics. These changes influenced the criteria by which Arab editors evaluated and selected foreign news. Future studies should reflect similar changes in the gatekeepers' attitudes because of the major political changes that took place in the 1970s. Regional alliances shifted as a result of the 1973 war between Israel and Egypt, Sadat's peace treaty with Israel, the fall of the Shah in Iran, the Iran-Iraq war, and the Sadat assassination. Most probably, the Arab-Israeli conflict will remain the delicate measure by which foreign news in the Arab media will be evaluated.

The Dajani and Donohue study also found that ideological affinity with foreign countries and former cultural ties established with foreign countries during the colonial period favorably affect the volume and content of news concerning these countries. The foreign news in all six papers studied was predominantly political news. The greatest amount of space in these papers was given to U.S. political news, which was found to be negative in direction because of the clear U.S. support of Israel. The Soviet Union, with its clear pro-Arab stand, received positive and wide coverage in all papers except those in Saudi Arabia (Dajani and Donohue 1973).

A third study of foreign news in nine Arab countries, conducted by Gehan Rachty in 1978, found a heavier reliance on news from Western news agencies than from Communist or Third World news agencies. The study found the percentage of news from the Arab states higher than the percentage of news from any other area, and news from Western countries higher than the news from Communist or Third World countries. The percentage of foreign political, military, and economic news in the Arab press was higher than news of science, human interest, accidents, and crime. The data suggested that the Arab press published more positive news (reports of socially desirable events) than negative news such as wars, conflicts, riots, corruption, poverty, and social ills (Rachty 1978).

A more recent study of news values as criteria for selection of national and international news in the Arab media, conducted by Yehia Aboubakr, examined a cross section of the Arab press and news items carried by Egyptian broadcasting services. The study found that a daily average of thirty-one nondomestic items was carried by each of five Arab dailies studied. Out of these, three stories dealt with domestic politics in another Arab country, ten concerned world news touching on political problems of the region, and fourteen were political news items about events or problems of a regional nature. An average of three items per day was given to socioeconomic and cultural categories distributed among economic news, science, art, education, crime, disaster, and human interest. This survey showed that the question was not merely one of interest in local compared with regional news but a question of availability and the continuous flow of news. According to Aboubakr, this explained why in the region, news items carried by international news agencies outweighed news items from other countries of the Middle East (Aboubakr 1980).

This survey also showed that the daily average of news stories presented by Egypt's television network was 31. Of these, 17 items were local news, 4 were regional, and 10 came from outside the region. The daily average of television news included 26 items of a distinctly political nature, reflecting the wide preoccupation of the Middle East media with the Arab-Israeli conflict. This preoccupation, according to Aboubakr, has been responsible for limiting a great part of television exchange within the region. The selection criteria of such news are more sensitive than those related to other media. Most often, news items coming from outside the region are preferred over regional items because of their high professional quality. But this choice is often limited by language difficulties and the need to translate and edit material coming from non-Arabic-speaking countries. Sometimes stories are rejected on the ground that they include too much violence, terrorism, unacceptable sex, alien political propaganda, material offensive to religion or against moral and spiritual values. In applying these taboos, Arab gatekeepers use a wide margin of relativity. Many things considered offensive in one Arab country may be considered progressive in another, although the general cultural background is the same (Aboubakr 1980).

CONCLUSIONS AND EVALUATION

This study has examined the factors that influence news values in the Third World and has analyzed the social, political, ideological, and cultural realities that determine the criteria by which gatekeepers evaluate and select the news. Third World audiences receive the news after it has been revised and reshaped by government or media gatekeepers, depending on the political or cultural realities in the country. Such realities often force journalists to reflect a partisan view and judge, evaluate, and select the news from a position of commitment. In a country where the news media are expected to play a political and ideological role, the journalist becomes an "educator" and "nation builder." Third World countries argue that Western news values are rejected because they do not meet their needs. In their view, news should promote national goals, support authority, and forge a new social order. The rejection of the Western news model underlies Third World complaints in the current debate over the domination of the international flow of news by Western countries. Resistence to such domination involves the major Western news agencies and their influence on the news values of Third World gatekeepers, who reject what they consider to be alien concepts, such as freedom of the press, objectivity in the news, and the press as a watchdog on government. Instead, they argue that their developing societies need "guided media," which must serve as instruments of national policy and mass education.

The problem lies in the concept of news. While Western journalists have come to see their role as members of an opposition party who must expose the misdeeds of government, Third World journalists have given priority to development news and to interpreting events in their due context. It is probably difficult to apply the Western yardstick of newsworthiness to the events of developing countries because their news values vary according to the needs of their societies. Third World complaints about the Western concept of news may be better understood if one appreciates the problems confronting developing nations. These problems range from illiteracy, poverty, and tribalism to a lack of understanding of the function of the modern state. The mass media in such societies simply cannot function by Western theories of media, which emphasize competition for mass audiences in a free market of ideas and focus on the news arising from the exceptional rather than the commonplace.

Third World gatekeepers use varying yardsticks to measure and select news for their media. This variation depends on their perception of events, which are determined by their cultural and political biases and also by the relativity of news values. What is judged to be news in Washington, London, or Paris may not have the same news values in Bogota, Dakar, or Kuala Lumpur. There is a tendency among Western news media to devote much time and attention to the Third World in times of conflict, crises, and disaster. So-called development news gets very little attention, if any, because it does not fit Western criteria of news judgment. The building of a new hospital in Dakar, for example, does not meet the criteria of proximity, impact, conflict, or human interest in a Western newsroom. It is understandable when a Western editor does not select such a story—it is too local and detached from audiences in the United States or Western Europe. To an editor in Dakar, however, the hospital story is a front-page item.

Some people might argue that facts are facts and that there is only one true version of factual news everywhere in the world. They might say that journalists from different countries, covering the same event, should produce similar factual reports. Such an argument cannot be carried too far because news reporting, by its nature, is subjective. Journalists are human beings and express themselves through their personal, political, and cultural biases. The criteria used by journalists for selecting and reporting the news depend largely on the "news culture" in a given country and on how gatekeepers view such concepts as news values, freedom of the press, credibility of the source, and government control of the media. Mohamed Hassanein Heikal, a well-known Third World journalist and former editor of the leading Egyptian daily *Al-Ahram*, notes that there is no such thing as objectivity in the news. "We separate news and views only in appearance; the way in which we present news reflects a certain position that we adhere to. There is no newspaper in the world whose coverage is not colored by one political position or another. It is humanly impossible for any person to filter views from straight news completely" (Nasser 1979).

Cultural anthropologist Edward T. Hall describes how culture affects the way a person sends and receives messages. Culture, he writes, "is a mold in which we are all cast, and it controls our daily lives in many unsuspected ways" (Hall 1959). Third World gatekeepers select certain facts as news and leave others aside because they structure their perception of the world according to their cultural and ideological frames of reference. Through this process, known as selective exposure and selective perception, reporters and editors select and interpret messages in terms of their experience and the ways they have learned to respond to them. They also select and interpret messages so as to resist any change in their cultural and ideological frame of reference (Schramm 1973).

The question of news values and news content cannot be considered without the question of credibility in Third World news media. As a result of many of the political and socioeconomic factors discussed above, the news media of many Third World nations have not achieved the high professional and technical status of Western media. Their weak economic base, the lack of trained journalists, and the increasing political pressures on the media have resulted in their losing much of their credibility and professionalism. Many Third World journalists today, especially in countries where the media are controlled by the government, are suspected of being mouthpieces of the government or party in power. The audiences in these countries regard their news media with a large measure of skepticism and do not accept news content at face value. During times of crises and military conflict, audiences usually turn to foreign broadcasts to learn about developments in their own countries. The lack of objectivity and reliability often forces the reading public to read between the lines for omissions and implied meanings. In many cases, the mixing of news and views makes it hard for the reader to distinguish between news and commentary.

Quite often, distortion in news handling and news management in Third World countries results in the loss of media credibility. In countries where journalism has not developed into an advanced profession, news distortion and outright fabrication are common practices. Even in well-developed press systems like that of Egypt, news management and fabrication take place. In 1973, for example, Cairo radio fabricated a news item claiming that the Israelis had launched an attack on an Egyptian military base on the Red Sea. This was followed by announcements about Egypt's counterattack, which triggered the 1973 war. Mohamed Hassanein Heikal, then editor of *Al-Ahram*, helped prepare these announcements and even planted fabricated news stories in *Al-Ahram* to camouflage Egypt's war plans (Heikal 1976). Later, however, Heikal became critical of Sadat's information policies for trying to conceal Egypt's military setbacks. He said that people lost confidence and went back to their habit of listening to foreign radio stations (Nasser 1979). Another critic of Sadat's news management during the 1973 war was his chief of staff during the war, General Saad El Shazly, who charged that Egypt's official statements had "succumbed to straightforward lying." In his memoirs, El Shazly accused the Egyptian media of hiding the truth and spreading lies about Egypt's military setbacks. He said that people in Egypt learned to trust rumor over their press (El Shazly 1980).

News values must also be considered within the context of freedom of expression in the Third World, especially freedom of the press. It is pointless to inquire into the news values of a journalist in a country where freedom to select what to report is curtailed by censorship, official policy, and regulations. The quality and credibility of journalism in many Third World countries suffers because governments cannot tolerate journalists who expose their failures or weaknesses. They want the press to apply the yardstick of newsworthiness, which only enhances a positive image of the leadership and the country. News suppression and truth perversion in many Third World nations have disillusioned many people, including those who believe in "guided journalism" and a "social role" for the mass media. Press freedom has been sacrificed in the interest of national unity. To many Third World leaders, it is more important to speak with a national voice than to encourage freedom of dissent. They claim that press freedom endangers the national security and welfare of the state. They argue that in a situation where the majority of people are illiterate and owe their allegiance more to family and tribe than to the nation, conditions that justify a free press do not exist. Such self-serving justifications are advanced by leaders who are afraid to experiment with freedom. But it is pointless to expect press freedom when other freedoms do not exist. Press freedom cannot survive in the absence of democratic institutions and political and social freedoms.

REFERENCES

Aboubakr, Yehia. "Towards an Intra-Cultural News Exchange in the Arab States." In UNESCO, *News Values and Principles of Cross Cultural Communication*, No. 85. Paris, 1980.

Abu Lughod, Ibrahim. "International News in the Arabic Press: A Comparative Content Analysis." *Public Opinion Quarterly* 26 (1962): 600–613.

Aggarwala, Narinder. "What is Development News?" *Journal of Communication* 29 (Spring 1979): 180–85.

ANPA. *News and Editorial Content and Readership of the Daily Newspaper*. Reston: American Newspaper Publishers Association Research Center, 1973.

Barton, Frank. *The Press of Africa*. New York: African Publishing, 1979.

Boyd-Barrett, Oliver. *The International News Agencies*. Beverly Hills: Sage, 1980.

Chopra, Pran. "Asian News Values: A Barrier or a Bridge?" In UNESCO, *News Values and Principles of Cross Cultural Communication*, No. 85. Paris, 1980.

da Costa, Alcino Louis. "New Criteria for the Selection of News in African Countries." In UNESCO, *News Values and Principles of Cross Cultural Communication*, No. 85. Paris, 1980.

Dajani, Nabil, and John Donohue. "Foreign News in the Arab Press: A Content Analysis of Six Arab Dailies." *Gazette* 19, no. 3 (1973).

Dennis, Everette, and Arnold Ismach. *Reporting Processes and Practices: Newswriting for Today's Readers*. Belmont, Calif.: Wadsworth, 1981.

El Shazly, Saad. *The Crossing of the Suez*. San Francisco: American Mideast Research, 1980.

Gerbner, George, and George Marvanyi. "The Many Worlds of the World's Press." *Journal of Communication* (Winter 1977): 52–66.

Golding, Peter, and Philip Elliott. *Making the News*. London: Longman, 1979.

Hall, Edward T. *The Silent Language*. Garden City, N.Y.: Doubleday, 1959.

Heikal, Mohamed Hassanein. *The Road to Ramadan*. New York: Ballantine, 1976.

Hulteng, John. *The News Media: What Makes Them Tick?* Englewood Cliffs, N.J.: Prentice-Hall, 1979.

Illustrated Weekly of India, October 10, 1976.

Matta, Fernando Reyes. "The Concept of News in Latin America: Dominant Values and Perspectives of Change." In UNESCO, *News Values and Principles of Cross Cultural Communication*, No. 85. Paris, 1980.

Nasser, Munir. *Press, Politics, and Power: Egypt's Heikal and Al-Ahram*. Ames: Iowa State University Press, 1979.

Ng'weno, Hilary. "All Freedom Is at Stake." In Philip Horton, ed., *The Third World and Press Freedom.* New York: Praeger, 1978.

Pierce, Robert. *Keeping the Flame: Media and Government in Latin America.* New York: Hastings House, 1979.

Pinch, Edward. "The Flow of News: An Assessment of the Non-Aligned News Agencies Pool." *Journal of Communication* (Autumn 1978): 163–71.

Rachty, Gehan. "Foreign News in Nine Arab Countries." Paper presented at the Conference on International News Media and the Developing World, Cairo, April 2–5, 1978.

Righter, Rosemary. *Whose News? Politics, the Press and the Third World.* New York: Times Books, 1978.

Rugh, William. *The Arab Press: News Media and Political Process in the Arab World.* Syracuse: Syracuse University Press, 1979.

Schramm, Wilbur. *Men, Messages and Media: A Look at Human Communication.* New York: Harper & Row, 1973.

———, et al. *International News Wires and Third World News in Asia.* Hong Kong: Center for Communication Studies, Chinese University of Hong Kong, 1978.

Smith, Anthony. *The Geopolitics of Information: How Western Culture Dominates the World.* New York: Oxford University Press, 1980.

Tatarian, Roger, "News Flow in the Third World." In Philip Horton, ed., *The Third World and Press Freedom.* New York: Praeger, 1978.

Tunstall, Jeremy. *The Media Are American: Anglo-American Media in the World.* New York: Columbia University Press, 1977.

4. WHAT IS NEWSWORTHY—AND WHAT IS NOT—IN THE COMMUNIST WORLD?

PAUL LENDVAI

Both Soviet and Western media experts, scholars, and journalists have been long debating the criteria and standards for judging what is "newsworthy" in the countries of "real socialism" where, so the theory goes, the very nature of society is the best guarantee for "responsible, comprehensive and objective reporting."

Critics of the Western media, particularly of the major agencies, often single out as weak points in the international flow of information the tendency to overrepresent the rich industrialized countries, to present events in personal terms, and, last but not least, the disproportionate stress on "negativism."

The charges of ignorance and wrong priorities in reporting on both current events and long-term developments in the Third World, in the lesser-known European countries, and in the Soviet bloc are not without foundation. Criticism, however, should be related to sub-

This is a shortened version of Chapter 2 of *The Bureaucracy of Truth: How Communist Governments Manage the News* by Paul Lendvai, published in 1981 by Burnett Books Ltd., London, and in the United States by Westview Press, Boulder, Colo. Reprinted here by permission of the author and publishers.

stantive matters and not motivated by transparent political interests. There is no reason to disagree with James Reston's self-critical assessment:

> We are pretty good at reporting "happenings," particularly if they are dramatic. We are fascinated by events, but not by the things that cause events....We are not covering the news of the mind as we should. Here is where rebellion, revolution, and wars start. But we minimize the conflict of ideas and emphasize the conflicts in the streets without relating the second to the first. (Reston 1967)

The priorities of Soviet information policy have of course always been different. As an American student of Soviet political indoctrination and communication methods succinctly put it: "What is news? In the Soviet context basically anything which can be used to illustrate current party policy or economic progress is considered worthy of publication and almost anything else is considered unimportant and unworthy" (Hollander 1972, pp. 37–40). This is naturally a somewhat oversimplified picture since it ignores the so-called gray area. Reporting on many major political events, particularly in crisis situations (the Cuban crisis of 1962, Czechoslovakia in 1968, the overthrow of the Idi Amin regime in Uganda, the revolution in Iran 1978–79, or the intervention in Afghanistan), is often affected by delaying tactics, sometimes subtle, sometimes crude. These are intended to gain crucial time to prepare, first the propaganda apparatus, and then the general public, for news which has eventually to be released.

The sensational defection of the Bolshoi Ballet star Alexander Godunov on August 22, 1979, while on tour in New York, may well rate only a footnote in the works of future historians. Yet the case produced not only a temporary crisis in U.S.–Soviet relations but also an illuminating insight into just how the Soviet media work. After Godunov's disappearance, his wife, Lyudmila Vlasova, who had also been performing with him at the Lincoln Center, was put on the next Aeroflot plane to Moscow. The American authorities, however, blocked the departure of the plane for three days until the ballerina personally told U.S. officials that she was returning home voluntarily.

For our purposes the main point is not the inept handling of the case by the State Department, nor the personal feelings of the ballerina, but the simple fact that the massive anti-American propaganda, accusing the United States of hypocrisy, inhuman behavior, and cold war strong-arm tactics left the Soviet public in the dark about the factual background. Thus it was not until Sunday morning, August 27, that Radio Moscow identified Vlasova as a Bolshoi ballerina. On Monday, for example, Belgrade *Politika* carried on its front page under a banner headline a report by its Moscow correspondent that the Soviets had sharply protested in the case of the blocked Aeroflot plane. However, it also added in a three-column subtitle that "the Bolshoi soloist, Alexander Godunov, Vlasova's husband, had asked for asylum in the U.S." But it was not until after the plane had departed that *Pravda*, in a lengthy, sharply worded piece—"End to a provocation"—indicated a reason for all the fuss. It informed the readers that "Vlasova did not want to find herself in a situation similar to that of her husband, Bolshoi ballet artist A. Godunov, who had disappeared earlier under circumstances which are not yet clear."

Not surprisingly, the way the Soviet media treated the sensitive affair, which was of course widely known in the East through international radio broadcasts, served as a model for the entire communication apparatus east of the Elbe. The East Germans were, as so often, overzealous. Twelve days later the East Berlin weekly, *Horizont*, published a whole page attack against the "incitement and hate campaign launched by the West German bourgeois media" over the Vlasova affair. The article rebuked the West German media for acting according to the principle "truth is what harms the Communists and socialism." The only thing the self-righteous weekly forgot to mention was the defection of the ballerina's husband (Huebner 1979).

SOVIET NEWS COVERAGE

The Soviet and East European coverage of a major topical news story confirms that the observations of a former TASS director general, and erstwhile head of the Moscow University Faculty of Journalism, N. G. Palgunov, are as valid today as they were some twenty-five years ago:

> News should not be merely concerned with reporting such and such a fact or event. News or information must pursue a definite goal: it must serve and support the decisions related to fundamental duties facing our Soviet society, our Soviet people marching on the road of gradual transition from socialism to Communism.... In selecting the object of information, the author of an informative report must, above all, abandon the notion that just any fact or just any events have to be reported in the pages of the newspaper. The aim of information must be to present selected facts and events....

One might think that this kind of reasoning at a so-called theoretical level is no longer in fashion, but only quietly practiced. A short, more recent, quote from an authoritative *Pravda* article dispels such assumptions: "The press should not provide a simple photograph of facts, an account of what happened, but a target-oriented description of events, phenomena and novelties" (September 16, 1968).

Nothing would be more misleading than to always look for some sinister exercise of censorship or political motive behind the often slow release of information by TASS or other Eastern news agencies. The delay is very often due to simple inefficiency, poor organization, or slow distribution. In February 1950, for example, when the Sino-Soviet pact was signed in Moscow, all Western news media immediately reported this significant event. However, in Hungary and elsewhere in Eastern Europe, everyone was waiting in suspense for the release of the text from Moscow. TASS finally began to cable the material 24 hours later: The morning newspapers never reached their subscribers. Two decades later, the publication of the Soviet Journalists Union itself revealed, among other examples, how the tradition of slowness hit the largest circulation newspaper in the city of Gorky with 1.2 million inhabitants (250 miles east of Moscow): The picture of a Soyuz space ship and its crew arrived only three days after the actual launching (*Zhurnalist*, 1970).

But delaying tactics, or genuine mishaps, which are after all not a privilege of the Communist media alone, pale into utter insignificance compared to the most striking and apparently immutable characteristic of the Soviet and (with the partial exception of Hungary and Poland) East European media as a whole. This is the total indifference to, and frequent suppression of, major news and reports of significant events that occur at home or abroad. This practice flagrantly contradicts Lenin's oft-cited statement: "The state gets its strength from the consciousness of the masses. It is strong when the masses know everything, can pass judgment on everything and do everything consciously."

These words are also quoted in the most comprehensive and, by all accounts, most important Central Committee decree adopted since the twenty-fifth Party Congress in 1976, on political indoctrination, communication policies, and the mass media. Its main points were discussed at an ideological conference where none other than M. A. Suslov himself, the 76-year-old guardian of orthodox ideology, delivered the (unpublished) keynote address. Certain formulations in the resolution about the "fierce offensive of the imperialists, assisted by the Peking chauvinists and aggressors" who seek, with the aid of "the most refined methods and modern technological means" to "poison the minds of the Soviet people" were clear indications that the Kremlin is increasingly worried about the widespread audience for the Russian-language broadcasts of the Voice of America, the BBC, Radio Liberty, and Deutsche Welle. . . .

The criteria for what is not "newsworthy" and what must be kept out of the papers have not been altered. At any rate, the media treatment of two serious accidents in August 1979, that is, more than three months after the publication of the resolution and the ideological-propaganda conference, shows no change for the better. In some ways it reflects an even greater contempt for the people's right to know.

The traditional way of informing the domestic public about a disaster, be it natural catastrophe or industrial accident, if a complete "blackout" of the news proves impossible, is the announcement of the event itself, always with one additional sentence, that the "competent authorities have started an investigation." If the communiqué says that the government and the party organs expressed their condolences to the families of the victims and promised measures to help them, then this is an unmistakable sign that there were many deaths and injuries. But we must stress the fact, repeatedly confirmed by private Soviet sources, foreign correspondents, and diplomats, that what gets known or reported of disasters is only the tip of an iceberg (see Udgaard 1979)....

When Robert Kaiser, the *Washington Post* correspondent in Moscow in the early 1970s, asked the head of *Pravda*'s Information Department, Mrs. Irina Kirilova, technically in charge of the coverage of such things as plane accidents, why the press did not mention plane crashes, she replied that "the reader must know something new and good." After recalling the story of a plane with jammed front landing gear, which nevertheless landed safely due to the skill of the pilot and ground crew precautions, Mrs. Kirilova declared: "If there is a connection with heroism, courage or overcoming a great risk, then we write about it." "What about unluckier occasions, when planes crash?" her visitor asked. "What's the point of writing about every one? It happens that accidents occur for technical reasons—that doesn't interest us very much," she replied.

We shall later see in detail what *does* interest Soviet media, but at this point we may as well recall the two previous disasters which had induced the American correspondent to raise the matter in the first place. In late 1972, an *Aeroflot* jet flying from Leningrad crashed in a muddy swamp outside Moscow, killing 176 people, among them 39 foreigners. The news was buried as a 42-word item on *Pravda*'s back page, most probably only printed at all because of the foreigners involved. In June of the following year, the mid-air explosion of a Soviet supersonic jet transport, in front of television cameras and thousands of spectators at the Paris air show, was the major news of the day in most of the world's newspapers. In *Pravda* it was tucked

away as a 27-word item at the bottom of page 6, its back page....
According to many informed sources the censorship regulations forbid
any mention of domestic plane, train, and bus accidents.

Such issues as industrial accidents and inadequate safety measures are not regarded as suitable subjects for debate in the media.
Only specialist Soviet journals are said to admit that safety precautions are inadequate and the level of mechanization is low. According
to a Western source, a 1978 survey revealed that two-thirds of the
deeper mines in the Donbas basin were "highly dangerous" and recommended the introduction of degassing techniques adopted in the
West about 36 years ago (*New Statesman*, April 13, 1979).

To go back to Mrs. Kirilova's point about heroism, the point
seems to be that good news is news—bad news is not really news at
all. Or not so far as the public at large is concerned, though for the
recipients of confidential bulletins it may be a different matter. To
dispute this attitude is to be guilty of "Western sensationalism,"
which pollutes moral standards and undermines responsible
journalism.

Perhaps the most potent argument against this kind of reasoning,
which makes the systematic suppression of unpleasant news an indispensable tool in protecting the population from "bourgeois" selection
criteria, is the example of other East European countries whose leaders had the courage and intelligence to break, albeit only partially,
with a ridiculous and—even from the regime's point of view—
counter-productive practice....

OTHER COMMUNIST COUNTRIES

In free-wheeling Yugoslavia the kind of information policy still
prevailing in the Soviet Union, Bulgaria, or for that matter in Romania, is regarded as a ghost from the distant past, even as something of
a joke. Bogdan Pešić, now retired, who edited the most influential
Yugoslav paper *NIN* after the war, recalled in an interview how, in
1952, he published a news item in *Politika* about the hijacking of a
Yugoslav plane to Italy by three armed men and the subsequent return of the plane and passengers. In those days the report was a
sensation and eventually led to Pešić's replacement as editor-in-chief.
What is fascinating, however, is his account of debates with the
"leading comrades in the party" and the letter in which he set out his
main arguments against restrictive and "paternalistic" news filtering. More than 25 years later, it is worth quoting some of his words,
now openly published in the mass circulation weekly.

> Ever since I worked in the daily press as a journalist, I have
> never agreed with the practice that newspapers should be

the last to report on some events, particularly when those
events are generally known, commented on and discussed by
the masses. Information usually comes first from Radio
London, which in this way has unfortunately acquired great
prestige as a very well-informed station among our citizens,
who listen to it regularly. We journalists find ourselves in a
very curious situation when we are asked from all sides, by
both well- and ill-wishers, whether we know about this or
that event and if yes, why we have not written about it. This
was the case for a long time with train accidents and natural
disasters. Although it was generally known that this or that
train accident had taken place, the daily paper did not write
anything about it for some days and in this way the public
was led to believe that there had been some kind of outrage
or sabotage, that there had been twice as many victims. . . .

Finally, Pešić concluded that the press is often reproached for
sensationalism, although it is often very difficult to draw a line where
objective information stops and sensation begins. . . .

Perhaps nothing could better illustrate the unbroken tradition of
secrecy than the treatment of the earthquake which hit Ashkhabad,
the capital of Turkmenia, in October 1948. According to the latest
edition of the *Great Soviet Encyclopedia*, it was one of the strongest
earthquakes registered in history, completely destroying the city,
which in that year had a population of 200,000. The disaster occurred
at 4 a.m., when most of the inhabitants were still asleep. The *Encyclopedia* lists the deaths caused by other quakes from Japan to Turkey;
but 30 years later the number of dead in the Ashkhabad earthquake
is still a secret. This case was related by the exiled Soviet biochemist
Zhores Medvedev in his book on the Soviet nuclear disaster of 1957,
to convince the skeptics that in the Soviet Union the number of victims is never revealed, even if the disaster occurred three decades
ago.

The nuclear accident which occurred in the Kyshtyn area, between the industrial centers of Chelyabinsk and Sverdlovsk in the
Urals, was kept secret by the Soviets for almost 20 years. . . .

The more sophisticated Hungarian approach to communications
is also evident in the nuclear debate. For example, the widely read
Budapest cultural and political weekly, *Élet és Irodalom*, carried an
editorial over three full columns on its front page (June 29, 1979)
under the provocative headline: "Do we need a nuclear power plant?"
The author described the worldwide unease and recent dramatic protests, and also admitted frankly that there was a crisis of confidence
over nuclear safety which could not be ignored since it had also
reached Hungary. Though he bluntly stated that the antinuclear attitude is a "reactionary phenomenon," public concern and the need to

deal with it was repeatedly stressed. It would, of course, be totally in-
conceivable, even in Hungary, to publish any substantial article in a
widely read journal spreading actual doubts about nuclear power and
safety precautions while the country was engaged in erecting a large
nuclear plant. Indeed, raising the matter so candidly, the article
cleverly responded to popular concern, without even remotely raising
the basic question of the wisdom of erecting a plant in a densely populated area....

ONE DAY IN PRAVDA

A scrutiny of *Pravda* of October 1, 1979, should help to judge
whether this shattering indictment was fair. What are the main news
items, published on the same day, in the *International Herald Tribune* in Paris and the German *Frankfurter Allgemeine Zeitung*? Both
Western papers feature, as the main news story on the front page,
Pope John Paul II's appeal for peace in Ireland on the eve of his flight
to the United States. The *Tribune* also reports on the front page the
purge of the armed forces in Iran, the talks between the United States
and Mexico about compensation for the oil spill, the Washington-
Bonn vow to press dollar support, a Chinese official accusing Russia of
encroachment, and, under a four-column headline, an interview with
Soviet foreign affairs spokesman Georgi Arbatov. The main political
news stories on the following pages deal with Bokassa, the deposed
Emperor, having killed students in the Central African Republic;
President Carter's consultations concerning the attitude to Soviet
troops in Cuba; the execution of Macias Nguema, the former dictator
of Equatorial Guinea, and indications that Senator Kennedy will run
as a candidate for President. Apart from topical domestic political
controversies, the Frankfurt paper carries on its front page, as third
lead story, Carter's efforts to produce proof of the presence of Soviet
troops in Cuba, followed by stories on the West German Defense
Minister's trip to Washington, a half-page feature on the Pope's activities in Ireland, a two-column analysis of Greek Premier Karamanlis' journey to Moscow, the Mexico-U.S. talks, and many other short
political items.

What, then, did *Pravda* report on the same day on its front page?
Two full columns out of eight are taken up by an unsigned editorial
calling for higher standards in political and economic work, firm action against indiscipline and the utilization of all reserves in order to
"succeed in the great overall cause of building communism." The
main news item in the right upper corner, under a two-column headline, is "Harvest completed," a report about the successful work of the

sovkhoz (state farm), "forty-year Kazakh SSR," in the *Oktober* region of Kazakhstan. In the center of the front page, two photos are grouped together: on the left, three outstanding young workers from an Odessa oil refinery; on the right, the factory hall of a ball-bearing plant in Moscow. Three brief one-column items about geological explorations, agricultural experiments, and new ships on Lake Baikal, and a long, four-column interview with the Minister of Power about new methods being applied in a power plant going up in Rjazan, occupy the center part. And what is the foreign lead story? Under a two-column headline "Important factor," a report from Vienna, quoting Franz Muhri, chairman of the Austrian Communist party, about the "importance for Austria of trade and cooperation with the Soviet Union and other Socialist states, in particular in the fight against unemployment and for the stabilizing of its energy supplies." One wonders which, if any, of *Pravda*'s readers know that in the 1979 Austrian general election Muhri's party received less than 1 percent of the vote, that the Communists have not been represented in parliament since 1959, and that, on top of that, Austria has had full employment for many years.

The second main foreign news item is an account of the situation in the Central African Republic, quoting the critical comments of the French Communist daily, *L'Humanité* about the dispatch of French parachutists. A brief, low-key telegram sent by the Soviet Council of Ministers and the Presidium of the Supreme Soviet (no names are given) to the equivalent Chinese bodies on the thirtieth anniversary of the founding of the Chinese People's Republic is the politically most important report. Finally, at the bottom of the front page, readers are informed of the arrival of Greek Prime Minister Konstantin Karamanlis, together with a brief biographical note.

The following pages are mainly taken up with long pieces by a deputy chief engineer of the Jaroslavski iron plant and a bookkeeper from a *sovkhoz* in Minsk about the year of political indoctrination and the application of Lenin's teachings; reports about the situation in the "Dimitrov" *kolkhoz* in the region of Novgorod and the contact between science and production in the city of Volgograd.

A cultural feature, describing how young poets respond to the challenge of building communism, is followed by a critical assessment of management practices. A long piece about China, stressing that the Soviets have always been willing to forge good-neighborly and friendly relations and that it is up to the Chinese to give up their "hegemonistic" policies, is followed by an article reproaching Western writers for falling prey to cheap anti-Soviet political propaganda.

The overall picture would not be complete without three short reports about "fraternal parties" from Hanoi, Tokyo, and Geneva, and an item about the reception of a Socialist International delegation by

Brezhnev. A picture of a smiling Mongolian girl from a factory in Ulan Bator strengthens the stamina of the reader before he turns to page 5, where the correspondents of *Pravda* and TASS report on the state of the world. At the top of the page, under a banner headline "Fight for justice," two separate dispatches, grouped together, report how "Americans are outraged by racist and political repression," and on mass demonstrations and protest meetings in Newark and Philadelphia (it is noted that in the latter city between 1970 and 1978, 469 people were killed by the police without trial and investigation). In Canada, the economic situation is deteriorating even further; in Australia, U.S. capital takes over the economy; and in Britain, the Conservative government brutally violates human rights by not allowing the unification of families from Asia and Africa. In the world of socialism, in Havana, East Berlin, and Sofia, new production records and educational successes are achieved; in Cambodia, the second congress of the United National Front draws a positive balance sheet of normalization; and in Afghanistan, the (progressive) government will issue new passports.

The last page of the newspaper is, not without reason, regarded by the readers as the most interesting. There they find the TV and radio programs, weather reports, and sports news; on October 1 there were also long reports on the performance of the Soviet participants at the water-skiing world championship in Toronto and on an international chess tournament. Nevertheless, the lead story on this page is a lengthy feature about the geographical museum in Vladivostok.

This, then, is the detailed content of *Pravda* on a normal day. It is not only completely different from the two Western newspapers, cited earlier, but also ignores the main news story of the previous day in the "non-Socialist" world, namely, the Pope's dramatic appeal against violence in Ireland. Scrutinizing a copy of *Pravda*, there is no reason to doubt the unanimous view of every new Western correspondent in Moscow, after an obligatory visit to the newspaper's offices, that when the editorial board conference in the morning begins, the following day's paper is already complete and ready for the printers except for a few small spaces left blank for late-breaking official announcements or a story expected from overseas. The editorial staff is in fact putting the final touches to a paper which will appear only two days later. No wonder that reports of events that actually occurred the day before, at home or abroad, make up only some 10 to 15 percent of the paper's content....

ONE DAY ON TELEVISION

At this point, a few words about the use of television in the selection, interpretation, and above all, transmission of political messages may be appropriate. The tremendous implications of the Soviet regime's capacity to reach tens of millions of viewers in a vast country and exert a politically welcome "narcotizing effect" become evident if one notes the rapid growth of TV sets, from 27 million in 1969 to 55.1 million by 1975. The best guide to an assessment of television as a tool of political persuasion is a brief glance at the main political newscast. Called Vremya, it is broadcast at 9 p.m. every evening and repeated the following morning at 8 a.m. Let us take April 14, 1979, a Saturday during the Easter weekend, with nothing extraordinary happening either in the Soviet Union or abroad. Here is the complete list of the items in the order they were shown (*Frankfurter Allgemeine Zeitung*, April 19, 1979):

The Central Committee issued its annual 68 slogans for the 1st of May celebrations, published in all papers on the front page. On April 21, Lenin's birthday, a *subotnik* will be staged, workers and farmers in the whole country will work free of charge on this day.

Film about a textile plant in Kirgisia showing the ever faster and better production; an outstanding female laborer who overfulfilled her norm is interviewed.

Leningrad.   Brezhnev sends greetings to a scientific conference discussing the "new Socialist man." A speaker quotes Lenin's words about the quality of labor. Pensioned miner talks about plan fulfilment. Film about an oil refinery with reference to cooperation with East Germany in this branch of industry.

Reports from the world of labor.   A car plant in the Urals increases production, more vegetables harvested in Azerbaijan, a film about new methods, with women harvesting cabbage.

The first Bulgarian cosmonaut and his Soviet colleague receive decorations.

Moscow.   Report about a conference on "science day," with an academician talking about science in the service of industry, agriculture and the Communist Party.

Tiflis.   Meeting of the Communist Youth Union on Lenin square.

Vienna. U.S.-Soviet talks about satellites in Sofia. Bulgarian President Todor Zhivkov receives unionists and speaks with them about disarmament.

Hanoi. Vietnamese note handed over to the Chinese. New accusations against Peking leadership.

Damascus. Protest meeting against the Egyptian-Israeli peace treaty.

Beirut. Palestinians protest against Sadat's "capitulation line."

Teheran. Premier Bazargan predicts further successes in the reconstruction of Iran.

Islamabad. According to a report by the *New York Times*, American citizens involved in "counter-revolutionary" conspiracy against the Afghan Government under Premier Taraki.

Rome. Film about the election campaign. The "conservative bourgeoisie and the monopolies" place their hopes on anti-Communist propaganda.

Nicaragua. Opposition against the Somoza regime increases: successes of the guerrillas.

Kampala. Calm in Uganda's capital, new Premier Lule sworn in. Western agencies report that Idi Amin still has some support in parts of the country.

Addis Ababa. Ethiopia recognizes Lule's government in Uganda.

Stockholm. Protest demonstrations in Swedish capital against unemployment. Film about a typical crisis symptom in a capitalist country.

Delhi. Chinese "bands" stir up unrest on India's borders.

Moscow. First night performance of the ballet "My Vietnam" in the congress palais in the Kremlin.

During the following two days of the Easter weekend the TV news continued to focus on "positive" items about the Soviet Union and her allies and on a negative picture of the West, this time with films showing mass demonstrations in Rome for "peace and disarmament" and in New York against youth unemployment, as well as reports on terror in Northern Ireland and fighting in Nicaragua.

Politically most revealing is the treatment of the Third World countries, both in television and in the central press. Thus the weekend newscast did not say anything about the background to the rebellion against Amin or about the dictator himself. Amin had been, during his rule, on very good terms indeed with the Soviets; between 1971 and 1979 the Kremlin provided Uganda with massive deliveries of heavy weapons. Nevertheless, Soviet press reports about the dictator were always low-key, on account of his poor image in the rest of the world. In view of *Pravda*'s sharp attack on Britain's "inhuman treatment" of immigrant families, it may be instructive to recall that on August 15, 1972, *Izvestia* supported Amin's expulsion of at least 50,000 Indians holding British passports, on the grounds that Uganda was quite capable of solving its domestic problems without "imperialist interference." During the war with Tanzania in 1978–79, Soviet media gave the public no background information whatsoever, and a TV commentator on March 29, 1979, restricted his remarks to the classic phrase that "fighting could only benefit foreign reaction." By the end of April 1979, however, *Pravda* discovered that the "forced wholesale expulsion of 70,000 Asians" had created an acute shortage of skilled labor, thus also reversing the previous line of tacitly supporting Amin's anti-Asian policy....

The treatment of Amin sheds a characteristic light on the Soviet model of "objective, responsible and comprehensive reporting" as admired by UNESCO experts. As long as Amin was in power and on the whole amenable to Soviet interests, albeit personally unpredictable and therefore sometimes embarrassing (for example, when he wanted to erect a statue of Adolf Hitler), one could have searched in vain with a magnifying glass for a single critical analysis of the situation in Uganda. The world's press had for years been reporting Amin's murderous regime in great detail, but *Pravda*, which according to its previous editor, Mikhail V. Zymanin (now Central Committee secretary), is different from all bourgeois papers because "it writes nothing but the truth," discovered the "bloody crimes" only at the end of April 1979. By then, Tanzanian forces had occupied the whole country and Amin had been forced to flee. Thus for eight years the Soviet media were either ignorant of the events in a "friendly" country—or had simply lied for reasons of state. This is the only possible conclusion....

The Soviet invasion of Afghanistan not only marked a watershed in East-West relations; it also provided the latest stunning examples of what an American analyst has called "the brutality of the lie" in Soviet propaganda. Thus Moscow did not admit publicly that there were any Soviet troops in Afghanistan until three days after the coup of December 27, 1979, which overthrew President Hafizullah Amin and installed Babrak Karmal as his successor. After months of fierce, if sporadic, fighting, and the presence of some 80,000 Soviet combat troops, of which thousands have been killed or wounded, the Kremlin still maintains silence over the scope of the military operations and casualties in Afghanistan. The official line is that "a limited military contingent" was requested by the legitimate government of Afghanistan under imperialist threats and that it will be withdrawn as soon as an end is put to "outside interference."

Today Soviet bloc media condemn Amin's rule as a "regime of terror and persecution." But when West German, French, and American newspapermen in the autumn of 1979 reported the methods of torture applied in Kabul's prisons, the Soviet and Eastern European press remained either silent or even complained about the "slanderous campaign against the patriotic revolutionary forces in Afghanistan." As to the role of Babrak Karmal, who at the time of writing is the head of the party and the state, he was flown by the Soviets into Afghanistan from his exile in Eastern Europe after the coup that ousted Amin. "Radio Kabul," which announced the news of the coup, was actually a Soviet transmitter at Termez in the USSR. At the very time when these prerecorded broadcasts were put on the air the genuine Radio Kabul was broadcasting "normal" programs....

EAST GERMAN MEDIA

The effort to imitate the Soviet system of indoctrination is perhaps nowhere so evident, and yet so ridiculous, as in East Germany. If we take, for example, *Neues Deutschland*, the central party organ, of October 1, 1979, it reads more or less like a German-language *Pravda* with slight local variations. There are, however, two differences. First, the paper announces under a four-column banner headline on the front page that a Soviet party and government delegation led by Brezhnev will arrive in East Berlin on October 4 for an official visit to mark the thirtieth anniversary of the founding of the German Democratic Republic (*Pravda* kept its usual silence until the actual arrival of Brezhnev four days later). Second, in contrast to its Soviet sister paper, *Neues Deutschland* reported on the Pope's trip to Ireland and to New York, even if only in six lines tucked away at the bottom of the front page, preceded by such "foreign briefs" as the arrival in Austria of a peace bicycle rally from the Netherlands and the South African bombing of Angola.

On the whole, however, *Neues Deutschland* conveys the same world view and the same stereotypes about a happy population, prospering citizens, and a powerful economy as *Pravda* does. The lead story on the front page, side by side with the announcement of Brezhnev's trip, is a report with a picture about a visit of Enrico Berlinguer, the Italian Communist leader, to an exhibition in Rome of the achievements of the GDR. Page 2 is dominated by a major news story about the opening of a dairy and meat plant and page 3 by a glowing three-column review of party leader Erich Honecker's book on the role of the trade unions. Who, then, could be surprised that, apart from the pieces about China, demonstrations in Newark, Portuguese unions, and the rest already familiar from *Pravda, Neues Deutschland*'s main foreign report is a long illustrated account of an international cycling rally "against the arms race and for peace" from Amsterdam to Bonn, Prague, and (by plane!) to Moscow?

Of course, what makes the 8 million copies of *Neues Deutschland*, and the 38 other dailies produced in East Germany, so unique is that they are written and edited for by far the best-informed population in the Communist world. All East Germans can listen to the news bulletins of the West German radio stations, and 80 percent can also receive TV transmissions from the Federal Republic. Nowhere in the Soviet bloc is the state's monopoly of information so thoroughly undermined as in East Germany. According to reliable audience surveys, only 7 to 10 percent of the viewers see the main evening newscast of the East Berlin TV, while the two main news programs of the West German networks are seen regularly by 22 percent and 40 percent, respectively, of East Germans. When there is a crisis, such as the assassination of prominent personalities by terrorists or the hijacking of a Lufthansa plane to Mogadishu, up to 87 percent of East Germans watch Western TV newscasts (see *Deutsch-deutsche Pressefreiheit*, 1978)....

Telecasts from the West threaten to create insurmountable problems of credibility for a regime which, alone in the Warsaw Pact, also lacks a national basis. Despite the recognition of the GDR by 127 states, 75 percent of young people between 16 and 25 described themselves as Germans rather than as "citizens of the GDR" (*Der Spiegel*, August 29, 1979), according to an opinion survey institute. Though Western penetration via the TV screen and radio alone cannot become a major threat to domestic stability, it does promote a climate of heightened social tensions, by accelerating the changes in values and cultural choices, and influencing the life style of the young and the cultural elite.

East German media executives are faced with insoluble problems. Their political output is eminently dull. In order to attract at least some audience, their programs must either copy Western trivialities, such as thrillers and revues, or purchase series shown years earlier in West Germany, thus discrediting their claim of seeking to "shape a new Socialist man." Even technically good documentaries using Western cameramen and newsreels to show the darker and seamier sides of West German capitalism backfire in the end because they consist mainly of reports about right-wing extremist groups, the unemployed, and people excluded from civil service jobs because of their Communist beliefs. The propaganda is so overdone that even ordinary people can recognize the exaggerations....

CONCLUSION

The deadening barrage of political messages directed at the ordinary people from East Berlin to Irkutsk reflects the cardinal weakness of Communist propaganda methods. What should all these messages convey to the readers and listeners? A world view dominated by a picture of capitalism and the West as periodically shaken by structural economic and social crises; haunted by growing unemployment, uncontrollable inflation, and a rising tide of protests, strikes, and demonstrations; ridden with crime and corruption; and last but not least, ruthlessly repressing Communist and other progressive, peace-loving forces.

On the one hand, the NATO countries are split among themselves, their differences continuously sharpened by domestic contradictions, popular pressures, and conflicts of class interests. On the other hand, they are ignoring the series of peace-loving propositions made by Brezhnev on behalf of the Soviet Union and the "Socialist community," and stubbornly carrying on with the arms race, assisted and even abetted by the Chinese great power chauvinists. On the other hand again, preceding trips by Brezhnev, Kádár or Husák to West Germany, France, and the United States, or on the arrival of a Western premier or president in Moscow, Budapest, or Prague, the local Communist media will suddenly paint a brighter picture of the state in question; the mutual advantages of economic cooperation are stressed, always indicating that the Soviet (or Comecon) orders provide jobs for so-and-so many people.

Now contrast the unstable mire of rapacious capitalism and imperialism with the calm confidence, steady progress, and full harmony between state policy and public interest radiated by the "world of socialism," and above all by its leading power, the Soviet Union! The leaders of these countries are firmly united and share the common concern for peace and the well-being of their people. Fuel problems, natural disasters, or common crimes can only momentarily disturb the general progress toward an ever higher standard of living and the birth (or further perfection) of the Socialist man who cares for the community first and only second for himself. Though the special conditions under which socialism is being built may vary from country to country, the common features—the leading role of the Marxist-Leninist vanguard, the means of production in public possession, and no compromises with the foreign and domestic class enemy—prevail elsewhere. The adherence to a firm party political line and the careful application of the generally valid laws of building socialism provide everywhere for law and order, growing prosperity, and the happiness of those lucky people already living under socialism. Last but not least, public opinion in the Socialist countries realizes the importance of strengthening the defense capacity of each country, and of the entire Socialist community, for as long as imperialist circles harbor expansionist plans and turn a deaf ear to the constructive proposals of the Warsaw Pact.

REFERENCES

Erich Böhme, ed. *Deutsch-deutsche Pressefreiheit*. Hamburg: 1978.

Der Spiegel, August 29, 1979.

Frankfurter Allgemeine Zeitung, April 19, 1979.

Hollander, Gayle Durham. *Soviet Political Indoctrination*. New York: 1972.

Huebner, Gerald. "Brunnenvergifter." *Horizont* (East Berlin) 39 (1979).

New Statesmen (London), April 13, 1979.

Pravda, September 16, 1968.

Reston, James. *The Artillery of the Press: Its Influence on American Foreign Policy*. New York: 1967.

Udgaard, Nils Morten. *Der ratlose Riese, Alltag in der Sowjetunion*. Hamburg: 1979.

Zhurnalist (Moscow), no. 11 (1970).

THE ROLE OF MASS MEDIA ▬

---

5. THE MASS MEDIA ROLE IN THE WESTERN WORLD

OSMO A. WIIO

> The hypothesis, which seems to me the most fertile, is that
> news and truth are not the same thing, and must be clearly
> distinguished.

Walter Lippmann, *Public Opinion*, 1922

Textbooks of human communication are full of different models
of mass communication. We have the two-step model, the uses and
gratifications model, the functional model, the Marxist model, the
agenda-setting model, and system models. None of these is generally
accepted in the field of communication research as the one and only
explanation for mass communication processes.

Quite rightly so! These models explain only a part of the situation. They have two main weaknesses: (1) They imply that the mass
media are one entity; (2) they imply that the mass media function in
some idealized social system, typically an American-type Western
country.

WHAT MEDIA?

If one stops to think about media functions even in the same country, it is easy to see how different are the roles and functions the different media have. Newspapers differ from magazines, weeklies differ from trade journals. Radio has a different role from television. Books differ from all the others. Film and recordings have their specific functions.

Thus our first question about mass media roles should be, The role of *what* media?

WHICH SOCIAL SYSTEM?

Even a superficial comparison of mass media in China, Nigeria, and the United States shows that the roles and functions of mass media in these countries are very different. No doubt, there are some common features and functions, but the differences may be greater than the similarities. In some societies mass media play a dominant role in the social interaction and political discussion. In other societies mass media have only a marginal role in the formation of "public opinion."

Our second question is, therefore, In *which* social system does the mass media system function?

THE CONTINGENCY MODEL OF COMMUNICATION

If anything, the differences in mass media roles and functions in different social systems support a contingency view of communication (Wiio 1975, 1982). According to this view, the communication processes and outcomes are influenced by internal and external contingencies (situations) as well as by the degree of freedom of the work processes of the system.

This view maintains that different contingencies create different combinations of internal and external system constraints; consequently, system outcomes (changes in the system and system environment) may be different. The same messages and the same communicators may create quite different effects in different communication situations.

The contingency approach explains many of the seemingly conflicting research results in mass communication research. In some cases mass communication seems to have a direct effect on public opinion; in other cases there seem to be no effects. The decisive factor may be whether it is a new topic or whether there are existing attitudes and opinions. Or it may be that the direct experience of the audience is different and the message is not accepted.

Klapper (1960) summed up some of the communication research findings into a somewhat pessimistic—but very influential—book titled *The Effects of Mass Communication*. In his concluding notes he wrote:

> Other situations and conditions which are not covered in this volume in which communication may have extensive effects may be readily imagined. For many of these situations and conditions, the primitive theoretical framework we have sketched may prove to be an inadequate model. It is to be hoped that its shortcomings may serve to stimulate the development of other models, at once refined and more widely applicable. (p. 256)

Such models have been abundantly created since Klapper's book, and some of them really explain research data that Klapper found to be conflicting and thus canceling each other.

According to the contingency view, however, there is no single model of explanation: All of the models may explain communication behavior only in some situations, whereas some other models are better in other contingencies. In the following pages we are going to analyze some contingencies of mass communication in different social systems.

OPEN AND CLOSED MASS MEDIA SYSTEMS

System openness is one of the main units of analysis in the general systems theory. A "closed system" has little interchange with the system environment; the more interchange there is, the more "open" the system is. The system states of an open system are unpredictable; the more closed a system is, the more predictable the system states are.

The openness of a communication system can be measured in many ways. Our first example shows two basic dimensions of national communication systems: receiver system and message system openness (Wiio 1975, 1977). An open *receiver system* means that anybody can be a member of the audience system. The more open a *message system* is, the fewer constraints (controls) there are for messages.

The relative openness of the communication systems can be regarded as in Figure 5.1. We have four contingencies of communication systems for any social system.

Type 1A: Controlled (Mass) Communication Controlled (mass) communication means a communication system in which the audience system is as open as possible but the message system is relatively closed. The constraints of the message system may be political (censorship) or any other kind that limits the selection of messages.

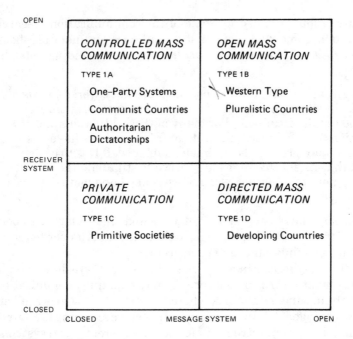

Figure 5.1.

This is a typical situation for communist countries, but also for any other centralized political system. In addition to political message control, there can be other message constraints such as religious or commercial pressures.

Type 1B: (Open) Mass Communication An open mass communication system is a system in which both the audience and message constraints are as open as possible. This system comes closest to the traditional Western form of mass communication as typified by the BBC in broadcasting or the *New York Times* in print.

Type 1C: Private Communication The opposite of an open mass communication system is private communication, where both the audience and the message systems are relatively closed. Typical examples are private letters and phone calls. In primitive societies—those with no mass communication system—this is the only mode of communication.

Type 1D: Directed (Mass) Communication Directed communication means a communication system in which the audience system is closed but the message system is open. There are few constraints in the selection of the messages, but not everybody can join the communication system. Typical audience constraints are economic or ethnic restrictions; for example, a linguistic minority may not know the language used by the dominant medium. Or media use is too expensive for a large part of the social system, as would be the case in many developing countries.

The types are, of course, idealized, and there are many middle values in different social systems. The model can be operationalized to some degree as shown in Wiio (1975, 1977).

This model, however, accounts for only a simple two-dimensional contingency. Communication systems can be analyzed in many other contingencies. Another contingency is shown in Figure 5.2, where the dimensions are the *ownership of the media* and the *control of the media*. The ownership dimension is *public-private* and the control dimension is *decentralized-centralized*.

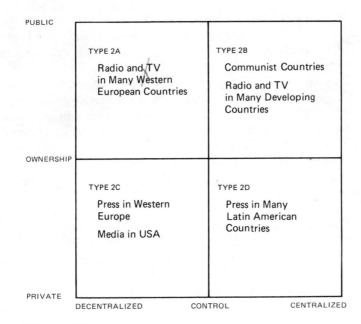

Figure 5.2.

Type 2A: Decentralized Public Model   This model is perhaps best typified by the broadcast media in Western and Northern European countries, such as France and Denmark. The broadcasting companies are publicly owned, but the control system is decentralized. No single political or any other interest group can totally control the messages. Even if a governing body is nominated by the political system (parliament or cabinet), there are many simultaneous control systems.

The model is not pure; there are mixed systems in Europe in which a part of the broadcasting system is owned by private interest. The United Kingdom and Finland are such cases.

Type 2B: Centralized Public Model This is a typical *socialist* or Communist model in which the media are owned by society and controlled centrally by the dominant political party. The Soviet Union, China, and many Eastern European countries are examples of this model.

Type 2C: Decentralized Private Model The Western European press and U.S. media in general belong to this category. The media are privately owned and there is no centralized control.

Type 2D: Centralized Private Model In many Latin American countries, in Turkey, and in Spain under Franco, the press is privately owned but centrally controlled by the rulers. Such was also the case in Germany during the Nazi era.

In recent years, much of the international discussion about communication has concentrated on the concept of the "right to communicate" (d'Arcy 1969), which is used as a general term to cover such aspects as freedom of expression, free flow of information, and access to media (Wiio 1977). We shall break the concept of the "right to communicate" into two dimensions of communication: the *right to receive* and the *right to send*. Thus our next model (see Figure 5.3) is based on these dimensions.

Type 3A: The Authoritarian Model In this model the right to send may belong to the individual, but the right to receive belongs to the society. Thus, in fact, message content of the media is, in the final stage, also controlled by the society. The society allows only certain kinds of messages to be sent by the media. This model is applicable to many authoritarian states and dictatorships, such as Nazi Germany or Franco's Spain.

Type 3B: The Communist Model According to this model, society controls both the right to send and the right to receive. Society can give these rights to individuals on certain conditions, and it has the absolute right to recall these rights when individual rights conflict with the interests of society. This model is applicable in the Communist countries. Events in Poland during 1981–82 are a very good example of this model in action.

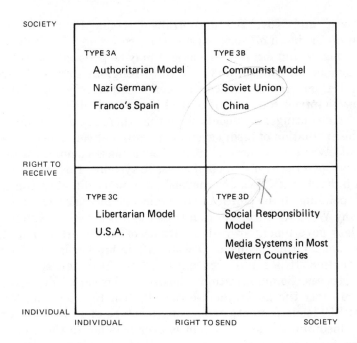

Figure 5.3.

Type 3C: The Libertarian Model   In the libertarian model, the individual owns both the right to send and the right to receive, and society can limit these rights only to protect similar rights of other individuals. This model in its pure form is not applied anywhere; but the U.S. media system may be closest to it.

Type 3D: The Model of Social Responsibility   In this model the individual owns the right to receive, but society owns the right to send. Accordingly, society also has some control over what is received. This right is used mainly to protect the members of society against "harmful" communication, such as too much violence, explicit sex, abuse of children, or unwanted advertisements. This model is used in most Western-type democracies, although there are large variations in the degree of societal control.

The designations in model 3 come from the famous concept of the "Four Theories of the Press" (Siebert, Peterson, and Schramm 1957).

A Comparison of Models

International media comparisons are often too simplified and biased in one way or another. They are often based on such dichotomies as "free" and "government controlled" media. First, one may argue that *all* media in *all* social systems are controlled. Controls differ only in degree and form. In one case it may be political control, in another commercial control, and in a third religious control. In the United States, government control is seen as inherently bad, but in Communist countries commercial control is seen as bad.

Our three contingency models show that there are many dimensions in the evaluation of media systems in different countries. Model 1 shows all "Western countries" in the "open mass communication" contingency: open receiver and open message systems. However, models 2 and 3 divide the "Western models" into many different contingencies, depending on the political, economic, and media systems.

In many Western European countries the broadcasting system is more or less government owned. In terms of the libertarian communication model, this means an Orwellian "big brother is watching" kind of situation. It is a use of media to control private citizens for political purposes. Communication scholars in Europe hardly accept this view. In fact the government-owned British Broadcasting Corporation (BBC) is often mentioned as an archetype of an independent and "free" medium, if such a system is ever possible in the modern world. The European argument often is that public ownership (of broadcasting media) ensures freedom for journalists from any particular interest groups: political, commercial, or whatever.

The BBC may be more of an exception than a rule, however. There are examples from Western Europe of government-owned and/or controlled broadcast media being used for blatant political propaganda purposes, government or otherwise. There are also plenty of criticisms by American writers of the U.S. broadcasting system for furthering only commercial interests.

Marxist writers, on the other hand, claim that Western "commercial media" are also political media in the sense that they further the interests of the capitalist society. They claim that Western media are entertainment oriented and that they dull the senses of the masses to their plight and misery. The Marxist media system is, of course, openly political. The function of the media in a Communist society is to serve the Communist ideology as interpreted by the ruling party. This is specifically stated by the media.

Table 5.1 shows some of the basic differences between Marxist and pluralistic communication models.

Our contingency analysis shows that there really is no "Western model" for mass communication; it all depends on what dimensions have been selected for analysis. Possibly the clearest difference is between a "monolithic model" and a "pluralistic model." The monolithic

TABLE 5.1
Communication Models

Communica- tion Function	Marxist Models	Pluralistic Models
Types of models	Mostly mass communication models.	All types of communication models: intra-, inter- and mass communication.
Sender	Emphasis on the political ideology of the sender.	Emphasis on gatekeeper functions of the sender.
Channel	Emphasis on the ownership of media and media economics.	Emphasis on legal and political control of the media.
Receiver	Who is exploited by communication process?	What are effects of communication on the individual? Who communicates and what?
Outcomes of communication process	Who benefits from communication process?	What are functions of communication? What are uses and gratifications of communication?
Messages	What "social facts" are behind news items? People do not perceive the real truth of events (criticism of "Gallup democracy").	What is content of messages? How do people understand messages? What is relationship between events and messages?
Purpose of communication	Social unity. Support for dominant ideology. Deviant information suppressed. Communication seen as a part of the political and administrative system.	Exchange of ideas and opinions between individuals. Support for dominant social, political, and economic system. Deviant and pluralistic information allowed. Communication seen as branch of industry.

model (or centralized model) of mass communication serves the purposes of one dominant ideology in the society. The pluralistic model (or decentralized model) has different goals and explanations. The monolithic model is sender centered, the pluralistic model is receiver centered.

REFERENCES

d'Arcy, J. "Direct Satellite broadcasting and the Right to Communicate."
EBU Review, 1969.

Klapper, J. *The Effects of Mas Communication*, Glencoe, Ill.: Free Press,
1960.

Lippmann, W. *Public Opinion*. Glencoe, Ill.: Free Press, 1922, 1965.

Siebert, F.S., T. Peterson, and W. Schramm. *Four Theories of the Press*.
Urbana: University of Illinois Press, 1957.

Wiio, O. A. *Systems of Information, Communication, and Organizations*.
Helsinki: 1975.

———. *Open and Closed Mass Media Systems and Problems of International
Communication Policy*. Tokyo: Studies of Broadcasting, NHK, 1977.

———. *Information and Communication Systems*. Ablex: 1982 (in print).

6. THE MASS MEDIA ROLE IN THE THIRD WORLD

AMDE-MICHAEL HABTE

Perhaps the most nagging problem facing international communication scholars today is the apparent lack of a comprehensive approach toward a better understanding of mass media systems in Third World countries. This problem is further compounded by the absence of a common pattern or a panoramic model, which may explain the political and socioeconomic settings of these media systems.

The immediate question that is difficult to resolve is, Which countries fall within the Third World camp? "Third World" is a term with an ideological overtone popularized ever since the Bandung Conference in 1955 when newly emerging nations of Africa and Asia resolved to pursue independent and nonaligned national goals amid the cold war between East and West. Such pursuit of nonalignment— irrespective of its merits—has not created a common ideological identity among these nations. Indeed, one observes Western-modeled democracies, Soviet-backed Communist regimes, Marxist and socialist governments, monarchies, military juntas, and a host of other combinations lumped together under the banner of the Third World. It is therefore misleading to speak of the Third World as a political camp. Instead, it is safe to simply state that this group consists of the less industrialized countries in Asia, Africa, and Latin America.

Communication—including social, public, and mass communication—reflects the political and economic structures and cultural expressions of a given society. These structures form the boundaries in which social interactions take place. Constructing a basic paradigm consisting of these social boundaries would obviously be an immense help to all scholars in the field. Unfortunately, there has not been any comprehensive and meaningful suggestion so far. The problem is indeed gigantic.

First, the Third World is a mosaic composition of all sorts of political platforms ranging from the extreme right to the radical left. It consists of a few of the most populated and democratic governments and many tiny and repressive states. Even neighboring nations within the same region practice opposing political ideologies. The Kingdom of Morocco nervously borders a one-party socialist regime in Algeria. The Saudi and Jordanian monarchies are in the midst of leftist national movements and radical governments in the Middle East. A Western-style democratic rule has so far been able to flourish in Costa Rica, although the region is a showcase of right-wing military regimes, Marxist and nationalist governments, and even a president-for-life in Haiti.

Second, the economic diversity of Third World countries defies any intelligent description. In GNP terms, there are some of the richest nations endowed with abundant exploitable natural resources; whereas many of the rest are so poor—the poorest nations have an income per capita of less than $100—that their populations lead substandard lives. Oil-producing nations, particularly in the Middle East with a few in Africa and Latin America, are able to generate enough surplus funds to invest in their infrastructure and social service programs.

Third, modern mass communication institutions are not indigenous to most Third World countries. Notwithstanding the remarkable communication networks that were in part responsible for the prosperity and might of the ancient Aztecs, Chinese, Indians, and Egyptians, the modern press, as an instrument of public information, has essentially remained a Western institution. The flow of ideas and information in traditional societies has always been a slow and toilsome effort often using interpersonal communication channels. The absence of rapid communication systems accounts in part for the retardation of the economic and social development in many Third World regions.

European missionaries, immigrants, and colonial administrators were primarily responsible for introducing printing presses to several African, Asian, and Latin American regions during the last two hundred years. These presses were often used to print periodicals and other publications that disseminated news and information among the European residents. Christian missionaries in a few instances printed translations of the Bible and other reading materials in indigenous African and the Indian languages of Latin America using European characters. Despite these efforts, the press was in most part confined to serving the information needs of European residents and the native employees in the colonial administrative bureaucracy.

Fourth, news and information media in Third World countries have not particularly enjoyed the respect and protection of their societies, as has been the case in many Western nations. From the beginning, the European press had assumed a catalytic role in fostering political and economic changes. Indeed, it would be hard to contemplate the modernization process of the West without the help of the press in general. Books, political pamphlets, and early newspapers rendered a revolutionary function, altering the basic characteristics of Medieval Europe. The emergence of nation-states carved out of major linguistic units, the destruction of feudal autocracies once exercised jointly by the nobility and clergy, the rapid rise of large urban centers, the expansion of trade and commerce leading to the industrialization of Europe, and the democratization of its political institutions could easily be traced in part to the advent of the printing press in the fifteenth century. By the middle of the eighteenth century, the press had become a strong social force and a respectable financial enterprise. In Europe and North America, it had mobilized public opinion in support of popular and democratic causes; and it later became an independent social institution.

Such was not the fate of the press in many Third World countries. Often newspapers in colonial Africa, Asia, and Latin America were first owned, managed, and edited by resident Europeans to serve the needs of the ruling communities. There were several instances in which nationalists used the press to advocate democratic rights and liberation from colonial rule (Legum, 1975; Kitchen 1956). This was particularly true of several Latin American colonies in their struggle against Spanish rule. But their case was similar to that of the American colonies, whose local inhabitants were essentially descendants of European immigrants. The press had very little to offer non-European natives during the colonial period. Thus the character of the press in most former colonial territories remained basically European, reflecting the dominant influences of the West. In other words, the press in Third World countries was not a major instrument of political changes and social development. Consequently, it has been relegated to a status of servitude without any strong social distinction.

Fifth, another characteristic problem shared by many developing nations is the nonexistence of a single national language. In many cases, this problem is compounded further by the fact that several of the languages in use have no alphabet. Latin American countries may be excluded from this category if one disregards non-Spanish-speaking and non-Portuguese-speaking Indians. Indeed only Arabic-speaking countries in the Middle East and North Africa are totally excludable. The absence of a common national language to close the communication gap between diverse nationalistic and ethnic masses dwelling in the same state accounts for much political and social turmoil in developing countries. Even in some Western democratic nations, such as Canada and Belgium, resentment of minorities subjected to domination by larger linguistic entities has resulted in much political strife.

There are some 1,250 languages spoken on the African continent. Even Swahili, which is now spoken in several contiguous states, is relatively new and not completely accepted as a national language by many in the region. In India alone, some 15 major languages are used for official communication and education. Asia—apart from Japan, China, and India—uses over 15 national languages (Katzner 1975).

These and similar problems have become common features of many Third World countries. Yet it would be naive to infer that these developing nations have similar mass media systems because of their common experiences. Ever since the "wind of change" began to sweep over the vast regions of Asia, Africa, and Latin America, newer political ideologies and contemporary economic and social conditions have given rise to different realities in the institutionalization of mass communication in these societies.

The remnants of colonialism are to be seen in those countries that remain heavily dependent on the metropolitan powers. European languages such as English, French, Spanish, and Portuguese have been adopted as the lingua franca in many parts of Africa and Latin America.[1] In the political spectrum, a few countries have retained some of the Western-modeled democratic institutions and made them work with some success. India is still a citadel of parliamentary democracy. Several states in Asia, Africa, and Latin America have managed to hold on to some form of representative government in spite of adverse pressures from neighboring authoritarian and totalitarian states. But in the greater part of the Third World, nations are developing their own political and economic structures. Even in states once ruled collectively by one colonial power, separate growth and different national objectives have become inevitable. Kenya, Uganda, and Tanzania were once not only governed under similar British colonial administrations but shared economic benefits under the East Africa community. In the 1970s these contiguous states found themselves in total opposition to each other—with governments ranging from a one-man dictatorship in Uganda and quasi-parliamentary democracy in Kenya to a one-party socialist government in Tanzania. The same could be said of several countries in other regions of the world.

The genesis of a press philosophy in a given society is to be found in political bodies and the public at large. Similarly, the institutionalization process of mass communication is often determined by the two operating social forces—the governing elites (constitutionally elected or otherwise) and the public. Whichever force emerges as the more dominant of the two will also call the critical shots in influencing the character of the media system. This is particularly true in many developing nations where central governments invariably assume the more active role in planning and implementing economic and social developments without the benefit of visible public participation. In such cases, the press and other national information media function within government-established prerogatives even in the presence of constitutional guarantees.

In order to appreciate the role of national news and information media in developing nations, a simple if somewhat loose classification is in order. Such classification is based on the extent of government control or intrusion in the national media system. Three kinds of national media systems are currently in use in the Third World: state-controlled, government directed or sanctioned, and independent media organizations.

STATE-CONTROLLED MEDIA SYSTEMS

The provision that underlies media operations in a state-controlled system is total control over the management of the system and strict censorship of the communication content. Under most leftist totalitarian regimes, the function of mass media is defined within the socialist and communist ideological concepts, which govern all political, economic, and social activities of the state. In a socialist country, the press is controlled by the state organ—the party—to serve the needs of the proletariat. The concept of a free and independent press under Anglo-Saxon libertarian philosophy is contrary to the ideological wisdom of a Marxist society. Lenin ridiculed press freedom in the Western capitalist society:

The capitalists (and with them, willingly or unwillingly,
many Social Revolutionaries and Mensheviks) define as
"freedom of the press" a state of affairs under which
censorship is abolished and all parties freely publish all
kinds of newspapers. In reality, this is not freedom of the
press, but freedom to deceive the oppressed and exploited
masses of the people by the rich, by the bourgeoisie. (Quoted
in Markham 1967, p. 103)

Scientific socialism and state capitalism under the aegis of
Marxist-Leninist theory have achieved remarkable penetration into
several societies of the Third World. In some developing areas
Marxist theory has been conveniently meshed with a traditional and
precolonial mode of communal life, justifying the establishment of
socialism by giving it a local character. Although the practices of
Western parliamentary rule may be rejected on the grounds that they
are alien and unworkable in many newly independent nations of the
Third World, the principles of democratic socialism with a quasi-
Marxist rationale seem to be acceptable. The concept of political freedom, which governs the extent of press independence, is somewhat
modified to conform to the traditional environment and contemporary
expediency of the state. President Julius Nyerere of Tanzania argues
this point of view with passion:

... where there is one party, and that party is identified with
the nation as a whole, the foundations of democracy are
firmer than they can ever be where you have two or more
parties, each representing only a section of the community.
After all, we do have it on a very reliable authority that a
house divided against itself cannot stand. (Nyerere 1962)

A few states, such as Cuba, have adopted the unadulterated form
of Marxist-Leninist press philosophy, but most developing nations
that espouse a form of socialism examine the functions of mass media
within the context of *national unity and economic and social development*. To no one's surprise, the preoccupation of Third World political
leaders with frustrating and often insurmountable problems of
nationhood and economic development has produced a narrower and
more independent definition of the role of mass communication from
the East-West polemics. Mass media are primarily expected to
function as parts of the national effort in the gigantic task of
modernization.

This argument draws strong support from several communication
scholars. News and information media are viewed as essential inter-
mediaries between policy decision makers and the public by mobiliz-

ing masses to accept new ideas and modern techniques without creating cultural and ethnic tensions and psychological frustrations and anxieties. The dynamics of modernization are complex and require multidimensional approaches. To think of national development or modernization in economic terms and scales alone is simplistic and unworkable. Hence, a critical task of mass media is the establishment of a sound and stable political framework in which a proper and congenial social environment is created that in turn promotes the expansion of other sectors of national development. Information media can mobilize the fragmented interests of the masses into a single national goal by reducing "the problems of changing the attitudes and behavior of others and of communicating across the barrier of differing culture" (Pye 1963).

Two distinct mass media functions are charted: (1) to integrate all people within the modern state, and (2) to make them participate in national development schemes. Several Western scholars have some cogent arguments on the need for a strong national communication system for a developing country. One such scholar is Wilbur Schramm. Unlike his more contemplative and speculative colleagues, Schramm (1964) offers a detailed description of mass media functions in Third World countries:

> To bring the people of the developing countries into the
> decisions of development, to give them a basis for
> participating effectively, to speed and smooth the changes
> decided upon. . . . It is not entirely an impersonal, inflexible
> process. If the flow of communication will permit, the people
> can have a great deal to do with setting goals and deciding
> when and how they should change and what they want their
> society to change to.

Schramm is optimistic about the role of mass media in national development. He continues:

> The mass media can contribute substantially to the amount
> and kinds of information available to the people of a
> developing country. They can widen horizons and thus help
> to build empathy; they can focus attention on problems and
> goals of development; they can raise personal and national
> aspirations; and all this they can do largely themselves and
> directly. (ibid.)

Other scholars are more cautious but equally excited about the prospects of mass media in the Third World. The Indian scholar Y. V. L. Rao, pays more attention to the "constant and cumulative" interactions between mass media and national development creating the proper environment for modernization:

While it is true that economic development leads to an
increase in the flow of information through the greater
purchasing capacity of the people, reflected in subscriptions
to newspapers, magazines and specialized journals as well as
the ownership of radio sets and travel, it is also true that
increased information in turn furthers economic
development. (Rao 1968)

What Rao says is that mass media may not be the prime movers
of development in general, but they provide part of the necessary social interactions in a development cycle. In essence, an increase in the
flow of information contributes to economic growth, and economic expansion in turn stimulates the supply of more information.

To Lucian Pye, another communication scholar, the ultimate
measure of national development lies in the success of achieving political modernization. This political modernization is the difficult task
of "changing attitudes and reducing the gap between the ruling elites
and the less modernized masses" (Pye 1963). Pye describes a sound
political structure as a critical prerequisite to national development.
He states:

We have learned that very few of the essential prerequisites
for economic growth are related to purely economic matters.
The habits of mind, the values and world views, the social
conditions of life, and the stability and effectiveness of
government are all clearly crucial factors determining the
prospects of economic growth. Thus for both policy makers
and scholars what began as relatively uncontroversial and
presumably narrowly technical problems have increasingly
become entangled in the most complex of social and political
issues. The inescapable conclusion seems to be that the
concept of development cannot be reserved for the economic
sphere alone. (ibid.)

Ithiel de Sola Pool (1963) similarly believed that mass communication could contribute to the unity of a newly developing nation
by focusing attention on salient problems and facilitating the ensuing
discussions and debates on a national level. Nevertheless, Pool was
careful to point out that such unity among members of a society may
not be of a political nature. But he felt that national problems discussed on common communication media could bring about the
necessary developmental climate of sharing and exchanging ideas
and opinions among culturally diversified peoples of the state:

A mass media system permits the unification of a nation in
many non-political ways. The existence of daily price
quotations facilitates the establishment of a national
market. Media encourage national art and literature by

holding up products against each other. The media broaden
the relevant reference groups in discussions. The same kind
of processes of national organization through the media
take place in social life, in cultural life, in economic life, and
in party politics. (p. 253)

Pool states further that not only do the media provide essential
forums in which relevant issues are raised and discussed but they
also help to produce possible future political leaders who win public
attention by attacking negative social values and the social elites
opposed to change. In other words, mass media assist in the creation of
new leaders who are issue oriented and ideologically committed to
national development. Indeed, many contemporary leaders, particularly those in the newly independent African and Asian countries,
came to national politics and prominence not only because of their
ability to articulate the needs and aspirations of their people but also
because they were proficient in utilizing mass media to their political
advantage. In several cases these leaders were at one time or another
editors, publishers, or regular contributors to publications.

Although there may be a lack of agreement on specifics, most
Western scholars invariably hypothesize one or more of the following
functions of mass media:

There is a positive interaction between economic
development and mass communication, and mass media act
as reflectors of the dynamics of the development process in a
society.
   Mass media exposure leads to the creation of and/or
increase in empathy in persons—an essential state in the
modernization process.
   Mass media can also create the necessary climate of
modernization—such vital ingredients as innovativeness,
achievement motivation, and educational and occupational
aspirations.
   Mass communication systems could be effectively
utilized to teach basic skills such as literacy and even more
complex technical knowledge.
   When properly used, mass communication is an effective
instrument to bring about national integration—the feeling
of belonging to one nation—among diverse tribal, ethnic and
religious groups of people in a country. Without the growth
of such common feeling of national loyalty, without the
participation of the mass in an integrated fashion, the
economic growth of a country is hardly attainable.
   Mass communication has to perform simultaneously in
conjunction with other political, social and economic
institutions to achieve national objectives. (Habte 1977)

Such arguments by media scholars, although speculative at times, carried tremendous leverage among decision makers in many Third World countries during the early crucial period of national development. Yet, although many social scientists orchestrated the necessity of a strong mass communication policy as a prerequisite for modernization and national development, hardly any of them offered any meaningful suggestions on the structure of media systems and their position vis-à-vis government. Western intellectual models of development posited by such scholars during the 1960s recognized only the importance of mass media functions and paid no attention to the nature of communication systems and their place in a transitional society. This development paradigm strongly suggested that the role of mass media in Third World countries is based on a one-way flow of communication from government, responsible for planning and implementing national development projects, to the people.

Lately, some scholars have revised and at times repudiated their earlier hypotheses on the role of communication in development. Daniel Lerner (Schramm and Lerner 1976), Wilbur Schramm (1964), Everett Rogers (1976), and others have recently amended their views on the presumed strong interplay between communication and development, partially because of "the discouraging realization that development was not going very well in the developing countries that had closely followed the paradigm" (Rogers 1978).

Despite this change of heart on the part of scholars, many Marxist and socialist countries in the Third World have combined Western intellectual arguments with their own ideological preferences to establish state-controlled media systems. Countries such as Cuba, Chile (in the 1970s), and now Nicaragua in Latin America; Tanzania and Guinea in Africa; Iraq, Syria, and Iran in the Middle East; and the Communist nations in Southeast Asia advocate a state communication apparatus that functions principally as an instrument of national integration and economic development.

GOVERNMENT-DIRECTED OR GOVERNMENT-SANCTIONED MEDIA SYSTEMS

The rationale for direct control by Third World governments over national mass media systems is not drastically different from the reasons given by the Marxist and socialist leadership. The rhetoric may change, depending on the political sophistication of each state, but the message is similar. Authoritarian governments, like their Marxist and socialist counterparts, justify the control of mass communication systems by their perceptions of the political and economic realities of their societies. Whether they are military dictatorships, autocracies, or monarchies, they all exculpate their form of government on the grounds that they offer better alternatives—at least for the moment—to protect their nations from alien incursions or internal corruption, in the hope of improving economic conditions. The military coup against the duly elected Marxist government of Salvador Allende in Chile in the early 1970s and the Ghanaian experience[2] over the last two decades are such examples.

The fortunes of mass media systems in most developing nations have been linked with the radicalization process of political structures. Except for a brief period after independence, many former European colonies in Africa, Asia, and Latin America began altering the structures and functions of their mass media systems according to their perceived social needs and national political persuasions. The means to do this were twofold: (1) to absorb the mass communication channels within existing national directives and goals through direct government ownership and management; and (2) when such drastic action was difficult or ill advised, to reconcile modes of operation with government policies by imposing a series of restrictions. The first method became a principal goal in many African states, whereas several Asian and Latin American countries pursued the second means.

By 1977 only six African countries—Gambia, Kenya, Liberia, Morocco, Rhodesia, and South Africa—allowed private ownership of newspapers. According to Dennis Wilcox (1977), more than half of the African states own all newspapers and other publications produced in their respective borders. Wilcox believes that "government ownership of the print media is a clear trend in Africa, and the extent of ownership domination has increased significantly in recent years" (ibid.). Even in some parts of Africa, such as Nigeria, Senegal, and Kenya, where press restrictions are not so severe, journalists walk on tightropes balancing between public credibility and government sanction. African governments see themselves in a state of war, struggling against poverty, illiteracy, disease, and factionalism, and the press is summoned to join hands with government and herald the theme of national unity. In many cases, press collaboration with government is even advocated by publishers of independent newspapers. Alhaji Babatunde Jose, former chairman of the largest and once-independent daily newspaper in Africa, the *Daily Times of Nigeria*, has this to say:

> ...in the new nations and traditional societies of Africa...a journalist has additional responsibilities to help in building a nation out of the multi-lingual, multi-cultured societies in countries where economic sources are inadequate to meet expectations of the people.... In the final analysis, the

> journalists are part of the Nigerian society. If a society
> decays, the journalist cannot claim to be healthier than the
> body and if law and order breaks down and there is chaos,
> there would be no newspapers, no journalists and no readers.
> (Legum 1975)

In general, national mass media systems in Africa perform two basic functions: (1) they orchestrate messages of the central government and amplify national unity; and (2) they educate and mobilize the masses for social and economic development.

In Asia, mass media face subtle pressures, and sometimes direct threats, even in countries where Western democratic institutions have managed to survive. Amitabha Chowdhury (1976) reports that the Asian press has undergone a series "of imposed restructuring" since 1975. India's one-time free and lively press was almost brought to its knees during the mid 1970s by Indira Gandhi's government. National goals and objectives prescribed by central governments have begun to prevail over independent editorial judgment. Social responsibility has been replaced by national responsibility, and the press reporter has become an entrepreneur of "developmental journalism." According to Chowdhury, this trend of press control is sweeping across the Asian continent, with the exception of Japan.

Government intrusion in independent mass media systems in Latin America has visibly increased during the last few years. John Lent (1976) believes that "such persuasive government interest in the news media was perhaps inevitable." Nonetheless, he blames UNESCO's "experts" who "concentrated on Latin America as the first region in which to propose and develop national communication policies and the projected regional news agency."

The San Jose Declaration of 1976, sponsored by UNESCO, unanimously recommended the establishment of new national and international communication policies, despite the consternation of and outright condemnation by many Western participants and observers. It must be noted, however, that this declaration was preceded by earlier UNESCO-sponsored preparatory meetings convened in Latin American states—Bogota (1974), Quito (1975), and again San Jose (1976). The substance of these meetings, a substance eventually incorporated in the San Jose Declaration, laid the ground for a redefinition of the role of national communication systems. The clear implication was that mass media's primary function was within the framework of national identity and social integration. An international crisis surfaced and soon developed into an East-West ideological conflict when the Soviet Union submitted a draft declaration at UNESCO's 1976 biennial general conference held in Nairobi, Kenya. The Soviet draft, which was included in Article XII, read: "States are responsible for the activities in the international sphere of all mass media under their jurisdiction." This draft went as far as mandating the role of mass media to be one of "strengthening peace and international understanding and . . . combating war propaganda, racism and apartheid."

Mass media systems in several Latin American countries are increasingly feeling nagging pressures, sometimes subtle and often direct, to align themselves with the national policies prescribed by central governments. As several of these states—notably those in Central America and the Caribbean region—are experiencing the challenge of political and social revolutions, it seems inevitable that their press and broadcasting services will be forced to buckle under to the declared ideology.

INDEPENDENT MEDIA SYSTEMS

In a few Third World nations, the media in the independent category enjoy a certain measure of freedom from direct government intervention. Print media in particular manage to show a fierce independence under adverse government pressures in some Asian and Latin American states. In spite of several attempts by central governments in the Philippines, Thailand, Malaysia, and India during the 1970s, the press remain a strong social force with a respectable margin of editorial independence. This level of press freedom is allowed to flourish in a few Western-modeled democratic states. But, surprisingly, several independent newspapers exist in Latin American states where governments are hardly democratic or tolerant of a free press (Pierce 1979). For instance, Brazil's O Estado in Sao Paulo manages to steer an independent course by criticizing government policies, thereby gaining the respect of its readers. Its crusading journalism against government corruption and consumer fraud is indeed remarkable considering the restrained political climate within which it operates. Two leading dailies in Argentina, La Prensa and La Opinion of Buenos Aires, so far remain relatively free and do not hesitate to criticize government policies. Even in Chile, where the Pinochet junta keeps a tight reign over the conduct of the national press, the leading news magazine Ercilla is a respectable voice with a combative spirit and investigative reporting. Aside from incidents arising out of partisan favoritism and corruption by underpaid reporters and writers, news media in Mexico and Costa Rica enjoy a relatively free and open political environment.

To get a comprehensive view of the role of national mass media systems in the Third World, a brief discussion of a few generalizations may be helpful. First, although modern news and information media systems in developing nations are not historical offshoots of economic and political experiences of their societies, they continue to reflect contemporary conditions. They exemplify the current trend of political centralization that is sweeping over most Third World regions. This process of centralization—a postcolonial vestige that stems from the absence of established political institutions and gigantic economic problems—has given rise to national mass media systems that are either totally controlled or partially regulated by their governments. Even in those few states where the press enjoys relative freedom, it has faced constant pressure and intimidation to conform to government policies and guidelines. As Western-type democracies rapidly diminished in many newly independent nations of Africa and Asia, most national news and information media systems have been stripped of autonomous status and forced to follow national directives dictated by the central governments.

Second, news media in many Third World countries are not expected to create or shape public opinion. Instead they are often instructed or encouraged to reflect national policies through a series of government directives. The press is expected to devote itself selflessly to the welfare of its citizens by emphasizing national unity and consensus. Political and social conflicts are often avoided in newspaper columns and on the air in order to discourage fragmented and dissenting voices being manifested along ethnic, tribal, and religious lines. This is the official government rationale. In many instances, however, the imposition of such restrictions on dissenting public expression spills over into political thought as well.

As is often the case, many developing countries are occupied with the difficult task of building modern nation-states out of masses of people with diverse linguistic and cultural backgrounds. It should not be too surprising, therefore, that government authorities in the Third World see an imminent threat from an unbridled press in their countries. These officials, many of whom were trained in Western Europe and North America, are ready to give an impassioned lecture on the rationality of a controlled press. To them, mass media are important agents of unity whose critical function is to smooth out conflicting contrasts in values and attitudes among their diverse people and create an environment conducive to national development. Government officials are often unabashed when they proclaim that information media ought to be dutiful mouthpieces of national policies.

Third, underlying the press philosophy that dictates the overall function of mass media systems in many developing nations is the concept of *national service*. None of the four theories of the press (Merrill 1974) spells out the scope and depth of the rationale for a controlled media system in the Third World. It is tempting for a Western communication scholar to conjecture, as many do, using ready-made

"Communist" or "authoritarian" pigeonholes. The functions of news media in many developing nations may indeed appear Communist or socialist or authoritarian, but nothing could be farther from the truth.

The libertarian concept of the press serving as a "watchdog" on government is perceived by many well-meaning bureaucrats in the Third World as a destructive force. The Western values of a free press take a back seat when freedom from poverty, disease, and illiteracy becomes the overriding issue.

Neither is the concept of a Communist press acceptable in many socialist states in the Third World. A Communist doctrinal approach to the function of the press in which news and information media are instruments to advance the causes of the proletariat is unworkable. The Communist propensity to identify every social and political institution within the context of class struggle is often rejected. Although some socialist states inject a Marxist approach in their analyses of the sociopolitical environment of their societies (Al-Qaddafi 1976), the classic Communist press model is not recommended. The ideal democratic model in the Third World is for the press to become an expression of the entire society. The press is the standard-bearer of the nation and provides the necessary news and information to all social segments under the watchful eyes of the central government.

Perhaps in this respect, Third World information media may deserve the term "mass media." As tools of nationalism and development, they are expected to serve a great number of societies within a state subscribing to diverse cultural, sociological, and political norms. They have charted an ideal scenario that may be hailed or deplored, depending on the critics' political and philosophical orientations.

NOTES

1. UNESCO estimates that more than two-thirds of materials printed are in English, French, Spanish, German, and Russian.

2. Since the end of Kwame Nkrumah's rule in the Republic of Ghana in the early 1960s, successive military juntas, alternating with brief periods of civilian rule, have plagued this nation.

REFERENCES

Al-Qaddafi, Muammar. *The Green Book*. Part I. London: Martin, Brian and O'Keefe, 1976.

Chowdhury, Amitabha. "Report to the Annual Assembly of the International Press Institute." *IPI Report* 25, no. 7 (September 1976): 1–2.

Doob, Leonard. *Communication in Africa*. New Haven: Yale University Press, 1961.

Ghose, Hemendra Prasad. *The Newspaper in India*. Calcutta: University of Calcutta, 1952.

Habte, Amde-Michael. "Mass Media and International Development Bureaucracies." Ph.D. dissertation, University of Minnesota, 1977.

Hachten, William A. *Muffled Drums: The News Media in Africa*. Ames: Iowa State University Press, 1971.

Katzner, Kenneth. *Languages of the World*. Toronto: 1975.

Kitchen, Helen, ed. *The Press in Africa*. Washington, D.C.: Ruth Sloan Associates, 1956.

Legum, Colin, ed. *African Contemporary Record—Annual Survey and Documents, 1972–73*. Ad quoted by Dennis Wilcox in "Mass Media in Black Africa," 1975.

———. *Pan Africanism*. New York: Praeger, 1962.

Lent, John. "Caribbean Press Hemmed in with Controls." *IPI Report* 25, no. 7 (September 1976).

Markham, James W. *Voices of the Red Giants: Communication in Russia and China*. Ames: Iowa State University Press, 1967.

Merrill, John C. *The Imperative of Freedom: A Philosophy of Journalistic Autonomy*. New York: Hastings House, 1974.

Nyerere, Julius. *Ujama: The Basis of African Socialism*. Dar-es-Salam: Tanganyika Standard, 1962.

Pierce, Robert N., *Keeping the Flame; Media and Government in Latin America*. New York: Hastings House, 1979.

Pool, Ithiel de Sola. "The Mass Media and Politics in the Modernization Process." In Lucian W. Pye, ed., *"Communication and Political Development*. Princeton: Princeton University Press, 1963.

Pye, Lucian W. *Communication and Political Development*. Princeton: Princeton University Press, 1963.

Rao, Y. V. L. *Communication and Development: A Study of Two Indian Villages*. Minneapolis: University of Minnesota Press, 1966.

Rogers, Everett M. "The Rise and Fall of the Dominant Paradigm." *Journal of Communication* 28, no. 1 (Winter 1978): 63–69.

———. "Comunication and Development: The Passing of the Dominant Paradigm." *Communication Research* 3 (1976): 213–40.

Schramm, Wilbur. *Mass Media and National Development*. Stanford: Stanford University Press, 1964.

———, and Daniel Lerner, eds. *Communication and Change: The Last Ten Years—and the Next*. Honolulu: University Press of Hawaii, 1976.

Wilcox, Dennis. "What Hope for the Press in Africa?" *Freedom at Issue*, March–April 1977, pp. 10–13.

7. NEWS AND ITS USES IN THE COMMUNIST WORLD

JOHN J. KARCH

THE MARXIST-LENINIST FOUNDATION

In the Communist world, media are designed to serve a politically purposeful role: an "enormous educational" function (Tolkunov 1977, Tsukasov 1978) in disseminating propaganda domestically and externally to ensure that only Marxist-Leninist ideology, current party policies, and purported achievements of Communist regimes are projected. Media are also an important instrument in the ideological struggle between communism and capitalism. This is possible because domineering Communist parties control rigidly all aspects of mass media. An extensive censorship network operates to ensure effective compliance.

In the Communist world, the media of communication are a state monopoly, under the control of the Communist party (CP). The CP exercises total control whether it is the only political party permitted to function (as in the Soviet Union) or one of several parties (as in East European countries). The significance of mass media is clearly evident from the high priority they are assigned bureaucratically. In the Soviet Union, under the ruling Politburo, the Central Committee exercises control and policy guidance through several departments, especially the departments of Propaganda, Culture, and International Information.

Generally, only the Communist party, the CP-controlled government, and party-directed "public organizations" such as trade unions are permitted to own and operate media; this ensures ideological and political "purity." Major newspapers and magazines are "organs" of these institutions, and targeting is an important consideration in establishing a newspaper or magazine. No individual or nonapproved organization, and certainly nothing that can be considered even remotely competitive, is tolerated. Competition is rejected as "subjugation to the monopolists." Accordingly, immediately following the Bolshevik takeover, with the October 28, 1917, Decree on the Press, the militant party abolished the media then in existence and established the foundations for the press and publications envisioned by Lenin.

Lenin had recognized the importance of media long before the Bolshevik Revolution. He believed that "ideas are power" and that a newspaper is "not only a collective propagandist and a collective agitator, it is also a collective organizer" (Lenin 1969, p. 161). Russian revolutionary publications had begun agitating even before Lenin—as early as the mid-nineteenth century. *Iskra* (*The Spark*), the forerunner of *Pravda*, was inaugurated in 1900. Two years later, Lenin wrote his famous propaganda treatise *Chto Delat'?* (*What Is to Be Done?*) in which he explained the necessary ingredients for a successful revolution—ideology and organization—with an all-Russian political newspaper for more effective communication and organization. In 1912, with Stalin as an organizer, the Bolsheviks began to publish *Pravda*, which became the organ of the Central Committee of the Communist party of the Soviet Union.

Following Lenin's principles, the CP considers media in military terms: "The press, radio, films, and television are the shock forces on the ideological front" declared *Pravda*, and they have the additional responsibility of combating "enemy propaganda." Subscription figures for 1981 indicate clearly the mass character of print media: *Pravda* (*Truth*) with 10.7 million, *Komsomol'skaya Pravda* (*Komsomol Truth*, organ of the Central Committee of the Communist Youth League) with 10.1 million, *Pionerskaya Pravda* (*Pioneer Truth*, published by the Central Committee of the Komsomol) with 8.6 million, *Trud* (*Labor*, organ of the Central Council of the Trade Unions) with 10.5 million, *Sel'skaya Zhizn'* (*Country Life*, published by the Central Committee of the CP for the agricultural sector) with 8.5 million, and *Izvestiya* (*News*, organ of the Presidium of the Supreme Soviet of the USSR) with 7 million. The party "organs" are the most authoritative

TABLE 7.1
Organs of Communist Parties

Country	CP Organ
USSR	Pravda (Truth)
Albania	Zeri i Popullit (People's Voice)
Bulgaria	Rabotnichesko Delo (Workers' Cause)
Czechoslovakia	
Czech	Rudé Právo (Red Right)
Slovak	Pravda (Truth)
GDR	Neues Deutschland (New Germany)
Hungary	Népszabadság (People's Freedom)
Poland	Trybuna Ludu (People's Tribune)
Romania	Scinteia (The Spark)
Yugoslavia	Borba (Struggle)
People's Republic of China	Jenmin jihpao (People's Daily)
Cuba	Granma (name of Castro's yacht)
Vietnam	Nhan Dan (The People)
North Korea	Radong Sinmum (Labor Daily)

and influential newspapers in Communist countries, reflecting as they do the current policies of the regimes (see Table 7.1).

Media are heavily subsidized by the regimes, and this allows for inexpensive newspapers, magazines, and books. Daily newspapers cost between three and six cents, and neither circulation nor advertising revenues is of major financial significance. The importance of mass media lies in their support of and contribution to the party, which, by its control of the content, deliberately seeks to reach audiences on a massive scale. Cost increases levied on readers are infrequent and minimal. On August 1, 1981, *Pravda* announced that beginning January 1, 1982, its newsstand price would be increased as a result of the higher cost of newsprint; the increase was to be from three kopecks (about four cents) to four kopecks (slightly over five cents) for six-page issues (Tuesday through Sunday editions), and from four to five kopecks for the eight-page Monday edition.

Government ownership, ensuring CP monopoly of the dissemination of information, extends logically to the news agencies. Unlike independent news agencies in Western countries (e.g., AP, UPI, and Reuters), those in Communist countries are "official," and thus no meaningful comparison between the two systems can be made.

According to the director general of TASS, "We are engaged in exten-
sive propaganda of the domestic and foreign policy of the Communist
Party and the Soviet state. . . ." (Losev 1981, p. 16). News agencies in
Communist countries are listed in Table 7.2.

TASS, established in 1925, is a model for Communist news agencies. This official news agency of the USSR is directly under the
Council of Ministers, on the All-Union State Committee level, a rank
equivalent to a ministry and of obvious importance. TASS is headed
by a director general who is always a high-ranking party official.[1]
With headquarters in Moscow, TASS controls the news agencies of
fourteen non-Russian Republics in the Soviet Union. In the RSFSR
approximately 500 correspondents and 360 photographers in three
TASS offices and 72 centers disseminate news, features, and photos to
the central and lower press. A special Soviet and foreign "news-in-
brief" service is provided to radio and television stations. TASS main-

TABLE 7.2
Official News Agencies in Communist Countries

Country	News Agency
USSR	TASS[a]
Bulgaria	BTA
Czechoslovakia	ČTK
East Germany (GDR)	ADN
Hungary	MTI
Poland	PAP
Romania	Agerpres
Albania	ATA
Yugoslavia	Tanjug
China (PRC)[b]	Xinhua
Vietnam	Vietnam News Agency
North Korea	Korean Central News Agency
Cuba[c]	Prensa Latina

[a] Telegrafnoye Agentstvo Sovyetskovo Soyuza (Telegraph Agency of the
Soviet Union).
[b] In 1952 Beijing established a second news agency, the China News Service, with an office in Hong Kong. It provides features and photographs for
overseas Chinese newspapers and periodicals.
[c] Prensa Latina maintains field offices in 35 countries, including 11 Latin
American and Caribbean countries, "and combines news gathering and
propaganda dissemination with intelligence operations" (State Department, December 14, 1981, p. 4). AIN (Agencia de Information Nacional or
National News Agency) was established in 1974 to provide news to Cuban
newspapers and radio and TV stations in the provinces.

tains bureaus and correspondents in 125 countries and has 3 offices in the United States—at the UN, in Washington, and in San Francisco.

The objectives of TASS have been authoritatively and clearly stated on numerous occasions. According to the current director general, TASS is "engaged in extensive propaganda of the domestic and foreign policy of the Communist Party and the Soviet state and informs the Soviet people and world community about the economic, political, and spiritual life of our society" (Losev 1981, p. 16).

While all East European governments have their own state news agencies (Kruglak 1976), most rely heavily on TASS reports for information and for indications of the official Soviet position on current issues. For example, the Bulgarian CP organ *Rabotnichesko Delo* carried a lengthy TASS report "Decisive Measures Adopted by the Military Council of National Salvation," while the BTA report from Warsaw dealt with food supplies and the black market. Discernible differences from TASS are observable in reports from news agencies of countries pursuing more independent policies, particularly Romania,[2] Hungary, and recently, Poland.

TASS and the other official news agencies have an additional important role. They provide confidential to top-secret domestic and foreign information earmarked for various echelons of media, government, and party officials; this material is not intended for publication because of its sensitivity. The level of classification is identified by color, either green, blue, or white (Hannah 1977, Lendvai 1981). These colored reports partly explain the need for the large number of TASS Bureau members (e.g., in Washington) compared to the volume of publicly filed reports.

Because mass media in Communist countries are government monopolies, control by party functionaries extends to the lowest echelon, thus ensuring ideological and political conformity. Officials make no secret of the importance of media's reflecting Marxism-Leninism and the party's interpretation of events. Former TASS Director N. G. Palgunov says: "Soviet information not only contains facts but analyzes them in a Marxist way . . . it serves the cause of Communism, the cause of fighting the bourgeois ideology hostile to us." While Western journalism prides itself on objective and factual reporting, Leninist principles reject objectivity as, in Lenin's words, "absurd, scandalous, and harmful." The role of the mass media is broader than one of simply reporting facts, Communist officials declare; the mass media must "correctly interpret" events.

The following are the "Basic Principles of the Soviet Press," cited as Leninist principles for a "new type" press. They are applicable to all Soviet media and are generally adopted by all Communist countries: Party-mindedness (*partiinost'*), high ideological/idea content

(*vysokaya ideinost'*), truthfulness (*pravdivost'*), national/popular character (*narodnost'*), mass character (*massovost'*), and criticism and self-
criticism in the press (*kritika samokritika pechati*). In a discussion of
high ideological content, Bogdanov and Vyazemskiy (1961), included
"Soviet patriotism" (*sovetskiy patriotizm*). Applied, these principles
are designed to enhance Marxist-Leninist ideology; the image of the
Communist party; Communist, especially Soviet, achievements and
superiority; conversely, they are intended to conduct propaganda
campaigns against implacable enemies, the bourgeois countries, with
the United States as the acknowledged leader of that group. This doctrinaire role of mass media rejects the reporting so familiar in Western countries, including human interest stories, entertainment, and
tragedies. "Yellow Journalism" is characterized by the *Great Soviet
Encyclopedia* (1975) as "the most reactionary, mercenary bourgeois
journalism" with "the basest bourgeois publications". Nevertheless,
Communist mass media do not proscribe "sensationalism" entirely.
Stories appear from time to time about alcoholism, economic crimes,
or hooliganism, but these are selectively designed for their "educational" value in solving socioeconomic problems in Communist
societies. Even "letters to the editor" are officially generated to serve
this fundamental purpose. To give the appearance that ordinary people have access to mass media and that the regime maintains contact
with the masses, the Soviet regime has established a network of *Rabselkor* (*rabochiye isel'skiye korrespondenty*—worker-peasant correspondents) and a "letters to the editor" system. According to Hannah
(1977), "the *Rabselkor* institution can be viewed as an attempt to co-
opt people to the Party's tasks, inviting them to play the role of volun-
teer journalist (under Party supervision) and thus become part of the
political system" (p. 15). In recent years, "Open Letter Days" (*Den'
otkrytogo pis'ma*), which permit workers and farmers to submit questions about their working and living conditions, have been given publicity and have even been sponsored by newspapers, such as *Trud*
(RFE-RL 1981).

The accounts stemming from the cliché-ridden press and radio
and television are predictable: heavily stylized, leaden, progagandis-
tic, tendentious, uninteresting, and repetitious. Readers, listeners,
and viewers of the Communist fare are evincing an increasing desire
for alternative sources of information and for interesting programming. Moscow and other Communist capitals have not been blind to
these trends. Through officially sponsored sociological surveys, the
regimes are seeking to improve their understanding of the concerns
and anxieties of their populations so as to deal more effectively with
them through the mass media (Alekseev et al. 1981, Mink 1976,
Mickiewicz 1981). Attracting youth—the "future of Communist con-

struction"—is a high priority. In their efforts to attract not only additional subscribers (many people subscribe for political purposes) but additional "readers," the media leadership, with the concurrence of the authorities, has been adopting some modern, Western-style techniques including more attractive layouts, genuine human interest stories, entertainment features, and eye-catching illustrations and photos rather than photos of "happy" collective farmers and industrial workers in "socialist realism" poses. But the regimes are not likely to succeed appreciably as long as their regulations and policies permit innovations only within rigid parameters. Under these conditions, people will continue to seek alternatives such as listening to foreign broadcasts and, for a small segment, even resort to the underground *samizdat*, or self-publication (Tökes 1975).

The party-government view of the role of the mass media—"educational," propagandistic, supportive of official policies and programs—is clear. Everyone involved in media understands the ideological-political primacy. Those who do not accept their expected and unqualified supportive role, those who possess a natural proclivity for expressing individuality, or those who wish to challenge the system face insurmountable obstacles.

EDUCATIONAL PREPARATION

In Communist countries the entire upbringing, education, and training of children is directed at imbuing them with the unquestioned "truth" of Marxism-Leninism and loyalty to the Communist party. In Communist China, "Maoism" was added. The educational process continues through higher education and beyond. Journalism is considered to be a "special" branch of education; it was initially entrusted to Communist institutions. Today, leading universities have journalism departments and faculties, and other institutions offer media studies including courses in electronic media. Student selection is carefully made by party-government authorities, who continue to monitor student progress, as do officials of the Union of Journalists and other CP-controlled unions. At the request of TASS, "special student groups" exist on the journalism faculty of Moscow State University and other institutions to prepare them for the "highly specific" work of the agency, especially abroad (Losev 1981).

The expansion of journalism studies has contributed to a qualitative improvement of mass media, but the aim is greater effectiveness, not diversity of opinion or competitiveness. An attempt at diversity has been evident in Eastern Europe more than in the Soviet Union, where alternatives for freer expression have been confined to the underground *samizdat* and *magnitizdat* (tape recordings), both primary targets of the KGB. Independent-minded and recalcitrant journalists are given warnings or dismissed; if accused of serious transgressions, they may be tried, usually under Article 50 of the RSFSR Law for "anti-Soviet agitation and propaganda."

CENSORSHIP

To ensure that mass media contain desired ideological and political content, the Soviet regime employs a censorship network that, with some exceptions, has been copied by other Communist regimes and today constitutes a vital element of control throughout the Communist world. In the Soviet Union the major censorship organization is the Main Administration for Safeguarding State Secrets in the Press, under the Council of Ministers. Popularly known as Glavlit, its jurisdiction is comprehensive: to exercise virtually total control over press and publications content, as well as over radio broadcasts, television transmissions, lectures, and exhibitions (Conquest 1967). Glavlit's "plenipotentiaries" are also assigned to all publishing enterprises. Other organizations with censorship responsibilities are the Communist party, which oversees the entire apparatus, the KGB (*Komitet gosudarstvennoy bezopasnosti*—Committee for State Security), and functionaries concerned with sensitive and secret areas. The KGB is entrusted with preventing objectionable information from entering the Soviet Union, the dissemination of information within the country, and the placement of disinformation (*dezinformatsiya*) abroad.

Censorship networks were established in East European countries following Communist takeovers and were modeled on the Soviet Agitprop (Agitation and Propaganda Department at the Central Committee) and Glavlit networks. For example, in 1946 Poland established the Chief Press Control Office, and in 1953 Czechoslovakia established the Chief Administration of Press Supervision. In Yugoslavia, on the other hand, censorship was exercised until 1952 through party-cleared materials disseminated by Tanjug, the news agency, whose supervisors received party guidances. Thereafter, control was less stringently imposed by the Press Commission of the Socialist Alliance of Working People (SAWPY), the major mass organization controlled by the League of Communists of Yugoslavia. Stronger party censorship was instituted in 1956 by the Workers' Councils, the alternative Yugpress news agency was abolished in 1958, and the 1960 Law of the Press further tightened the press. Interestingly, no preventive or prior censorship exists in Yugoslavia.

While Hungary has no formal government censorship apparatus, effective controls are applied here and elsewhere through the party bureaucracy; the offices of press, radio, and television; the writers' and journalists' unions; and through the most insidious means—"self-censorship." As indicated, the entire upbringing and educational processes seek to condition conformity. In adult life one's professional, party, and social behavior are closely monitored, with any signs of deviant behavior rapidly corrected. Accordingly, journalists and other professionals are cognizant of their responsibilities and limitations regarding independent expression. Whatever one's private feelings, a journalist must compose articles that are ideologically sound and within the party's guidances; that is, portraying communism, led by the Soviet Union, highly favorably, and the bourgeois world, led by the United States, critically.

For upward mobility, or indeed simply to maintain a position in mass media, and for such attractive perquisites as foreign travel, journalists and commentators have to be unchallenged experts in conformity. They are among the higher echelons of society in terms of creature comforts and prestige. As members of the Union of Journalists or the more prestigious Union of Writers, they can publish for additional remuneration. Without membership, which can be denied or withdrawn if one is deemed "unworthy," they cannot publish and in effect lose employment in the media profession.

The great majority of journalists obviously accept these party-imposed conditions; some may even believe their own propaganda. Nevertheless, numerous instances in the Soviet Union and in other Communist countries of reservations, challenges, and rebellion by journalists and writers against controlled and censored information indicate a calamitous failure in persuasion. And substantial evidence exists that mass media in these countries lack credibility and prompt people to seek alternative sources of information.

Communist officials frequently cite Marxism-Leninism for their rationale, legitimacy, and justification of policies. But censorship extends even to Marx and Lenin when their writings do not "conform" to current reality. For example, one never sees such views by Marx as: "a censored press remains bad even when it produces good things" or "the censored press has a demoralizing effect."

To ensure Communist control of mass media, the entire distribution apparatus is under the jurisdiction of the government, unlike the situation in the United States where distribution is made by individual newspapers or private distributors. For example, in the Soviet Union *Soyuzpechat'* (Main Administration for the Distribution of Printed Matter), which is within the Ministry of Communication, is the official distributor of newspapers and magazines. *Soyuzkniga* distributes books within the Soviet Union, and *Mezhdunarodnaya Kniga* (an All-Union organization under the Ministry of Foreign Trade) is charged with the export and import of books, periodicals, and sheet music.

PROMISE AND REJECTION IN HUNGARY, CZECHOSLOVAKIA, AND POLAND

Even under stringent Communist control, and the watchful eye of Moscow, mass media in several East European countries have exhibited the powerful potential recognized by Lenin and feared by Communist regimes. During the 1954–56 "New Course" period in Hungary, following Stalin's death, journalists and writers sparked the movement for a more liberalized atmosphere, and contributed significantly to the revolutionary ferment of 1956. During the "October Revolution," when tolerance created opportunities for greater expression, "freedom of the press" blossomed. Tragically these halcyon days were short-lived as the revolution was crushed by Soviet military intervention; purges, persecution, and oppression of the mass media followed, and the world learned of the exacting limits of Communist tolerance for freedom.

Nevertheless, there was no return to the "Stalinist" press. Janos Kadar exercised rule under the slogan "He who is not against us is with us," and mass media and writers functioned under less stringent conditions but within certain limits of tolerance. These are the well-known areas of Marxist-Leninist ideology, party leaders and programs, and criticism of the Soviet Union. Many articles were not permitted to be published, and writers and journalists resorted to underground publications. Today, while seeking the cooperation of the intelligentsia, regime officials simultaneously monitor their behavior and harass them. During the 1980–81 developments in Poland, Hungarian writers and others attempted to achieve greater liberalization, and young writers demanded an uncensored newspaper and an independent publishing enterprise. The Writers Union was compelled to discontinue its youth chapter in February 1981. Deputy Prime Minister György Aczel warned the Writers Union of the party's limits to toleration.

Albeit delayed, "De-Stalinization" extended to Czechoslovakia during the 1960s. Here, as in Hungary, intellectuals were in the forefront of liberalization, especially Slovak journalists and writers, who reflected the spirit of those who suffered the political stigma of "bourgeois nationalism" during the 1950s. One of the most significant developments of the remarkable Prague Spring was the appearance of a relatively free press (Skilling 1976). Inquisitive journalists probed long-held secrets, inquired about Soviet involvement, and printed revelations about the trials of the 1950s and the "cult of personality" of Czech and Slovak party leaders. Czech and Slovak journalists and writers, faced previously with the rigid censorship that produced sterile propaganda tracts, now flowered in reflecting Alexander Dubček's "socialism with a human face." The ubiquitous censors seemed to disappear as the daily and periodic press, and radio and television, became more informative, interesting, and exciting. Original commentaries and analyses were carried; open conferences were held by leading political figures; public opinion polls were conducted even on previously sensitive sociological and political issues; and unrehearsed political debates were televised. No area seemed exempt from media scrutiny as reporters led the liberalization movement. As secrets were revealed, compromising the party and implicating Moscow, emboldened media leaders campaigned for political reform as well as for cultural freedom, freedom of the press, and the end of censorship. The Action Program provided for a new press law that eliminated "preliminary" censorship, and the intelligentsia demanded legislative guarantees to abolish "all" censorship, which ended in June 1968 (*Rudé Právo*, June 19, 1968). However, there were "antireformists" and Soviet "interventionists" as well, the latter "making good use of the Soviet press" (Valenta 1979).

The Soviet-led Warsaw Pact invasion of Czechoslovakia in August 1968 crushed Alexander Dubček's political liberalization and reinstated the party's rigid control over the media, including censorship the following month, with the establishment of the Office of Press and Information (Skilling 1976). Unbridled mass media were considered infectious and a threat to effective Communist rule—an intolerable situation for Moscow. As in Hungary in 1956, widespread purges of mass media followed the invasion, and the clandestine radio and press, which sparked temporary "resistance," were silenced within a few days (Eidlin 1980).

The Polish mass media reflected closely the character of the population and political developments in the country, including their significant role in the emergence of Solidarity (*Solidarność*). During the Stalinist period the media were as rigidly controlled by the party as elsewhere in Moscow's new satellites. An elaborate censorship apparatus was established. During the "thaw" (1953–56) the mass media began to reflect popular discontent and contributed significantly to liberalizing tendencies, as in Hungary. Although it was still on the books, censorship virtually ceased to exist in 1956; ironically, the media that were in large measure responsible for Wladyslaw Gomulka's return as the party's First Secretary in October 1956 were to be harnessed by his regime, albeit not to the degree of the Stalinist period, as a modicum of freedom continued to exist. With the ascendancy of Edward Gierek (1970), control was centralized to mobilize popular support—so-called propaganda of positivism—for his policies. The worsening socioeconomic situation in the late 1970s led to great popular discontent, however, and more stringent controls over the media by the party's press department were imposed, leading to greater alienation of journalists and writers, who increasingly resorted to *samizdat* (Curry and Johnson 1980).

Among the numerous worker demands in the summer of 1980 was one for greater liberalization of the mass media, including free access to them by the Roman Catholic Church. The Gdansk Agreement (August 31) between Solidarity and the government provided for a reformed censorship law and radio broadcasts of Sunday masses. A Sunday mass was broadcast on September 21, 1980, the first on state radio since the CP seized power in Poland. On November 11, one hour a week was granted to independent trade unions to broadcast labor developments.

While censorship was a burning issue, realistic proposals focused on its "reform" rather than its outright abolishment. The regime's draft bill was submitted to the *Sejm* on April 1, 1981, rather than within three months (end of November 1980), as stipulated in the Gdansk Agreement. The law, adopted July 31, 1981, reduced substantially the rights of censors from the Main Administration for the Control of Press, Publications, and Public Performances, and exempted Solidarity publications from prior censorship.

As Solidarity's membership and power increased, mass media underwent a cataclysmic change heretofore not experienced in any Communist-ruled country. Many new newspapers and periodicals sprouted and flourished. Radio and television reflected revolutionary developments through their programs. Solidarity achieved a kind of communication revolution. Despite a shortage of newsprint and price increases, the popularity of newspapers and journals increased circulation figures. For example, the circulation of the Cracow Catholic weekly *Tygodnik Powszechny* grew from 25,000 to 75,000; the circulation of this quality publication had been deliberately limited by the authorities. Even some party papers—for example, *Gazeta Krakowska*, the Cracow daily—became supporters of the Solidarity-generated developments and found themselves in an unaccustomed position, that of "best sellers." The most impressive publication was *Tygodnik Solidarność (Solidarity Weekly)*. It began publication on April 3, 1981, with a circulation of 500,000 copies, which disappeared from public view as soon as they were offered for sale. *Solidarność* became a collector's and black market item. For the first time, Solidarity organizations in all parts of Poland were informed of current developments—union, political, economic, social, and cultural. A newspaper indeed became an "organizer"—an organizer of the proletariat. However, party First Secretary Stanislaw Kania warned at a CC Plenum (April 29, 1981) that "the party will never renounce...the right to... control over the means of information and propaganda," and the party-controlled media became more aggressive against Solidarity during the second half of 1981. Addressing Poznan workers in late August, Kania declared, "The mass media cannot be apolitical. We will not allow any actions that could serve to paralyze means of mass communication" (*New York Times*, August 31, 1981, p. 3). A week later, September 3, 1981, Kania warned that a threatened Solidarity strike against state radio and TV would be countered by a declaration of a "state of emergency" (*Trybuna Ludu*, September 4, 1981).

Following a Solidarity resolution on December 12, General Wojciech Jaruzelski[3] announced the imposition of martial law on December 13, restricting civil rights and suspending activities of Solidarity (FBIS). According to the proclamation, "The dissemination of all kinds of publications and information, by any means, is banned, as is the public display of works of art and the use of all kinds of printing equipment without first obtaining the permission of the appropriate organ." Strict limitations were placed on the press; only *Trybuna Ludu, Zolnierz Wolności,* and system local dailies were to be published. The ruling Military Council for National Salvation imposed information restrictions immediately with the obvious objective of rendering totally ineffective the internal nongovernment communication network and placing the population under quarantine against outside information sources (Dobbs 1982).

Rigid application of censorship was immediately imposed on mass media. Nothing was to be published without official authorization. The Foreign Broadcast Information Service (FBIS) of the United States reported on December 14, 1981, that Poland's radio broadcast a Radio and TV Committee Statement immediately after the proclamation of the Military Council. The head of the committee claimed that "hostile forces" were "aiming at taking over the radio and television," and "in order to ensure their correct and essential functioning," ordered the following:

1. Production and broadcast of one central 24-hour radio program and one central television program.
2. Cessation of remaining radio programs and the second television program.
3. Switching off of regional broadcasting stations and regional television centers and limiting the activity of the television center and the central radio station in Warsaw to the minimum essential in the current situation.
4. Undertaking of program, technical, and organizational work by the assigned team of employees of the committee. Persons assigned to this work report to agreed places immediately.
5. Remaining employees given a special holiday until further notice.

The independent-minded Poles made courageous efforts to maintain communication links.[4] The conference of bishops sent messages to both Jaruzelski and the Polish people protesting the regime's curbing of freedoms and calling for their restoration. The appeal was supported by Pope John Paul II. On Sunday, January 24, in a mass broadcast throughout Poland, Archbishop Jozef Glemp, the primate, said in a sermon that there must be "honest information" in the news media, both domestic and foreign (*New York Times*, January 25, 1982). Over one hundred Polish intellectuals signed a petition and sent it to the parliament (Sejm) and Archbishop Glemp. The petition cited as a consequence of martial law "the blockade of communications in the whole country," and demanded the lifting of the "state of war" (*New York Times*, January 22, 1982, p. A10).

FOREIGN PROPAGANDA, DISINFORMATION, AND ACTIVE MEASURES

The propagation of Marxism-Leninism is extensive and unrelenting. Soviet and other Communist media serve as major instruments of foreign policy. They have a dual function abroad: (1) to propagate Marxism-Leninism, publicize Soviet policies, and extol Communist achievements; and (2) to systematically and continually denounce real or imagined enemies of Communism, especially the United States. "Peaceful coexistence" and "détente" provide excellent environments for the dissemination of pro-Soviet and anti-Western propaganda.

Communist countries utilize both electronic and print media for foreign programming. For example, TASS has exchange agreements with other major news agencies and national news services. It provides materials, including photographs, of approximately 300 reports on domestic and foreign topics daily to over 400 news and press agencies, information ministries, editorial boards of newspapers and journals, and television and radio broadcasting companies in over 90 countries. Soviet policies are clearly reflected (Losev 1981). TASS has especially intimate working relationships with news agencies in other Communist countries.[5]

In 1961 Moscow established a second agency—"Novosti" (Agenstvo Pechati Novosti, or APN—The News Press Agency). It is allegedly nongovernment because of its founding members. Nevertheless, Novosti is a CP-inspired and controlled "public information service" designed officially "to aid the development and strengthening of mutual understanding, confidence, and friendship among peoples." Also, of course, it was to disseminate favorable Soviet materials to counter "hostile capitalist propaganda." Novosti is a vast propaganda network that operates in over one hundred countries, including the United States.[6] It publishes periodicals, newspapers, brochures, and books for foreign consumption, and operates Radio Peace and Progress (RPP) for foreign transmissions.

Communist countries provide substantial investments—human and financial—for foreign propaganda. The Soviet Union alone is said to spend over $3 billion a year for propaganda and covert action (U.S. Congress 1980). This includes the KGB's active measures (*aktivnyye meropriyatiya*). Soviet allies add substantially to this effort. According to the State Department, active measures "refer to operations intended to affect other nations' policies" (State Department, October 1981). These include written or spoken disinformation, efforts to control media in foreign countries, use of Communist parties and front organizations, and clandestine radio broadcasting. Disinformation consists of "rumor, insinuation, and distortion of facts to discredit foreign governments and leaders" (*ibid.*). Fundamentally, disinformation is a mental process, but the combination of the psychological and physical, or "propaganda of the deed," results in effective propaganda (Martin 1981). Soviet disinformation is a global problem requiring intense study (Douglass 1981).

In its design to influence behavior and mold attitudes, Soviet propaganda themes have been, allowing for updating and modifications, impressively consistent over decades. These themes are deliberately and frequently repeated not only by mass media but by the highest party leaders (including, in their day, Josef Stalin, Nikita Khrushchev, and Leonid Brezhnev), through ministers and other functionaries down to the lowest party agitators. By their repetition, catchwords become a part of the language, used wittingly or unwittingly even by officials and the intelligentsia of targets of Communist propaganda. Specifically, these themes have been as follows: "Socialist superiority" and the "inevitable triumph" of communism as opposed to the "decadent" Western, especially U.S., society; "democracy" (Soviet) versus "capitalism" (United States); "war" and "peace" (the Soviet Union is pictured as "peace-loving," favoring "peaceful coexistence," or "détente," and the supporter of "wars of national liberation"; the United States is "imperialist," "militaristic," "warmongering," and "aggressive"). Soviet propagandists have arrogated to themselves such meaningful words as "socialist" (rather than "Communist"), "democratic" (rather than "totalitarian"), and "peaceloving" (rather than aggressive).

Communist propaganda techniques include selection and exclusion, overemphasis, underemphasis, repetition (e.g., "ruling circles," "imperialists"), campaigns (e.g., "peace," "détente," "neutron weapon"), argumentation, emotionalism, diversion (e.g., use of massive countercharges), indirection (e.g., citing non-Soviet sources), satire, ridicule, and mockery.

The vast Soviet foreign propaganda network includes international front organizations encompassing various disciplines and sponsored, supported, and controlled by Moscow. They reflect pro-Soviet and anti-U.S. policies without the appearance of direct Kremlin sponsorship. Several front organizations were specifically organized in the field of political communication. The Prague-based International Organization of Journalists (IOJ) provides both a propaganda platform through its monthly, *The Democratic Journalist*, and training for Third World journalists (U.S. Congress 1978, Lendvai 1981).

Cuba has the major responsibility for conducting propaganda activities in support of Communist revolutionary movements in Latin America and the Caribbean. These programs, plus Havana's activities in Africa, are supported by the Soviet Union. Soviet assistance amounts to over $8 million daily. Cuba conducts exclusive cultural exchanges and propaganda programs "to support covert operations and elicit support for armed struggle." Specifically, Havana's propaganda has actively supported insurgents in El Salvador, Guatemala, and Colombia; and Radio Havana broadcasts to Paraguay have called for the overthrow of the Paraguayan government (State Department, December 14, 1981).

Several East European countries have the major responsibility for the indoctrination of Third World journalists (Lendvai 1981). Since 1963, the East Berlin "school of solidarity" has been giving intensive training to journalists, especially to those from African countries; in 1964, the Association of Hungarian Journalists, in a cooperative project with the International Organization of Journalists, established the Center for Training of (foreign) Journalists, with scholarships awarded to journalists from Third World countries (Erdei 1968). Sofia's International School offers graduate study, and Bucharest University has a three-year course for journalists. Efforts are made to maintain contact with all graduates (Novosti 1981). Cuba also provides opportunities for foreign students, especially those from Latin America. Its various educational institutions include the Nico Lopez National Training School, the party's highest, where courses include "political training for journalists." Cuban mass organizations are assigned the major responsibility for the indoctrination of foreign students; their training schools include courses in "agitation and propaganda" (State Department, December 14, 1981).

Another organization serving Soviet objectives is the Prague-based International Radio and Television Organization (OIRT) whose program contents "reflect the integration and cooperation of the Socialist community" (Wygledowski 1978, p. 27). OIRT's Intervision

TABLE 7.3
Foreign Broadcasts by Communist Countries,
December 31, 1981

Country	Number of Hours Weekly	Number of Languages
USSR	2,100[a]	80
Albania	564	21
East Germany	433	12
Poland[b]	298	12
Bulgaria	282	12
Czechoslovakia	262	11
Romania	208	13
Yugoslavia	150	14
Hungary	124	7
People's Republic of China	1,318	43
North Korea	590	8
Vietnam	301	12
Cuba	410	8

SOURCE: U.S. International Communication Agency.
[a] Radio Moscow added 35 hours weekly in Polish on February 11, 1982.
[b] Radio Polonia went off the air on December 13, 1981, when martial law
   was established; it resumed transmission on December 22, with 87½ hours
   weekly in four languages—Polish, English, German, and French.

and the European Broadcasting Union's (EBU) Eurovision networks
have an agreement for the exchange of news. Since 1958, pro-Soviet
policies have been disseminated worldwide through the multilan-
guage *Problems of Peace and Socialism*, a monthly published in
Prague.

The Soviet Union is by far the most ambitious of the major broadcasters, but other Communist countries also engage heavily in foreign propaganda, as indicated by their radio broadcasts. Soviet overseas radio programs are broadcast by Radio Moscow, Radio Peace and
Progress, and two clandestine radio stations, National Voice of Iran
(NVOI), and Radio Ba Yi, which broadcast to Iran and China, respectively (State Department, October 1981). The latter are instruments
of KGB's "active measures" and portray themselves as "progressive,"
national (local) organs. During the Iranian revolution, NVOI carried
scurrilous disinformation charges of the CIA's killing Iranian religious leaders and planning to kill Khomeini. Among other clandestine stations, North Korea broadcasts 80 hours a week. See Table 7.3.

The People's Republic of China is a major target area for Soviet propaganda. Radio Moscow broadcasts 119 hours weekly in Mandarin, while RPP carries 49 hours in Mandarin, 17½ hours in Cantonese, and 10½ hours in the Shanghai dialect. Radio Moscow's World Service began around-the-clock transmissions in 1979; of the week's 168 hours of English broadcasts, 63 hours were specially directed to North America, while 105 hours were audible in this region.

Of the East European countries, the most concerned with the momentous events in Poland were Czechoslovakia and East Germany. A major factor was the fear of Polish "infection" on these Polish neighbors. In mid-April 1981 Czechoslovakia began broadcasting 3 hours a day in Polish; East Germany initiated Polish-language broadcasts in October 1981 with 19 hours weekly with a strong signal (750 KW transmitter); and the USSR doubled its output in Polish on April 1, 1981, going from 17.5 to 35 hours weekly. The Soviet increase in Polish broadcasts followed a crisis policy established in 1956 when Moscow stepped up Hungarian-language transmissions from 4.5 to 21 hours weekly, continued in 1968 with Czech/Slovak from 7 to 84 hours, and in 1980 with Dari and Pashto (to Afghanistan) from 21 to 60 hours.

Cuba's Radio Havana shortwave broadcasts total over 350 hours a week in eight languages worldwide; its medium-wave Spanish-language broadcasts over "La Voz de Cuba" are carried nightly by a network of high-powered transmitters located in different parts of Cuba. To the Caribbean alone, Radio Havana's weekly transmissions include 14 hours in Creole to Haiti, 60 hours in English, 3 hours in French, and 125 hours in Spanish. According to the State Department, Prensa Latina and Radio Havana, in close coordination with TASS and Radio Moscow, regularly use disinformation to distort news reports transmitted to the region, especially those concerning places where Cuban covert activities are most intense.

JAMMING OF WESTERN BROADCASTS

Faced with tightly controlled access to domestic and foreign information, and lack of credibility in their media, the inquisitive population turns to alternative sources, especially Western broadcasts. To counter these programs, the Soviet Union has resorted to jamming, interference by radio "noise" on the same frequency. Moscow has jammed Radio Liberty transmissions continuously and resumed jamming VOA, BBC, and Deutsche Welle broadcasts on August 20, 1980, prompted by Polish Solidarity-generated developments. In Eastern Europe, RFE broadcasts continued to be jammed in

Bulgaria, Poland, and Czechoslovakia, but not in Hungary and Romania. Nevertheless, some transmissions were received and were of concern to the authorities. For example, in a January 1982 *Newsweek* interview, Jerzy Urban, the Polish regime's spokesman, responded to the question "Can martial law last six months?" as follows: "Yes, if the reasons for its introduction persist, i.e., if broad-scale, illegal anti-state attempts continue. Radio Free Europe, financed by agencies of the U.S. Government, calls, for instance, to organize a conspiratorial network in Poland. In this way it backs up martial law and acts in favor of its prolongation...." (p. 47).

NOTES

1. Sergei A. Losev since May 1979. In 1978 Leonid M. Zamyatin, Director of TASS, became Director of Information Department of the CP's CC, where he is a full member.

2. Agerpress (e.g., December 3, 1981) and other Romanian media reported mass peace demonstrations throughout Romania during November and December 1981, culminating in President Nicolae Ceausescu's declaration calling for a U.S.-Soviet agreement at Geneva on limiting intermediate-range nuclear weapons in Europe.

3. Jaruzelski had replaced Jozef Pinkowski as Prime Minister on February 9, 1981, and Kania as Party First Secretary on October 17, 1981; he was also Minister of Defense.

4. See Dobbs (1982) for an informative summary of the council's actions, Solidarity countermeasures, and the role of foreign broadcasts during the early weeks of martial law.

5. For closer coordination of international propaganda, conferences of chiefs of Communist news agencies are held periodically—for example, in Prague during November 30-December 2, 1981 — which discuss their supportive role in propaganda campaigns for peace and disarmament. (See *Rude Pravo*, December 2, 1981.)

6. For example, the *Christian Science Monitor*, December 31, 1981, p. 26, carried a Moscow-datelined article by Novosti's political commentator Gennady Gerasimov, "Soviet View of 1981: 'A Year Without Dialogue' "; and the *New York Times*, January 7, 1982, p. A27, Genrikh Borovik's "A Russian Views U.S. News." Journalist and playwright Borovik was in the United States for Novosti.

REFERENCES

Alekseev, B., B. Z. Doktorov, and B. M. Firsov. "The Study of Public Opinion: Experiences and Problems." *Soviet Review* 22, no. 1 (Spring 1981): 3–19. Translated from *Sotsiologicheskiye issledovaniya*, no. 4 (1979).

Board for International Broadcasting. *Eighth Annual Report 1982*. Washington, D.C.: January 31, 1982.

Bogdanov, N., and B. Vyazemskiy. *Spravochnik zhurnalista (Handbook for the Journalist*). Leningrad: Lenizdat, 1961.

Conquest, Robert, ed. *The Politics of Ideas in the USSR*. New York: Praeger, 1967.

Curry, Jane Leftwich, and A. Ross Johnson. *The Media and Intra-Elite Communication in Poland*. Summary Report. Santa Monica: Rand, December 1980. Pp. 14–15.

Dobbs, Michael. "Solidarity Seeks to Salvage Vital Information Network." *Washington Post*, January 10, 1982, pp. A1, A22.

Douglass, Joseph D., Jr. "Soviet Disinformation." *Strategic Review* 9, no. 1 (Winter 1981): 16–26.

Eidlin, Fred H. *The Logic of "Normalization": The Soviet Intervention in Czechoslovakia of 21 August 1968 and the Czechoslovak Response*. East European Monographs, Boulder, Colo. Distributed by Columbia University Press, New York, 1980. Pp. 93–156.

Erdei, Ferenc, ed. *Information Hungary*. New York: Pergamon Press, 1968.

Foreign Broadcast Information Service. Eastern Europe. April 30, 1981.

———. Eastern Europe. December 14, 1981. Contains texts of Address, Military Council Proclamation, Decree, Communiqués, and Resolutions.

Great Soviet Encyclopedia. Translation of 3rd ed. New York: Macmillan, 1973–81.

Hannah, Gayle Durham. *Soviet Information Network*. 1977.

Hurd, Douglas. "Freedom of the Press and the Threat of State Intervention." *NATO Review* 29, no. 6 (December 1981): 10–12.

Izvestiya, May 2, 1981.

Kornilov, Yu. "Rejoinder: Vain Endeavors." *Izvestiya*, October 22, 1980, p. 5.

Kruglak, Theodore E. "The Role and Evolution of Press Agencies in the Socialist Countries." In Bohdan Harasymiw, ed., *Education and the Mass Media in the Soviet Union and Eastern Europe*, pp. 80–98. New York: Praeger, 1976.

———. *The Two Faces of TASS*. New York: McGraw-Hill, 1963.

Lendvai, Paul. *The Bureaucracy of Truth: How Communist Governments Manage the News*. Boulder, Colo.: Westview Press, 1981.

Lenin, V. I. *What Is to Be Done?* (February 1902). Moscow: Progress Publishers, 1969.

Levshina, I. S. "The Educational Potential of the Mass Media." *Soviet Education*, 21, no. 1 (November 1978): 28–39.

Lewis, Paul. "West's News Organizations Vow to Fight UNESCO on Press Curbs." *New York Times*, May 18, 1981, pp. A1, A14. Text of Declaration of Talloires, adopted by Voices of Freedom Conference of Independent News Media, Talloires, France, May 15–17, 1981.

Losev, S. "Increasing the Quality and Rapidity of Information Is the Main Thing." *Zhurnalist* (Moscow), no. 4 (April 1981): 16–18.

Maksudov, L. "Efforts to Regulate the International Mass Media." *International Affairs* (Moscow) (March 1980): 101–3.

Martin, L. John. "Disinformation as a Form of Propaganda." Paper presented at the World Media Conference, New York, October 1–5, 1981.

Mickiewicz, Ellen Propper. *Media and the Russian Public*. New York: Praeger, 1981.

Mink, Georges. "The Conceptual Approach to Public Opinion Surveys in the

Soviet Union." In Bohdan Harasymiw, ed., *Education and the Mass Media in the Soviet Union and Eastern Europe*, pp. 116–24. New York: Praeger, 1976.

Mlynář, Zdeněk. *Nightfrost in Prague*. New York: Karz Publishers, 1980.

Newsweek, February 1, 1982, p. 47.

New York Times, August 31, 1981, p. 3.

———, January 21, 1982, p. A10. Contains excerpts from message by Poland's bishops.

———· January 22, 1982, p. A10. Contains text of the petition.

———, January 25, 1982, pp. A1, A8.

Novosti Press Agency. *1981 Yearbook USSR*. Moscow: 1981.

RFE-RL. *Radio Liberty Research* (by Elizabeth Teague), no. 401/81, October 7, 1981.

Robotnichesko Delo, December 21, 1981, p. 5.

Rudé Právo, December 2, 1981, p. 2; June 19, 1968.

Shishkin, Gennadiy. *New York Times*, August 31, 1981, p. A17.

Skilling, H. Gordon. *Czechoslovakia's Interrupted Revolution*. Princeton: Princeton University Press, 1976.

State Department. "Cuba's Renewed Support for Violence in Latin America." *Special Report No. 90*, December 14, 1981.

———· "Forgery, Disinformation, Political Operations." *Special Report No. 88*, October 1981.

———. *Gist*. "New World Information Order," October 1981.

———. "Implementation of Helsinki Final Act," June 1, 1981–November 30, 1981. Eleventh Semiannual Report, *Special Report No. 89*.

———· "President Reagan: Situation in Poland." *Current Policy No. 357*, December 23, 1981, p. 2.

TASS, June 2, 1981.

Theberge, Leonard J. "UNESCO's 'New World Information Order': Colliding with First Amendment Values." *American Bar Association Journal*, June 21, 1981.

Tökes, Rudolf L., ed. *Dissent in the USSR: Politics, Ideology, and People*. Baltimore: Johns Hopkins University Press, 1975.

Tolkunov, Lev. "The Responsibility of the Mass Media." *New Times* 6 (1977): 13–15.

Trybuna Ludu, September 4, 1981.

Tsukasov, S. "Enhancing the Effectiveness and Quality of the Soviet Press." *Soviet Education* 21, no. 1 (November 1978): 53–71.

U.S. Congress. House. Permanent Select Committee on Intelligence. *The CIA and the Media. CIA Report on Soviet Propaganda Operations*. Appendix R., pp. 531–627. Washington, D.C.: Government Printing Office, 1978.

———. House. Permanent Select Committee on Intelligence. *Soviet Covert Action (The Forgery Offensive)*. Washington, D.C.: Government Printing Office, 1980.

Valenta, Jiri. *Soviet Intervention in Czechoslovakia, 1968*. Baltimore: Johns Hopkins University Press, 1979.

Washington Post, Jaunary 31, 1982, p. A7.

Wygledowski, Waclaw. "Intervision: The Growth of an Exchange." *Intermedia* 6, no. 3 (June 1978): 24–27.

PART 4

MASS MEDIA AS VEHICLES OF EDUCATION, PERSUASION, AND OPINION MAKING

8...IN THE WESTERN WORLD

HENRY F. SCHULTE

The media of mass communication may not shape the way readers and viewers react to their messages, but there is no question about one thing—they shape perceptions of reality and set certain priorities. "The press may not be successful much of the time in telling people what to think, but it is stunningly successful in telling its readers what to think about" (Cohen 1963, p. 13). Were it not for media, most individuals would be unaware of what happens beyond the reach of their vision and hearing. The average user of media is not aware of matters unreported by media. Often, it is the size of the headline or the duration of the film clip or videotape, not the inherent importance of an event or trend, that establishes its importance in the minds of readers or viewers. Media set the agenda. They certainly play a role in the process of educating the public and in the formation of public opinion.

That concept is fundamental to the image of media in the democratic Western world. At a basic level, media are viewed as suppliers of information to the electorate. The broader in scope the information and opinion supplied to the voter, the more likely it is that he or she will make "the right decision" in the secrecy of the voting booth. As Alexis de Tocqueville (1836) put it more than a century ago, "When the right of every citizen to cooperate in the government of society is acknowledged, every citizen must be presumed to possess the power of discriminating between the different opinions of his contemporaries, and of appreciating the different facts from which inferences may be drawn."

It has been traditional to consider the media as purveyors of information or attitudes toward an event. But that may no longer be the popular view or the whole truth. During a syndicated television talk show dealing with American media, a member of the audience expressed one facet of contemporary public opinion. "I am concerned about the power of the press," she said. "In presidential elections, they make or break the candidates." Her statement reflected concern that mass media influence goes far beyond that of a channel which carries information and opinion. By now, Thomas Jefferson's statement about newspapers and government has been repeated so often that it may be a communication cliché. Writing to a friend in 1787, Jefferson said, "...were it left to me to decide whether we should have a government without newspapers or newspapers without a government, I should not hesitate to prefer the latter." The addendum to that letter came twenty years later when a somewhat disillusioned Jefferson reflected, "It is a melancholy truth that a suppression of the press could not more completely deprive the nation of its benefits than is done by its abandoned prostitution to falsehood. Nothing can now be believed which is seen in a newspaper. Truth itself becomes suspicious by being put into that polluted vehicle." The same ambivalent attitudes toward media prevail today. Media are perceived as doing more than reporting on how opinion is shaped. They are seen as shapers of opinion.

Jefferson was not alone in recognizing the potential of the press. In eighteenth-century Britain and France, the press was labeled "the fourth estate." In Spain, the press became known as "the fourth power." In the United States it has been called "the fourth branch of government." In each case, the nomenclature reflects a recognition of the role played by media as a communication channel linking those who govern with those who are governed—a channel that is not always passive and that may have its own impact on events or policy. The press is a carrier of information about government to the people. It performs the function of relaying information about "public opinion" to those in government who are assumed to find such information relevant.

The notion of public opinion—or even the opinions of multiple publics—is fundamental to the democratic system of government.

When a system assumes that those who make decisions should carry out the wishes of the voters, public opinion plays a major role in the patterning of political behavior. The election of officeholders at specified intervals is not a terminal act. Public opinion is assessed on a continuous basis. There may be more than one reason for that. In some cases, it is done so that decision makers can adjust their acts to public opinion. Sometimes it is done so that strategies may be developed to change public opinion, to bring it into line with the decisions of those who govern.

What is public opinion? It is the way in which people react to the social and political issues brought to their attention, usually via media. High on the agenda of issues to which people respond are those emerging from elections, especially the postures and personalities of candidates, matters of domestic policy, and international affairs. Since World War II, there has been a great increase in the importance attached to public opinion. There are two major reasons for this:

1. An increase in literacy and the extension of education to a broader section of society. This has resulted in better informed and more activist publics.
2. The development of more sophisticated print and electronic media technology. This has made it possible to bring news, and reactions to it, instantly to a large segment of the human race. Even the illiterate have access to information about local, national, and international events through radio and television.

Recognition of these facts has more and more focused national and international attention on public opinion. In a complex society, those who seek office, those who sell a product, or those whose goal is the modification of the social, political, or economic structure of a nation, state, community, or institution seek the approval of one or more publics. They seek access to media with messages that will advance their goals and through those messages reach public opinion.

Soon after movable type was introduced into Europe in the fifteenth century, rulers recognized the potential impact of such technology. They saw it as a tool of education, but they saw it also as a threat to their claims to power. European history is dotted with laws and regulations designed to control the production and content of books and broadsides. By the end of the eighteenth century—the period of the American and French revolutions—there was a clear delineation between those committed to freedom of the press and those committed to controls. Napoleon Bonaparte once said that "four hostile newspapers are more to be feared than a thousand bayonets." When his lieutenants invaded France's neighbors, they carried with them detailed instructions about the control and management of the newspapers they found.

As Western Europe plowed through the political wrenches of the nineteenth century, newspapers became a direct part of the political process. (At about the same time, newspapers in the United States, influenced among other things by the birth of the "penny press," moved away from alignment with or subservience to political parties.) Most European nationalist movements were traditionally aided by newspapers. Even now, newspapers in many nations reflect the position of political parties. As electronic technology introduced new communication channels, new techniques were developed by political leaders to reach mass audiences. President Franklin Delano Roosevelt turned to the radio "fireside chat" to find access to millions of Americans and present them directly with his solutions for the economic ills of the United States. Adolf Hilter used radio to mobilize hundreds of thousands of listeners.

Politicians today use increasingly sophisticated techniques as they attempt to manipulate the messages carried by those channels. They stage events to capture media attention, and they often coordinate those events with media deadlines. Given the opportunity, they will time "events"—or as Daniel Boorstin has called them, "pseudo-events"—to upstage an opponent or an advocate of an opposing point of view. Absolute monarchs and dictators have used—and continue to use—communication monopolies to regulate the flow of messages. Among the first acts of the government of Poland when it declared a state of martial law in late 1981 was to seize control of all channels of communication, censoring internal and external media messages and cutting off domestic and international telephonic communication.

Revolutionaries include radio and television transmitters among the primary targets of insurrection. Some of the great growth in the size and cost of government can be traced to the increase in the numbers of official information specialists. Small businesses have become large and prosperous through the effective persuasive use of communication channels. Business and industry allocate sizable portions of their operating budgets to support public relations and advertising operations—aimed, obviously, at presenting their point of view or their product to some part of the public. That the media can and do influence opinion has been a "given" in democractic societies. Robert Ezra Park (cited in Frazier and Gaziano 1979), student of public opinion, wrote: "Through the newspaper, the common man ... participates in the social movements of his time." At about the same time, Walter Lippmann called a free press "... an organic necessity in a great society. Without criticism and reliable and intelligent reporting, the government cannot govern. For there is no adequate way in which it can keep itself informed about what the people of the country are thinking and doing and wanting." Lippmann (1922) went on to note that "within the life of the generation now in control of affairs, persuasion has become a self-conscious art and a regular organ of popular government."

The counterpart, of course, is the control exerted by the citizen in the act of voting. That is established by national constitutions. But that right, as Fischer and Merrill have put it, "is supplemented, and indeed usually overshadowed, by other mechanisms through which the citizen can influence officials: the public media, pressure groups, lobbies, communications to administrative agencies, and public opinion. Public opinion polls offer a relatively new device through which popular views on a large range of issues can be made known to policymakers" (Fischer and Merrill 1976, 31).

Official concern with public opinion and press relations varies. It can be the often heavy-handed, sometimes negligent treatment of media and their publics in dictatorships. It can manifest itself in the constructive use of subsidies in one form or another, as in Sweden or Spain: subsidies supposed to provide the economic base for a communication system that serves the needs of a democracy.

In Spain the government grants a small subsidy to a newspaper for each copy sold, as well as a subsidy for each kilo of domestically produced newsprint a newspaper buys. Any attempt to use the subsidies to manipulate the press would result in uproar and outrage in the nation's parliament. As Juan Luis Cebrian, editor of the Madrid newspaper *El Pais*, says, "The role of the press is to challenge power. The press itself is a power and its basic function, along with that of informing, is to criticize others." By "others," Cebrian understands the government, especially its relations with the media of mass communication (Smith 1980, p. 168). In Sweden, in 1981, a plan to reduce government subsidies was defeated in the face of declining newspaper circulations. In fact, a substantial increase in subsidies was paid to print media.

The role of government can take the shape of television in France, which oscillates between freedom and government intervention. In 1964 the Office de Radiodiffusion Television Française (ORTF) was created to counter criticism of the then existing system. "Specific complaints about the program service and inadequate personnel were accompanied by charges that French radio and television were dominated by the executive branch of government" (Wells 1974, p. 19). The advent of the socialist government of François Mitterand in 1981 caused a renewal of concern about ORTF's impact on public opinion that was followed by drastic changes in the management of radio and TV organizations.

In Japan, on the other hand, there is "a concordance of views on the formulation and conduct of national policies among government, industry, press, and general public that is unique in an industrialized country outside the Communist world" (Smith 1980, p. 200). In the United States, the politician and the public official are possibly even more concerned with public opinion than are their counterparts in other countries.

UNDERSTANDING MEDIA

Much is known about the techniques of both overt and covert control or manipulation of the press. Working journalists and academic scholars, sometimes in harness, explore the techniques of controlling media message content and flow. They understand the process of mass communication and analyze the impact of media structure on messages. An example is Breed's classic work (1955) on the socialization of the newsperson to the "norms" of the company for which he or she works. They understand the impact of media "gatekeepers" on media messages. They treat of "pack journalism." Reporters, by design or by accident, tend to cover events in groups. Often they perceive the news from the same perspective. In many cases they share sources, transportation, and communication channels. Be it Vietnam or Nicaragua, they inhabit the same lodgings, meet similar deadlines, and try out ideas on one another. Students of media are especially aware of the effect on the reportorial process of the masses of information churned out by government agencies. They know about "trial balloons," stories planted in the media to determine the reaction of other decision makers, as well as of the public, about the uses and misuses of the "leaked" story, which gives the governmental official an anonymous voice in the decision-making capitals of the world. That official can measure and even structure public opinion—or the reactions of peers—without making the commitment of the attributed statement. They understand the corruptive influence on the newsperson of prolonged intimate association with the powerful of the political world. They know the impact of advertising on television and radio, where content is often designed not necessarily to inform but to deliver an audience to the income-producing message of the advertising. They know that a large percentage of consumers buy newspapers for access to advertising messages.

There is a general tendency on the part of the media consumer, media practitioners, and those whose messages are carried by media or who are the subjects of media messages to treat media as if they have power. By so doing, they enhance the power of media. That power is twofold: It is the power to provide information to people, to supply or add to a data base; it is also the power to persuade, to shape and change attitudes. Blumler and McQuail (1968), in an analysis of the campaigning that preceded the 1964 general election in Great Britain, note that ". . . the politicians behaved as if the mass media mattered and used them avidly to project their parties' refurbished images to the public" (p. 7). It is accepted today in the United States that television reportage of battlefield scenes in Vietnam helped change public opinion and led to the withdrawal of American armed forces from that country. It is also accepted that the persistence of newspapers, most notably the *Washington Post*, in investigating what has become known as "Watergate" led to the resignation of an American President. "Public opinion polls show that most of the new orientations and opinions that adults acquire during their lifetime also are based on information supplied by the mass media," Graber concludes (1980, p. 9). "People do not necessarily adopt the precise attitudes and opinions that may be suggested by the media. Rather, mass media information provides the ingredients that people use to adjust their existing attitudes to keep pace with a changing world."

PRINT VERSUS ELECTRONIC MEDIA

Though the newspaper has been the traditional means of mass communication, evidence suggests that the electronic media now play a more crucial role in the education of great masses of people whether that education be formal and systematic or informal. In many countries newspaper circulation has not kept pace with population growth. For example, in Spain newspaper circulation per 1,000 population dropped from 104 in 1970 to 98 at the end of the decade. That was in spite of an increase of 7 percent in the national literacy rate during the period. In the United States, to cite another example, newspaper circulation remained relatively static during the decade, declining very slightly from a total of 62.1 million copies published daily in 1970 to 62 million in 1978. But if one considers the increase in population, the statistics represent a loss. Copies per 1,000 population dropped from 305 in 1970 to 285 in 1978. The decline in circulation appears to be mainly among younger readers. During roughly the same period, newspaper circulation declined in Belgium, Canada, Denmark, France, and the United Kingdom, as well as Spain. It held steady in Italy, Japan, the Netherlands, Norway, and Sweden; and it increased in Austria, Finland, Israel, West Germany, and Switzerland. To pinpoint the causes of the differences is difficult in many cases. The reasons are individual to the country, the media system, or both.

At one time, the newspaper was the major source of information available outside the school system. But newspapers were not always fully trusted. Charles Y. Glock (1961) expressed the opinion that "in Western Europe, it is taken for granted that most newspapers are the organs of the political party. Because this orientation is reflected in the news as well as the editorial columns, readers tend to be cautious in their willingness to accept what they read" (p. 472). Today polls show that print journalists command less public confidence than they may have in the past. Shortly before Watergate, the American newsmagazine *Newsweek* surveyed perceptions of the coverage of the Nixon administration. Forth-five percent of the respondents said they found such coverage to be slanted. Twenty-three percent thought media were prejudiced against the Nixon administration; 22 percent thought media were biased in favor of it. As Warren H. Phillips (1976), president of Dow Jones and Company, put it, "... nearly half of America thought the press slanted the news, but they were split down the middle on which way we were slanting it" (p. 11). *Christian Science Monitor* editor John Hughes (1979) reported on other research. "Editors," he told a lecture audience, "... are finding out in research sessions that their readers often regard their newspapers as arrogant, unresponsive, and committed to the pursuit of various self-interests" (p. 8).

A 1981 Gallup poll showed that the public ranked journalists about average in terms of honesty and ethical standards. At least eight job categories—clergymen, druggists, dentists, medical doctors, engineers, college teachers, policemen, and bankers—ranked ahead of TV reporters and commentators and newspaper reporters in the poll. TV reporters and commentators ranked slightly ahead of print journalists, perhaps a reflection of the successful challenge of electronic media to the dominance of newspapers since World War II; television and radio have come to have a major impact on mass media consumers. By 1979 television and radio, at least in the United States, were so ubiquitous that the Carnegie Commission (1979) on the future of broadcasting would report: "Sixty-four percent of the Americans rely on television as their principal source of news. The average high-school graduate has spent nearly 50 percent more time in front of the television set than in the classroom" (p. 254).

At the same time, the usefulness of print media vis-à-vis electronic media, especially television, was being challenged. In 1970 a Canadian Special Senate Committee on Mass Media reported the results of a nationwide survey of reactions to the various media. Thirty-seven percent of those questioned found television to be the "most factual" medium, 28 percent responded in favor of newspapers. Fifty-nine percent found television "most influential"; 25 percent, newspapers. Sixty percent found television "most educational"; 21 percent, newspapers. Polls in the United States have produced similar results. Nevertheless, experts such as George Comstock warn against taking such survey results too literally, in spite of the fact that with major breaking stories, such as the assassination of President John F. Kennedy, only a minuscule percentage of the population learn of the event from print media.

> Survey evidence shows that the public names television as the source of most of its news, the most rapid disseminator of news, the most fair and unbiased of sources, the most comprehensive in coverage, and the more credible when the two media disagree on a report. Newspapers, magazines, and radio all rank lower, although they once either rivaled or exceeded television.... But for regional and local news, newspapers equal or exceed television as the principal source. Furthermore, far more people actually see a daily newspaper within any two-week period than watch a national network evening news program. This is as true today as it was a decade ago. (Comstock 1981, p. 236)

Obviously, different media attract different audiences. For example, there is an inverse relationship between hours spent viewing television and the educational level of the viewers. In 1976 the A. C. Nielsen Company reported that the average individual in the United States spent 28.7 hours a week in front of the television set. In homes where the head of the household had less than four years of college, that rose to 29.9 hours a week. In homes where the head of the household had four years or more of college, it dropped to 22.9 hours. There is evidence to suggest that a positive relationship exists between educational level and use of print media—newspapers, magazines, and books. There are other distinctions. For example, in the United States, those who watch public television (where there is more emphasis on educational/informational functions compared to commercial television, which is more oriented to entertainment) are slightly better educated than the average. The audiences of public television number 4 percent more college graduates than the national average. There is also an above average representation of the "professional, owner, managerial" class in the public television audience (Rhodes 1981).

The Madrid newspaper *El Pais*, which has become, since its founding in 1976, one of the world's influential, elite newspapers (so ranked by Merrill and Fisher 1980) claims to be "the newspaper of the men and women belonging to a social class which is above the average professionally, educationally, economically." A study published by *El Pais* in 1979 reported that 54 percent of its readers belong to that small percentage of the Spanish population that attends or has attended a university or a technical school (*Pais* 1979). Merrill and Fisher (1980) conclude that great newspapers aim at audiences different from those of run-of-the-mill newspapers, audiences that seek diversity and depth rather than sensationalism. The elite press, they argue, "will not appeal to the typical reader looking over a wide assortment of journals at a newsstand." They go on to note that ". . . there is little in any of the great newspapers of the general levity, splash, crackle, and pop that characterizes the general press of the world. The elite press actually attempts to do what the Commission of Freedom of the Press said the press should do for society in its 1947 report—'to present a truthful, comprehensive, and intelligent account of the day's events in a context which gives them meaning'" (p. 7). Influential newspapers in Europe are not written for the masses but are aimed at an influential elite; these are newspapers such as *Le Monde*, the *Times* of London, the *Neue Zürcher Zeitung*, and, most recently, *El Pais*.

In the United States and Canada there is a relatively clear line drawn between news and editorial content. That is not always the case in the European press, where opinion and fact may merge in the columns of a newspaper. The tradition is different, partly at least because of the historic association of newspapers with political parties or movements.

MEDIA AS EDUCATORS

In most countries of the democratized world, there is some emphasis on the use of TV and radio as educational tools, a practice in many ways pioneered in the United Kingdom. As early as 1924, three years before the British Broadcasting System was chartered, radio was used to provide programming for schools. In 1952 the BBC used closed-circuit television to reach school systems, and began regular broadcasting to schools in 1955. The Independent Television Authority (ITA) joined the BBC in the production and transmitting of educational programming after its inception in 1954. There has been correlation in Great Britain between the use of television in homes and schools. Radio grew between 1922 and 1948 to the point that it reached 75 percent of the homes in Great Britain. Between 1924 and 1953, radio grew until it was used in 75 percent of the nation's schools. Television reached 75 percent of the homes between 1946 and 1963: it reached 75 percent of the schools between 1957 and 1974. It was estimated that color television would reach 75 percent of the nation's homes between 1968 and 1982. Experts predict that color television, whose use began in the schools in 1971, will be in 75 percent of the schools by 1983 (Cain 1980).

As part of its commitment to the use of radio and television for educational purposes, the BBC worked closely with Great Britain's Open University. Even before it began operations in 1971, the Open University had been promised access to up to 30 hours a week of television time (the weekday 5:30 to 7:30 p.m. slot, as well as weekend daytime hours) and an additional 30 hours of radio time. By the time the Open University began its third year, in January 1973, it had a student body of about 48,000 and offered 43 undergraduate courses as well as 3 "post-experience courses" (BBC Handbook 1973). The image inspired by the BBC link with the Open University was such that many referred to the operation as "the BBC University" (Ferguson 1976).

Great Britain is not the only European nation involved in educational broadcasting. The Austrian Television Service is responsible to both the Ministry of Communications and the Ministry of National Education, an arrangement that underlines the commitment to educational telecasting. Since 1959, the service has included television programming for the nation's schools. France began its educational service, *Television Scolaire*, in 1951. Italy, in 1958, inaugurated its Telescuola, a semiautonomous branch of the RAI (Radio Audizioni Italia), which works closely with the Ministry of Public Instruction. As a part of its programming, it broadcasts courses in a variety of subjects to pupils living in areas remote from regular secondary schools. In 1973 Spain began using radio as part of its extended education program (Universidad Nacional de Educácion a Distáncia). Within three years, enrollment nearly doubled. The Spanish program is aimed at four categories of students: those who have jobs and are therefore not free to attend conventional institutions, students living in rural areas, those who wish to complete unfinished studies, and those who want to master a second profession. Norway introduced educational television in 1962, while the Netherlands began its Schools Television in 1963. (One might note that most educational television operations in Europe share an interest in teaching foreign languages, a concern fostered by the Council for Cultural Cooperation of the Council of Europe. There is a widespread exchange of language instruction materials.) In Japan, the NHK network sets aside a TV channel for educational purposes, a channel that operates 18 hours a day (Krisher 1972).

There have been attempts at international educational television and radio. The International Radio-Television University, whose forerunner was the International Radio University, was created in 1961. Its charter states:

> The URTI's object is to exchange and promote broadcast programmes or programme components of a cultural nature.

The general orientation of its programmes, while being
nonetheless of a university level, does not lay claim to being
a form of teaching given official recognition by examinations
and diplomas and must be able to appeal to the real radio
and television audiences in all its diversity. (URTI 1977,
p. 13)

In 1976 twenty national broadcasting organizations made financial contributions to the support of the organization. In addition to the
major European countries, several former French colonies in Africa
supported the URTI, as did Canada and Mexico. Among the activities
of the organization are the distribution of lectures received from contributing members; broadcasting documentary-type programming
developed and supplied by members; and the maintenance of a
catalogue of color television programs made available by members.

MEASURING MEDIA IMPACT

As noted at the beginning of this chapter, political systems and
media operate as if media create or change attitudes, motivate to action, tell people *how* to think. It would be unrealistic to suggest that
media, one way or another, cannot have such effects. Nevertheless, it
is extremely difficult to measure their precise impact. As Maxwell
McCombs (1972) put it, "While public and some scientific opinion
seems inclined to attribute sweeping political power to mass communications, empirical evidence gathered by journalists and be-
havioral scientists suggests a more circumspect approach. There are
few documented instances of real political or ideological conversion"
(p. 170).

London's *Sunday Times* editor Harold M. Evans put it succinctly
a decade ago: "I am skeptical of the currently fashionable picture of
the media as kingmakers" (Evans 1972, p. 13). In a somewhat different way, a French communication researcher came to much the
same conclusion. On May 10, 1974, an estimated 23 million French
viewers watched a television debate between Giscard d'Estaing and
François Mitterand. Campaign analysts had access to public opinion
polls taken on May 9, May 11, and May 13. "By examining the polls it
is noted, however, that it was after the debate that d'Estaing most
clearly surpassed his rival during the campaign. But the lead recorded the day after the debate disappeared completely in the polls
carried out three and four days later. Therefore, if the debate is really
the cause of that lead in the polls, it certainly must be admitted that
its effect on the modification in voting intentions was very short-
lived" (Gerstle 1979, p. 38).

For the average adult, the forming or changing of attitudes is not
a self-generating process taking place in isolation from external influ-

ences. In years after formal education ends, the major sources of information for the individual are the media of mass communication. The typical person in the literate, democratic world is probably exposed to all the traditional media—newspapers, radio, television, magazines—on a regular basis. In some cases, the individual may be subjected to massive doses of some media. In addition, the individual is exposed to media messages as they are filtered through others—friends, family, co-workers, employers, and employees. The mix and the impact may vary from country to country, from society to society, from issue to issue. But part of that mix comes from media.

REFERENCES

Blumler, Jay G., and Denis McQuail. *Television in Politics: Its Uses and Influence.* London: Faber and Faber, 1968.

Bogart, Leo. *Press and People.* Hillsdale, N.J.: Lawrence Erlbaum Associates, 1981.

Breed, Warren. "Social Control in the Newsroom." *Social Forces* 33 (1955): 323–35.

British Broadcasting Corporation. *BBC Handbook 1974.* London: Whitefriars Press, 1973.

Cain, John. "Communications Technology—An Education View." *EBU Review,* November 1980.

Carnegie Commission on the Future of Public Broadcasting. *A Public Trust.* New York: Bantam Books, 1979.

Cater, Douglass. *The Fourth Branch of Government.* New York: Vintage Books, 1965.

Cohen, Bernard C. *The Press and Foreign Policy.* Princeton: Princeton University Press, 1963.

Comstock, George. "Social and Cultural Impact of Mass Media." In Elie Abel, ed., *What's News: The Media in American Society.* San Francisco: Institute for Contemporary Studies, 1981.

———, et al. *Television and Human Behavior.* New York: Columbia University Press, 1978.

Davison, W. Phillips, James Boylan, and Frederick T. C. Yu. *Mass Media Systems and Effects.* New York: Praeger, 1976.

Evans, Harold M. "Is the Press Too Powerful?" *Columbia Journalism Review,* January/February 1972.

Ferguson, John. *The Open University from Within.* New York: New York University Press, 1976.

Fischer, Heinz-Dietrich, and John C. Merrill, eds. *International and Intercultural Communications.* 2nd ed. New York: Hastings House, 1976.

Frazier, P. Jean and Cecilie Gaziano, "Robert Ezra Park's Theory of News, Public Opinion and Social Control." *Journalism Monographs,* no. 64 (1979).

Gallup Poll. "Honesty and Ethical Standards." *Gallup Report No. 192.* Princeton, N.J.: Gallup Poll, 1981.

Gerstle, Jacques. "The Study of Campaign Debating on Television: A Comparative Analysis of U.S. and French Approaches—A French Perspective." *Political Communication Review* 4 (1979).

Glock, Charles Y. "Communication and Opinion Formation." In Wilbur Schramm, ed., *The Process and Effects of Mass Communication*. Urbana: University of Illinois Press, 1961.

Graber, Doris A. *Mass Media and American Politics*. Washington, D.C.: Congressional Quarterly Press, 1980.

Hughes, John. *Is the Press an Endangered Species?* Riverside, Calif.: Press Enterprise Lecture Series, 1979.

Krisher, Bernard. "What Public Television Can Be: Japan's NHK." *Columbia Journalism Review*, July/August 1972.

Lippmann, Walter. *Public Opinion*. New York: Macmillan, 1922.

McBride, Sean. "The Most Important of Human Rights." *IPI Report*, 30, no. 7. London: International Press Institute, 1981.

McCombs, Maxwell E. "Mass Communication in Political Campaigns: Information, Gratification, and Persuasion." In F. Gerald Kline and Phillip J. Tichenor, eds., *Current Perspectives in Mass Communication Research*. Beverly Hills: Sage, 1972.

Merrill, John C., and Harold A. Fisher. *The World's Great Dailies: Profiles of Fifty Newspapers*. New York: Hastings House, 1980.

Nielson, A. C. *Nielson Report on Television*. 1981.

Pais, El. *Una Ojeada a El Pais*. Madrid: El Pais, 1979.

Paletz, David L., and Robert M. Entman. *Media, Power, Politics*. New York: Free Press, 1981.

Phillips, Warren H. *A Free Press—If You Can Keep It*. Riverside, Calif.: Press Enterprise Lecture Series, 1976.

Pool, Ithiel de Sola. In Elie Abel, ed., *What's News: The Media in American Society*. San Francisco: Institute for Contemporary Studies, 1981.

Rhodes, Dale. *Who's Watching: Public Television Audience Report*. Washington, D.C.: Public Broadcasting Service, 1981.

Shiono, Hirosh. "The Development of Broadcasting Technology and Related Laws in Japan." In *Studies in Broadcasting No. 14*. Tokyo: Nippon Hoso Ryokai, 1978.

Smith, Anthony. *Newspapers and Democracy*. Cambridge: MIT Press, 1980.

Special Senate Committee on Mass Media. *Mass Media Good, Bad, or Simply Inevitable*. Vol. 3. Ottawa: Information Canada, 1970.

Statistics Canada. *Perspectives Canada III*. Ottawa: Statistics Canada, 1980.

Tocqueville, Alexis de. *Democracy in America*. Translated by Henry Reeve. London: Saunders and Ottey, 1836.

UNESCO. *Statistical Yearbook*. Paris: UNESCO, 1980.

URTI (International Radio-Television University). "A Footnote to the General Assembly of the International Radio-Television University." *EBU Review*, 1977.

Wells, Alan, ed. *Mass Communication: A World View*. Palo Alto, Calif.: Mayfield, 1974.

9...IN THE THIRD WORLD

KULDIP R. RAMPAL

The role of mass media in education, persuasion, and opinion making in the Third World can best be understood in the context of the origins and aspirations of the Third World movement. It was in Bandung, Indonesia, that twenty-nine newly independent, developing nations of Asia and Africa organized a "nonaligned" movement in 1955. This effort was defined as a third force to act as a buffer between capitalism and communism, or more specifically, between the so-called First World (or Free World) led by the United States and the Second World led by the Soviet Union (Stavrianos 1981). The members of the Bandung Conference also planned economic and cultural cooperation and opposed colonialism.

The developing, nonaligned countries, or the Third World as they have come to be called since the early 1970s, have been struggling to overcome problems of poverty, illiteracy, and rapidly growing populations. In addition, these largely agrarian societies are engaged in the process of industrial development. In the 1950s and 1960s it was widely believed that after some transitional difficulties, the independent, developing countries would resolve their socioeconomic problems through international development efforts and become full and equal members of the international community. By the end of the 1960s, these hopes remained largely unfulfilled. The international development efforts did not deliver what they had seemed to promise (Sauvant 1979). Sauvant says that "if anything, the gap between North and South had increased. At the same time, it became obvious that political independence is a mere chimera unless based on economic independence. Economic decolonization and development thus came to be viewed with new urgency" (p. 10).

In hopes of realizing that goal, the nonaligned nations embraced the concept of Third World self-reliance in the early 1970s. This concept required that economic structures linking developing countries to colonial nations be altered to promote economic interdependence among Third World countries. Meanwhile, as more countries gained independence, the Third World grew in size. At their Algiers conference in 1973, leaders of the Third World formulated proposals for a New International Economic Order. In May 1974 the UN General Assembly adopted the Declaration of the Establishment of a New International Economic Order. The declaration called for replacing the existing order, which was characterized by "inequality, domination, dependence, narrow self-interest and segmentation," with a new order based on "equity, sovereign equality, interdependence, common interest and cooperation among States irrespective of their economic and social systems" (UN Resolution, May 1974).

Linked closely to Third World's endeavors toward socioeconomic progress has been the issue of the role that mass media should play in national developmental efforts. Communication research in the late 1950s and '60s had shown much optimism for the positive role that mass media could play in fostering socioeconomic development in the Third World. Lerner (1958) in his landmark study of the modernizing process had asserted that "a communication system is both index and agent of change in a total social system" (p. 56). Schramm (1964), in another pioneering study, indicated that

> the mass media, the great multipliers, are a nation's best
> hope of filling in some of its informational lags, and keeping
> (so far as information can help to keep) its timetables for
> national development. Therefore, a developing country needs
> to look hard and carefully at the use it is making of these
> tools of modern communication. (p. 254)

Two years later, Rao (1966), in a study of two villages in India, found that mass communication was important in smoothing development. Rogers (1969) supported the previous research as to the use of mass media in national development. He claimed that "a small but growing body of research in less developed nations ... indicates the crucial, integral role of mass media in modernization" (p. 99). He noted, however, that governments had not fully utilized the media for accomplishing developmental objectives: "National development planners have...tended to neglect the potential of the mass media, even though these communication channels may well be one of the sharpest tools in the developer's kit. Few (noncommunist) developing countries have given much emphasis to mass communication in the past decade" (p. 99).

NATIONAL COMMUNICATION POLICIES

It was not long before serious attention was focused on communication policies by the Third World under the aegis of the United Nations Educational, Scientific, and Culture Organization. UNESCO, since the early 1950s, has helped create skills and programs that primarily benefit developing people. Its activities in the area of mass communication have been generally guided by the UN General Assembly resolution of December 1962 that "information media have an important part to play in education and in economic and social progress generally and that new techniques of communication offer special opportunities for acceleration of the education process" (Schramm 1964, p. vii).

UNESCO sponsored several studies[1] on media use in education and development. Apparently convinced of the substantial impact of media in these areas by independent and UNESCO-sponsored research, the general conference of UNESCO passed a resolution in 1970 authorizing the director-general "to assist Member States in formulating their policies with respect to the mass communication media" (UNESCO 1976, p. 5). Two years later, a similar resolution was approved that said, "The Director-General is authorized to further development of communication research, especially in its application to the formulation of communication policies and the elaboration of national strategies and plans for communication in the service of development" (ibid.).

Communication policies, as envisioned by UNESCO, would delineate coherent sets of principles and norms designed to act as general guidelines for communication organs and institutions in individual countries. Amadou-Mahtar M'Bow, director-general of UNESCO, stated that communication policies "provide a frame of reference for the elaboration of national strategies with a view to the setting up of communication infrastructures that will have a function to fulfill in their educational, social, cultural and economic development" (ibid., p. 52).

At its Intergovernmental Conference on Communication Policies in 1976 in San José, Costa Rica, the UNESCO general conference formally recommended that "governments begin to revise existing mass communication and information standards in their respective countries with a view to bringing them up-to-date and integrating them coherently into policies consistent with the national communication and information systems called for by the overall panorama of development" (ibid., p. 28).

The developing Third World countries thus began to reevaluate their media patterns and look for ways to effectively integrate mass media in development processes. Communication policy studies began to appear in the mid-1970s. Sixteen countries from Asia, Africa, Latin America, and even Europe had issued such studies by 1980 under the sponsorship of UNESCO. The policy studies included a section on the use of media for development. A statement typical of what many developing countries would like to do with their mass media is noted here from the policy study of the Indian media. Desai (1977) says that "the communicators' engagement with problems of poverty, disease, ignorance and deprivation has to become real. To remove them is not the job just of a planning commission or government" (p. 79). Tatarian (1978) echoes Desai's point:

> Nothing is more important to the Third World than national
> development. Even among many Third World journalists
> who prize free press traditions, it is widely acknowledged
> that a higher priority must often, and perhaps usually, go to
> national development—the monumental, uphill struggle to
> weld often disparate ethnic, tribal, or religious groups into
> cohesive new nations while bettering their social well-being
> through economic progress. (p. 42)

It is in this context that the role of media in education, persuasion, and opinion making in the Third World is discussed in this chapter. The term "education" is used to mean the imparting of traditional, formal education primarily through media, although teachers and supporting materials are also used. "Persuasion" is used to mean developmental communication or nonformal education in support of a development campaign, for example, a family planning campaign, a campaign to change agricultural practices, or a campaign to improve sanitation and public health. By "opinion making" is meant the editorial function of media. We shall see to what degree the three functions are coordinated in the Third World to obtain developmental objectives. A brief glimpse of the Western and Communist media's role in these areas is provided here for comparative purposes before we go on with the Third World.

THE WESTERN WORLD

According to Western tradition (which embraces the countries of Western Europe, North America, Japan, and some countries of the Third World), the role of the press is not only to inform people but also to scrutinize and criticize the social order, in particular, government policies and the government itself. The emphasis is on discussion of controversy rather than fulfilling goals of the government. The press, which is usually privately owned and independently operated, is one of many checks and balances essential for the functioning of a democratic society.

Thus, since media are comparatively independent by virtue of press freedom guarantees and financial support through advertising revenue, information and entertainment become their primary content. Privately owned media, or even government-controlled broadcasting outlets, are generally under no obligation to engage in systematic educational or mobilization objectives. There are, nonetheless, good examples of the educational role of media in Western countries within the larger role of information and entertainment.

Britain's Open University is considered to be the most successful experiment in the use of media for formal education. Since 1971, the Open University has offered a complete university curriculum by a combination of television, radio, correspondence study, and tutorial opportunities. Since its foundation, more than 65,000 students have enrolled and over 21,000 have graduated with the university's bachelor of arts degree (Seligman 1978).

The university has a contractual agreement with the British Broadcasting Corporation under which the BBC transmits each week 36 hours of television and about 30 hours of radio programs. The programs are mostly produced by members of the faculty course teams in collaboration with the BBC's department of Open University Productions. Briggs (1979) indicates that "the most successful programs have been those where producer and academic have brought the most creative imagination to bear on their joint understanding of a particular subject" (p. 41). Students, says Briggs, do not want programs to be a simple regurgitation of what is in their correspondence texts. Apart from the quality of programs, the success of the Open University is also attributed to the availability of support materials, study centers, tutors, and the opportunity for short-term residential study in the summers.

Another notable example in the use of radio and television for formal education is that of the Japan Broadcasting Corporation (NHK). Since 1973, it has offered *NHK Gakuen*, a radio-television-correspondence high school curriculum for students who do not find places in residence high schools. The broadcasting lessons are supplemented with correspondence lessons, texts, and one day a month and five summer days in classes. Other countries offering formal education through broadcasting are Australia, France, West Germany, the Netherlands, Sweden, and the United States (Schramm 1977, Lee 1981).

THE COMMUNIST WORLD

Galliner (1978) says that Soviet political ideology is based on the premise that the government and the people are one—that the state and the masses have a single common purpose and that the government is the only true representative of the people. According to this logic, says Galliner, "there is no inconsistency or lack of 'freedom' in the fact that the media are owned and controlled exclusively by the government and the Communist party. Newspapers act as instruments of information, propaganda, and education and journalists are agents of the government" (pp. 93–94).

With this philosophy, persuasion and opinion making along doctrinaire lines become very important functions of the Soviet media and media of other Communist countries. The role of the Soviet journalist is defined by *Pravda*, the Communist party newspaper: "A journalist is an active fighter for the cause of the party. It is not enough for him to have good intentions, he must also have clear views, a knowledge of life and the ability to present his thoughts convincingly and brilliantly from Leninist positions" (Lendvai 1981, p. 12).

Party-mindedness, the most frequently mentioned personal characteristic demanded of a Soviet or East European journalist, means that a Communist must judge every issue from the point of view of his proletarian party, thus implying an absolute devotion to the party and obedience to its instructions (ibid.). Thus the educative function of the Communist media goes much beyond the formal education provided by some broadcast media in the Western world.

Formal education is also offered through media in the Soviet Union. One television channel offers lessons in chemistry, physics, German, English, and Russian for high school students preparing for university entrance examinations. Courses in science, mathematics, and applied technology have been offered by Poland's Television Technical College since 1966. The courses supplement study in correspondence and evening technical schools (Schramm 1977). East Germany's Television Academy offers a variety of adult vocational subjects. Nonformal education is also provided in Soviet media. Hopkins (1970) says that "a major segment [of the Soviet media] is educational or instructive.... One can learn how to manage a farm, how to increase labor productivity, how to improve customer service in a department store, how to enter a university, or how to construct an apartment building" (pp. 48–49).

Print or broadcast media in the Soviet Union and its satellite countries of Eastern Europe do not take a critical view of major decisions or suggest alternative solutions. Instead, they engage in political persuasion exercised in behalf of decisions already taken, usually behind closed doors, and provide for their acceptance and active support by the population (Lendvai 1981).

THE THIRD WORLD

We now return to the Third World and examine how it has used the media for education, persuasion, and opinion making. A point needs to be made here about ownership patterns of media in order to better understand the objectives of these media. In its annual survey of political rights and civil liberties around the world, Freedom House found that in 1980 governments in three-fourths of the 161 countries had a significant or dominant voice in determining what does or does not appear in media. Most of the world's 100-plus Third World nations were listed in this category (Gastil 1980). Thus, even though media, in particular print media, are generally privately owned in the Third World, their contents are carefully watched by governments. Broadcasting, with very few exceptions, is government controlled and government operated in the Third World nations of Asia, Africa, and Latin America (Katz and Wedell 1977). It is also state owned and operated in the Arab countries, with very few exceptions (Rugh 1979). Thus, Third World media are generally patterned after the authoritarian press theory.

With this partial or full control over media, Third World countries have found it easier to use media for accomplishing their socioeconomic objectives. Also, UNESCO's calls for the formulation of national communication policies, as indicated earlier, have encouraged developing nations to include media use in their development strategies. "Development journalism" and "developmental journalism" are terms used frequently by Third World journalists and governments. Sussman (1980) defines development journalism as "concentration by objective journalists on the news, the newness, of developments in education, agriculture, industry, communications, and applied science; developments that leaders hope will eventually produce economic success and a secure sense of national unity" (p. 87). Whereas "development journalism" is nongovernmental, it is defined as the use of communication outlets by the government for socioeconomic development. Sussman (1978) says elsewhere that developmental journalism has become a widely shared concept and goal among Third World countries, crossing all lines of political and economic doctrine. Broadcasting, since it does not require literacy to consume its messages, has been used increasingly for formal and nonformal education in the 1970s.

We shall discuss some major experiments in selected Third World countries in the use of mass media for formal and nonformal education; look at the media role in opinion making; and finally draw some comparisons and conclusions.

FORMAL EDUCATION THROUGH MASS MEDIA

Indian broadcasting, owned and operated by the government, has been used for instructional purposes since the 1950s. In the 1970s broadcasting seemed to take an increasing role in the government's development plans. Nonformal education, which we discuss later, has been provided more through broadcast media than has formal education. India has been using its limited television service for formal education since 1961. In that year, 250 schools in Delhi were installed with television sets for in-school viewing. The lessons covered chemistry, physics, English, and general science. By 1964 over 100,000 students were studying various subjects with the aid of television.

An impact study made a year later by Paul Neurath, an American professor of social research, indicated the following: (1) Television is a useful aid to teaching; (2) students learn more with television; (3) the teaching process, and the performance of teachers, undergoes a change for the better; (4) instructional television is especially useful in teaching physics and chemistry (Desai 1977). Over 300,000 students in more than 500 schools in India were benefiting from television instruction in 1977.

In Thailand instructional school radio, started by the Ministry of Education in 1958, reaches more than a million primary school students. It is used to teach social studies, music, and English. The total time of different programs on the air is about 165 hours per year, and the estimated total number of student listening hours to these programs is over 8 million. Studies to evaluate the learning from instructional radio indicate that, in general, radio students scored higher than the control groups (Schramm 1977).

In 1969 the government established Ramkhamhaeng University to offer a complete college curriculum by closed-circuit television. The university, located in Bangkok, provides educational opportunities to students not admitted to traditional universities for lack of space. Approximately 43,000 students enroll at this university. Schramm (1977) says that some Ramkhamhaeng classes enroll over 7,000 students. Textbooks are used in each course. Large-group discussions constitute an important part of the educational experience. Degrees are awarded to students who complete the courses satisfactorily.

El Salvador was the first developing country to use educational television on a large scale for formal education. Under the 1968–72 development plan, educational reform was introduced to educate a large number of people and to improve the quality of curricula of secondary schools. Grades 7 to 9 were chosen for an educational television project because a study indicated that "it was the lack of opportunity and the low quality of instruction at this level that was believed to constitute a 'bottleneck' to El Salvador's development" (Clippinger 1976, p. 41). Instructional television was also expected to compensate for many unqualified secondary school teachers, who in turn could be trained in a short time to become effective monitors within the television classes (ibid.).

With financial and technical aid coming from international agencies including UNESCO, the Ministry of Education began to televise programming in 1969 by renting air time for a period of four years. The initial programs were tried out on 32 seventh-grade classes. In the second year these programs, some with revisions, were broadcast to all seventh-grade classes able to receive them. Also in the second year, eighth-grade programs were tried on 32 classes in the eighth grade. At this pace, the reform moved through the three years of Plan Basico—seventh through ninth grades.

The reform was accompanied by an extensive program of retraining teachers. With few exceptions, every teacher in Plan Basico assigned to a classroom with television received a year's retraining before going to his new assignment. The retraining course included both subject matter and teaching method. Schramm (1977) says that "this is the only case to our knowledge when a school system has made use of a new media project to upgrade its teacher corps by such an extensive program of retraining" (p. 153).

By 1973 educational television, teacher training, and extension of universal free education to the Plan Basico made it possible to triple enrollments in those three grades. According to an evaluation of the project, educational television students were learning 15 to 25 percent more than their counterparts (Clippinger 1976). The success of the project led the government to extend free universal education through the ninth grade.

Other projects in educational broadcasting in Latin America that are attracting attention are Mexico's Radioprimaria and Telesecundaria. Radioprimaria has been used to allow a school with four teachers to offer all six grades of primary schooling in the state of San Luis Potosi since 1971. Three teachers handle the first three grades in the traditional manner; the fourth teacher has the fourth, fifth, and sixth grades in one classroom and instructs them with the assistance of radio lessons. Some instructional radio programs are grade specific, while others are directed to all three grades in common. When grade-specific lessons are broadcast, students in the other two grades are supposed to engage in work of their own.

Instructional radio lessons, based on the official primary school curriculum, are broadcast from the University of San Luis Potosi radio station. Emphasis is placed on Spanish, arithmetic, history, and geography. During the school year, about 1,200 14-minute programs are broadcast. About 80 percent of the programs are directed at the combined fourth, fifth, and sixth grades with the remaining 20 percent distributed among three grades (Jamison and McAnany 1978).

Data suggest that students in radio schools performed better than those in nonradio schools in both Spanish and mathematics, and the difference in Spanish was statistically highly significant (Jamison and McAnany 1978, Schramm 1977). Jamison and McAnany point out, however, that "there would be risks in adopting some variant of the Radioprimaria approach in another country, or in expanding it in Mexico, before more rigorous effectiveness comparisons have been undertaken.

The Telesecundaria offers a complete secondary school curriculum to groups assembled in towns that have no secondary schools. Television instruction is supplemented with textual materials. There is usually one teacher for the entire school. As of 1977, the program was attracting about 29,000 students (Schramm 1977).

Researchers compared samples of schools in each of four districts of Mexico from among the schools teaching face to face and from Telesecundaria groups taught with the aid of television. They used before-and-after tests and found that Telesecundaria students had higher test scores in mathematics, Spanish, and chemistry than did students from traditional schools (ibid.).

Another successful experiment in the use of broadcasting for education is Nicaragua's Radio Mathematics Project (RMP), which began in 1975. RMP uses radio for direct instruction in mathematics at the primary level in Masaya to several thousand students. A daily lesson consists of a 30-minute radio presentation followed by approximately 30 minutes of teacher-directed activities, for which instructions are contained in a project-developed teacher's guide. No textbooks are used. During each radio lesson "two main characters join with one or two subordinate characters to sing, play, and talk mathematics, usually inviting the children to join in. The children are asked to respond orally, physically and in writing, and they do so up to 100 times during each 30-minute lesson" (p. 38).

Studies of the project indicate that radio students scored higher in tests than students who had no radio. Jamison and McAnany state that the difference in scores between the two groups is "highly statistically significant" (p. 41).

In Africa, Ivory Coast began in 1971 the kind of educational reform sought by El Salvador two years earlier. Ivory Coast, with only a fraction of its school-age population in primary schools, wanted to achieve universal primary school education by 1985. The national planners needed a system to reach the greatest number of people and at the same time give training to teachers. UNESCO and French experts suggested instructional television in 1967. The government accepted the idea and established a center for teacher training in 1968, with the intention of training teachers to be principals and directors of the new schools. The Ministry of Education, with the cooperation of UNESCO, France, and Canada, began to broadcast instructional programs in 1971.

In the first year, 20,000 pupils were taught with the aid of television in the first grade. By the 1976–77 school year, educational television programs were broadcast for about 325,000 pupils in the six grades of the primary school system (Lenglet 1980). Teachers have adapted to the use of instructional television as a result of their extensive inservice training. Schramm (1977) says that it is evident that the project is "moving forward very strongly" toward the goal of universal primary education (p. 168).

Elsewhere in Africa, broadcasting is utilized for formal education and teacher training in Niger, Nigeria, the Gambia, and Kenya. Kenya will expand its educational services and introduce nonformal education when a new Educational Media Service Complex is completed around 1982.

NONFORMAL EDUCATION THROUGH MASS MEDIA

Broadcasting has been used for nonformal education in India since 1956. In that year UNESCO and the government of India began to experiment with the concept of radio rural forums, which has since been tried in other developing countries. In India the radio rural forum is a group of about twenty villagers who are willing to come together twice a week to listen to a radio program dealing with agriculture, health, literacy, education, local self-government, or other aspects of economic and social development. The radio program lasts from 30 to 45 minutes and is followed by discussion. Discussions are intended to increase participants' understanding of subjects heard on the radio. When appropriate, decisions are taken by participants to improve village life. Every forum has a chairman and a secretary-convenor, a literate person who keeps records and corresponds with the radio station.

The UNESCO-sponsored radio rural forum project in 1956 lasted for ten weeks. It was extensively evaluated by an independent body, the Tata Institute of Social Sciences in Bombay. The evaluation team compared the 145 forum villages with villages that had no forum. The team interviewed every forum member before and after the project, and made before-and-after interviews with samples of twenty adults from each of the control villages. During the project, each forum was visited and observed four times (Bordenave 1977, Schramm 1977).

A number of findings resulted about the forums. Bordenave (1977) says that

> the study showed that forum members learned a good deal more than non-forum members; most of the non-forum members who made knowledge gains were in villages with radios and thus could have listened to forum broadcasts. Literates started and finished with more knowledge than non-literates, but in the amount of knowledge gained non-literates did just as well as literates, indicating that the forum is an effective means of teaching non-literates. (p. 41)

In 1978, some 22,500 radio rural forums were operating in India (Khan 1978).

Television has also been used in the Delhi area since 1967 to teach farmers to improve agricultural productivity. Evaluations of programs indicate that television has a greater appeal to the illiterate and small farmers, a population the Indian government has tried to reach through a much larger experiment using the direct broadcasting satellite technology.

A Satellite Instructional Television Experiment (SITE) in India was conducted in 1975–76 by using a direct broadcasting satellite on loan from the United States to the Indian government. The experiment brought mostly nonformal but some formal education to community viewing centers in 2,400 villages. The goals of SITE were to contribute to general school and adult education; contribute to teacher training; improve agricultural practices, health and hygiene, and nutrition; and contribute to family planning and national integration. Specially prerecorded television programs were broadcast for about 4 hours a day. Criteria for choosing villages for reception of SITE programs were backwardness, common agro-socioeconomic conditions, availability of infrastructure, and probability of their continuing to receive television programs from other local transmitters after this experiment. Villagers who participated in SITE had no previous television exposure of any kind (Agrawal 1981, Desai 1977).

Several independent evaluations of the experiment indicate that some gains were made toward the stated objectives. Some of the major findings were these:

- Very little gains were found in the students' knowledge of subjects taught other than language development, where statistically significant gains were found.
- Statistically significant gain was found in training school teachers for teaching science as a result of multimedia (print media, interpersonal discussion, radio, television and actual experimentation) package training. Television rather than radio was preferred for the training.
- More females than males changed or gained in health innovations and family planning. However, literate viewers showed a greater desire for a small family than illiterate viewers.
- Adoption of innovations in agriculture was found more feasible in innovations that did not involve additional expenditure or dependence on agricultural development agencies and their infrastructure.
- Statistically significant gains were found in empathy and educational and occupational aspirations for sons. In the area of political socialization, the illiterate rather than literate male viewers showed greater gain (Agrawal 1981).

Some of the important lessons of SITE are these:

- Planning for software requires more time than planning for hardware. Formative research in the deliberate use of communication facilities for predetermined social change should start many years prior to the planning of hardware aspects.
- Involvement of social scientists in a team mode from the policy formulation stage to the evaluation stage is necessary to maximize the benefits of instructional television.
- Training of communication researchers and media evaluators should be an integral part of the development communication plans (ibid.).

SITE was a learning experience to provide planning inputs for a future national satellite-based television system in India. In 1982 the Indian National Satellite (INSAT) is scheduled to go into operation. INSAT will also be a direct broadcasting satellite, and its nonformal education programs will reach community receivers in rural areas in most parts of India (Venkateshwarlu 1981).

In the Philippines radio was used extensively in a new land-reform program that lasted from 1973 until 1978. The program was accompanied by a scheme for the formation of farmers' cooperatives and the institutions and services required to support them. The cooperatives were expected to help improve the quality of life for the Filipino farmer by training him to become a better producer, allowing him to pay off his debts, giving him a means of saving, and encouraging him to perform economic activities such as buying supplies and selling produce collectively. The program was also intended to develop marketing outlets for farm products. The project was national in scope, involving 25,000 villages. In addition to radio, print materials were used to support the program. Fieldworkers were also used to facilitate the development of cooperatives.

Radio communication included a jingle, spot announcements, slogans, and discussion programs. Supplementary radio support came from occasional radio news items, interview programs, and press releases. Print communication included color leaflets, brochures, and posters. Bordenave (1977) says that in general the strategies governing the media campaign were to use economic motivational appeal by stressing the benefits offered by cooperatives, positive social motivational appeal by associating membership with prestige, and negative social motivational appeal by bringing social pressure to bear on members and officers remiss in their responsibilities to the cooperatives.

An evaluation study of the project was carried out by the University of the Philippines. The researchers interviewed 17,400 persons from 2,479 villages, 30 percent of whom were not members of cooperatives, to determine the extent to which various aspects of the program, as taught by the educational and promotional campaign, were understood. The study showed that fieldworkers were the major source of information for both groups. Mass media were found to have significantly improved and reinforced the fieldworkers' effectiveness (Bordenave 1977).

Another notable case of media use for nonformal education is that of a family planning campaign in Iran's Esfahan Province in 1970–71. Radio and print materials were used in this six-month campaign to increase the acceptance and use of family planning methods in the province. A number of experts collaborated on such activities as carrying out surveys, preparing and pretesting media materials, and devising a work schedule listing project objectives for each month of operation. A relatively small staff of health corps women was given the task of persuading large numbers of women of child-bearing age to accept and practice family planning (ibid.).

During the first three months of the campaign, a one-minute spot was on the air three times daily, at times indicated the survey to be the most suitable. The spots were changed monthly. Address and telephone numbers were given where listeners could get further information. Announcements by various officials were broadcast about once a week.

During the last three months, all available media were used: banners, posters, mailings, one-page advertisements placed five times in the two leading newspapers, and an insert in other papers and magazines. About fifty news items related to the project appeared in newspapers.

A careful evaluation of the project indicated that the net increase for all methods of contraception during the six months of the project was 64 percent. A total of 1,000 men and women in the province were interviewed before the project, and 968 afterward. Both groups were probability samples, comparable except for a slight urban bias in the second. The postproject survey showed a significant increase in the knowledge, acceptance, and practice of family planning (ibid.).

The systematic use of broadcasting and other media for nonformal education has also been made since the early 1970s in Tanzania. Radio Tanzania, which emphasizes adult education and mobilization programs of various sorts, has reported success with several campaigns. Jamison and McAnany (1978) indicate that a health campaign obtained particularly impressive results. A 47 percent gain on a knowledge test from pretest to posttest was reported among the health study groups. In terms of action, about 750,000 latrines were constructed and public health measures such as boiling water or clearing away mosquito breeding areas were adopted. In a sample of participant villages, there was 60 percent improvement in health-related practices. Ghana and the Gambia have pushed the radio rural forums concept practiced in India.

Meanwhile, developing countries are looking at the potential of television in meeting their developmental objectives. Ugwu (1980) says:

> Television has not yet gone into the classrooms, into the farms, into work places, into village communities the way it must do if it is to influence quickly the lives of so many who are in a hurry to acquire education, learn new skills or improve existing ones in order to improve their social and economic circumstances generally. The signs are that developing countries are on the road to this. . . . (p. 16)

OPINION MAKING THROUGH MASS MEDIA

At the risk of making unwarranted generalizations, we now take a look at the opinion-making role of media in the Third World. As mentioned earlier, media in most Third World countries were operating under considerable governmental control in 1980. Therefore, any criticism of governmental policies in most developing countries seemed to be muted at best. Indications are that governments, instead, solicited the support of privately owned media to their educational and developmental objectives. Lent (1978) says that three interrelated concepts that have caught on in most of Asia are the "guided press," "development journalism," and "development support communication." He adds:

> Asian authorities continually state that because most of
> their societies are newly emergent, they need time to develop
> their institutions. During this initial period of growth,
> stability and unity must be sought; criticism must be
> minimized and the public faith in governmental
> institutions and policies must be encouraged. Media must
> cooperate, according to the guided press notion, by stressing
> positive, development-inspired news, by ignoring negative
> societal or oppositionist characteristics and by supporting
> governmental ideologies and plans. (pp. 42–43)

Indeed, the Freedom House survey of the press in 1980 showed that the editorial policies of the press in Pakistan, Bangladesh, Burma, Sri Lanka, Nepal, Indonesia, Malaysia, Thailand, and the Philippines were influenced by government controls or pressures (Gastil 1980). In India the press was strong and independent following the lifting of the state of emergency in 1977, but there was much talk of development journalism among the country's journalists.

Opinion making takes the form of positive criticism in Africa also. Wilcox (1974) states that one of the themes of African journalism is the pressure for "constructive" or "responsible" criticism (p. 79). He adds that this term is subject to broad interpretation but generally means that a dim view is taken of any press content perceived as negative comment on the performance of a government official or policy. Editors are encouraged to applaud development news and not to comment on abuses or shortcomings such as corruption and maladministration.

In 1980, the press in Angola, Chad, Ethiopia, Ivory Coast, Niger, Senegal, Somalia, Sudan, Tanzania, Uganda, Zaire, and Zambia was operating under strict government controls. Print media were said to "have considerable editorial independence" in Nigeria, although all but two of the major newspapers were government owned

(Gastil 1980). Even the press of Kenya, which is privately owned and relatively free, was operating under government pressures to avoid criticism.

In general, Latin America also presents a gloomy picture in the area of the opinion-making role of the press. Pierce (1979) in his study of media in Latin America says:

> Media criticism of governments can have three types of effects—it can anger the leaders enough to retaliate, stir up the public enough to throw out the government by force or election, and spur the government to alter its behavior. There is ample evidence of the first, but the other two are difficult to document. (p. 211)

He claims that the 1970s produced a high tide of retaliation in the form of closures, suspensions, seizures, censorship, jailings, beatings, murders, etc., in Latin America. He explains that "these actions are often channeled through the courts and are explained as the result of legal offenses such as sedition or incitement. But everyone concerned always is aware that the real cause is the fury of a civil or military official who has felt the jab of criticism" (p. 211).

The Freedom House survey indicates that in 1980 media in Bolivia, Brazil, Chile, Colombia, El Salvador, Mexico, Nicaragua, Peru, and Uruguay were operating under direct or indirect government pressures resulting in limited critical ability. The press in Costa Rica, Dominican Republic, Ecuador, and Venezuela was listed as free in its editorial role (Gastil 1980).

Finally, the press of the Arab countries is also generally supervised by government. Rugh (1979) has called the press of Algeria, Egypt, Iraq, Syria, Libya, South Yemen, and the Sudan as the "mobilization press" that does not criticize the basic policies of the national government. He explains: "Similar social, economic, political, and even cultural goals are enunciated by the leadership in all seven countries, and it is toward these objectives that the press is supposed to help mobilize public support" (p. 35). In Jordan, Tunisia, Saudi Arabia, Bahrain, Qatar, and the United Arab Emirates "newspapers are consistently loyal to and supportive of the regime in power despite the fact that they are privately owned" with very few exceptions (pp. 71–72). Rugh says that the loyalist press "avoids the language and opinions of aggressive revolutionary journalism which are characteristic of the mobilization press, in which writers continuously do battle with enemies and evils, real or imagined, and loudly exhort the public on to victory for the goals of the regime" (p. 75).

It is clear from the above discussion that Third World countries are finding an important place for media, in particular broadcast media, in their socioeconomic development strategies. In the 1970s, Third World journalism began gradually to shift its emphasis from news values left by the colonial past to news values dictated by unique societal conditions and needs for development. A new journalistic concept is taking shape in the Third World, and perhaps it may not be long before media scholars begin to identify it as "developmental journalism" just as the Western press is labeled as "adversary journalism" or the Communist press as the "Marxist-Leninist journalism." Such identification suggests a fundamental difference between Third World media and media in Communist states when there may be a temptation to call the two essentially the same. The Communist press is the product of a totalitarian system guided by Marxist-Leninist ideology, or very slight variations thereof. The Third World, on the other hand, represents a variety of authoritarian ideologies, and in some countries even large elements of libertarian ideology. Private ownership of print media in many Third World countries is another key difference from the Communist press.

We have seen that although there is some similarity in the use of media for formal education in all three areas of the world, there are differences in the use of media for persuasion and opinion making in the Western world, Communist world, and Third World. Western media are generally not used for any systematic mobilization campaigns of the kind discussed under nonformal education through media. They are also generally free in their editorial, opinion-making function. In the Soviet Union and its East European satellites persuasion and opinion making are integral functions of media, in keeping with the Marxist-Leninist ideology. In the Third World the use of media for formal and nonformal education reflects a genuine need in these countries to progress. Nevertheless the editorial or opinion-making function of the press is often conveniently regulated in developing countries in the name of national unity and development. This is decried by many Third World journalists who are otherwise sympathetic to the concept of developmental journalism.

In any event, various case studies on the use of media for formal and nonformal education indicate that media can be effective in accomplishing socioeconomic objectives if they are used with a carefully devised strategy. Media use for developmental purposes may not yield expected results unless such use is accompanied by adequate field personnel and support materials. India's satellite experiment in developmental journalism left a clear lesson that the planning of software—programming, team work, support systems, and materials—requires more time than planning for hardware. Britain's Open University has been successful because of the good coordination of educational programming and support systems for its students.

Communication policy studies, mentioned earlier in this chapter, are recommending an increasingly important role for mass media in the development plans of Third World countries. There is a good hope that with appropriate use, mass media will accelerate the process of socioeconomic development in developing countries in the 1980s.

NOTES

1. See UNESCO publications numbers: 23, *Cultural Radio Broadcasts: Some Experiences*, 1956; 25, *Adult Education Groups and Audiovisual Techniques*, 1958; 38, *Social Education Through Television*, 1963; 48, *Radio Broadcasting Serves Rural Development*, 1965; 49, *Radio Television in the Service of Education and Development in Asia*, 1967; 51, *An African Experiment in Radio Forums for Rural Development*, Ghana, 1964/1965, 1968; 55, *Television for Higher Technical Education of the Employed. A First Report on a Pilot Project in Poland*, 1969.

REFERENCES

Agrawal, Binod C. *SITE Social Evaluation: Results, Experiences and Implications*. Ahmedabad, India: Space Applications Centre, 1981.

Bordenave, Juan E. Diaz. *Communication and Rural Development*. Paris: UNESCO, 1977.

Briggs, Asa. "Open University: First Ten Years." *Combroad* 43 (April/June 1979).

Clippinger, John H. "Who Gains by Communications Development?" *Program on Information Resources Policy: Working Paper 76–1*. Cambridge: Harvard University Press, 1976.

Desai, M. V. *Communication Policies in India*. Paris: UNESCO, 1977.

Galliner, Peter. "Improving News Flow in the Third World." In Philip C. Horton, ed., *The Third World and Press Freedom*. New York: Praeger, 1978.

Gastil, Raymond D. *Freedom in the World: Political Rights and Civil Liberties 1980*. New York: Freedom House, 1980.

Hopkins, Mark. *Mass Media in the Soviet Union*. New York: Pegasus, 1970.

Jamison, Dean T., and Emile G. McAnany. *Radio for Education and Development*. Beverly Hills: Sage, 1978.

Katz, Elihu, and George Wedell. *Broadcasting in the Third World: Promise and Performance*. Cambridge: Harvard University Press, 1977.

Khan, A. W. "Non-Formal Educational Broadcasting for Rural Development in India." *Combroad* 38 (January/March 1978).

Lee, S. Young. *Status Report of Public Broadcasting 1980*. Washington, D.C.: Corporation for Public Broadcasting, 1981.

Lendvai, Paul. "The Party's Sharpest Weapon." *IPI Report*, July 1981.

Lenglet, Frans. "The Ivory Coast: Who Benefits from Education/Information in Rural Television?" In Emile G. McAnany, ed., *Communications in the Rural Third World*. New York: Praeger, 1980.

Lent, John A. "Press Freedom in Asia: The Quiet, but Completed, Revolution." *Gazette* 24, no. 1 (1978).

Lerner, Daniel. *The Passing of Traditional Society.* Glencoe, Ill.: Free Press, 1958.

Pierce, Robert N. *Keeping the Flame: Media and Government in Latin America.* New York: Hastings House, 1979.

Rao, Y. V. Lakshmana. *Communication and Development: A Study of Two Indian Villages.* Minneapolis: University of Minnesota Press, 1966.

Rogers, Everette M. *Modernization Among Peasants: The Impact of Communication.* New York: Holt, Rinehart and Winston, 1969.

Rugh, William A. *The Arab Press.* Syracuse: Syracuse University Press, 1979.

Sauvant, Karl P. "Sociocultural Emancipation." In Kaarle Nordenstreng and Herbert I. Schiller, eds., *National Sovereignty and International Communication.* Norwood, N.J.: Ablex Publishing, 1979.

Schramm, Wilbur. *Big Media, Little Media.* Beverly Hills: Sage, 1977.

————. *Mass Media and National Development.* Stanford: Stanford University Press, 1964.

Seligman, David. "The Open University Centre for International Cooperation and Services." *Combroad* 40 (July/September 1978).

Stavrianos, L. S. *Global Rift: The Third World Comes of Age.* New York: William Morrow, 1981.

Sussman, Leonard. "Freedom of the Press: Problems in Restructuring the Flow of International News." In Raymond D. Gastil, *Freedom in the World: Political Rights and Civil Liberties 1980.* New York: Freedom House, 1980.

————. "Developmental Journalism: The Ideological Factor." In Philip C. Horton, ed., *The Third World and Press Freedom.* New York: Praeger, 1978.

Tatarian, Roger. "News Flow in the Third World: An Overview." In Philip C. Horton, ed., *The Third World and Press Freedom.* New York: Praeger, 1978.

Ugwu, Goodwin. "Managing Television in Developing Countries." *Combroad* 49 (December 1980).

UNESCO. *Intergovernmental Conference on Communication Policies in Latin America and the Caribbean. Final Report.* Paris: UNESCO, 1976.

United Nations. General Assembly Resolution 3201 (S-VI), General Assembly Resolution 3202 (S-VI). Adopted May 1, 1974.

Venkateshwarlu, K. "TV Training for INSAT in India." *Combroad* 52 (September 1981).

Wilcox, Dennis, "The Black Press in Africa: Philosophy and Control." Ph.D. dissertation, University of Missouri, Columbia, 1974.

10 ... IN THE COMMUNIST WORLD

RILLA DEAN MILLS

Media in the Communist world have always been seen by their shapers as primarily tools of persuasion and education, and only secondarily as transmitters of information. Lenin, who invented the pattern on which all subsequent Communist media systems are based, decreed that the Communist press be not only a partisan of the revolution but also a partner in its accomplishment. In a dictum quoted to this day as the distilled essence of Communist press theory, Lenin (1961) said that the Bolshevik newspaper must be

> not only a collective propagandist and a collective agitator,
> [but] also a collective organiser.... With the aid of the
> newspaper, and through it, a permanent organization will
> naturally take shape that will engage, not only in local
> activities, but in regular general work, and will train its
> members to follow political events carefully, appraise their
> significance and their effect on the various strata of the
> population, and develop effective means for the revolutionary
> party to influence those events. (pp. 22–23)

A temptation for the Western reader of such phrases is to interpret them as meaning that the Communist press is expected to be nothing more than a gigantic public relations operation for the government, carefully orchestrating media content to mold public opinion to the government's will. Often, this temptation is not resisted. In a classic cold-war description, Wilbur Schramm (1974) said that the Soviet press

> exists to do a job specifically assigned it by the leaders of the state. Over-all, this job is to contribute to the advance of the working class and world Communism in the class struggle, and to maintain and advance the power of the Soviets. Specifically, the media are assigned certain tasks within that large assignment.... The point is, that Soviet mass communications do not have integrity of their own. They are "kept" instruments, and they follow humbly and nimbly the gyrations of the party line and the state directives. (p. 122)

Soviet press theoreticians themselves encourage such a view with their constant reminders of the press role in supporting the party in its work with the masses. The authors of a handbook for Soviet journalists write:

> The principle of the Party spirit of the press is seen above all in the ideological ties of journalists with the party and the people. Our press is one of the most important means of ideological, political, and economic education, and also of the organization of the masses. It could not fulfill these huge goals if it were not constantly tied to the Party organizations. (Bogdanov 1965, pp. 30–31)

Yet it is not so simple. Even in the Soviet Union, where media have remained the most faithful to the Leninist model, the role of the press as educator and persuader has been changed dramatically by the metamorphosis from a furtive underground operation printing a few revolutionary sheets to a vast bureaucratic structure of some 63,000 journalists. The modern Soviet propaganda-information apparatus oversees 7,985 newspapers in 56 different languages, radio broadcasts blanket the country in 68 different languages, and a multichannel television service reaches almost all Soviet citizens (*Zhurnalist*, April 1977). Some of the changes, of course, have had to do with the increased efficiency and sophistication that come with vast increases in the quantity and quality of personnel and technology. Others suggest fundamental shifts in the conception of media's role in the state. In some ways, those shifts come intriguingly close to a Western conception of journalistic roles. At the center of these changes stand Soviet journalists. The rise in the status of information relative to persuasion can be seen in their debates with one another over their proper role in Soviet society.

In other Communist countries, departures from Leninist press theory are even more complex. They range from the relatively minor variations on the Soviet theme seen among close Soviet allies (minor, that is, except for the occasional and so far short-lived departures from the norm of the kind that occurred in Czechoslovakia in 1968 and Poland in 1980–81) to the more dramatic innovations of China and Yugoslavia.

One of the most significant changes in most Communist countries has been the appearance of a phenomenon external to the press apparatus—an unofficial press. In most cases, dissident media have chosen not only to challenge the official press version of the truth but also the official ideology's assumptions about how truth is to be found. In one sense, the persuasive power of these unofficial media lies precisely in their decision to avoid the traditional techniques of persuasion used by the official press. At its extreme, this more neutral approach to the news, this preference for information over argument, can make for a style of journalism somewhat like the Western, so-called objective approach to the news.

JOURNALISTS AS PERSUADERS

The rhetoric of today's Soviet journalists—and, with modifications, of other Communist journalists—can be traced to Lenin's days as an underground revolutionary in tsarist Russia. In Lenin's early professional life, journalism and revolutionary activities were related, sometimes almost synonymous occupations so that the identification of journalism with the demands of the party—so strange in Western eyes—seemed natural to a Soviet journalist. As editor of *Iskra* (*The Spark*), the turn-of-the-century Russian Social Democratic predecessor of *Pravda*, Lenin was already emphasizing the integration of journalism and party. The newspaper staff was to be both recruiter and drill sergeant for the revolutionary troops. *Iskra*, Lenin (1961) wrote,

> would become part of an enormous pair of Smith's bellows
> that would fan every spark of the class struggle and of
> popular indignation into a general conflagration. Around
> what is in itself a very innocuous and very small, but regular
> and common, effort, in the full sense of the word, a regular
> army of tried fighters would systematically gather and
> receive their training. On the ladders and scaffolding of this
> general organisational structure there would soon develop
> and come to the fore[leaders] who would take their place at

the head of the mobilized army and rouse the whole people to settle accounts with the shame and the curse of Russia. (pp. 508–9)

By the time Lenin took over the new Soviet state in 1917, he had a clear view, thanks to Lenin the revolutionary journalist, of what the Soviet press should be. As Mark Hopkins (1970) points out, in Lenin's view the press had a double role, as a government institution and a medium of communication. The press in the new Soviet state would not merely report information; it would also work toward a goal, just as the revolutionary press had. The goal had changed from revolution to consolidation of the power of the Soviet state and the Bolshevik party that stood at its helm. But the approach remained the same. There was to be no such thing as neutral information. Even reports of current events would be presented from a distinctly ideological viewpoint. All facts and opinions would be published with an eye to their relevance to the well-being of the new state.

Lenin called for a Soviet press that would avoid constant discussion of political events. Instead, the new Soviet media would concentrate on "economic education" of the masses—helping them to repair an economy severely damaged by revolution and civil war and preparing them for the new Soviet order. He also ordered the press to eschew the twin evils of capitalist media: advertising and sensationalism. The press, in short, was to be like Lenin himself: serious, practical, and goal oriented. In the pure Leninist conception, then, all media content was to be educative and persuasive. There was no line to be drawn, as in the West, between opinion and information because all information was to be used in the war to reshape opinion.

This was not simply a matter of cynical manipulation of the facts. It was based on a central tenet of Marxism-Leninism, one that to this day undergirds a Communist attitude toward the press that Westerners, particularly Americans, find puzzling. In the Marxist-Leninist conception, truth cannot be synonymous with "objectivity," in the sense of being non-partisan, since every point of view is partisan—an expression of some class interest, whether hidden or open. Truth is to be identified with the best interests of the working class, whose ultimate victory over the bourgeoisie is assured by historical forces:

> Bourgeois journalism tries to hide its class nature under a mask of "classlessness" or "nonpartisanness," tries to present itself to the eyes of public opinion as supposedly "objective," independent of the social forces of the source of information, issuing from the "neutral" position of the commentator. The Marxist theory of journalism exposes these inventions, proving that objectivity in journalism can be achieved not by an ostentatious refusal to ignore the class struggle, but by

the expression and defense of the interests of those forces
which are the vehicles of progress and embody the
requirements of social development. (*Bolshaia Sovietskaia
Entsiklopedia* 1972, 9:252)

Such a point of view not only allows an integration of opinion with information but virtually demands it.

At the level of theory, then, there is no Western distinction between opinion and information. The main purpose of media, say the
authors of a recent theoretical work on mass information, is to "influence people's consciousness, impart the desired properties and qualities to this consciousness and bring it closer to the ideal that accords
with the political, cultural and ideological norms and values of socialist society" (*Current Digest of the Soviet Press*, March 25, 1981, p. 25).
In other words, all information is simply material to be used in the
service of the party's task of shaping public opinion along desired
socialist lines.

The educational goals of the Soviet media—the determination to
pull together the fragmented events of reality into an integrated
whole—enable Soviet journalists to avoid, at least in theory, two
problems that have long troubled observers of the Western, particularly the American, press. Critics of the American press have long
noted its fragmented and episodic nature. Walter Lippmann, in his
classic *Public Opinion* (1946), compared the press to "a searchlight
that moves restlessly about, bringing one episode and then another
out of darkness into vision" (p. 275). Such a press, Lippmann believed,
threatened to overwhelm the reader with a continuing series of
apparently chaotic and unrelated images, which could not be brought
together into a coherent and usable picture of the world.

For Soviet journalists who accept the ideology of their party, the
Soviet approach seems clearly superior. All events are interpreted in
the light of Marxist-Leninist "reality," all facts fitted into a coherent
picture of what the world is like. It is a continuing process of educating the reader in the proper orientation to events:

V. I. Lenin saw the goal of the ideologues of the working class
as giving the masses "an integral picture of our reality"
satisfying scientific standards and answering the needs of
the working class. This picture must give the people not
some kind of separate, fragmented events from separate
areas of life—but a system of knowledge in unity of the
contributory parts of Marxism—philosophy, political
economy, scientific Communism, a system of knowledge
founded on a creative study of the real processes of societal
development, on a deep penetration into the heart of these
processes. (Shkondin 1978, p. 19)

So the journalist in a Communist system is concerned less with un-covering the latest news event and more with explaining unfolding truth (by Marxist lights). "The function of news," Lippmann (1946) wrote, "is to signalize an event, the function of truth is to bring to light the hidden facts, to see them into relation with each other, and make a picture of reality on which men can act" (p. 271). Lippmann's definition of truth might well serve as a summary of the Communist journalists' mission—with the amendment that Communist journalists are expected not only to provide a picture of reality but also to instruct the audience how to react to it.

Because control over media content in a Communist system rests with the party, the content of educational and persuasive material has changed through the years along with changes in party priorities. Under Lenin's leadership, from the founding of the Soviet state in 1917 to his death in 1924, media, like the rest of the Soviet propaganda apparatus, had three basic missions: to replace the old, bourgeois and peasant mentality with the new socialist consciousness, to generate enthusiasm for the new Soviet state (and erase remnants of sympathy for the old order); and to educate a predominantly illiterate peasant population in preparation for industrial modernization.

During the Stalinist years, media, like all arms of the state, were enlisted in the forced industrialization campaign and, eventually, in the personal glorification of Stalin. In the post-Stalin period, as the Soviet economy moved from its almost exclusive concentration on heavy industry toward a more complex configuration in which consumer concerns played an increasingly important role, media propaganda adjusted accordingly. Articles and broadcasts highlighting the feats of dairymaids who dramatically increase milk production or factory workers who turn out a record number of tractors have not disappeared during this new stage. But they have been joined by articles exposing rude service in restaurants and the poor quality or shortage of popular consumer goods.

The present-day content of educational and persuasive material can be grouped into three main categories:

1. *Socialist ideology.* Print and electronic media continue the Leninist tradition of trying to shape public opinion along suitably socialist lines. Newspapers continue to print front-page editorials that educate readers in the correct interpretation of one or another development in current events. Philosophical articles of 4,000 words and up, with heavily academic subject matter and language—the kind of article that in the United States would appear only in an obscure scholarly journal—continue to play a prominent role in the Soviet daily newspaper. In less heavy language, Soviet journalists interpret the ideological significance of foreign affairs and internal econ-

omic developments. Antireligious propaganda continues to make up a significant component of this category, although it is now considerably less heavy-handed than in the priest-baiting 1920s and '30s.

2. *The economy.* Soviet media are expected to praise good performances by workers and managers—and to expose shortcomings. In this category the Soviet media come in for the most criticism; the human qualities of laziness and greed appear less tractable than the fine points of Marxism-Leninism. A 1979 resolution of the Soviet Communist Party Central Committee, for example, exhorts the media to do more

> to eradicate ugly vestiges of the past—vestiges hostile to socialism—that frequently are still present in our life, such as money-grubbing and bribery, the desire to grab whatever one can from society without giving it anything in return, mismanagement, wastefulness, drunkenness, hooliganism, red tape, a callous attitude toward people and violations of labor discipline and public order. (*Current Digest of the Soviet Press*, May 30, 1979, p. 8)

3. *Personal Life.* From the campaign to wipe out illiteracy in the 1920s and '30s to the present-day concern with rock music, Soviet media have tried to guide Soviet citizens in leading productive and moral personal lives. A constant flow of articles and television programs helps citizens get their proper share of government health and welfare benefits; advises them on proper health and diet habits; and gives counsel on marriage, childrearing, divorce, and even, on occasion, sex. This "personal life" category seems to draw the strongest and most varied reactions from audiences, perhaps because it is more remote from Communist dogma than the other two categories. Some years ago, one provincial paper conducted a heated debate over the course of several weeks on the case of some women factory workers ejected from a restaurant because one of them wore a pants suit. (The newspaper eventually came down against the maitre d' and in favor of pants suits.)

The second feature of the American press that Lippmann (1946) criticized was its "preference for the curious trivial as against the dull important, and the hunger for sideshows and three legged calves" (p. 271). In the Soviet Union, journalism might be understood as an attempt to bring to its audience the "dull important" (importance being determined, of course, according to criteria of Marxism-Leninism defined by party leaders). In the United States, the "hunger for sideshows and three legged calves," critics of the American press have long argued, distorts even the news that centers on public affairs. Emphasis is accorded the unusual, even the bizarre. The audi-

ence's picture of reality must be constructed from atypical materials—
the malfunctioning political unit, not the efficient one; the lying
statesman, not the honest (though dull) one; the airplane crash, not
the thousands of flights that are routine. For the Soviet journalist, because the ultimate goal is to give the audience a monistic view of
reality (and because, it must be added, the journalist's success is not
measured by the number of newspapers sold or the Nielsen ratings of
his or her newscast), there is no premium on the unusual. An account
of the routine functioning of societal processes has at least as much
claim to the front page as malfunctions do.

In sum, the monistic world view of Soviet journalism—a quality
Western analysts generally find distasteful—gives Soviet journalists
an ideological rationale for overcoming the episodic and relent-
lessly negative content typical of American journalism. The Soviet
journalist is expected to aim for a comprehensive, integrated view of
reality, and he or she is expected to give more attention to what is
right with society than what is wrong with it. The publicist, not surprisingly, fits more neatly into this activist role than does the reporter. The four functions of publicism, as listed by a Soviet media
scholar, underline the activist nature of the role: "The formation of
public opinion, the creation of the history of the contemporary period,
participation in the formation of the mass consciousness, and the
stimulation of practical activities" (Prokhorov 1975, p. 105).

The result is that the Soviet publicist has powers—and responsibilities—undreamed of by the American journalist. Unlike the American journalist, the Soviet publicist falls on the truth side of Lippmann's news/truth dichotomy.

Illustrations of journalists' successes and failures in trying to
meet their responsibilities may make clear how difficult the task can
be. Empowered to present a comprehensive rather than episodic view
of reality, and to emphasize the positive rather than negative aspects
of Soviet society, the Soviet journalist escapes two constraints that
narrow the scope of American daily journalism. But it is more difficult to pursue truth—even a limited, Marxist-Leninist view of truth—
than to pursue "facts." Aleksandr Maryamov, himself a celebrated
publicist, discussed the difficulties of presenting an "integrated picture of reality" in an article in *Zhurnalist* (December 1967), the
monthly journal of the Soviet Union of Journalists. He compared a
stack of *ocherki*—roughly, feature stories—submitted to him from
provincial papers for criticism with a rider who has forgotten his
horse: Most had superficially pleasing styles, he wrote, but no substance. For example, the *ocherki* from the Novgorod region had totally
failed to come to terms with the region's most pressing problem, the

decline and gradual abandonment of villages in the rich agricultural area.

> [T]he *ocherki*, written by journalists working in those areas, and devoted in the majority mainly to agriculture in those regions which developed on those ancient Novgorod plains, should have, if not exhausted this problem, at least have come close to turning up an accurate answer. But it didn't happen.
> Having sadly come to this conclusion, I tried to recall: What did I find in this pile of articles which was new and interesting for myself? I recalled portraits of several people, some written more clearly and sharply, some more boring, and others which seemed to be constructed, like a modern standardized building, from uniform builders' parts. I recalled, too, the descriptions of several cities and villages, often with well-done historical descriptions, but also done by the simple method of direct attack: This is the way it had been, this is the way it became. But what of the problem?
> What did the authors of the *ocherki* think about?
> What did they make me think about?
> The authors hold the reins elegantly, they look beautiful in the saddle, but where the devil are their horses? (p. 31)

Maryamov contrasted the provincial writers' superficial approach to the desired method of A. Agranovsky, a prominent publicist who writes for *Izvestia*. Agranovsky wrote about a trial in the Moscow *oblast*, not for the sake of giving the readers an account of the trial, Maryamov noted, but rather "in order to comprehensively, convincingly and cleverly present one of the urgent problems of economic reforms in the *kolkhozes*—the question of the existence of subsidiary enterprises, of initiative, of profitability."

The court case was only a peg for a commentary on a problem the publicist had long been studying. His observations at the trial, Maryamov said, "only confirmed the conclusions he had already made and the answers he had already found." By contrast, one of the provincial articles, also about a trial, failed to probe beyond the immediate case—the trial of some hoodlums who had fallen on an innocent passerby and crippled him.

> In the first instance, an economic problem, in the second, a moral one. But in both cases the goals of the *ocherkist* pass more often than not into the sphere of sociology and demand that he search into the roots of serious social phenomena and find answers which by no means lie on the surface. A. Agranovsky did not recoil from these goals. In his *ocherk* he

became a research-sociologist and presented the reader with
clear, well-founded conclusions. The [provincial journalist]
limited himself to a declaration. (*ibid*)

Or, put another way, Agranovsky took a Soviet approach to the story,
whereas the provincial journalist took an American one.

For American journalists, perhaps the most objectionable duty of
the Soviet publicist is that of finding and describing successes of the
Soviet system. Here, Soviet journalism is nearly a mirror image of
American journalism. For many American journalists, the supreme
goal is exposing failings in the American system and failings of its
functionaries. The philosophy was described bluntly in a speech by a
prominent American television journalist. Political reporting, she
said, "means biting these politicians in the ankle. We get them by
hook or by crook, that is the name of the game" (Lund 1980). The attitude has alarmed even some journalists, who believe it encourages a
reporter to write only the negative story—and sometimes to play
loose with the facts in search of it. As a result, the audience receives a
permanently alarmist picture of the universe. Every politician is a
crook. The sky is always falling.

Acceptance of this practice of accentuating the negative as the
norm of journalistic conduct may explain some of the abhorrence
shown by American analysts for Soviet journalism, where the norm is
the reverse. The Soviet journalist, particularly in his or her role as
publicist, is seen, not as a journalist, but as a public relations person
for the Soviet government. There is enough truth in this view to
make it appealing. Certainly the Soviet journalist is frequently engaged in efforts to put the best possible light on governmental policy.
But, although an examination of the Soviet publicist in action turns
up the portrait of a journalist who leans over backward to present his
audience with a reassuring rather than frightening view of the world,
it is not a portrait of the passive propagandist and simpleminded
booster of American (and, occasionally, Soviet) description. To the
contrary, a picture of the journalist as activist emerges. Indeed, in
some ways the Soviet journalist's goals (if not always his or her
accomplishments) are more ambitious and sophisticated than those of
American journalists. For the Soviet journalist has been trying all
along to do what some American journalists are only beginning to see
as a journalistic task: to sort out, from the myriad facts of each day, a
connected version of reality—in other words, to get at the truth.

"The problem with newspapers," the managing editor of the Los
Angeles *Herald Examiner* said in a recent update of Lippmann's criticism of the press, "is that they have too many facts and not enough
truth. [During the Watergate scandal] the facts were what the White

House was telling us; the truth was what Woodward and Bernstein were writing....Facts—even if they are right—aren't enough anymore. There are too many of them. We like to know what's going on. But we know more than we can understand (Dolan 1980).

A detailed description of how a Soviet publicist goes about her work may offer some insight into the challenges of tying facts together into a positive version of reality. Vera Takchenko, a special correspondent for *Pravda*, described in 1978 the process of researching and writing "portrait *ocherki*"—articles describing the New Soviet Man, "the worker and warrior, reared in the spirit of Communist morality, honing in himself those fine qualities and characteristics of the personality which are expressed in the moral code of a builder of Communism" (*Zhurnalist*, July 1978, p. 28). Takchenko made it clear that the hero of an *ocherk*, although an exemplary member of the new order, must be a real, and credible, person, "not a misty angel with transparent wings and halo, not a demonic superman . . . but a human in the large and proud sense of the word, a bearer of the new morality, a fully accredited representative of the epoch of mature socialism—he is the positive hero of our time. To just such a hero should our brother-*ocherkist* turn in his effort to tell the reader about the best of the best[11] (ibid.).

The search for the best, Takchenko wrote, leads in Soviet society to those who excel in their work. It is not necessary that the choice be an officially recognized hero, the recipient of some government award: "Frequently the journalist's attention is drawn to more modest contributions in the workplace. But never, not under any circumstances, will our publicism sing the praises of some 'talented' loafer or some 'charming' parasite—these are definitely not our heroes!" (ibid.).

But the hero of an *ocherk* must be more than a hard worker. "And it's a fact that not infrequently a hard worker, an excellent contributor to production who systematically overfulfills the plan [is also someone] who, once beyond the factory gates, in no way distinguishes himself by good citizenship." Moral defects that would disqualify a candidate for the honor of appearing in one of Takchenko's *ocherki* include "an uncontrollable attraction to moneygrubbing," "rudeness to family and acquaintances," and "personal slovenliness."

In their search for positive portraits, *ocherkisti* are advised to pursue a research strategy that underscores the difference between the attitude of Soviet journalists, who consider themselves integrated with (though not identical to) their government and society, and American journalists, who traditionally see themselves as outsiders by choice. To ensure the moral and occupational trustworthiness of their heroes, the *ocherkisti* must without fail consult local party, government, and institutional authorities who know them.

Yet the publicist's job is far more complex than the mindless boosterism Western analysts have often pictured as the chief role of Soviet journalists. Although the overall goals may be to present a harmonious, integrated, and generally positive view of Soviet society, the negative aspects of real life are not ignored. Indeed, the publicist is expected to explore negative aspects and offer suggestions on how they can be dealt with. But in contrast to the normal American approach of isolating and highlighting the negative, the Soviet journalist treats negative phenomena within Soviet society as departures from the norm, as more or less minor ripples in an otherwise smooth reality. The exercise is normative as well as descriptive. A discussion of somebody or something that has gone wrong can serve both as a warning and, to the extent that the journalist explains how the problem was (or should have been) dealt with, as a pattern, a strategy for handling similar problems.

Takchenko described a story that illustrates those "dramatic moments in the biography of my hero which helped form his character, which strengthened it as a personality." The *ocherk*'s heroine was a dairymaid from Karelia. The *ocherk* illustrated how proper and sensitive action by one's fellows can turn personal tragedy into triumph. The dairymaid had been beaten constantly by her husband and was "therefore shy, lacking in any self-confidence." But with the encouragement and support of members of her work collective, she gained confidence in herself and became a Hero of Socialist Labor.

Such descriptions of negative aspects of Soviet life undoubtedly have an entertainment, as well as a pedagogical, purpose. Soviet journalists seem to recognize this other side of the question; but they write about it only indirectly, perhaps because exploiting the entertainment value of negative phenomena may seem dangerously close to bourgeois sensationalism. The chief editor of programming for Moscow Central Television complained in 1967 of the dullness of unrelentingly positive material:

> Why are so many news telecasts so amazingly similar? Why does a news item about the foremost workers in a Gorky factory resemble a piece on a Moscow factory? It's the same kind of machinery and the same kind of workers standing next to it. And all taken from real life, and all authentic. But dull. A piece without a striking conclusion, without its own particular view of the world cannot attract a viewer. Particularly when it gets on the air only on the grounds that "it's accurate." How often news ceases to be news simply because it is conventional, unexpressive. (*Zhurnalist*, January 1967, p. 47)

Soviet journalists who want their product to be entertaining (for even in the Soviet system, it is recognized that journalism without an audience is not journalism) are placed in a bind by the dictum that it must also present a harmonious view of the world.

An American television producer would sympathize. But note that the editor does not suggest emphasis on conflict or negative news as the solution. Rather he wants the interest to come from a "particular view of the world" or a "striking conclusion"—changes in form rather than content. And while many writers in *Zhurnalist* stress the need for "well-rounded" stories, including the good with the bad, in order to maintain readership, seldom if ever do they consider negative phenomena desiderata *in themselves*. The goal is always a "well-integrated" picture of the phenomena being discussed. It is clearly not the boosterist, cover-to-cover optimism of the Western stereotypical view of the Soviet press. Neither is it the unrelieved conflict and mayhem of the American press. It is a holistic, calm view of the world with the accent largely, though not entirely, on normality. In a sense it is closer to a nineteenth-century novel or one of those Hollywood movies of the 1930s: The world is interesting, challenging, puzzling, even sometimes frustrating—but never overwhelming.

PUBLITSIST VERSUS *REPORTYOR*

In theory, the *publitsist*—the journalist as educator, persuader, and molder of public opinion—remains very much the ideal figure of Soviet journalism. But in practice, in the modern Soviet state, the *publitsist* is getting some tough competition from the *reportyor*—the journalist as aggressive and sometimes relatively objective reporter of news. Discussions in *Zhurnalist* of the reporter's role make it clear that more attention is being given to relatively unadorned information—something close to news in the American sense. What is more, at times there emerges an admiring word for objectivity, not in the Soviet sense of the proper Marxist interpretation of reality, but in the American sense of detached, neutral news coverage. Respect for information and for the reporter who delivers it has grown during the post-Stalin period. "The well-known underestimation of information is behind us. The reporter is recognized, he is respected. The section of reporters is one of the biggest in the Union of Journalists. Reporters publish book after book. Books are also written about their work" (*Zhurnalist*, June 1968, p. 5).

Three considerations seem to be behind the rise in status of reporting. First, the Soviet authorities have discovered that ignoring an unpleasant event—a practice that has been natural under a system that abhors sensationalism and wants to present the most positive possible picture of itself—can lead to a worse public image than reporting the event can. Rumor, Western broadcasts to the Soviet Union, or both may present a more damaging version than a straightforward Soviet account would. "There is no such thing as an information vacuum," wrote one Soviet journalist advocating more and speedier news, even about unpleasant events. "People will satisfy their curiosity in one way or another, but in that case the news may come to them from dishonorable sources. It has been pointed out more than once that lack of information in the periodical press is one of the reasons for the presence of rumors and idle talk" (*Zhurnalist*, June 1968, p. 6).

Second, audience feedback is encouraging journalists to work for more aggressive and efficient coverage of the news. A readership survey in Kharkov, for example, found that a newspaper's popularity is tied directly to the quality of its news. Ninety-two percent of the readers were interested first of all in information (*Zhurnalist*, December 1974).

Finally, some evidence suggests that the Soviet authorities, despite the Leninist dictum that no information is nonideological, recognize that the modern Soviet state demands copious amounts of relatively unadorned information simply in order to function. Recurring official appeals to Soviet reporters to be more aggressive and more efficient indicate that the very nature of a modern industrial state requires a steady diet of information.

> There hasn't been a single business meeting, seminar, scientific conference devoted to information at which there hasn't been talk of the necessity for full and comprehensive elucidation of the work of party and government organs. As L. I. Brezhnev has emphasized, "publicity, informing the masses and all the working class of the activity of the party is a principle of our party life, and we firmly observe this principle." (ibid., p. 33)

As the hunger for more information grows, so does a more Western-style approach to news coverage. In Soviet theory, even information is not neutral. The journalist is expected to fit it into its correct place in the Marxist theoretical framework. In practice, the proper ideological viewpoint on breaking news is not always clear. Reporting on events from abroad presents relatively little difficulty—the party's position on relations with various countries dictates the tone of coverage. But how to choose between conservation values and demands for high production from a polluting paper factory? How to decide who is right in a dispute between a construction firm and the people who live in its shoddily built apartments? One way out, Soviet reporters have discovered, is an approach that—although they of course do not de-

scribe it in those terms—comes close to American-style "objectivity."
Thus, the editor of a newspaper in Sverdlovsk argues:

[It] seems to me the development of norms, even if very
general ones, of professional ethics for journalists is a vital
necessity. One of those norms, in my view, should be a
comprehensive study of his subject matter and, of special
importance, an absolute impartiality, a lack of preconceptions
in his research, which guarantees that he will not take a
onesided approach to people, to events. It is a very strict
standard. (*Zhurnalist*, July 1969, pp. 9–10)

This is not to suggest that Soviet journalism is about to adopt entirely American standards of "objectivity" and abandon its educative
and persuasive role. The *publitsist* clearly retains more status within
the Soviet journalistic hierarchy than does the reporter. "Just a reporter" remains pejorative, a description of the Soviet journalist who
has not yet paid enough dues to achieve a more prestigious title. But
clearly the more Western-style role of the reporter is gaining respect not only among some journalists but also, and more crucially
for the reporter's continuing role in the Soviet system, among the
authorities.

THE SOVIET AUDIENCE: ARE THEY PERSUADED?

The most difficult aspect of Soviet media dynamics to analyze is
audience reaction. Communication effects research, decades old in the
West, is a new and fragile discipline in the Soviet Union. Much of the
audience research that has been done is unsophisticated by American
standards, and all of it is subject to the doubts attendant on any survey research in an authoritarian society: To what extent will the respondents dissemble in their eagerness to give the politically safe
answer?

Fragmentary evidence suggests that Soviet media have not had
the simple, direct "hypodermic-needle" effects that Western critics have
sometimes assumed and that Soviet propagandists have hoped for.
Vladimir Shliapentokh, a former senior research fellow at the Institute of Sociological Research in Moscow who emigrated to the United
States in 1979, believes Soviet readership studies establish that readers largely share the values promulgated by media. On the other
hand, one survey revealed that Aleksandr. I. Solzhenitsyn, the
émigré writer attacked loudly and long by *Literaturnaya Gazeta*, was
one of the three favorite writers of that newspaper's readers (Dionne
1980). Mickiewicz (1981), in her study of the Russian media public,
concluded that Soviet officials have found out through opinion poll-

ing that the public's "structure of demands and tastes is quite different from what they had imagined or wished, and that the blanketing of the public with constant repetitive messages was not producing the desired effect" (p. 147). A study in Kostroma found that, despite the years of constant atheist propaganda, one-quarter of the population surveyed were believers. And 88 percent of the strong believers and 95 percent of the moderates were also regular consumers of newspapers, magazines, and radio and television broadcasts. An *Izvestia* survey showed that 75 percent of the readers had admitted to disagreeing with one or more *Izvestia* editorials. Eleven percent were willing to cite specific editorials with which they disagreed. Clearly, then, Soviet media are not entirely successful in their efforts at persuasion.

THE COMPETITION: DISSIDENT PERSUADERS

In almost all Communist societies of any duration, graphic proof of another kind of the partial failure of the Communist propaganda apparatus has appeared: Dissident journalists, usually operating illegally, have published—and have occasionally broadcast—versions of reality at odds with the official Communist version. The importance of the phenomenon is sometimes underestimated in the West because Westerners often interpret it in a Western context. A few hundred dissenters distributing smudgy carbon copies of unofficial news would have no more importance in the United States than would high school students publishing a newsletter attacking the principal. In the Soviet Union, officials apply a different test of relevance. They may recall that Lenin improvised a revolution with a handful of hard-core disciples. Within that Soviet context, the numbers have been significant, even under the policy of increased repression pursued by the party for the last several years. Since the mid-1970s, more than 400 dissidents have been imprisoned or have had their activities restricted by the authorities. Between June 1979 and May 1980 alone, 71 dissidents were convicted and 86 others arrested. Between 1978 and 1980, "thousands of other people" have had their houses searched, been subjected to police interrogation, or otherwise come afoul of Soviet authorities in connection with their presumed human rights activities (Sharlet 1980).

The Chronicle of Current Events, which first appeared in 1968, has been the most important Soviet underground newspaper. It has offered a journalism strikingly different from the official one, not only in content but also in approach. The *Chronicle*'s typescript pages have provided a dry, neutral, almost American-style reportage of events that remain beyond the pale of official Soviet journalism. News of the court cases of political dissidents, and of the arrests of dissenting

Jews and Baptists, is presented without commentary. It is, as its practitioners have often explained, an attempt to persuade through nonpersuasive journalism. The dissidents hope that an alternative channel of information (whose contents, they anticipate, will be amplified by Western broadcasts back to the Soviet Union) will provide the leaven for reform within Soviet society. Such an alternative remains a constant challenge to the integrated view of reality that the Soviet Communist party wants to promulgate. Sharlet (1980) noted the implicit challenge of such a phenomenon to the official system of persuasion:

> Workers have begun to organize unofficially; the first
> *samizdat* feminist journal has appeared and a second one is
> soon expected; psychiatric internees, religious believers,
> prisoners, and even handicapped people all now have
> unofficial specialized groups defending their rights and
> interests. The growing strength of the Soviet contra-system
> suggests that if the official system does not or cannot provide
> for the multiplying needs of its citizens in a changing society,
> unofficial groups will emerge to fill the vacuum and meet
> their needs. This problem, which shakes the power of the
> KGB, and is not susceptible to police solutions, will surely
> plague Brezhnev's successors in the coming decade. (p. 100)

NON-SOVIET COMMUNIST COUNTRIES

In the non-Soviet Communist world, the media have remained more or less faithful to the Leninist model in theory while, as in politics and economics, departing from Soviet practice—sometimes dramatically. In none of these countries—including Yugoslavia, probably the farthest from Soviet practice—have Communist journalists abandoned their role as educators and persuaders for the party. But national differences in the practice of communism have meant differences, too, in the practice of Communist journalism.

The Soviet Union's close European allies have remained, except for occasional dramatic reverses, closest to Soviet journalistic orthodoxy, as they have to Soviet orthodoxy in general. They also have dissident journalists who challenge the party's claim to a monopoly on truth.

In the two countries where dissidence came briefly above ground —Czechoslovakia and Poland—dissatisfaction with Soviet-style persuasive journalism played an important role. Czechoslovak journalists were at the center of much of the brief liberalization of the Prague Spring of 1968, and journalists have continued to be arrested for dissident activities. Polish journalists did not lead the liberalization movements of the 1970s and early '80s. But they did take advantage of these movements to fill the media with an unprecedented range of opinions, and probably more important, with neutral reportage of political and economic events. Significantly, an aggressive and objective press was near the top of workers' demands in their negotiations with the Polish government.

The Yugoslav media have more diversity of opinion than those of any other Communist country. In the system evolved since Tito began his de-Stalinization of Yugoslav communism in 1948, journalists do not take their orders directly from party committees on the press. The party leads, but it does not command. Yugoslavs can buy and read Western publications freely. Yet even here the party dominates publicly expressed opinion. A purge of party and media officials in the early 1970s assured a narrower range of debate even than in the preceding decade. Yugoslavs who want to offer a public alternative to official viewpoints are thwarted and sometimes arrested. Attempts by a group of prominent intellectuals to publish a "free and democratic" magazine in 1979 brought charges that they were trying to establish a political opposition (Petrovic 1980).

Nowhere has Communist press theory run a more tempestuous course than in China. Mao built a rigidly Stalinist media system, with modifications he considered appropriate to the Chinese experience. For Mao, as for Lenin, media were tools to be used in the building of communism. Radio, particularly, was important to Mao's plans for a continuing revolution fired by peasant zeal. In a kind of Chinese version of the two-step flow of communication, radio broadcasts to loudspeakers in public squares were to be reinforced by group conversation led by local agitators.

During the Cultural Revolution, the determination to rid the country of all non-Maoist thought led to a ban on nearly all Western writings and cultural productions. In the post-Mao era, the pendulum swung back toward tolerance. At one point, Chinese dissidents demanded, in notices on Peking's "Democracy Wall" and in underground newspapers, a democratized political system.

China's new leaders have reasserted their firm monopoly on publicly expressed opinion. But media remain very different from those of the Maoist era. Under the leadership of Vice-Premier Deng Xiaoping, the old Maoist priorities of bringing about a classless society and, secondarily, of improving economic conditions have been reversed. "The immediate goal now is to use mass media to bring about a higher standard of living through increased productivity. The political goal is, at least temporarily, on the back burner" (Robinson 1981).

To accomplish those changed priorities, Chinese media have downplayed the old emphasis on bringing about the classless society. In its place is advertising—urging workers to buy goods that Deng hopes will stimulate the productivity needed to raise China's standard of living. Mass rallies at which hundreds of thousands waved Mao's Little Book and pledged to remain pure in Maoist thought have disappeared. Orientation to the world outside the village now comes in more Western-style news broadcasts. Robinson (1981) suggested, perhaps rashly, that the Chinese media "may one day be indistinguishable from their Western counterparts—promoting consumer goods, fostering viewing of (individually owned) TV sets, dampening group discussion and active political interest, and presenting a conception of the world as an arena for unresolvable social conflict and drama" (p. 72).

CONCLUSION

Jay Jensen (1959) has shown how the Western liberal theory of the press has been cast adrift from its metaphysical moorings because of the changes in life and thought since the eighteenth century, when both liberalism as a world view and the liberal theory of the press were born. Something of the same sort may be taking place with Communist press theory. All Communist media systems owe their theoretical underpinnings to Lenin and Marx (though some, particularly Yugoslavia and China, may pay their Leninist origins very little attention). Indeed, Marxist monism has made Communist press systems much more efficient as educators and persuaders than are liberal press systems—at least on paper. The educational function, particularly, can be more smoothly performed in Communist systems. Once the government decides on a goal, whether it be mass literacy or hygiene education, it can pursue it singlemindedly in a way no pluralistic system can. There are no publicly dissenting views as to the wisdom or the methods of the campaign. Media can command the services of the education establishment or the health establishment because they, like media, are arms of a single government apparatus.

Yet it is clear that efficiency on paper does not assure efficacy in practice. At least some human beings remain, at least some of the time, perversely resistant to being persuaded, however monolithic and insistent the message. Some Russians remain stubbornly religious despite more than six decades of relentless atheist propaganda. Given the slightest opening, dissenters spring into view in the home of Maoist mass thought. And the hunger for pure information seems to grow, even in societies that deny its possibility.

REFERENCES

Bogdanov, N., and B. Vyazyemskiy. *Spravochnik Zhurnalista*. Leningrad: Lenizdat, 1965.

Bolshaia Soviestkaia Entsiklopedia. 3rd. ed. Moscow, 1972.

Current Digest of the Soviet Press, 31, no. 18 (1979): 8; 33, no. 8 (1981): 25.

Dionne, E. J. "Opinion Polling by the Russians Is Oblique Art." *New York Times*, February 3, 1980, p. 7.

Dolan, M. A. Quoted in Los Angeles *Herald-Examiner*, April 21, 1980, p. A9.

Hopkins, M. W. *Mass Media in the Soviet Union.* New York: Pegasus, 1970.

Jensen, J. W. "Liberalism, Democracy and the Mass Media." Manuscript, 1969. Available from University of Illinois at Urbana-Champaign.

Lenin, V. I. *Collected Works.* Vol. 5. Moscow: Foreign Languages Publishing, 1961.

Lippmann, W. *Public Opinion.* New York: Pelican Books, 1946.

Lund, C. Quoted in *Los Angeles Times*, April 23 1980, sec. 6, p. 7.

Mickiewicz, E. P. *Media and the Russian Public.* New York: Praeger, 1981.

Petrovic, B. "Yugoslav Media Gaining Freedom." *Los Angeles Times*, December 17 1980, sec. 8, p. 9.

Prokhorov, Y. P. *Publitsist i Deistvitelnost.* Moscow: 1975.

Robinson, D. C. "Changing Functions of Mass Media in the People's Republic of China." *Journal of Communication* 31, no. 4 (Autumn 1981): 58–73.

Schramm, W. *The Soviet Communist Theory of the Press.* In S. S. Siebert, T. Peterson, and W. Schramm. *Four Theories of the Press.* Urbana: University of Illinois Press, 1974.

Sharlet, R. "Growing Soviet Dissidents," *Current History*, 79 (October 1980), pps. 96–100.

Shkondin, M. V. "Zhurnalistika Razvitogo Sotsializma." *Vestnik Moskovskogo Universiteta, seria 10, Zhurnalistika*, January–February 1978, pp. 16–27.

Zhurnalist. January 1967, December 1967, June 1968, July 1969, December 1974, and April 1977.

PART 5

MASS MEDIA AS VEHICLES OF ENTERTAINMENT

---

11. MEDIA ENTERTAINMENT IN THE WESTERN WORLD

DONALD R. BROWNE

Entertainment may well be the most prominent mass media activity, at least in terms of amounts of time people devote to reading, watching, and listening. Yet media entertainment is exceptionally difficult to analyze because it is so difficult to define (Fischer 1979). Is it synonymous with relaxation, distraction, escape, pleasure? And are we not frequently informed through entertainment? Do we not have our societal values reinforced through it?

Put another way, most of us have no difficulty acknowledging that the news we read, hear, and see through newspapers and radio and television programs informs rather than entertains (although U.S. radio and television newscasts often conclude with a bizarre or humorous item). But entertainment may have several primary and secondary functions for us, depending upon how much or how little we already know about the situation, characters, and setting portrayed, how we feel at the time, and the events we may be experiencing. For example, when we read a popular novel set in a foreign country, we may feel that we are being informed as much as entertained. A television drama portraying criminal activities in a major city may reinforce our impressions of what city life is like. A cartoon strip such as *Mary Worth* may "tell" us how we should and should not treat one another. Yet we also are capable of reacting to these entertainment messages as amusements or distractions.

Because mass media in the Western world are so all-pervasive—almost everyone can read and can afford to purchase newspapers, magazines, paperbacks, radio and television sets, and tickets to the movies, all of which are available in the smallest towns—mass media entertainment, too, is all-pervasive. Whether we consume it or not, we are bound to be reminded of it in conversations with friends, in sermons delivered at church, even in news items. Yet, ubiquitous as it is, there is no agreed-upon definition for it, and certainly no agreement as to its impact on society—although it *is* analyzed and criticized throughout the Western world.

For purposes of this analysis, mass media entertainment is defined as that which appears to have as its *primary* purpose the amusement, distraction, and/or relaxation of its audience. Its forms would include comic and serious dramatic presentations (movies, radio and TV dramas, popular novels, comic strips), game and quiz contests (crossword puzzles, TV game and quiz shows), variety shows (TV and, in a few countries, radio), and music (radio, TV, recordings). I have excluded sports from this list on the grounds that, for much of the audience, sports fall primarily into the category of information.

It will be noted that there are few great differences among Western nations in terms of how each conveys entertainment through mass media and what kinds of entertainment are conveyed. (However, the limited quantitative data to which I have had access do indicate differences in balance; for example, Japan's public broadcasting service seems to devote far more time to television drama with historical settings than does U.S. public television.) But there are some interesting differences in message content, as well as some interesting similarities; and it is message content that forms the principal basis of this analysis. First, however, let us consider communication policies and laws regarding entertainment. Then we shall examine briefly the entertainment media themselves.

THE REGULATION OF MEDIA ENTERTAINMENT

Aside from regulations on the distribution of "pornographic" material—and even these regulations vary a good deal, from the relative looseness of Denmark's to the relative strictness of Australia's—there are few legal prohibitions governing mass media entertainment in the Western world. Where prohibitions exist, they are more likely to apply to broadcasting than to print media, which enjoy a private enterprise status throughout the Western world, whether under capitalist or socialist governments. Furthermore, any regulation of broadcast entertainment usually takes the form of very general prohibitions or exhortations that are difficult to apply in specific cases and for which no specific penalties are prescribed.

If references must be made to physical deformities, particular care shall be exercised. (Standards of NHK (Japan) Domestic Broadcast Programs, Sec. 8*b*)

The station shall prevent the dissemination of ideas or conceptions that would grossly offend the moral sentiments of wide circles of the audience. (Statute Articles for South German Radio, Stuttgart, Art. 2, Sec. 4*j*)

Presentation of the details of violence should avoid the excessive, the gratuitous and the instructional. (Television Code, National Association of Broadcasters (U.S.), Sec. IV, 1A)

The national broadcast/service should contribute to the development of national unity and provide for a continuing expression of Canadian identity. (Broadcasting Act, Canada, Pt. 1, Sec. 2*g*)

Nor do the various regulatory devices, whether laws, codes, or guidelines, do much to encourage the dissemination of specific kinds of entertainment. Many broadcast systems have quotas on the amounts of foreign programming that may be shown over television or, more rarely, played over radio. A few nations have quotas on the number of foreign movies that may be imported. But foreign comic strips, comic books, and entertainment magazines enjoy generally unrestricted entry unless they are deemed "pornographic." And while the quota system may increase the sheer volume of domestic radio, television, and film production, it does not guarantee that the material produced will be reflective of specific national cultural values, as anyone who has seen Japanese, British, or Australian equivalents of American TV hosts Johnny Carson or Mike Douglas will attest.

Where there is specific promotion of entertainment that reflects national culture, it is likely to come through "understandings" within media organizations that certain elements of society—particularly religious, cultural, ethnic, and linguistic minorities—should be served. Such understandings are rarely made explicit in broadcast laws or codes. Nor do they prevent broadcasters, newspaper and comic book publishers, or movie producers from satirizing religion, homosexuality, blacks, or devotees of opera. Great Britain, for example, which is synonymous in many people's minds with tolerance, politeness, and respect for the ways of others, is home to some of the more flagrantly sexist and racist entertainment on television that may be seen anywhere ("The Benny Hill Show," "The Black and White Minstrel Show").

Most Western nations with linguistic minorities, and many with racial minorities, have newspapers and other media directed to those minorities, but they did not come into existence as a result of any specific national cultural policy or regulatory act, and sales and ad revenue rather than public funding keep most of them in existence. Such movies as are made to cater to minorities have the same *raison d'être*, as with the "blaxploitation" films made in the United States during the 1970s. Broadcast services often include portions of the schedule set aside for linguistic and ethnic, as well as cultural, minorities, but broadcasters generally determine how much of this shall be done, when, and in what manner. Australia and the United States have radio and television stations that broadcast "exclusively" to racial and ethnic minorities. Those in Australia are supported by public funds, but those in the United States usually operate as commercial, profit-making ventures, although the Federal Communications Commission gives specific encouragement to their creation.

Various Western nations have less formal manifestations of regulation of mass media entertainment. Several nations have advisory or supervisory councils drawn from among the citizenry; these most often function with respect to broadcasting. There are press councils, often composed of citizens and media professionals, in a few countries, but rarely do they concern themselves with entertainment. Movie "censorship" committees and councils exist at the local, state, or national level in most Western countries and are responsible for conferring specific ratings on films (suitable for general viewing, suitable for adults only). Citizens' groups can and do organize to protest excessive violence and sex on television (e.g., Great Britain's Viewers and Listeners Association, Japan's Parent-Teacher Association, Action for Children's Television in the United States). But most of these, with the exception of the movie censorship committees, do not have the force of law behind them and are limited to giving advice and applying pressure. In Western nations where national communication policy has been discussed in any depth (West Germany, Ireland, Canada, Australia, Sweden), informational policies seem to have been the primary subject of discussion, and some reports on the subject (UNESCO 1974) say next to nothing about entertainment. It is almost as if entertainment were unworthy of serious policy consideration!

MASS MEDIA

The channels through which entertainment reaches Western audiences are common to Western nations and, as stated, of generally equal availability in each nation. All nations have a number of daily newspapers, magazines, cinemas, nationwide radio and television services, in addition to whatever comes in from other countries. Despite this universality of the media, there are a number of interesting differences (as well as similarities) in the ways in which they have grown and exist today.

Newspapers. In Western nations, newspapers are almost always published by private industry and devote relatively little space to entertainment. The United States seems to be a clear leader in its devotion to comic strips as a staple offering of the daily newspaper, with Canada second in that respect. Some dailies in France, Great Britain, and a few other Western European nations carry a more limited number of comic strips, many of them originally from the United States (e.g., *Popeye, Tarzan,* or *Blondie*). Certain newspapers in Western European nations—perhaps most notably those in France—carry serialized novels, sometimes from the "classics" but occasionally original works. Crossword puzzles are common in newspapers throughout the Western world. "Cheesecake" photos of scantily clad women appear regularly in many "popular" daily and weekly newspapers (e.g., Great Britain's *Daily Express*). Little else in Western newspapers seems to be intended primarily to entertain readers.

Magazines. Like newspapers, magazines are also in the hands of private industry throughout the West. Magazines have experienced a spectacular growth in most Western nations over the past thirty years, as a comparison between the 1951 and 1981 editions of *Willings Press Guide* will reveal. The growth has come largely in the form of specialized magazines for cooks, homemakers, and so on. Whether these magazines should be considered as information or entertainment is an open question, although some of them, especially those intended for homemakers, young parents, and sexually active (in mind if not in body) adult males contain considerable fiction and light entertainment. One entertainment/information magazine, *Readers' Digest,* has developed a considerable international circulation: In the late 1970s, its per issue figure outside the United States was 11.5 million, and it was available in 13 languages in 32 countries (Schreiner 1977).

One category of magazine clearly associated with entertainment is the comic book. It exists in all Western nations, although many comics may be imported and still others may be translated from comics originating abroad. Unlike comics in some developing nations (e.g., Mexico's *Chanoc*), those published in Western nations rarely set out to "teach" moral lessons. (The "underground" comics published in the United States, for example Freakx Comics, are a major exception to this rule, but do not enjoy widespread circulation.) This does not discount the possibility that readers learn certain moral values. One analysis of Donald Duck comics finds their "hero" imperialist, colonialist, racist, and classist (Dorfman and Mattelart 1977), but that does not appear to be the intent of the publisher.

Movies. Although they have been used for other purposes, such as newsreels and documentaries, movies are largely synonymous with entertainment throughout the world. The growth of "art films" for limited audiences over the past few decades does not alter the fact that most movies are produced for mass audiences. Almost all Western nations produce at least one or two feature films a year; Japan, France, Italy, Great Britain, and the United States produce them by the dozens. Television has decreased cinema attendance in all Western nations. In some cases, this has resulted in government support for an ailing cinema industry; in other cases, for example, Australia and New Zealand, it has resulted in the virtual creation of a government-subsidized film industry where none existed before. Still, the production of movies remains largely in private hands, even though most governments practice censorship in one form or another (Phelps 1975), usually through film boards. Most boards pass judgment on whether films, both domestic and imported, should be exhibited as originally shot or whether they should be cut, and what category of rating they should receive (e.g., an *R* in the United States means that admission to that movie is restricted to those over 17 years of age, unless accompanied by parent or guardian). Although several Western nations are major exporters of movies—France, Sweden, West Germany, Italy, Great Britain, and the United States are particularly active—their governments rarely attempt to impose restrictions on the content of those exports.

Radio. In most Western countries the early years of radio saw the medium used for a variety of purposes, but entertainment was chief among them and remains so to this day. No Western nation is without at least one radio station of its own, and most have a variety of separate (but often jointly administered) radio services ranging from two or three in some Nordic countries to hundreds and even thousands in Canada, Italy, and the United States. Countries with some provision for private enterprise radio also tend to have large numbers of stations;[1] even in Great Britain, where commercial radio has been in existence for only a decade, there are about three dozen local commercial stations on the air, and the parent company, IBA, projects a total of nearly seventy by the mid-1980s. Most commercial radio stations feature a far heavier diet of entertainment (largely popular music) than do their noncommercial counterparts, but many of the latter have also increased the amount of popular music they play.

Thus, while radio is regarded as an excellent medium for receiving up-to-the-minute news, people in most Western countries spend most of their radio-listening time on music of one sort or another. Very few radio stations, public or private, attempt to present the wide variety of entertainment that they did in the days before television. The BBC continues to broadcast many radio plays, however, as do the West Germany ARD stations, France-Culture, some other West European stations, CBC in Canada, the ABC in Australia, and increasingly, National Public Radio in the United States. Most West European stations also have their own symphony orchestras and commission a number of original works each year. Plays and concerts usually appeal to no more than a small portion of the audience, but they permit broadcasters to serve as patrons of the (often contemporary) arts. A few broadcasters, such as the BBC, continue to air quiz shows and even serial drama ("The Archers") and comedy ("Tony's"). Radio is regulated by the government in all Western countries, but the regulation of radio entertainment content is usually left to the stations themselves, although regulatory agencies and legislative bodies in some countries have at times expressed concern over the broadcast of popular music that appeared to encourage a "liberal" attitude toward sex or the taking of drugs.

Television. The sheer cost of television, plus the fact that radio was present and thriving when TV arrived, meant that few who had not worked with radio would be inclined or permitted to try their hands at this relatively new medium, basically a phenomenon of the past three decades. As a result, television tended to follow in the programmatic footsteps of radio, borrowing most of the older medium's entertainment and information formats. Television remains to this day a medium of entertainment, first and foremost, not only in the Western world but throughout the world. (Television was a medium of education in India and American Samoa during its early years, but entertainment has grown in importance over the past decade or so.) Not only did television co-opt much of radio entertainment; it also turned to movies as a major source of supply, to the point where film industries in some countries (e.g., Austria, New Zealand, and Sweden) rely heavily on income from television to sustain their work.

All Western nations have television stations, and as with radio, it is rare to find a nation with only one TV channel. Most have two or three, a few have several dozen, and the United States has nearly a thousand, not counting cable services. Patterns of finance and regulation are similar to those for radio, although television entertainment seems to have provoked more criticism from government officials, religious leaders, parents, and educators than have any other entertainment media, even film. This has resulted in legislative hearings, critical newspaper and magazine articles and books, and calls for stricter government control of the medium. Few laws governing television have been changed from the time of their initial adoption, but internal codes of regulation (e.g., the NAB Codes in the United States, the Japanese NAB Broadcast Standards, the British IBA Television Programme Guidelines and Code of Violence) have become more specific and detailed as regards acceptable program standards.

COMPARATIVE MEDIA CONTENT

Just as there is no agreed-upon definition of entertainment, there are no agreed-upon categories for the analysis of entertainment. I have devised my own categorical system in order to bring a measure of organization to something that seems to defy such efforts. I have chosen to develop categories that would, as much as possible, rest on media content rather than producer intention or audience perception. My use of the term "portrayers" is not meant to convey the impression that this is what producers necessarily seek to show or what audiences necessarily understand, but what is the primary content of the material.

Portrayers of National History

It is not uncommon for Western mass media to use national history as a basis for entertainment. American movies with "Wild West" settings, British TV series about Ivanhoe and Robin Hood, French cartoon books about the Gauls and the Romans (Asterix), and Australian novels about frontier days in the outback all draw upon their national histories. In some cases, history is incidental, serving as just another backdrop for the endless conflict between good and evil, wisdom and folly, love and hate. In others, it is integral to the plot and may even acquire something of a documentary air so that it becomes difficult to tell where fact leaves off and fiction begins. In almost all cases, it is the history of the dominant or mainstream culture: Cowboys defeat Indians, Christians triumph over Moslems, and so on.

Rarely is there evidence to suggest that Western media deliberately set about to "teach" history to readers, viewers, and listeners through entertainment. Rather, the use of history seems to be based on its story-telling potential; its ability to attract and hold a sizable audience on the basis of the emotional value of the material; its capacity to make them smile, fear, and sympathize. Learning may or may not take place.

Revisionist historians active throughout the Western world have cast doubt on many time-honored interpretations of national history, but little of their work has had an impact on entertainment media. When revisionist history does appear as entertainment, it is likely to be in the form of movies with limited circulation (although the U.S. film *Little Big Man* did well at the box office) or radio plays for specialized audiences, and not as major TV series (with the possible exception of the U.S. "Roots"), popular novels, or comic books.

Perhaps those in charge of Western media are reluctant to challenge their audiences' long-held images of national history; perhaps those in charge are not even aware of the changes. But it is at least as likely that history, in and of itself, simply is not that important to media producers. In contrast, Communist media frequently provide entertainment where historical settings are of paramount importance: World War II or the struggles of the people against their oppressors in pre-Communist times. Soviet movies on these two aspects of history are well known to moviegoers outside the USSR; but Soviet, East German, Czech, and other Communist television, popular novels, and songs present them as well.

Portrayers of Artistic Culture

When one considers the range of artistic culture—including popular, folk, jazz and classical music, ballet, painting, sculpture, and drama—it is clear that Western mass media devote considerable attention to it. Radio's predeliction for popular music has already been mentioned; in some countries (Canada, Australia) domestically composed, performed, and recorded music is specifically encouraged through mandatory quotas. Televised performances of popular music also are becoming more frequent. Some radio services, especially in Great Britain, France, and West Germany, as well as public stations in the United States and Canada, devote large amounts of time to classical music. Most West European television stations manage to include at least one classical music concert, ballet, or opera in the schedule each week, and some broadcast two or three. Most radio and television music broadcasts include considerable music from other Western nations, although British and American artists tend to dominate popular music broadcasts, whereas Western European music, ballet, and opera dominate classical music schedules. As has been mentioned, many West European stations are important patrons of classical music.

"Serious" novels and plays written for theatrical presentation, as well as dramas written for mass media, also find their places on many radio and television services, in movies, and even (for short stories and novels) as serializations in newspapers; several daily newspapers in France regularly serialize novels, almost all of them French. Such "serious" media presentations are more likely to be prominent in systems with license fees, government subsidies, or other forms of non-commercial support, although the IBA's television companies, despite rising costs and low ratings, produced nearly forty single and often original (written for TV) plays in 1980. Yet, as IBA remarked in its 1982 report, "If the viewer doesn't show much enthusiasm for the single play, how many of them can the [broadcaster] afford?" (p. 36). The same would pertain to filmmaking, where rising costs of production and the failure of certain lavish productions to recoup their costs at the box office—the American *Heaven's Gate* is a recent example—seem to have diminished the enthusiasm of many film organizations for some kinds of original material.

Where television in particular is concerned, many Western nations have placed a premium on low production costs and more or less guaranteed hits, many of them "guaranteed" because they resemble, or are thought to resemble, past successes. This is especially true of the dramas most often available and most widely viewed over commercially supported systems, as in Great Britain, Australia, Japan, Canada, and the United States. There is little originality to most commercial TV drama, situation comedy, or variety (which generally includes at least a few "minidramas" or comic sketches).

Yet another problem arises with television and film adaptations of novels or dramas. While TV and film producers in most Western European nations take great pains to remain faithful to the original work, producers in the United States often feel free to adapt the original as they wish, until in some cases only the title of the work remains intact! There may be a fundamental difference between the viewpoints of European and American producers. The former seek their creative outlets through the attainment of the best possible translation of the original material through a new medium; the latter use the original material as the basis for a display of their own originality. And while certain laws protect authors from depredations, authors long dead (and often most closely associated with the nation's cultural heritage) have little protection.

But the picture is not unreservedly bleak. As mentioned, some media in Western nations are active as sponsors of artistic culture, and at times, even serve as archivists of it. Film has been used in many countries to preserve records of "dying" cultural traditions: crafts, dances, and the like. Radio and television systems in most Western countries commission musical compositions, ballets, and plays; occasionally, the latter will even be adapted for theater, as was Edward Albee's radio play *Wings*.

One thing seems quite clear about Western mass media support for artistic culture: Except for popular music, most Western media organizations *not* supported by public funds (license fees, taxes, direct contributions) have little interest in promoting original artistic expression.[2] That was not always the case. The NBC radio network in the United States had its own symphony orchestra from the late 1930s through the early 1950s, and all three U.S. commercial TV networks carried numerous plays by then unknown but later relatively famous playwrights such as Paddy Chayevsky and Reginald Rose in the early to mid 1950s. Few advertising dollars go to support original artistic expression nowadays, although that may change with the spread of cable TV, videocassette, and other "new technologies."

Portrayers of Ethnic Minorities

Ethnic minorities vary in size, number, and diversity in Western nations, but no nation is without them. Mass media entertainment reflecting ethnic cultures also varies. Print media seem to pay the least attention to ethnic minority cultures, although some comic strips (*Gordo, Fat Albert, Short Ribs*) appearing in U.S. newspapers have portrayed Chicanos and blacks. This is a risky venture, however, simply because comic strips are comic and can so easily be interpreted as mocking the individuals and groups they portray. Also, the possible lack of majority culture interest in minority cultures may reduce the audience to such a small size that the activity is not economically viable.

In fact, these two conditions—the risk of insulting minorities and a lack of economic viability—have held down the development of media reflections of ethnic cultures in most Western nations where the media are largely private enterprises. Most ethnic minorities are not large enough, or well enough concentrated, to be worth the attention of private enterprise media, including not only print but also movies, radio, and television. Ethnic minorities usually lack the economic wherewithal to invest in media operations, and even if they do invest, they may still face difficulties in sustaining a profit if they concentrate on serving their minority compatriots.

Popular music is the one exception to this general rule, but even it is a limited exception. The chief minority to "benefit" from commercial media attention has been blacks in the United States. Black popular music is extensively recorded and played over commercial radio stations, not only in the United States, but in other parts of the Western world. Whether the majority culture actually perceives black popular music as a reflection of black culture is another question, but at least it is available. Certain commercial television programs, especially in the United States, have featured black casts and black environments ("Good Times", "The Jeffersons"), but they have been heavily criticized in some quarters for perpetuating some of the worst stereotypes of blacks as lazy, clownish, and stupid (U.S. Commission on Civil Rights 1977, 1979). The spate of U.S. "blaxploitation" films in the 1970s met with much the same criticism (Murray 1973), although a few, such as *Sweet Sweetback's Baaadass Song*, were hailed by critics as authentic expressions of black culture.

Noncommercial media operations, mostly broadcast services, do a somewhat better job of reflecting the cultures of ethnic minorities through entertainment, but the record is not an exemplary one. BBC local radio stations serving areas with concentrations of South Asian or black residents may devote a few hours a week to their music and may on rare occasions produce a play or poetry reading by one of their number. Australia's ABC initiated a special Aboriginal radio service in the fall of 1981 from an ABC station in Alice Springs and has experimented with "ethnic" radio and TV services for European immigrants to Australia, with programs in Greek, Italian, and so on. However, the entertainment on such services—and on similar broadcast services for "guest workers" in Western Europe—is usually limited to music. Very rarely are there attempts by stations to present entertainment that will help the majority culture understand minority cultures. Minority cultures of other Western nations fare about as poorly in broadcast terms.

The situation is only slightly better in the various government-subsidized film industries. Canada's National Film Board has done a number of stunning short films about Inuit (Eskimo) life, and Australian filmmakers have sometimes turned to Aboriginal cultures for subject matter (e.g., the highly acclaimed feature film *The Chant of Jimmy Blacksmith*), but these are exceptions that appear to prove the general rule: What majority cultures see and hear in their movies, TV, and radio programs is themselves.

Portrayer of Foreign Cultures

Most Western mass media pay considerable attention to at least some foreign cultures, but this often has economic rather than artistic or philosophical causes. U.S. movies gained a major share of the European market during World War I and have enjoyed a prominent, if not predominant, share of the market ever since. Disney cartoons were particularly successful in Europe, and they helped pave the way for Disney comic books. U.S. radio programs had limited distribution in other countries, aside from Canada; but U.S. television entered overseas markets in a major way in the early to mid 1950s when there was little competition from other nations. Even if other nations had had much to sell abroad, they would have found it difficult to match the low U.S. prices. U.S. comic strips, too, found a place in many foreign newspapers, where they were something of a novelty. Few other countries have developed many comic strips of their own. Some U.S. entertainment magazines have also built up something of a foreign market—*Playboy* is not only sold in many Western countries but seems to have spawned a host of imitators (Tunstall 1977).

The decline of U.S. movie production in the early 1950s weakened American dominance of overseas movie markets and helped increase the proportion of British, French, Italian, Swedish, and other entertainment films throughout the Western world. Several nations began in the late 1950s and early '60s to impose quotas on the importation of U.S. television entertainment. By the late 1960s, Great Britain, West Germany, and Japan were beginning vigorously to promote the sale of some of their own television entertainment programs in other Western markets, thus challenging U.S. dominance in that sphere as well. Recorded popular music was a U.S. prerogative throughout the West during the late 1940s and most of the '50s, but began to face stiff competition from abroad: the Beatles and the Rolling Stones from England in the 1960s, the Swedish group ABBA in the 1970s.

At present, the number of countries contributing to the Western mix of "foreign" entertainment is greater than ever, and shows every sign of continuing to grow (Chapman 1981). But whether the imported entertainment tells its audiences anything about the cultures of the nations from which it comes is another question. It is sometimes hard to find anything particularly Swedish in the music of ABBA, anything particularly American in Donald Duck, anything particularly Australian in the TV series "Women in Cell Block H," anything particularly Canadian in the Harlequin Romance novels.

National origins are no guarantee of national characteristics. In fact, media products may do much better in international markets if they are not too "nationalistic." The growth in the number of international co-productions of television and film entertainment also tends to reduce the culture-specific character of some mass media entertainment.

Media entertainment produced within a given country rarely chooses to present a foreign culture, aside from the playing of classical music of largely European composers. Although it is not unheard of, it is rare for British television to present plays by American playwrights such as Eugene O'Neill (although West German television gave a fine performance of O'Neill's *Mourning Becomes Electra* in the early 1970s); for French radio to present dramatizations of novels by German writers such as Heinrich Böll; for German film to adapt the works of English writers such as Robert Bolt. Several television services do have a modest commitment to broadcasting dramas by foreign writers—West Germany's ZDF produced plays by Jean Anouilh and Ivan Bukovcan and imported television plays from several West European nations in 1980—but such productions are far outnumbered by domestic fare. Some of that domestic product draws upon material originally produced in other countries for its inspiration, as did the popular U.S. situation comedy "All in the Family," which was based on the equally popular British TV series "'Til Death Do Us Part," but there was nothing remotely British about the American version.

Perhaps audiences in most Western countries are happiest seeing, hearing, and reading about themselves when they turn to mass media for entertainment. Granted, the Rolling Stones can still draw huge crowds on their overseas tours, and the U.S. prime-time soap opera "Dallas" can place among the top ten in the program popularity charts in England, France, West Germany, and elsewhere in the Western world (although it has not done well in Japan). American movies such as *Jaws* and *Raiders of the Lost Ark* have been smash hits in almost every Western country where they have been shown. But when reasonably well-produced domestic entertainment is available, it usually will outdraw the foreign competition.

Portrayal of Social Norms

In all the media functions that have been discussed to this point, there is the implication that media act as mirrors of society. There have been many discussions about whether media set the tone for society or follow in its wake (Loevinger 1968); but it seems to be agreed upon throughout the Western world that media are closely linked with societal norms, and that media entertainment in particular is connected with their formation, perpetuation, and destruction. This is partly because so much media entertainment has contemporary domestic society as its principal setting. Popular literature may sometimes feature historical settings, and certain television organizations—Japan's NHK and Britain's BBC and IBA in particular—are famous for their historical dramas (Makita 1979, BBC 1982, IBA 1982). But such offerings are in the minority in the West, and certain media in certain Western countries (e.g., television in the United States and Australia) rarely present historically based entertainment.

Furthermore, most of the entertainment has an urban setting, just as all Western nations themselves are far more urban than rural. And while the characters and situations portrayed certainly do not present a balanced picture of society, most of them are people, places, and circumstances we can recognize.

With these various conditions in mind, and given the widespread consumption of media entertainment throughout the West, it is easy to see why some have assumed that the media are a major influence on society's perceptions of how it behaves and how it should behave. Those working within media organizations generally reject the notion that they attempt to decry or prescribe desirable or undesirable behaviors, aside from upholding certain "basic" moral values: Evil should and will be punished, good rewarded; law enforcement agencies have the good of society at heart; the "ordinary" person can be a success in life. Some media producers are willing to acknowledge that some members of the audience will treat fictional entertainment as if it were fact—writers of novels and dramas centered on hospitals are usually very careful to get their facts straight because of the tendency for readers and viewers to diagnose their own ailments—but there is still a widespread tendency for producers to claim that "the audience knows it's just a story."

Perhaps the first line of criticism of Western entertainment media as reflectors of society, however, is not that the portrayals are so inaccurate as that they are so selective. Police and law enforcement agencies appear in the movies, television dramas, and popular novels of virtually every Western nation, and account for a large share of media imports as well. Almost never are law enforcement officials depicted as unkind, incompetent, venal, or unsuccessful, and rarely do they have uninteresting cases. In hospital dramas, which are more common in English-speaking Western countries than elsewhere, the portrait is much the same from country to country: Doctors and nurses generally are kind, courteous, attentive, and thoroughly competent. Yet, while there are indeed police, judges, nurses, and doctors who are models of virtue and professionalism, there are others who are not. A patient who goes to a hospital expecting the level of care shown in a typical episode of the American TV series "The Nurses" is likely to be in for something of a surprise, if not a shock.

Occupationally, the story is much the same. The "professional" occupations such as doctor, lawyer, engineer, and professor usually are shown as white- and male-dominated (except, of course, in Japan); ethnic minorities and women rarely enter their domains. Women appear as homemakers, but rarely as wage earners; when women do have jobs, they are often at a low level. If the jobs involve managerial work, the woman frequently is shown as secretly or unconsciously anxious to have a man take over the responsibility (a common theme in Canada's Harlequin Romance novels).

Portrayers of Violence

Mass media in the Western world have come in for considerable criticism over the years in terms of their portrayal of violence and the presumed effects of that portrayal on society. Some Western nations, including the United States, Great Britain, and West Germany, have undertaken studies of possible causal links between violence in media and violent behavior, but the results have been inconclusive. Even the "million dollar" set of studies financed through the U.S. Office of the Surgeon General in 1969–71 (*Television and Social Behavior*) led only to the cautious conclusion that television might serve to stimulate violence in certain people viewing under certain conditions. Nevertheless, the lack of conclusive results has not stopped parents, teachers, law enforcement officials, and other critics from claiming that mass media, television in particular, encourage violence.

It is true that a goodly amount of violence is available through the mass media of the Western world—far more than there is in Communist countries. The United States produces and exports a fair share of it, principally through movies, television programs, and comic books. Japan has become increasingly prominent as an exporter of violent television cartoon shows, and its *samurai* films and television programs can be exceptionally violent. Japanese commercial TV shows crime dramas that closely resemble the U.S., UK, and West German counterparts (Iwao et al. 1981), leading to many public protests and parliamentary debates over the "superabundance" of violence available to Japanese audiences, especially children. Yet Japan has the lowest violent crime rate of any major Western nation, which simply adds more fuel to the controversy over the connection between media violence and violence in society.

Many Western nations have imposed controls of various sorts on the importation and/or exhibition of violent material. Films, as noted, are often screened prior to distribution by "censorship" offices, and material judged to be excessively violent is cut, the film is given a more restrictive rating, or it is banned. The television services of several Western nations will not show violent entertainment before the mid-evening hours, in order to limit children's access to it. Great Britain's BBC and IBA both follow this practice. Swedish television allows little violent entertainment at any time. American TV stations, on the other hand, are relatively free to choose how much violent material they may broadcast and when they may broadcast it—this despite a self-regulatory Code of Good Practices that contains several sections reminding broadcasters of their obligation to maintain some control over the portrayal of violence.

Portrayers of Sex

Scarcely less controversial than mass media violence, "mass media sex" has led to much the same criticism from people throughout the Western world. For example, Mary Whitehouse's Viewers and Listeners Association was organized in Great Britain in the mid-1960s primarily to combat what its members saw as sexually overpermissive television programing. Some groups indict mass media for their alleged encouragement of loose sexual behavior, which, it is further alleged, leads to a breakdown of family life, increases in abortions, and illegitimate births. Again, television and movies are prime targets of criticism, but "pornographic" magazines and popular music, whether broadcast over radio or offered for sale on records and tapes, are the objects of many of the same accusations.

There are far fewer scientific studies of possible causal connections between mass media sex and sexual behavior than of connections between media violence and violent behavior. Interestingly, several studies by U.S. researcher Dolf Zillmann and his associates (1979) have suggested that mass media sex may provoke some of the same effects as does mass media violence, and that those effects may last much longer.

Many of the controls imposed on sexual material throughout the Western world are similar to controls imposed on violent material. Film censorship and ratings systems deal as often with sex as they do with violence, although this varies according to the individual country, Sweden and Denmark being somewhat more permissive with respect to sexual material than is, say, Spain. But many Western societies are adopting the attitude that it is permissible for adults to expose themselves to such material as long as it is not readily available to children. Thus, sexual intercourse would not be shown over a public or commercial television service (although it may be suggested in ways that leave little to the imagination), but it might be allowable over a special cable TV service if it is at the subscriber's request and available only late at night. As with violence, sex receives little exposure in Communist media.

THE AUDIENCE FOR ENTERTAINMENT

One of the greatest problems facing the scholar who wishes to know how entertainment media are perceived by their audiences is that, with the exception of television, there is little qualitative research available. Radio, film, and print media entertainment have received little attention from Western researchers in recent years. Quantitative data reveal something about audience preferences: box office receipts, newsstand and subscription sales figures, and broadcast ratings and other data from numerical surveys give us some idea of what people seem to prefer based on what is available to them, but they tell us little about why people prefer what they do, or how their preferences may influence their behavior.

Numerical data seem to indicate that if well-made domestic entertainment is available, it will fare well in comparison with imported material. For example, the top twenty films in terms of gross box office receipts shown in Sweden between July 1, 1974, and December 31, 1976, included eight Swedish films, and numbers three, four and six were Swedish (*Swedish Film 1977*). Ratings figures for the West German and British top ten television programs in October 1981 saw ten West German and nine British shows in the lists, and the top five in each case were entertainment shows, only one of them (the American movie *Jaws*) foreign (*TV World*, November 1981).

The data also show that mass audience tastes from one Western nation to another are similar, at least when similar fare is available, as it often is. If crime dramas are available on TV, and they are in most Western nations, they will generally be popular, especially among younger viewers (Wober 1978). So will prime-time TV quiz shows, which do especially well in West Germany, the Netherlands, and Great Britain. "Spectacular" movies, particularly of the "disaster" variety (*Towering Inferno, Earthquake*) seem to do well throughout the Western world, whether on cinema screens or over television. Conversely, broadcasts of "serious" music, even if made available in prime time and with little competition from other TV services, do very poorly in quantitative terms: West Germany's ZDF reported ratings (percentages of all television homes) of between 1 and 14 percent for its many offerings of serious music in 1980, and the higher ratings were for concerts of light classical music (e.g., Johann Strauss).

Many TV services in Western nations are not content to limit themselves to quantitative measurements of the audience; they also collect data on what is usually called "audience appreciation." Viewers are asked to indicate on 1–10 scales how much they like the shows they watch. On that basis many serious plays, concerts, and other entertainment programs that attract small audiences receive very high scores for audience appreciation. The public broadcasting systems of many countries use such figures to help justify the continuation of certain shows that might be canceled on the basis of audience size alone. Commercial broadcasting systems rarely conduct audience appreciation research (Great Britain's IBA is a notable exception), but then, most of them do not devote as much broadcast time to "serious" entertainment as do their public broadcasting counterparts.

Research studies that take demographics into account reveal some interesting similarities and differences around the Western world. For example, moviegoing seems to be far more frequent for people in their teens and twenties in the United States, but seems to be spread quite evenly throughout the population in Sweden. Radio listening studies in Great Britain and the United States have shown that many listeners who became accustomed in their teens to listening to certain popular music groups and soloists (the Beatles, the Rolling Stones, Elvis Presley) carry that habit with them in later life.

A number of qualitative studies have been conducted on specific TV shows or series in various countries. Perhaps the most heavily studied show has been the American situation comedy "All in the Family," which featured a rather bigoted and earthy blue-collar worker. It was the subject of several dozen research investigations in the United States, Canada, Holland, and elsewhere (Adler 1979). While the figures did not match exactly from study to study or country to country, they did show a fairly common tendency for a majority of people to think of the show primarily as entertainment, and a minority primarily as a "message" drama which told viewers that Archie Bunker, the lead character, showed societally undesirable behavior in his prejudiced remarks and actions. Yet each country where it was shown also had a small minority of viewers who identified with Archie and saw his statements and acts as acceptable and even desirable.

BBC and NHK audience research has been notable for its sheer quantity and scope (see, for example, "Til Death Do Us Part," *BBC Annual Review of BBC Research Findings*), but few broadcasting organizations elsewhere come close to matching their efforts. Some organizations, especially the French broadcasting services, have kept the studies they conduct very much to themselves instead of making them publicly available as BBC, NHK, and a number of other services do. Comparative (cross-cultural) studies of audience reactions to media entertainment are very rare, partly because they are difficult and expensive to undertake. Those studies that do exist usually are limited to investigating how people spend their time with media (Robinson 1972). It would be interesting to see how audiences differed from and resembled one another in their reactions to some of the more universally distributed media entertainment, such as "Dallas." But it does not seem likely that such research will be forthcoming in any quantity, especially when so many of the entertainment media are the subject of so little quantitative or qualitative research at the domestic, let alone international, level.

SOME CLOSING OBSERVATIONS

We said at the outset that there seem to be few great differences among Western mass media in terms of how each of them conveys entertainment. It should also be apparent that there are several common concerns among the Western entertainment media: violence, sex, the depiction of society. The absence of a discussion of "cultural imperialism" among the common concerns may be striking. But although U.S.-produced entertainment has entered all Western nations in one form or another, in my travels in the Western world over the past fifteen years I have heard expressions of substantial concern over the U.S. "cultural invasion" only in Canada and Australia, where it was connected specifically with television. Concern over American comic books, comic strips, movies, and popular music has been minor, where it has been expressed at all. Perhaps the various quota systems and "censorship" offices have reduced the level of con‑cern in some countries—it was quite high with respect to U.S. television shown in Japan and Great Britain during the 1950s—but the increasing sophistication of most Western nations in producing their own media entertainment must have played a role too.

Perhaps Western nations have certain shared values and tastes that make the media entertainment of any one country less of a threat to other countries. Or perhaps the media have contributed to a certain homogenization of taste throughout the West. Or perhaps there is indeed deep concern over cultural imperialism and/or homogenization that fails to find its expression through mass media themselves. Or perhaps there are subtle differences in the values and tastes of Western audiences that are not being detected because so few researchers are looking for them. My chief hope in connection with my own consideration of this subject is that it will stimulate others to conduct research on it—to learn more precisely whether, how, and why Western mass media entertainment and its audiences are similar and different.

NOTES

1. "Passive" relay stations would increase the numbers still further.
2. Great Britan's IBA is a notable exception.

REFERENCES

Adler, Richard, ed. *All in the Family: A Critical Appraisal.* New York: Praeger, 1979.

BBC Annual Report and Handbook 1982. London: BBC, 1982.

BBC Annual Review of BBC Research Findings, no. 1 (1973/74). "Til Death Us Do Part," pp. 26–35. London: BBC, 1974.

Chapman, Graham. "International Television Flow in West Europe." Paper presented at Annual Conference of the International Institute of Communications, Strasbourg, France, 1981.

Dorfman, Ariel, and Armand Mattelart. *How to Read Donald Duck: Imperialist Ideology in the Disney Comic.* New York: International General, 1977.

Fischer, Heniz Dietrich, and Stefan Melnik, eds. *Entertainment: A Cross-Cultural Examination.* New York: Hastings House, 1979.

Hines, Harold. "Chanoc: Adventures and Slapstick on Mexico's Southeast Coast." *Journal of Popular Culture* 14, no. 3 (Winter 1980): 424–36.

IBA. *Television and Radio 1982.* London: IBA, 1982.

Iwao, Sumiko, et al. "Japanese and U.S. Media: Some Cross-Cultural Insights into TV Violence." *Journal of Communication* 31, no. 2 (Spring 1981): 28–36.

Loevinger, Lee. "The Ambiguous Mirror: The Reflective-Projective Theory of Broadcasting and Mass Communications." *Journal of Broadcasting* 12, no. 2 (Spring 1968): 97–116.

Makita, Tetsuo. "Television Drama and Japanese Culture with Special Emphasis on Historical Drama." In H. D. Fischer and S. Melnik, eds., *Entertainment: A Cross-Cultural Examination.* New York: Hastings House, 1979.

Murray, James P. *To Find an Image: Black Films from Uncle Tom to Superfly.* Indianapolis: Bobbs-Merrill, 1973.

Phelps, Guy. *Film Censorship.* London: Victor Gollancz, 1975.

Robinson J. P. "Television's Impact on Everyday Life: Some Cross-National Evidence." In E. A. Rubinstein et al., eds., *Television and Social Behavior.* Vol. 4, Television in Day-to-Day Life: Patterns of Use. pp. 410–31. Washington, D.C.: Government Printing Office, 1972.

Schreiner, Samuel A. *The Condensed World of the Reader's Digest.* New York: Stein and Day, 1977.

Swedish Film 1977. Stockholm: Swedish Film Institute, 1977.

Television and Social Behavior. 5 vols. Washington, D.C.: Government Printing Office, 1972.

Tunstall, Jeremy. *The Media Are American: Anglo-American Media in the World.* New York: Columbia University Press, 1977.

TV World. Monthly publication of Alain Charles Publishing Ltd., London.

UNESCO. *Communication Policies in . . .* (Germany, Sweden, Ireland). Paris: UNESCO, 1974.

U.S. Commission on Civil Rights. *Window Dressing on the Set* and *Window Dressing on the Set: An Update.* Washington, D.C.: Government Printing Office, 1977, 1979.

Wober, Mallory. "Who Views Violence in Britain?" *Journal of Communication* 28, no. 3 (Summer 1978): 172–75.

ZDF Jahrbuch 80. Mainz, West Germany: ZDF, 1981.

Zillmann, Dolf. *Hostility and Aggression.* Hillsdale, N.J.: L. Erlbaum Associates, 1979.

12. MEDIA ENTERTAINMENT IN THE THIRD WORLD

SUNWOO NAM

All work and no play makes Jack a dull boy.
—English proverb.

Play has always been an important component of human existence. Play or amusement has taken forms ranging from the wholesome recreation that refreshes body and mind to the sadistic enjoyment of a Nero playing his fiddle over burning Rome. In addition to people enjoying themselves by various pursuits requiring strength and initiative, people have enjoyed watching professional entertainers (gladiators, artisans) perform; this latter activity requires not only leisure time but also a certain standard of living. With the increasing "modernization" of society, entertainment has become the major source of play.

Webster's Dictionary defines entertainment as "the act of diverting, amusing or causing (someone's) time to pass agreeably." The value of amusement in providing diversions from the doldrums of everyday existence has been recognized among practically all races and cultures of the world. Roman rulers maintained the status quo by keeping Roman citizens satiated with food and fun through vast entertainment facilities, such as arenas and coliseums.

As society has moved from a tribal arrangement to a complex system, entertainment has become more and more diversified as well as institutionalized. For example, the ballad singer or troubadour of medieval times, who not only provided news of faraway places but also entertained or amused his listeners, has given way to modern means of communication that provide specialized media for different functions. Not that such functional and structural differentiation of communication is always rigid and watertight. In the Third World, the last region of the world to be "modernized," one still finds remnants of traditional means of entertainment, such as professional storytellers and acrobatic troupes visiting villages on market days. But, increasingly, the mode of mass or popular entertainment is by means of mass media, which may or may not include traditional approaches and elements in their outputs, be they newspaper serial novels, (historical) dramas on radio and television, or movie offerings.

As was the case with the Western world, the first modern mass media that appeared in the Third World were print media—newspapers and magazines of various kinds began to appear in the late nineteenth and early twentieth centuries. While the key function of newspapers in the Third World admittedly was to raise people's political consciousness so that they would be rid of their colonial yokes, entertainment was also provided readers by way of caricatures and serial novels. In fact, to this day newspapers in Korea, Taiwan, and other countries carry novels written for the papers by popular writers, often two or three in one paper. There may be a historical yarn of adventure and love, and a contemporary story of the romance and sex genre.

The American syndication phenomenon has also hit newspapers in the Third World. One can find *Blondie, Peanuts*, or *Popeye* in the newspapers of many different countries. Whether or not something is lost in translation, American comic strips and their characters have become household words for many newspaper readers. Of course, humor is difficult to transfer cross-culturally; some years ago, when Art Buchwald wrote a hilarious piece on President Johnson going to Lady Bird's bedroom on his knees so as not to wake up their daughters, to pray with her before making an important (bombing) decision in the Vietnam war, it came out as a straight story in a Korean newspaper because the paper's American correspondent was not familiar with Buchwald's specialty of satire.

Magazines have long been a major source of entertainment for literate segments of Third World populations. They range from movie fan magazines to women's magazines with all sorts of entertaining articles and pictures.

The Third World as a convenient shorthand encompasses diverse cultures and countries; for example, in terms of religious background, the diversity includes India's Hinduism, Arab countries' Mohammedanism, and Southeast Asian Buddhism. In terms of ethnicity and language, some countries are monoethnic and monoglot, although, more often than not, polyglotism and polyethnicity are found. Some have a history and culture thousands of years old, whereas others are a hodgepodge of different backgrounds thrown together by the colonial mapmakers of the nineteenth century. Economic development is also at different stages in different countries. Some Third World countries boast $2,000 to $3,000 GNP per capita, whereas others cannot provide a standard of living for their people beyond "absolute poverty." The literacy rate in the Third World ranges from over 90 percent to less than 30 percent, depending on the country. All these factors have implications for various systems of their countries including mass media, which are increasingly major deliverers of entertainment for the masses.

What are the entertainment media in the Third World? Generally speaking, Third World countries have all the forms of mass media found in more developed countries, albeit in different stages of development. As one cynic has said, the first two things that the leadership of any two-bit nation wants for the prestige of the country are a national airline and national television, never mind the poor penetration of the latter because of the absence of widespread electrification. Therefore, it all depends which country is being discussed. For example, India and several African countries share a British colonial experience. Jeremy Tunstall, in his book *The Media Are American* (1977), divides the population of these countries into three groups: "The top 1 percent, the next 10 percent and the rest in terms of income, education and media use (all of which tend to correlate very strongly in Africa and Asia)" (pp. 109–10). The following brief excerpts from his book about these segments are relevant to entertainment-related mass media.

The 90 percent or majority
These live in the country or urban shanty towns without electricity and with very low cash income. They never see television; even those who can read cannot afford regular reading matter.... A mobile cinema may come occasionally, but many adults have never seen a film show. The radio is more familiar.... What these people hear on the radio, then, is mainly music....
The 10 percent or so middle class
They mainly live in or near a city, and are likely to have an electricity supply. They may or may not see television—but the cinema will be relatively familiar.... The adults may

read a daily newspaper . . . film magazines, paperback books
or comics. The household will contain a working radio
set. . . . Music will still be the most popular radio fare—and at
least some of it will be American or British in origin or
influence.
The top 1 percent or so
. . . They will live in or near cities in comfortable houses, with
servants, just like the remaining expatriate Britons and
other Europeans. . . . They will speak and read
English. . . . They may have television. They can attend films
easily if they so wish. . . . They read imported
publications. . . . They buy books and records which are either
imported or produced locally by a subsidiary of a British
company. . . .

Such a broad sweep of generalizations provides a useful context
that helps us understand mass media situations in most developing
countries. But, as was pointed out, there are many differences in the
details. Even for the medium of movies, there are a number of differences between Africa and India. African nations have always depended on Hollywood productions. The Indian film industry, which in
its infancy was influenced by American films, has developed to such
an extent that in 1975, 475 feature films in 13 Indian languages were
produced, whereas Hollywood imports to India dropped.

Indian films undoubtedly have immense popular appeal.
Indian film music dominates the record market and provides
the most popular radio fare; film magazines are the only
really buoyant part of the magazine industry. "Film
Hindi"—a market-tested, colloquial spoken version—may
slowly become the most effective popular language of India.
Unattached youth, drink, romantic love, night clubs, cars and
palaces constitute the standard obsessions of Indian films. In
a land of poverty, prohibition, arranged marriages and with
hundreds of people sleeping on the streets, the demand for
film realism has been limited. (ibid., p. 20)

Tunstall's point that mass media are mainly urban phenomena,
neither accessible nor understandable to the teeming masses of people in the hinterland who may not even speak the same language(s) of
the media, is still valid. For example, Diana Lancaster, who lived
eighteen months in a remote village studying relationships between
local entertainment patterns and social change, opens her report as
follows:

A monk in a yellow robe climbed into a sermon chair, and for
three hours, sat talking and giggling for the entertainment
of about 1,000 villagers sitting below him on the concrete

floor. A few months later, heralded by vans with loudspeakers, a film show drew much the same audience to the triangle of rough grass just outside the same temple compound. On both occasions there was free entertainment which gave pleasure to a mixed audience of young and old, farmer, trader, and professional. But with the impact of the moment, the similarities ended. The sermon stayed alive through the ensuing year in the social life of the small farming community in northern Thailand. Snippets were recalled with laughter whenever groups formed and the tapes I had made were requested over and over again for funeral wakes, housewarmings, and working parties. The film failed to make its point and was quickly forgotten. (Gerbner 1977, p. 165)

Why the monk's success as an entertainer? "To sponsor an entertainment was a certain way to earn merit for advancement in the Buddhist cycle of rebirths, and to be present was valuable. . . . Because the gods were guardians of entertainment and social well-being depended on participation, entertainment was in no way trivial or escapist. Rather than competing as categories, work and entertainment were complementary duties" (ibid., p. 170). Furthermore, his sermon was full of improvisations, including quotations from popular songs banned from the radio for their suggestiveness, to show the teenagers that Buddhism was as up-to-date as they were.

As for the film, which was "the most coherent, logical, smooth Thai production" that Miss Lancaster had seen in two years, it had a health message in the plot. The plot hinged on a young doctor and his nurse-wife who, upon returning to their native village to pass on the benefit of their learning, were trying "to promote an awareness of basic hygiene and nutritional values against opposition from more conservative elements. . . . When I could recognize the purpose of some specialized form of entertainment and relate to its message, the form was justified and I was edified. The audience around me had different expectations—and they saw a 'different' film. Their training was to evaluate and enjoy the film as entertainment" (ibid., p. 177). So down the drain went the government effort to instruct the people, through an entertaining film, on the need to build a community water tank.

Still, the onslaught of nation building and modernization is inexorable, especially among the young generation. Even in northern Thailand, schoolchildren are taught the central Thai dialect, because of which they began to "have difficulty understanding their grandfathers' dialect and the local stories, music, songs and dramas that gave them pleasure. Instead, young people use the central language for access to popular and rock music from Bangkok and they read stories of urban life in magazines" (ibid., p. 181).

The author describes the pains of the transitional stage in the process of moving from the traditional way of life toward development via nationalism and modernization. He says two contradictory approaches of entertainment communication—the sermon by the monk and the modern developmental film—are sanctioned by the government. The author concludes:

> During the lifetime of the present students in that northern Thai village, radio, film, records, and television have been introduced and begun to usurp the place of the live entertainer. The need to fill an exact time slot with material that will appeal to a sponsor, the government, and as many city and country people as possible immediately imposes constraints on the media. Their items have to be structured with a beginning, a middle, and an end, like much of the foreign material already broadcast. Soon people in rural areas will have to adjust their way of listening and watching to appreciate the single bold points emphasized in developmental productions. *They probably will come to believe that the individual rather than a community of people is the significant unit.* They probably will take their prosperous place in the developed world. *But the price for that place will have included their cultural heritage and identity.* (ibid., p. 183; emphasis added)

However, the impact of mass media on a Third World country's populace may not always end in the capitulation of tradition. What has happened in Iran recently illustrates how mass media, especially television, can contribute to a "revolution of rising frustration," which can bring traditionalists back to power. Iran, a country of the Shi'ite Moslem sect with its strict code of behavior based on the Koran, was suddenly thrown into cultural turmoil when the Shah began to push his modernization programs, among which television was a big item. Iran provided "perhaps the world's most extreme example of an attempt to expand the media rapidly—or at least the electronic media" (Tunstall 1977, p. 246). The Shah tried to "use television as a weapon to consolidate power, confer prestige, divide the bureaucracy, to project a single national culture—and generally to identify his personality and office with national plans and prestige.... Despite the great concern with cultural elevation there [was] heavy importing of American TV series and films. Imports accounted for about 70 percent of programming in 1972 and 40 percent in 1974" (ibid., p. 247).

One can quite imagine how a movie like *Midnight Cowboy* or *The Boys in the Band* may have caused consternation among devout Shi'ites; in fact, the beginnings of the anti-Shah revolt took the form of burning down a movie theater. What about the half-naked female bodies abounding in American television series? The mullahs' agitations against the Shah for his ruthless rule must have been strengthened in the minds of the masses when they could see the connection between the Shah's modernization and subversion of their religious values. No wonder two remarkable features of the Ayatollah Khomeini's "cultural policies" are the execution of homosexuals and the banning of immodest attire for females with the preferred mode of dress for women being the chador.

American television entertainment programs may also have contributed to a sense of relative deprivation when the higher standard of living with the requisite material goods failed to materialize for the urban and rural poor. This led to frustration, which in turn led to participation in the movement to overthrow the Shah.

According to Daniel Lerner, quoting from Marshall McLuhan's *The Medium Is the Message*, President Sukarno of Indonesia, while visiting Hollywood, accused movie moguls of being "unconscious revolutionaries" because, in nearly all their films, somewhere or other appeared a refrigerator. Indonesian moviegoers were curious about these big white boxes, and when they found out the purpose they served, they wanted one for themselves. Sukarno was reported as saying: "So you see that, in a hot country like mine, a refrigerator is a revolutionary symbol. In two hours any of your films can stimulate desires for more refrigerators than Indonesia can produce in 20 years" (Schramm and Lerner 1976, p. 293). Therein lies the kernel of "the revolution of rising expectation" leading to "the revolution of rising frustration."

Ironically, even programs that tried to incorporate a traditional form of storytelling on Iranian television (Fischer and Melnik 1979) may have strengthened the hands of the anti-Shah mullahs because those programs recited traditional stories that, among other themes, emphasized "manliness, fellow-feeling, support of the deprived, encounter with the oppressor and other moral virtues." Indeed, the Iranian Islamic revolutionaries' slogan of "America, Great Satan" not only refers to the long-standing U.S. government support of the Shah and his Savak but may also refer to the moral degradation pictured in American media.

Real or imagined effects of foreign entertainment programs on a receiving country become a major headache for the political elite of that country. The limited resources of a Third World country are already too strained with the start of a television network or station to program all that is shown on it. Hence the need to import programs from a developed country, most likely the United States. As Robert C. Shayon says: "Students of international television are accustomed to cries of 'sovereignty, integrity, defence' emanating from nations intent on protecting their vulnerable indigenous cultures from the "imperialist' thrusts of American exporters who 'gobble up the international TV market' and dump programs at low prices in nations too weak to resist the cultural invasion" (Gerbner 1977, p. 41). Shayon quotes from two Third World sympathizers, Frantz Fanon and Timothy Green:

> It is to the youth of an underdeveloped country that
> industrialized countries most often offer their
> pastimes. . . . But in underdeveloped countries, young people
> have at their disposition leisure occupations designed for the
> youth of capitalist countries: detective novels,
> penny-in-the-slot machines, sexy photographs, pornographic
> literature, films banned to those under sixteen and above all
> alcohol. . . .

> The realities of television in the Third World can overwhelm
> high hopes even when the latter are not mere rhetoric.
> Timothy Green cites the case of Ghana, which originally
> planned to operate its television system with more than 80
> percent of its own programs, mostly educational. The
> planners were determined not to develop the appetite for
> cowboy pictures. The only trouble was that the money supply
> was not there to sustain them. With less than 15,000 sets in
> the country, the annual license fee of $12 could not provide
> enough revenue. After a while, Ghanaian television began to
> accept advertising and as a corollary, the advertisers
> demanded popular shows. So the floodgates to the west
> opened after all, and today Ghana's television service
> provides only 40 percent of its output. (ibid., p. 51)

One is reminded of Herbert Schiller's (1969) "American media imperialism" thesis here, but it is probably not a case of American business moguls, including ABC and CBS heads, getting together to conspire to dominate the Third World market by purposefully saturating American programs pushing American products. The end result of the predominance of American entertainment forms may simply be the superiority of U.S. communication equipment, especially from the inception of television to the early 1970s, the importation of which necessarily implied importation of programs as well, at least until the media-importing countries attained the status of media self-sufficiency. In short, the dominance of American media output may have been a developmental concomitant of the emergence of the United States as the leading superpower, even in entertainment communication.

TV Malaysia's one-week schedule for May 27 to June 3, 1974, for its Networks I and II, may not be atypical of what is offered to Third

World television viewers. Network I offered the following programs from the United States: "The Magician," "Rin Tin Tin," "Dusty's Trail," "Merrie Melodies," "Wrestling Forum," "Make Room for Daddy," "The Partridge Family," "Here's Lucy," "Bonanza," "The Brady Bunch," "The Untamed World," "The Virginian." Network II during the same week offered so-called sophisticated programming by airing the following imports: "The Wild, Wild West," "Marcus Welby," "Owen Marshall," "The Bob Newhart Show," "Laramie," "Bewitched," "The Name Game," "Disneyland," "Kreskin," "The Carol Burnett Show," "My Three Sons," "Cannon," "Mannix." "Streets of San Francisco," "Kojak," and "Hawaii 5-O" (Gerbner 1977).

For the ruling elite of any Third World country experiencing challenges to its legitimacy due to its being new in the power game or its failure to deliver the promised good life to its people fast enough, the strain upon the political system created by excessive demands of people exposed to Western (entertainment) media content cannot be ignored. Hence, as soon as a country is reasonably well off by modest successes in industrialization and modernization, its government assumes a more active role in its cultural policies including its entertainment policies.

A case in point is South Korea. For a country steeped in Confucianism, which among other things used to emphasize the harmonious unity of the collectivity, such as the family unit, respect for the aged, a strict segregation of sexes from the age of seven (necessitating the system of arranged marriages), and sacrifice of self for the good of a larger unit in life, the onslaught of alien phenomena such as independence, individualism, and moral laxity evident in American movies and television programs would produce cultural chauvinism. Periodic campaigns to purge the entertainment world of "decadent" foreign influences are to be expected.

For example, back in 1975, after 261 Western songs or music— protest songs such as "We Shall Overcome," folk ballads by Joan Baez, some rock and psychedelic music—were banned, the then President Park was reported to have said in a cabinet meeting that Koreans should be more "selective" and discriminatory in absorbing cultural influences. Park referred to the campaign against youth culture including long hair, marijuana smoking, and the banning of music considered objectionable and said: "Good influences we must retain, but bad ones we must reject, and reject at their very inception" (New York Times, December 5, 1975, p. 10). While political motivations behind such moves cannot be discounted, a sincere desire to preserve one's cultural and moral heritage may also have been present there.

After studying the development of Korean television and the use of foreign TV programs, Hye-Ra Kim (1980) concluded that television in Korea developed along Western lines, relying heavily on programs supplied by American companies at low cost. However,

> from 1971 to 1973, the Korean television which developed as an entertainment [medium], changed to a more informative, educational role as [the] Korean government sponsored a nationalistic political reform movement. In addition, foreign entertainment programs, which contributed to the development of Korean television for a decade, decreased slowly as local programs began to dominate entertainment programs on commercial TV stations, and the government increased restrictions on the importation of foreign entertainment programs. . . . In 1976, when the government provided certain guidelines on TV programming for the Korean TV networks, foreign entertainment programs were [assigned] to the late evening hours and the weekend program schedule. (pp. 69, 70)

In 1980 the Korean government took the ultimate step of control by engineering the merger of one independent network into the government network.

If Schiller's American media imperialism thesis can find a ready-made example anywhere, it is Latin America, which figuratively lives under the shadow of Uncle Sam. Luis Ramiro Beltran of the Division of Information Sciences at the International Research Center in Bogota, Colombia, says that like "many other things in their [Latin Americans'] life, the intoxicating TV images that assail their minds, indeed are, to a large extent, 'made in U.S.A.'" (Fischer and Melnik 1979, p. 194). Dr. Beltran cites some cogent examples and arguments. He quotes a Peruvian, Gorki Tapia, for an analysis of images projected by *Los Picapiedras* ("The Flintstones"):

1. The environment is that of a consumer society plentiful in material well-being and assumedly free of contradictions and conflicts. . . .
2. One central value proposed is selfish individualism coupled with rugged competitiveness. . . .
3. Success and happiness in life consists of being on top of others in terms of material well-being expressed in an ever-growing possession of goods and enjoyment of services. This represents prestige and power.
4. Society rewards those who win this game and punishes the losers.
5. Those who remain losers must accept their lot as a product of "fate," "the will from above," and their own incompe-

tence and inferior endowment. Conformity and resignation should characterize their behavior, not rebelliousness
and aggressiveness. For such is the natural order of
things, and it should not be altered. (ibid., p. 192)

He adds that

on the average, close to one third of one week's television
programming in eighteen cities of Latin America was found
to directly originate in the United States. Latin America
spends close to eighty million dollars per year in importing
TV material from the United States.... As a result of the
control the United States exercises over technology,
materials, technicians, and capital in Latin American
television, most of the television programs produced in Latin
America itself, can hardly be distinguished from United
States programs. (ibid., p. 193)

Print media are another source of readily available entertainment, at least for urban literate citizens. They include newspapers
and "cheap pulp" magazines and novels. Klaus Madings, who analyzed 219 short stories and novels written in Chinese in Hong Kong,
reported that they enjoy high circulation and are published either in
journals, newspapers, or cheap book series.

The reading of such mass circulated literature constitutes an
important cultural activity for the four million people living
in the colony, 98 percent of which are
Chinese.... Entertainment in the form of stories,
photographs and caricatures occupied an average of 20
percent of the total space in the daily newspapers included in
the study.... For readers in Hong Kong, entertainment is an
outstanding quality of such literature. (ibid., p. 181)

The author concludes that "mass-circulated literature can supply us
with an insight into the legitimation processes operating in a dependent society. Such literature avoids presenting its readers with a critique of the political system. At the same time it bears the imprints of
the dependent society within which it is produced in the way it contributes toward upholding status quo" (ibid., p. 188).

Because of the wide disparity among Third World nations, some
observers divide them into rich-poor categories by splitting off a
"Fourth World" of 40 countries with about 900 million people. "The
Fourth World is concentrated in the Indian subcontinent, sub-
Saharan Africa, and in pockets within Latin America" (Schramm and
Lerner 1976, p. 51). Given the low rates of literacy, urbanization,

TABLE 12.1
Mass Media in the Third World

REGIONS	NEWSPAPERS			RADIO BROADCASTING		
		CIRCULATION			RECEIVERS	
	Number	Millions	Per 1,000 inhabitants	TRANSMITTERS	Millions	Per 1,000 inhabitants
WORLD[1]	7,900	408	130	25,510	218	293
Africa[2]	190	6	14	700	28	71
Asia (inc. Japan)[1,2]	2,230	90	64	2,730	108	76
Northern America	1,935	66	281	8,470	424	1,793
Latin America	1,075	23	70	4,270	78	240
Europe[3]	1,660	115	243	5,980	158	334
Oceania	120	7	305	330	6	284
USSR	690	101	396	3,030	116	455
(Arab States)	(115)	(3)	(20)	(250)	(17)	(123)
Industrialized countries	4,620	350	312	18,840	758	676
Developing countries	3,280	58	29	6,670	160	80

| REGIONS | BOOK PRODUCTION NUMBER OF TITLES | | PERCENTAGE DISTRIBUTION | | TELEVISION | | |
	Thousands	Per million inhabitants	Book production	Population	TRANSMITTERS	RECEIVERS Millions	Per 1,000 inhabitants
WORLD[1]	568	182	100	100	24,980	366	117
Africa[2]	11	27	1.9	12.8	200	2.4	6
Asia (inc. Japan)[1]	88	62	15.5	45.3	6,610	35.5	25
Northern America	92	389	16.2	7.6	4,360	131	554
Latin America	29	89	5.1	10.4	450	27	83
Europe[3]	264	558	46.1	15.1	11,250	112	237
Oceania	5	235	0.9	0.7	360	4.6	216
USSR	79	310	13.9	8.2	1,750	53	208
(Arab States)	(5)	(35)	(0.9)	(4.5)	(190)	(3.2)	(23)
Industrialized countries	388	346	68.3	35.8	23,840	327	292
Developing countries	180	90	31.7	64.2	1,140	38	19

SOURCE: UNESCO Statistical Yearbook 1976, pp. 802, 921, 993, 1020. From Anthony Smith, The Geopolitics of Information (New York: Oxford University Press, 1980), pp. 62, 63. Permission granted by the publisher.
[1]Exclud. China, Dem. Peop. Rep. of Korea, Viet-Nam.
[2]Exclud. Arab States.
[3]Exclud. USSR.

electrification and industrialization in Africa, it is not surprising that radio rather than newspapers or television is the dominant mass medium of entertainment. As Table 12.1 indicates, in comparison with most regions of the world or the world as a whole, radio is the only medium that has meaningful distribution among the African people. Even on radio, it is difficult to propagate urgent information via a regular information format, say, on the need for family planning for countries faced with a food shortage coupled with a population explosion, because of strong cultural attitudes and taboos. That is where entertainment modes can come in handy as a vehicle of instruction. For example, a UNESCO project at the University of Lagos commissioned a Nigerian playwright to write *Ayitale* (*The Story of the Fruits* [children] *That Crush the Trunk* [mother]) as "an indisputable, creative and timely family planning communication strategy of our time. In a subtle manner *Ayitale* presents pertinent information on family planning to the rural, Muslim and traditional community of Igbogbo without offending any party" (Opubor 1980, p. iii). Testifying to the effectiveness of such an approach was an aftereffect research study that showed that 85 percent of the sampled villagers witnessed the play with 96 percent of the sampled interviewees saying that the play communicated the intended messages to them.

This cursory look at mass media as entertainment vehicles in the Third World would not be complete without some generalizations. First, the diversity of Third World countries needs to be emphasized. They range from relatively well off countries like Taiwan, Singapore, and South Korea to countries hovering around the "absolute poverty" level sometimes described as the "Fourth World." The degree of development notwithstanding, practically all countries of the Third World have a full range of mass media, at least in form. But among the less developed countries, these mass media, with the exception of radio, are mainly the playthings of the middle- to upper-middle class in urban areas. For rural areas, traditional entertainment forms survive or a transitional state exists, in which both traditional forms and modern mass media intrusions precariously coexist. Table 12.2 sums up entertainment in mass media and their audiences in the Third World.

As Table 12.2. indicates, the principle that "the rich are getting richer and the poor are getting poorer" works even in mass media entertainment in most countries. Most Third World countries rely heavily on imported programs (mainly from Western developed nations, with the United States playing the dominant role) for their television systems (see Figure 12.1). Table 12.3 shows that the United States also dominates in the exportation of feature films to the world.

TABLE 12.2
Entertainment in Mass Media and Their Audiences in
the Third World

	Contents	*Audiences*
Newspapers	Comic strips, color pictures, serialized novels	Upper class, middle class, and literate working class
Magazines	Popular biographies (e.g., of movie stars), photo features of female bodies	Same as above
Movies	All kinds	Urban middle class and up
Radio	Radio dramas, music, comedy hours	Rural poor and up
Television	Made in America entertainment ("Dallas," "Love Boat"), domestic programs	Middle class and up in urban areas
Books	Romances, science fiction, biographies, others	Upper class, middle class, and literate working class

A few developing countries, such as India, Egypt, Mexico, and Hong Kong, also export movies, even though their share of the market is negligible.

As Third World nations move toward more developed status, their reliance on imports decline. The irony here is that the poorer a country is, the more dependent it is on foreign imports for entertainment. The dominance of American programs sometimes brings about a cultural backlash, a recent example being Iran.

There an indigenous information system, Shi'ite Islam, discovered itself intact at the end of a decade or more of vigorous importation of Western culture and on the crest of a wave of oil prosperity. The whole quest for modernization was rejected along with the Shah and the electronic culture, technically advanced though it was, was suddenly seen to

TABLE 12.3

Feature film imports by these countries (in percentages)

Sources of film imports	7 EEC countries	13 Other W. Europe and developed countries	7 East European countries	3 Latin American countries	7 African countries	7 Middle-East countries	10 South Asian countries	Total of 54 countries
USA	45	39	10	61	26	38	38	34·6
Italy	13	12	8	7	28	15	10	13·2
UK	14	13	3	6	10	7	7	8·8
France	12	10	8	7	15	5	3	8·7
West Germany	6	5	1	2	2	1	2	2·8
4 EEC COUNTRIES	44	41	21	22	54	28	23	33·5
Japan	1	1	3	2	1	—	2	1·1
Spain	1	1	1	4	2	—	—	·9
Greece	—	1	—	—	—	2	—	·6
Sweden	1	—	—	—	—	—	—	·4
4 OTHER W. EUROPEAN AND DEVELOPED	3	4	4	7	3	2	2	3·0
USSR	1	2	19	2	2	1	3	3·6
Czechoslovakia	—	—	6	—	—	—	—	·8
East Germany	—	—	7	—	—	—	—	·8
Poland	—	—	6	—	—	—	—	·7
Hungary	—	—	4	—	—	—	—	·5
Romania	—	—	4	—	—	—	—	·5
Yugoslavia	—	—	3	—	—	—	—	·4

	A	B	C	D	E	F	G	%
7 EAST EUROPE	1	2	49	2	2	1	3	7·3
Mexico	1	1	1	2	—	—	—	·5
Egypt	—	—	1	—	3	5	—	1·0
Turkey	—	—	—	—	—	4	—	·6
Iran	—	—	—	—	—	—	2	·4
3 MID-EAST	—	—	1	—	3	9	2	2·0
India	—	—	—	—	9	5	17	4·5
Hong-Kong	—	—	—	—	—	—	7	1·0
2 FAR EAST	—	—	—	—	9	5	24	5·5
ALL OTHERS	6	13	14	6	3	27	8	13·6

SOURCE: Unesco (1975) *World Communications*. From Jeremy Tunstall, *The Media Are American* (New York: Columbia University Press, 1977), pp. 280, 281. Permission granted by *Journal of Communication*, Columbia University Press, and Arnold Constable and Co. Ltd.

NOTE: These figures incorporate the 54 countries for which Unesco's *World Communications* details the origins of feature film imports. In many cases the total number of feature films imports is indicated, but incomplete details are provided for country of origin. This is unlikely to distort figures for the top half of the table but probably does underestimate the weight of exports from the lesser exporters in the bottom half of the table.

The least reliable figures are for imports into the three Latin American nations (Costa Rica, Mexico, Argentina), the seven African nations (Ethiopia, Madagascar, Somalia, Ghana, Ivory Coast, Sudan, Tunisia) and the six Middle-East nations (Bahrein, Cyprus, Israel, Kuwait, Egypt, Iran, Lebanon).

Mexican film exports are certainly underestimated, as are those of Egypt; this occurs mainly because sufficiently detailed data are not available from the smaller central and south American and the smaller Middle-East nations which provide Mexico's and Egypt's strongest film export markets. These discrepancies, however, merely inflate the bottom 'all others' line of the table.

For most importing nations the figures relate to 1972 or 1971, but in some cases to an earlier year—usually 1970.

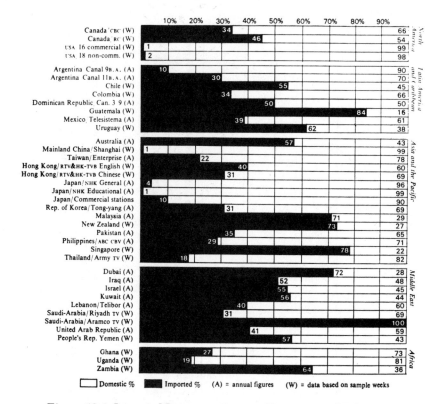

Figure 12.1 Imported Programming as a Percentage of Television Time, 1970–71.
Adapted from Tapio Varis, *Journal of Communication* Vol. 24:1 (Winter 1974). Permission granted by *Journal of Communication* and Arnold Constable and Co. Ltd.

have been an excrescence, an imposition, a conflict-bearing overseas culture which appealed to a particular Westward-leaning elite, but which had not and could not penetrate the entire culture. (Smith 1980, p. 59)

The Americanization of world culture, or possibly only of world youth culture, is evident in the familiar sight of young people in any Third World metropolis, dressed in blue jeans, drinking Coca-Cola, singing the latest "rock" hit. As a Greek philosopher long ago realized, vulgar (in the original sense of the term) entertainment can and does corrupt youth. If "all work and no play makes Jack a dull boy," too much play with little discipline or self-control makes him a dissipated boy. The decline and fall of Western civilization may be all but inevitable.

REFERENCES

Center for Communication Studies (Chinese University of Hong Kong). *Asian Messenger*. Hong Kong: 1981.

Fischer, Heinz-Dietrich, and Stefan Reinhard Melnik, eds. *Entertainment: A Cross-Cultural Examination*. New York: Hastings House, 1979.

Gerbner, George, ed. *Mass Media Policies in Changing Cultures*. New York: Wiley, 1977.

Kim, Hye-Ra. "Development of Korean Television and the Use of Foreign TV Programs." Master's thesis, University of Maryland, 1980.

New York Times, December 28, 1975.

Opubor, Alfred E., ed. *Ayitale (The Story of the Fruits That Crush the Trunk), A Play by Bode Osanyin*. African Family Planning Communication Series No. 6. Lagos: University of Lagos, Department of Mass Communication, 1980.

Schiller, Herbert I. *Mass Communications and American Empire*. New York: Augustus M. Kelley, 1969.

Schramm, Wilbur, and Daniel Lerner, eds. *Communication and Change: The Last Ten Years—and the Next*. Honolulu: University Press of Hawaii, 1976.

Smith, Anthony. *The Geopolitics of Information*. New York: Oxford University Press, 1980.

Tunstall, Jeremy. *The Media Are American*. New York: Columbia University Press, 1977.

UNESCO. *World Communications*. Paris: UNESCO, 1975.

13. MEDIA ENTERTAINMENT IN THE COMMUNIST WORLD

PAUL S. UNDERWOOD

Officially, entertainment is not a primary function of media in the Communist world. Newspapers, magazines, radio and television, and even movies are supposed to be, first and foremost, educational tools devoted to socializing people in accordance with approved doctrine.

Nevertheless, all the media present material that is considered entertainment by their audiences. The amount varies from country to country, as well as from medium to medium. Although both print and broadcast media in all Communist-ruled countries except Yugoslavia follow the Soviet pattern, the entertainment role is more openly acknowledged in the Eastern European states. As a result, media in these countries are, in general, livelier than those in the Soviet Union.

The Yugoslav situation is unique. Unlike media in Soviet bloc states, Yugoslav print and broadcast media are commercial operations that must earn their own way through circulation and advertising. Satisfying audience interest in entertainment is essential to the maintenance of their market positions; hence, the content of

Yugoslav media is much more like that of their Western counterparts.

In the Communist bloc, newspapers are the most didactic media, although even the Soviet press has been devoting increasing space to features on fashions and hobbies, sports coverage, light fiction, satirical articles, and other such material.

Radio is still a major propaganda vehicle, but it too has been moving toward more varied fare, with blocs of time devoted to popular music, utilitarian features, weather information, and news summaries.

Magazines have always been considered less important vehicles of mass persuasion in the Communist scheme of things. As a result, although they are subject to the same censorship and controls as newspapers, magazines have somewhat more leeway to cater to audience interests and have become increasingly popular. Circulation has risen markedly in all the bloc countries in recent years.

Television, like all other media, was developed primarily as a propaganda and agitation tool, but as far as the general public is concerned, it has become a major source of entertainment. One study of Soviet audiences describes television as "the primary source of entertainment," as well as "*the* medium for following sports" (Mickiewicz 1981, p. 44).

Movies have always been looked to for entertainment by the people of Communist-ruled states, although film, too, is subject to ideological taboos. Comedies, musicals, adventure stories (particularly spy thrillers and American cowboy pictures), and historical epics are the most popular films, though they are not necessarily the films that ruling parties encourage.

Another medium that has a special importance, particularly in the Soviet Union, is the book. Russians are voracious readers of almost any form of writing but are particularly fond of poetry and fiction, serious as well as light.

Audience uses of media in the Communist world are similar in many ways to those in the West. Probably the biggest difference is that, on the whole, women spend less time with media—except possibly radio—than their Western sisters do, a situation that probably reflects the fact that most married women hold full-time jobs outside the home, as well as doing the family shopping and caring for the household.

As in the West, the more education a person has, the more likely he or she is to be a consumer of a variety of media. The less educated tend to rely largely, if not entirely, on radio, television, and movies. The better educated are more likely to consider newspapers and magazines as the more thorough and more reliable sources of factual information. In contrast to the United States, television has not yet become the medium most relied on for news. It has been gaining acceptance, but print still holds first place. One reason for this is that news and information about other countries is more apt to appear in print than on the air. Interest in such material, particularly concerning major Western European nations and the United States, is high in most Communist countries, even in the Soviet Union.

Human interest stories; short, humorous, or satirical pieces; and features about people are generally popular items in newspapers, even though such material is given a relatively small share of total space. More such stories are found in the Eastern European than in the Soviet press, if for no other reason than that Eastern European papers tend to be larger than the four to six pages characteristic of even major Soviet dailies.

Stories of this kind in some Eastern European papers—the principal Hungarian dailies, for example—are also more likely to be written in a style Western readers would find familiar. Soviet versions of the human interest story, as well as other features, usually stress the ethical or moral issues involved, thus serving as a kind of lesson on approved behavior. In fact, the Russians, officially at least, consider much Western press treatment of such stories as "sensationalism," a taboo for Soviet periodicals, as *Pravda* made clear some years ago when it declared: "It cannot be considered normal that some newspapers and magazines try to please low tastes, at times chase after cheap sensationalism and loudness and sometimes descend to saccharine sentimentality" (Hopkins 1970, p. 121).

Of course, Soviet editors cannot be completely oblivious to reader preferences. They have to have some concern with circulation. But surveys suggest that other considerations carry much more weight. For example, Mickiewicz (1981) cited a four-month study of *Trud*, the principal Soviet trade union paper, which showed that the most popular topics as far as readers were concerned—humor, entertainment, and leisure time—were given little space compared with that allotted official announcements. In fact, for one whole month during the survey period, the paper printed no articles that fell within the favored categories.

The official party papers in all Communist countries are uniformly serious and heavy, devoting the least possible space to material that could be classified as entertainment. This kind of material is much more likely to be found in the regional or specialized press, journals, and magazines. Some observers have suggested that in the Soviet Union even these periodicals print less entertainment material than they did during the late 1950s and early '60s when then-Premier

Nikita S. Khrushchev let his son-in-law, Alexei Adzhubei, introduce human interest stories and other features into the previously painfully staid pages of *Izvestia*.

On the other hand, the entertainment component of radio has shown a steady increase. Some of these changes are the result, in part, of the need to compete with Western broadcast organizations like the BBC, VOA, and Deutsche Welle for audiences, particularly among young people, who seem to be increasingly looking for diversion. This competition with Western broadcasters is much more difficult for smaller Communist states, which are closer to the West culturally and geographically, and are much more exposed to its influences than is the Soviet Union. Thousands of Eastern Europeans living in border areas can even tune in Western television. In consequence, the shift toward entertainment has been more pronounced there than in the Soviet Union.

In most countries, a casual listener might find it difficult to determine whether a particular radio program was produced in the East or West, unless it included news or commentary, which are always presented in an unambiguously Marxist style by bloc stations. Such a listener would be less likely to be confused as to the origin of Radio Moscow newscasts. Although the amount of time devoted to entertainment has increased, Russian programming is still heavily larded with industrial production reports and other "striving-for-communism" segments. There may be a greater shift on the part of Moscow in the future, however, not only because of complaints at home and competition from abroad but because Soviet radio has been losing audiences to television, the same phenomenon noted in the United States.

Moviegoing also has declined, in step with the development of television, in the Soviet Union and in the other bloc states. People in the East, like those in the West, prefer to stay at home and watch films on TV. Soviet surveys indicate that movies are the most popular category of TV offerings. The decline in moviegoing has also been attributed to the relatively small number of popular films produced at home or imported. In her study, Mickiewicz (1981) noted:

> What has happened in the film industry, as has happened in other of the media, is that the failure of the government to provide for the satisfaction of audience demand has distorted that demand in a way that runs counter to government goals. In this case, there is a huge demand from masses of the people, many of whom have little education, for movies the Soviet movie industry refuses to produce or produces in very small numbers. (p. 81).

Typical TV fare, meanwhile, includes an assortment of educational and entertainment features that are not unlike the programming available in Western Europe. In fact, a number of these features are produced in the West. In East Germany, for example, a government-set quota permits up to one-third of the national TV programming to be imported from the West. Even the Soviet Union has aired some Western programs, although they represent a much smaller share of total offerings.

The bulk of the programming in all bloc countries is domestic, although there is some sharing of offerings among them through the Intervision network, Eastern Europe's answer to Western Europe's Eurovision system. Plays, movies, variety shows, serials, and even game shows are common in the Soviet Union and in the bloc states. One popular Russian game show is called "Papa, Mama and I—the Soviet Family." It has families competing in athletic and other skills for prizes that include refrigerators and other household appliances. Contestants are cheered on by enthusiastic studio audiences. Even in this kind of program, the regime's concern that the media promote what it deems proper social purposes shows through. "Papa, Mama and I" is clearly designed to promote activities involving the whole family.

A 1978 article in the *New York Times* referred to another show as designed to "popularize various professions and encourage initiative and good job performances." The same article described a popular Soviet crime series, which carefully avoids any suggestion of sensationalism, as underscoring "the social origins of 'anti-social' activities" along with "the infallibility and efficiency of the police."

Although the time devoted to most other media has declined since the development of television, magazines have succeeded in more than holding their own throughout the Communist bloc. As a general rule, circulation has risen, particularly for the more popular periodicals. Few of these are what most Americans would consider light reading. Most periodicals are specialized publications written for specific societal or occupational groups—women, children, professional people, teenagers, party members, writers and artists, trade unionists, and the like. One scholar, writing about Soviet periodicals, noted that even the most popular ones are not, like their Western counterparts, "escapist publications." Hollander (1972) added:

> Many of these are published for specific occupation groups and their aim is to increase the reader's concern with his everyday activity rather than divert attention from them.
> This means that the Soviet magazine will probably never come to closely resemble Western magazines in content and style. They, too, are bound by political demands

which seem to inhibit any extensive proliferation of
stimulating and varied materials. (p. 47)

The same can be said about magazines anywhere in the Communist
bloc, although there are some general interest publications even in
the Soviet Union. These include illustrated weeklies and monthlies,
satirical periodicals like Moscow's *Krokodil*, and literary journals
that, because they are sometimes daring and exciting, enjoy wide
readerships. Literary journals publish poetry, fiction, and nonfiction,
mainly about the arts, although some also deal with subjects of general concern. Some of the illustrated magazines also print poetry and
fiction, as well as informative articles, travel essays, fashions, and
news items, complete with photographs and drawings.

The satirical magazines have no real equivalent in the United
States. Their contents include political cartoons—some reprinted
from Western publications—and short satirical essays critical either of
foreign actions seen as inimical to Communist interests or domestic
shortcomings that can be blamed on specific individuals or groups—
never the system. The humor is political and usually heavy-handed,
with a distinct anticapitalist, anti-U.S. flavor.

Although there are obvious and profound differences between the
various Soviet bloc countries—Hungarian humor and music are different from Bulgarian, for example—the kinds of material used in all
countries are oddly similar. The reason, of course, is that in each it is
the party, not the audience, that determines content priorities, and
Communist parties are interested in entertainment only insofar as it
serves as a sugar coating for their indoctrination pills.

While each party knows it cannot ignore the cultural and historical background of its own country, it tends to minimize differences
with others in the bloc—particularly the Soviet Union—to keep in
step. As a result, a Hungarian newspaper may titillate its readers
with a story about a party functionary who deserted his wife for a
younger woman—something no Soviet paper would print—but it
takes care to stay within the Leninist pattern when it comes to important political or economic matters. The Warsaw weekly *Polytika* could
publish comment that clearly riled hard-line party members and
papers representing their point of view. When the military crackdown came late in 1981, however, the paper's editor was a part of the
regime.

These and other instances of differences within Eastern European states point up the fact that for these countries, the Soviet
media model does not fit well. Historically and culturally, the people
of most bloc countries feel closer to the West than to the Soviet Union,
and their media expectations are closer to Western patterns. As a re-

sult, their rulers have had to permit, albeit reluctantly, a greater responsiveness to consumer desires on the part of media than is true in the Soviet Union.

This trend is more apparent in some countries than in others, but in all countries the amount of general information made available through media has increased markedly in recent years. The entertainment quotient also has risen, more or less commensurately, although this has been less apparent in the case of newspapers than in broadcast media.

There are two exceptions among the Eastern European states—Albania and Yugoslavia. They are not members of the Soviet bloc, although at one time both paid allegiance to Moscow. The Yugoslavs were expelled in 1948 and the Albanians jumped ship in the 1960s after Khrushchev's denunciation of Stalin and his efforts to improve relations between Moscow and Belgrade. Since stepping out on their own, the two countries have taken diametrically opposite paths. The Albanian leadership has remained adamantly Stalinist, and except for a brief flirtation with permissiveness in the 1970s, has cemented the media into a rigidly Leninist mold. Entertainment is a small consideration. The Yugoslavs, on the other hand, have developed a system that is different from that of any other Communist-ruled country. Economic self-management of enterprises including media, and administrative decentralization coupled with the opening of frontiers to the West and freedom of movement have promoted media that are more like Western Europe's than like Moscow's, particularly insofar as entertainment is concerned.

Comics and cartoons, gossip about favorite entertainers, and features of all kinds are regular fare for the Yugoslav reader. Magazines run the gamut from very serious, scholarly journals to "girlie" books. Yugoslav television was begun with U.S. equipment and programming advice. By now the content is heavily Yugoslav, but the entertainment quotient has remained high.

Foreign newspapers and magazines, as well as foreign radio services, have unrestricted access to the country. Many Yugoslavs living in border areas can watch foreign television without problems. This kind of competition, plus the fact that Yugoslav media have to operate on a commercial basis, paying their own way, ensures that media will continue to respond to their audiences.

The Yugoslav experience suggests that the interests of media audiences in the Communist-ruled lands of Europe are much the same as those in Western Europe and America, a hypothesis supported by Soviet studies of media audiences and reported by Mickiewicz (1981). The media may be different, but the readers, listeners, and viewers have a lot in common.

In fact, many Soviet findings virtually duplicate those of American audience studies. For example, in addition to rating television as the primary medium for entertainment, they showed the following:

- Older people watch much more television than younger adults do.
- Generally speaking, education has a negative effect on TV viewing; that is, the higher the level of education, the less time a person will spend with TV.
- The more highly educated are more likely to be critical of standard TV fare, desiring more cultural programming, such as opera, serious drama, and ballet. However, the proportion of the total Russian audience for this kind of program apparently is about the same as public broadcasting's share of the total audience in the United States.
- Undoubtedly because of the shortage of alternative entertainment, rural people spend more time with television than do city dwellers.
- Poorer people, both urban and rural, spend more time with television than those in middle and upper-income brackets.
- In the Soviet Union, as in the United States, the better educated are more likely to be newspaper readers. But despite the comparatively small size of Soviet papers—four to six pages an issue—people read only parts of the paper. One-third to one-half is the average. Men are more likely than women to be systematic consumers.

One finding showed a striking variance from the U.S. experience. It concerned audience satisfaction with the paper or papers subscribed to. Forty-one percent of people who canceled their subscriptions to *Izvestia* in one particular year gave dissatisfaction with the content of the paper as the reason for their action. Mickiewicz (1981) compared that figure with results of a U.S. study that showed only 3.4 percent of Americans canceling subscriptions for content dissatisfaction.

The number of subscription cancellations, even considering the enormous circulation figures for central Moscow dailies, is surprisingly large. For example, several million names are taken off or added to *Izvestia*'s subscription lists every year. This turnover apparently represents, at least in part, a reaction to the disregard by editors of reader interests, as indicated in the *Trud* study. It also lends support to reports from many visitors to Moscow who maintain that their Soviet acquaintances—most of whom are educated people—seem to have little use for much of the press (Smith 1976). Party functionaries and ambitious bureaucrats may actually read their copies of *Pravda* carefully to make sure of the latest party line, but other Russians have been heard to say they take the paper primarily because its six pages will wrap more garbage.

A young American who spent several years in Moscow maintains strongly that the only central daily that is truly popular in the Western sense is *Komsomolskaya Pravda*, the principal paper for youth. However, the weekly *Literary Gazette* can cite the ultimate proof of popularity: Its copies sell out so quickly that it is frequently difficult to find one the day after publication.

Except for the statistics on newspaper subscription cancellations, the Soviet findings not only pretty well duplicate American surveys but are nearly identical to results of studies in other Communist bloc countries. In some, audiences look to television for information as well as entertainment to a somewhat greater degree than the Russians do, but the difference is not great. In all, television primarily means entertainment. And in Eastern Europe much of this is Western material—American serials, German rock-and-roll programs, British dramas, and movies from a variety of countries.

All imported material is prechecked for political and cultural suitability and can disappear if the ruling regime so decides. How quickly this can happen was made clear in 1980 when Romanian party chief Nicolae Ceausescu canceled the showing of all American and British serials, despite the fact that 90 percent of the nation's TV set owners reported watching them. Writing later in the Bucharest literary journal *Flacara*, a Romanian journalist recalled the Saturdays when "we used to put all other activities aside because they had become unimportant and looked forward to our serial. Colombo, The Sheriff in New York, Mannix, The Fugitive have paraded in front of us, with more or less talent. But now? Please give us our serials back" (Radio Free Europe 1980).

Even more than television, movies are almost universally regarded as entertainment as far as the public is concerned. Nevertheless, wide differences exist when it comes to subject and treatment preferences. Soviet bloc regimes, of course, seek to use films to support their general propaganda efforts. A heavy emphasis on movies based on historical themes, particularly World War II, reflects this desire. For Moscow particularly, the perpetuation of memories of patriotic resistance to invasion is a key ingredient in its indoctrination efforts. Rulers of other Eastern European states favor films that portray past heroics, that emphasize ties to the Soviet Union, or that, in one way or another, promote the idea that socialism is good and capitalism is bad. The East Germans, for instance, have been making spy thrillers that are shown throughout the bloc in which the villains are uniformly Western—usually American—capitalists or military people.

Movies with contemporary themes have become more common in recent years, but these, too, are supposed to consider issues from a "socialist viewpoint" so that they can serve the goal of helping create a social consciousness conducive to the development of communism.

What these regimes want, they usually get because they control the purse strings. Some films that do not exactly fit the desired patterns are made occasionally, and there have been times when moviemakers in one country or another have been able to practice their art more or less freely. Poland in the 1950s and Czechoslovakia in the 1960s are well-known examples. But such periods are brief, coming at times when divisions within the leadership over policy leave moviemakers more or less on their own. Sooner or later, however, unified central control is restored and imaginative filmmaking disappears. The content of the film is once more subject to government administration and party dictates which hold that adherence to doctrine is more important than art.

What the regimes want does not match audience preferences very well. Throughout the Communist bloc, comedies, adventure films, musicals, folk epics, and light entertainment features are favorites among all age groups and in all countries. Movies with current settings tend to be the least popular, apparently because audiences feel they treat everyday life in a superficial way. Movies about historical events, including the "Great Patriotic War," as the Russians call World War II, are popular with older audiences, but the young are far less enthusiastic about them. Among the favorites of youth, on the other hand, are science-fiction films, which rate low with their elders. Western films from serious drama to American cowboy pictures are highly popular. A visitor to Warsaw noticed one evening that a theater, which the night before had appeared all but deserted, had come to life with a vengeance. A line of would-be patrons stretched down the street and around the corner. A glance at the posters advertising the current attraction supplied an explanation: A John Wayne movie had replaced the Soviet film featured the night before.

Russian audiences provide one surprising exception to the general pattern throughout the Soviet bloc: Arab and Indian films are highly popular with the Russians. This is particularly true in rural areas, suggesting it may have something to do with the level of audience sophistication. In commenting on this phenomen, Mickiewicz (1981) cites an observation by a Soviet critic:

A long time ago the genre of melodrama in our cinema was reduced from art to the situation of an "old worthless lady," thanks to the efforts of zealous administrators and vulgar theoreticians. The balance between audience demand and their real satisfaction was destroyed.... The theme of

> everyday family life, which is the most accessible
> melodrama, was "farmed out" to foreign films. (p. 81)

As in the United States, those under thirty are more likely to go to the movies than their elders, and there has been at least a limited effort to respond to the special interests of the young—science-fiction films are an example. But the impact of youth on filmmaking has been minuscule in comparison with their impact on the music scene.

Pop music, which not too many years ago was officially condemned as a manifestation of Western decadence, is taking over. Gone are the days when Moscow youngsters tape the Voice of America or other shortwave broadcasts for the latest hits. The Kremlin's hierarchy of values emphasizes European classical music, to which nineteenth- and twentieth-century Russian composers were notable contributors; but it seems to be pretty much of a lost cause. The first floor of the big Melodia record store on Moscow's Kalinin Prospect, where pop records are sold, is almost always crowded; the classical record section on the second floor seldom has more than a few customers.

Radio stations forgo classical music in favor of pop. Pop concerts are commonplace. In Eastern European states, where the official strictures against pop were never as severe as in the Soviet Union, imported as well as home-grown versions are featured on television. Some of the imports are contracted for directly. Others are relayed through Eurovision and Intervision—the TV programming exchange networks set up by West and East during the cold war. Although originally there was no link between them, recent years have witnessed program exchanges.

The most common network exchanges are in news, but the two networks also link up for other programs, especially sports spectaculars but also major public events, cultural and scientific coverage, variety shows, and even pop concerts. The exchanges are made both via land lines—usually through neutral Austria, which has ties with both systems—and satellites.

All this means that there has been a small adjustment in the doctrine that has determined the shape and content of Soviet media since 1918 and of Eastern European media since the inception of Communist rule in the post–World War II period. With the triumph of the Bolshevik Revolution, Lenin set out to transform the Soviet press "from an organ which primarily reports the political news of the day to an organ earnestly educating the masses, teaching them how to live the new life and work in a new way." This is still the official role of media in all Soviet bloc countries.

Pravda much later spelled out the assignment in greater detail:

> The Soviet press actively assists the party, and fulfills well
> its important role as shock force on the ideological front. It
> struggles for the achievement of the party program and
> during the creation of Communist forms of social
> organization, contributes in all ways to the even deeper and
> stronger confirmation of Communist principles in life, labor
> and relations between people, so that there will be developed
> the skill to utilize wisely the blessing of communism.

This role as a sterile, obedient servant of the party, actively influencing and leading "public opinion," does not provide much room for entertainment and largely explains its relative dearth in the Communist media.

Much of what does appear seems to be a result of leadership feelings that some sugar coating is essential to get the public to swallow their indoctrination pills. This is the probable explanation for Khrushchev's encouragement of greater diversity in media during his period of rule, since he never wavered from the view that the press was the party's servant. Some of this diversity has been lost since Khrushchev's ouster and the succession of Leonid Brezhnev. A cautious, gray dullness, reminiscent of earlier times, has crept back into media. In fact, it got so bad at one point that Brezhnev himself felt obliged to call for more interesting treatment.

Nevertheless, the system does not offend the Russians to the same degree that it does thousands of Eastern Europeans. The Russians have never known an uncensored, uncontrolled press. Private communication channels, the political joke, *samizdat* publishing of officially disapproved writing, and the like are nothing new. There are some different twists—a number of Russian balladeers have become famous in recent years as a result of privately recorded and circulated tapes of political protest songs. The technique is new, but the underlying purpose is the same.

The people of Eastern Europe also have not had that much experience in the past with a free press. Czechoslovakia was almost the only country in the area to enjoy that privilege during the period between the two world wars. But the Eastern European cultural ties historically have been with Western Europe, and their expectations— for media as well as other things—coincide more closely with those of Western Europeans than they do with those of the Russians. This has meant pressure on Eastern European regimes for media that are less didactic, more informational, and more entertainment oriented. One could hardly describe the media in any of these countries as lively by Western European standards, but generally speaking, they are more entertaining than their Soviet counterparts.

REFERENCES

Hollander, Gayle Durham. *Soviet Political Indoctrination, Developments in Mass Media and Propaganda Since Stalin.* New York: Praeger, 1972.

Hopkins, Mark. *Mass Media in the Soviet Union.* New York: Pegasus, 1970.

Mickiewicz, Ellen Propper. *Media and the Russian Public.* New York: Praeger, 1981.

Radio Free Europe. *Situation Report No. 31.* October 1980.

Smith, Hedrick. *The Russians.* New York: Quadrangle, 1976.

PART 6

MASS MEDIA ECONOMICS

---

14. MEDIA ECONOMICS IN WESTERN EUROPE

MILTON HOLLSTEIN

Every country's mass media are involved not only with the country's history, values, and social organization but also with its economic institutions. The number, content, and quality of media depend on the resources that can be mustered and, especially in broadcasting, on national decisions about how resources should be allocated. Increasingly in Western Europe, as in the United States, media must deliver at bearable cost messages that compete swiftly and efficiently for readers and viewers, for advertising revenue, and with international or multinational systems.

Countries differ widely on how much government intervention or assistance is desirable to provide this support. All nations agree on the importance of media, which may generate as much as 3 percent of the gross national product. They have different approaches to two fundamentals: How much national planning should be done? And must media make a profit to survive? In Communist countries and much of the developing world, government and its organizations own or control all media, which may accept advertising but may not need to be profitable. In many developing nations, the shape of communication is not left to chance but is the result of nationally determined goals and priorities (UNESCO 1978). Small wonder that in less developed countries the press is usually tied to government—there is a direct correlation between freedom and gross national product (Nixon 1960). In an abundant society, American media luxuriate in the philosophy that free expression and public access are best served when government acts only to prevent predatory and restrictive practices from squeezing out competition and diversity. Otherwise, media are presumably subject to free market forces—they succeed when they correctly identify and stimulate the buying decisions of readers and advertisers. Rarely do they endure when they lose money. Media are marketed like any other product.

Europe fits between the American and Communist models. Most countries have socialist regimes or insecure coalition governments that are to the left of American liberal Democrats. Europeans have relied on the reports of literally dozens of parliamentary and crown commissions to legislate on the media. The recommendations have been shaped, however, not only by what these advisers see as the best ways to meet the information needs of the nation but also by the onrush of new technologies and the dramatic reshaping of political and social organizations in the past thirty years.

Even some ambitious proposals for supporting the media have gone ahead despite recession and inflation, although not so rapidly as during the days of the "economic miracle" that regenerated economies laid waste in World War II. The Continent's economic growth outpaced America's for twenty years, bringing a higher standard of living to seven European nations than that enjoyed in the United States, and enormous public outlays for public services. In 1974–75, however, Europe was staggered by a recession that followed the quadrupling of oil prices by the OPEC. Europe's economic problems have been so severe that they affect all issues more deeply than at any time since the Great Depression of the 1930s (*IPI Report*, February 1981). Stagflation has cut heavily into advertising revenue, especially newspaper classified ads, and has sent costs soaring. At the same time, government price commissions have restricted advertising and cover price increases, permitting them only when they could be justified within certain criteria.

Competition for dwindling advertising revenue also is changing because of the appearance of "small scale" electronic media such as cable and low-power TV and small newspapers, handbills, and direct mail advertising, and may imminently be profoundly affected by direct satellite broadcasts, in which all northern European countries have considerable interest. Equally important to how well media reach audiences have been vast changes in consumer life styles—

where and how people choose to live and make use of their time—and population changes, especially the trend toward zero population growth and, in northern Europe, immigration from the impoverished southern European countries.

In such an economic climate, only the fittest presumably survive and prosper. But European socialists see no necessary relationship between economic fitness and excellence. UNESCO (1978), too, has criticized the top-down communication system "decided by certain groups, aimed at mass audiences, and limited to a number of standardized messages, often with a commercial and/or ideological basis [that] treats the people as consumers of materials." This outlook is in tune with the socialist argument that support systems based on advertising are antidemocratic because the "fittest" are those that can deliver an audience to an advertiser (Williams 1962). Throughout the Western world, the death of editorially excellent but unprofitable newspapers is part of an increasing trend toward declining numbers of metropolitan dailies or their consolidation into fewer and fewer hands.

THE PRESS

Ownership

Most American newspapers were owned by tightly held companies dominated by family groups and heirs of the founders. These are being snapped up by newspaper chains (or "groups," as they prefer to be known); 155 groups now own 72 percent of weekday circulation (*Editor & Publisher*, October 1981). Rarely have U.S. papers been owned by great industrial concerns, and not for more than a century have they spoken for political factions. In Europe, some of the press is still dominated by banks and other industrial giants, although, except in Italy, such ownership is less common today than before World War II. Papers also were once owned by political parties, labor unions, and social movements. These groups provided a guaranteed readership and often direct financial support, although the sheer numbers of their papers also fractionated the audience and permitted few papers to flourish.

In the past quarter-century, the press has moved from a political and opinion medium to an information and entertainment function, with the old special interest and propaganda papers increasingly thrown into competition with community papers that seek a wide, secular readership. Relatively few speak outright for political groups, except in Scandinavia, where the party press is still important, though no longer dominant.

These changes have followed profound realignments of social and political groups and the overthrow of old governments. In Germany, and in most of Europe occupied by the Germans in World War II, a new press system has emerged. Some papers sprang from the clandestine resistance papers, others from the transitional press or from old publications "purified" of political affiliations. Some of these papers are now controlled by nonprofit trusts and foundations, grounded in the old special interest groups but no longer directly responsible to or dependent on them.

The European press started in the great capitals and spread much later to the hinterlands. In northern Europe a more vigorous local press, less encumbered by archaic labor problems and machinery or ideological baggage, and, more often than not, as local monopolies facing less intensive direct competition than the national papers, has matured in the provinces, offering comprehensive news and local information and entertainment.

The circulation of dailies in Europe declined slightly in the two decades to 1975, from 252 to 243 per 1,000 people, compared to a slight growth worldwide. The number of titles dropped from 2,000 to 1,660. Weeklies and monthlies, many circulated free like the American "shoppers," have proliferated, sometimes as adjuncts to the dailies. The great Copenhagen daily *Politiken* owns ten free-distribution suburban papers and is associated with a dozen others (Thorndahl 1981).

There were predictions that bankruptcies would shrink the number of dailies much further in the late 1970s because of high costs, especially for newsprint, which on the average nearly doubled in five years, and the need for costly new photoelectronic computer-based printing equipment. These fears have not been realized, but only because of government subsidies, the fact that national newspapers are sustained more than ever as adjuncts to other publishing enterprises, and the growth of chains. Six of the ten companies that control the largely unprofitable British national newspapers have substantial outside interests. The Beaverbrook papers were bought out by Trafalgar House, a conglomerate; Atlantic-Richfield Oil Company stepped in to save the great Sunday newspaper *The Observer*, subsequently selling the majority interest to another publishing group; *The Guardian*, a great liberal daily, is perpetuated under a trust arrangement and supported by its sister paper, *Manchester Evening News*. Some of the group-owned papers contribute substantially to the parent company, of course, as is the case with the *Financial Times*, the *Wall Street Journal* of Britain, though its circulation and revenue were stagnating in 1981 (Rattner 1981). It is part of a diversified publishing and financial services group owned by Pearson Longman, which in turn is owned by S. Pearson and Son, a multinational company.

Although 70 percent of the national circulation in Britain is in the hands of three companies, which also have magazine and provincial newspaper holdings, Britain, like most European governments, has recognized the impracticality of legislating to restrain the growth of chains when it is evident that only chain ownership has saved many papers. The trend to local monopoly in the provinces and chain ownership has been studied by three Royal Commissions on the press, which reported in 1949, 1962, and 1977. These reports have seen the potential danger that concentration of ownership could limit competition, but there is no evidence that chain ownership has limited the accurate presentation of news and free expression. The 1962 report noted several benefits of group ownership that enabled an apparently unprofitable paper to contribute to the parent company and said strength "frequently rests on multiple ownership." The 1977 report said it would be unrealistic "to prevent a sale if the owners of a paper are determined to sell," even though in Britain all such sales must be scrutinized by a Mergers and Monopolies Commission.

The most dramatic case in point is the sale by the Thomson Organization, after the death of Roy Thomson, of the early 200-year-old voice of the British establishment, the *Times*. The paper had been beleaguered by repeated strikes and an eleven-month shutdown and in the end was costing Thomson's vast media, oil, and industrial empire at least $25 million a year. While the paper's sales had increased from 270,000 to 450,000, the extra copies made the paper no more attractive as an advertising medium because the market was less well defined. Rupert Murdoch, the Australian newspaper magnate identified chiefly with two bosomy British papers, the tabloid *Sun* and Sunday *News of the World*, was chosen by Thomson as the only buyer who could absorb all the *Times* properties, including the *Sunday Times* and two supplements. Had a deal not been reached, the *Times* group would have had to pay some $96 million in payoffs to staff members.

In France, some old newspaper dynasties have given way to new. Hachette, once the nation's biggest advertising and distribution firm and the owner of many magazines and newspapers, sold off its unprofitable papers in the 1970s while retaining several magazines. But in 1981 it became part of Groupe Matra, an industrial conglomerate that also owns the Saar-based radio station Europe One (*IPI Report*, February 1981). Robert Hersant, who came to world attention in the 1970s with his acquisition of three Paris newspapers, added to a string of provincial papers and magazines, holds about 15 percent of the nation's newspaper circulation. Much criticized as a monopolist (as well as a wartime collaborator), Hersant faces the probability of antitrust action by the socialist government that came to power in 1981 (*Economist*, May 1981). Hersant insists that his purchases of ailing papers saved them from extinction.

In Germany, the most visible and most criticized publishing group is the aggregation of newspaper, magazine, book publishing, recording, and news service companies headed by Axel Springer. His company owns more than 25 percent of the daily newspaper circulation and about 80 percent of the Sunday, although the latter figure is misleading in its suggestion of monopoly because few German newspapers publish on Sunday. His is also one of four publishing companies that together account for 70 percent of the circulation of consumer magazines in Germany. There were rumors in 1981 that Springer wanted to sell off a quarter of his holdings to a rival company but was running into objections from the West German Cartel Office. Springer was forced to sell five of his most successful magazines in the mid-1960s after a commission found his share of the market above what it considered a danger point, but he has continued to create magazines. Like Hersant, Springer pleads free market economics, saying his publications are criticized for their success and survive because readers choose them. He also argues that larger and fewer production units are typical of contemporary economies and necessitated in the printing field by the trend toward expensive color printing and competition from television.

Joint publishing ventures, for which American newspapers have had to get legislated exemption from antitrust laws, have not been discouraged in Europe. The newspaper agency plan, under which two competing newspapers in the same locality pool mechanical, distribution, and advertising departments to realize economies of scale, have been encouraged by subsidy arrangements providing incentives for such joint arrangements. In Holland, an agency plan has combined an unlikely duo in Amsterdam—*Het Parool*, once a socialist paper, and *De Volkskrant*, once the organ of the radical Catholic labor unions. Any combination in which each paper maintained its own editorial staff and inclination would have been unthinkable before the 1960s. Then the great national dailies began losing readership and began to free themselves from sectarian and party affiliations because of enormous changes in the political and social behavior of the Dutch. The merger was brought about by economic difficulties, which found the number of newspaper ownerships dropping from 60 to only 24 in the late 1960s, spiraling labor costs, heavily disproportionate reliance on ads as opposed to circulation, competition from TV and from other papers aiming for a general rather than ideological readership. The two papers are owned by self-perpetuating nonprofit trusts.

In Norway, more than a third of the dailies are still aligned with the Social Democratic party and by and large are organized as cooperatives in which local party organizations and trade unions own shares. Most of the other papers are limited companies, and a few are owned by individuals. In Denmark, half the papers are now owned by closed foundations (Ejbye-Ernest 1979).

A strong current of "staff democracy" runs through the European press with workers, especially journalists, demanding a greater role in editorial decisions. In Holland, a nationwide charter agreed to by newspaper owners and journalists requires that an editorial council be consulted on important policy decisions and appointment of the editor (*IPI Report*, September 1976). However, staff ownership is still not a common phenomenon. The best example is *Le Monde*, the great Paris leftist daily and one of the few profitable French national papers. In 1951 an organization of insurgent journalists forced *Le Monde* to allot it minority stock ownership (28 percent) including veto power over major decisions. In 1968, the journalists' share was increased to 40 percent, the remainder divided among executives, managers, and other staff. All shareholders are elected by an administrative council, and no chief editor can be chosen without the journalists' approval.

Outright government ownership of papers also has not been a significant feature of Western European systems, except in Spain and Portugal. Under the Spanish dictatorship of Francisco Franco, the National Movement, or Falange, the only permitted political party, owned about 30 of the 109 daily papers, most radio stations, and news agencies. After Franco's death in 1975 and the restoration of the monarchy, the Ministry for Culture took over the papers. Ownership has since been an embarrassment to a government that has reformed itself from within, and throughout the late 1970s there were rumors that these papers would be transferred to a foundation, auctioned off, or closed. Former Premier Adolfo Suarez's Union of the Democratic Center urged that they be kept, hoping to make use of them, and the unions urged that they be kept in order to save 5,000 jobs. The rest of the press argued that the money needed to sustain these largely unprofitable papers would be better spent on subsidizing newsprint for the independent press. The government has sold six papers, but despite an expenditure of $40 million a year and a boom in newspapers competing in a suddenly "turbulent, unmanageable free market" (*IPI Report*, February 1980), the government in the early 1980s still had no effective plan for getting rid of the remainder (*Economist*, April 1978). In Portugal, after a 1974 coup that ousted a forty-six-year dictatorship, the military junta nationalized the banks and reluctantly became the guardian of eight money-losing newspapers in Lisbon and Oporto that the banks had been using as tax writeoffs. Subsequently elected governments, ranging from the left to moderate right, grappled with the problem of closing or restructuring these papers, but it was not until the late 1970s that the government began to stop supporting most of them (Reed 1979).

Subsidies

In the United States the press has insisted that its existence is independent of government, not a right conferred under the First Amendment. The natural extension of this is that government has no obligation to support the press and should not maintain its own press. Americans view government aid for the press as inevitably corrupting and hold that a subsidized press can never enjoy true freedom or wield influence. Almost every authoritarian government has used subsidies to reward papers in tune with it. Subsidies are common in the less developed countries; in sub-Saharan Africa at least 85 percent of media are either owned outright or heavily subsidized by governments.

Nevertheless, even those governments most chary of interfering in the free market spread of information have provided some incentives as *general* and *indirect* subsidies. These are in the form of reduced distribution costs, usually through favorable postal rates, favorable telecommunication rates, and tax concessions. In Europe, most countries grant exemption or reduction in the Value Added Tax on sales of copies. In the United States, second-class and favorable third-class bulk mailing rates have greatly benefited some papers; and in Canada, the indigenous magazine industry has been favored by a tax policy discriminating against foreign magazines.

In the past twenty years governments have moved boldly into the terrain of *direct* and *selective* subsidies, and every European country either has adopted or has flirted with such subsidy schemes. In some countries, especially Portugal and Spain, publishers have insisted that governments pledged to maintain a free press must support it.

The Nordic countries have plunged most enthusiastically into widespread direct subsidy schemes, especially to support the party press, and most particularly the press of the Social Democratic party. The Swedes argue that since broadcasting is obligated to remain impartial, it is essential that newspapers speak from a political viewpoint to maintain a political dialogue, even if they cannot compete successfully for advertising against dominant papers in their circulation areas.

Sweden built a system of supports for the daily and weekly press based on a decline in the number of competing dailies. By the early 1960s the number of cities with more than a single newspaper had halved—to seventeen—since the early 1950s. Nine of ten newspaper deaths involved the weaker of two competing papers, increasingly the papers owned by the Social Democratic party that had held power for forty-four years until unseated in 1976. The Social Democrats still control about 20 percent of the newspaper circulation. But with the death of Stockholm's *Tidningen* in the 1960s they have only two in metropolitan centers and only one in the capital, Stockholm. On the basis of a royal commission report, parliament in 1964 gave subsidies to ten political parties, some of which elected to distribute money to their papers. When that aid proved inadequate, the government in 1971 approved direct subsidies in the form of production grants distributed to papers with circulation smaller than that of their competitors. The grants were financed in part by a 6 percent tax on the advertising of daily newspapers and a 10 percent tax on weeklies, so dominant papers were indirectly subsidizing their rivals.

In 1976 the subsidies were widened to provide grants for morning newspapers (there are few evening newspapers, and these are sold on the streets) with coverage of less than half the households in the primary circulation area. Other support went for the launching of nondailies; aid for weak papers that otherwise would not qualify for support; payments for participation in joint distribution, printing, and advertising ventures; low cost loans; and government advertising. Altogether the Swedes are paying about $130 million a year for these subsidies.

The Swedish parliament decides on the amounts to be allocated, and the fund is administered by an independent agency, the Swedish Press Subsidies Council. The Swedes argue that safeguards have avoided government interference and all arbitrary judgments. And despite a few dissenting voices, even publishers who support the more "bourgeois" parties accept the subsidy plan on the grounds it has prevented monopolies that might have brought more obnoxious government action. The Swedes also insist that the subsidies have had their intended effect of stemming the high mortality rate of papers; the Press Council says that half the subsidized papers would have disappeared in the difficult 1970s without aid. No newspapers have died since 1973 (Hollstein 1978d). They also insist that subsidy money has helped papers improve.

In Finland, subsidies are granted through a parliamentary commission, according to the proportion of representatives in parliament of each paper's party. Some publishers believe it inevitable that there will be more losses in titles, down to 92 from 110 in 1965, but that subsidies have slowed the trend. Most conservative papers are not owned by a party, and most party papers are heavily dependent on subsidies. In Norway, subsidies also go to "second position" papers in each market; and a loan fund, government advertising, and other supports bring the total government contribution to nearly one-fifth of all newspaper income. But Denmark has no subsidy schemes, although they have been debated for years. The Newspaper Publishers Association, which represents the larger papers, is flatly against supports. The closest thing to a subsidy is the payment, totaling less than $1 million, to papers that print the results of the national lottery.

In France, the government provides by decree exceptional aid to newspapers with a daily press run of fewer than 200,000 copies that derive less than 30 percent of their total income from advertising. Other aid includes reduced postal and telephone rates, exemption from certain business and license taxes, and a 30 percent personal income tax deduction for all holders of press cards. Misgivings over even this relatively modest aid have been inevitable because the venal prewar press was for hire by special interests and government agencies. At least one publisher entitled to subsidies refused them (Hollstein 1978b). In Italy, a 1981 subsidy scheme is tied to a requirement that no publishing house control more than 20 percent of the total number of papers. The subsidy plan followed the bankruptcy of a 133-year-old paper, *La Gazzetta de Popolo* of Tavein, and it was feared that without some government aid, many others would die (*IPI Report*, August 1981).

In both Britain and Germany, publishing groups have argued about possible aid schemes. The chief proposal in Germany was for a press foundation into which all money saved by Value Added Tax (VAT) concessions would be given to papers losing money. One plan provided for publishers to contribute 11 percent of the costs (Hollstein 1978d).

Two of the three British Royal Commissions on the press considered subsidies, the third making a deep inquiry into European plans. It rejected "once and for all" subsidies, but urged government loans where papers could not qualify for commercial loans. The 1962 Royal Commission rejected subsidies out of hand because "if subsidies were available to all newspapers it would leave their respective positions unchanged; if it were discriminatory it would involve dangers of government interference."

Despite the apparent success of Scandinavian subsidies, large questions remain: Will readers tolerate a subsidized press indefinitely? Will governments continue to carry the costs as they struggle with revenue gaps and staggering welfare costs? Will subsidies keep marginal papers afloat in the long run when competing newspapers deliver saturation readership to advertisers? Will subsidies enable the press to meet the competition of newer electronic media? Do subsidies merely penalize papers that have succeeded in the marketplace because they have met reader needs and satisfactions? And, most profoundly, are subsidies pointing the way to the day when the taxpayer rather than the advertiser will be expected to shoulder the burden of media services?

Labor Problems

Newspaper unions throughout Europe have been among the best paid, most organized, and most left-inclined in the world. Overmanning has been common throughout the Continent because strict labor laws make it difficult to trim staffs—it is unpopular at best to fire workers in any socialist nation. This is particularly true in the blue-collar craft unions, but editorial shops often carry considerable staff deadwood. "We have 206 editorial employees but a quarter of them do nothing," says Milan's *Corriere della Sera* (Fleming 1971).

The cost squeeze on publishers has been accentuated by the militancy of the unions. The issue is not simply wages. All unions are eager to limit the influence of employers and enhance their own power. Craft unions have been reluctant to permit new electronic production equipment that would cost jobs or to yield their entrenched control over production facilities. Management–union strife became especially acute in the early 1970s, coincidental with the availability of computer typesetting technology, which allows any skilled typist to set type. In much of Europe printing plants are archaic. Despite some recent gains in Britain, a newspaper using conventional methods in Fleet Street today would be, as a British lord put it in a debate on the press in 1980, "as recognizable to a journalist in an era pre-dating the telephone, although the truth is that the new technology is a fact of life as real as the spinning jenny" (*UK Press Gazette*, May 1981).

Workers' councils that are required by law, and giving rank-and-file workers a voice in management (Bernstein 1978), have helped smooth the transition to new printing in Scandinavia and the Netherlands, but elsewhere have been largely adjudged failures in bringing about management–labor solidarity (Jacobs 1973). Throughout Europe, publishers have had trouble getting agreement from three groups of workers affected by the new composition methods—clerical workers, journalists, and graphic workers. One authority comments that "a sensible approach has failed all the way around," with journalists sometimes negotiating with the composing room about who is allowed to use what electronic devices, and employers having to negotiate with each group separately (Schlottz-Christensen 1978).

In England, union woes can be traced back to the turn of the century when, as one union leader expressed it, papers deliberately countenanced overstaffing and other union practices to put their rivals out of business and stop others from starting (Taylor 1978). The current difficulties in most of Europe go back to the expansive 1950s when most papers were getting fat on advertising and were willing to concede to demand after demand from unions for overmanning and featherbedding practices. Management came to rue these practices when circulation and advertising began to lag and costs went rocketing.

The result has been a pattern of losses, strikes, and sometimes suspensions of publication. Few labor disputes have been solved to the satisfaction of either side and then often only after government intervention. The most spectacular strike was at *Le Parisien Libéré*, which had grown from a Resistance paper in the early 1940s into a large, popular paper whose various editions serve the Ile de France region. Management locked horns with the Communist-led Sindicat de Livre in November 1974 when the company asked for changes to permit electronic typesetting. Faced with the loss of four hundred jobs, the union struck in May 1975. The strike turned ugly, with strikers occupying the paper's two Paris plants, demonstrating and sabotaging distribution. After twenty-nine months, the strike was settled when the government agreed to pay about $2 million to a printers' retirement fund.

In West Germany, fifteen months of negotiation between publishers and the graphic union only led to a strike in February and March 1978, against papers carefully selected by the union. The publishers responded by locking out workers at 326 of 350 papers, until the federal government stepped in as mediator and drafted a compromise agreement on manning of the computer typesetting.

The bitterest newspaper strike in Denmark in thirty years shut down the great Copenhagen daily *Berlingske Tidende* and two other papers in 1977. Again the problem was overmanning, featherbedding agreements allowed during a period when classified advertising swelled. In the lean 1970s the paper tried to reduce its technical staff by half and to trim benefits by 10 percent. Another strike, from the end of March to mid-June 1980, shut down 35 of the 45 Danish dailies over the issue of whether typographer wages should be regulated by a special price index (Thorndahl 1979).

But it is the British press that is having the greatest difficulty with craft unions in modernizing plants. (Both the British national and provincial press have been beset by unrest in the 25,000-member National Union of Journalists in recent years over the issue of the closed shop.) The four British production units control the labor market at the papers—hiring, firing, and distributing benefits. The unions have more data on cost-benefit analyses, number of man-hours expended and required, and other data than management does, and have exploited that knowledge to the fullest (Cleverly 1976). The unions in each shop have been divided into as many as 54 "chapels," each telling men what to do and when to do it, instead of leaving it to the nominal supervisors (Jenkins 1979). A truly complicated system of payments has been allowed to grow for late and early shifts, extra pages, extra work, work surrendered to another chapel, and the like, so that only a third of the money paid in wages has been covered by a man actually working on a job. Featherbedding has included the hiring of ghost crews for additional or unneeded jobs, with pay shared by the regular production crew; "blows," or workbreaks, in which a worker is entitled to one hour for every three worked regardless at what point in the production process the break occurs; "fiddles" paid to any compositor spotting an error in proof, although one was required to correct it; and "fat," payment for putting together an ad that was in fact delivered ready-to-print (Cleverly 1976).

The Royal Commission Report of 1977 noted that newspaper workers' wages were not out of line with the rest of Britain's labor force, but did not take into account the methods unions have of increasing printers' wages. The commission studied the American transition to the new technology and concluded that the hard line of locking out recalcitrant union members and training strikebreakers would be questionable in the British context.

For years, work stoppages have occurred almost daily in Britain's national press, and millions of copies of papers have been lost each year. When the *Times* shut down, virtually no copy was leaving the plant on time. Union leaders have seen the writing on the wall and have tried to cooperate in recent years in de-manning and other reforms. After the Royal Commission's 1977 report there was some optimism that solutions could be found on a range of problem, but production workers voted down a planned program for action.

The *Times* was shut down after Lord Kenneth Thomson gave the unions notice in May 1979 that he wanted to negotiate agreements the management characterized as "management's right to manage." Although the agreements provided that no workers should be made "redundant" against their wishes and offered generous terms to those leaving voluntarily, most workers refused to sign, and the paper closed on November 30, leaving Thomson with $80 million in overhead and wage obligations for workers who did sign. Rupert Murdoch took over the *Times* early in 1981, announcing that he had reached agreement on staff cuts and the new technology, although he got less than he sought. He failed to win agreement on a pay freeze and a 40 percent staff cut, and in August an interunion squabble on a pay raise halted publication of the *Sunday Times* and three issues of the *Times*. The dispute was settled when the Trades Union Congress general secretary acted as mediator and Murdoch threatened the two papers with permanent closure (Long 1981).

BROADCASTING OWNERSHIP AND SUPPORT

European broadcasting is on the whole far less commercially oriented than U.S. broadcasting. Television in Europe is operated by state-owned or chartered companies, responsive to government though often nominally independent, and controlled by huge bureaucracies. In a few countries, some private radio exists side by side with the government authority, but the intrusion of private television has been permitted only in Italy.

There are many ways to support a broadcasting system. Until the late 1960s, Americans accepted as a fact of life that broadcasting should be totally supported by commercial announcements. Now the noncommercial public broadcasting system, which provides Americans with a form of "duopoly," shows three other means of support: grants, public contributions, and federal subsidy (through the Corporation for Public Broadcasting).

In radio's early days, European parliaments rejected advertising as the way to finance broadcast services, partly to preserve a system's public character and partly to placate the existing print media, for private enterprise always objects when government competes with the private sector. European broadcasting has been mainly supported by license fees paid by owners of radio and television sets, and in some countries by import duties on the sale of receivers as well. Some broadcasting companies also receive money from sales of the programs they originate and from publications such as program guides.

But in response to escalating costs and a slowing of fee revenue, all Western European countries except Belgium, Denmark, Sweden, and Norway have turned, largely in the past fifteen years, to television advertising, and some to radio ads as well. (Even many Communist countries, including China, allow ads on the air.) In France and Britain, advertising-supported government systems compete with strictly noncommercial channels.

Advertising is rigidly controlled. No programs are sponsored. Commercials usually do not infringe on broadcasts and typically are seen in blocks of several minutes at designated early-evening times. They are not aired on Sundays or national holidays in most countries. Ad acceptability is spelled out in regulations and monitored by a government agency. Ads are often sold by an agency separate from the program companies.

In the late 1970s the fragile edifice of government control of both the companies themselves and advertising began to crack under the tremors of cable television, pay TV, satellite transmission, and low-power microwave transmission. These grew by fits and starts but threatened a rush of commercial services that might overwhelm the established noncommercial systems. They also intensified complaints of unfair competition from print publishers, who either wanted protection from the new media or to own a part of them.

Belgium anticipated a parliamentary debate in 1982 over whether TV commercials should be allowed, but the question has become academic. Belgium's two state-owned channels, broadcasting in Flemish and French, are not atypical; no European nation allows more than three channels, many only two, and Norway and Denmark only a single channel. But almost every Belgian home can receive eleven television signals from neighboring countries, either radiated or on community antenna cable systems (Menier 1981).

The fee on set ownership is levied in half the world and in every major Western European country except Spain and Greece (*EBU Review*, May 1980). This fee has been favored to buffer the systems from both direct government and business interference, although the rate is voted by parliaments, and they have used that power as a means of control. In Spain, the fee was abolished in 1966 because collections were low and on the rationale that television "as a vehicle of culture" should be free to all citizens in that aural culture. Advertising from the great department stores also helps support the two channels, which are operated by the Ministry of Information and Culture (Gorostiaga 1977).

In Greece, television is supported by a service charge on electricity bills. All set owners are assessed the fee, even though they may turn exclusively to an ad-supported program or to spillover signals from neighboring countries. Typically, a separate fee is imposed for radio sets and TV sets. In five countries—Finland, Ireland, Norway, Portugal, and the United Kingdom—the radio license fee has been abandoned, usually as uneconomic because of the high cost of collection. Most radio set owners also have television. In most countries, the fee for a color television set is substantially higher than for black and white, ranging up to nearly $100 a year.

The license fee has some inherent drawbacks. Collections are widely erratic, ranging from near noncompliance in Portugal (Hollstein 1978a) to virtually universal payment in Germany. Where a separate authority, such as Posts and Telegraphs, collects the fees, program companies often regard the collection charges as exorbitant. Moreover, fees rarely keep pace with inflation because of the reluctance of parliaments to raise taxes. The escalation of collections year after year, as color sets were being bought, peaked out in the 1970s, when the market was saturated.

The problem of trying to live without commercials has been particularly acute in the British Broadcasting Corporation. The Company was formed in 1926 when the government bought out six commercial companies. The BBC had a monopoly in radio until 1972 and in television until 1954. Fees have been insufficient to offset the eroding effects of inflation and to maintain the BBC's widely admired program quality. As a result, the BBC operated under deficit financing for 14 of the 21 years to 1980 and incurred interest charges that in 1979–80 amounted to $13.2 million. The BBC considered fee increases granted by Parliament "bold" but insufficient, the increase to £46 ($92) a year in 1981 being £4 under the BBC request. The result has been some cutbacks in services. The BBC says its aim is to concentrate on network programming and allow some expansion plans, such as for regional services, to mark time. One major priority is modernization of equipment.

Some Britons believe the BBC cannot continue to rely indefinitely on license fees that fail to rise as fast as the cost of services, and the BBC itself has begun to explore some alternate means of financing, including collaboration with a London pay-TV company to provide a selection of first-run BBC films (*Economist*, November 1981). But the concept is much at variance with the traditional British posture that everyone should pay the same price and receive the same service.

A British parliamentary commission (under Lord Annan) that exhaustively inquired into broadcasting and made recommendations for its future in 1977 explored alternative means of financing the BBC and found the license system "the least unsatisfactory" method yet devised. Among other possibilities, it cited direct taxation for the total service or portions of it (such as educational broadcasts); allocation of a portion of the Value Added Tax on the sale, rental, and servicing of TV and radio receivers; a tax on the sale or rental of broadcasting equipment; sponsorship of programs; and, of course, advertising. It also considered whether the license fee should be indexed to rise automatically with inflation, reinstituting the radio fee, and improving methods of collection (Annan 1977).

The BBC's overseas broadcasting, long the model for objective world services, has been funded by outright government grants, as is typical in Europe. However, these funds were pared by the austerity imposed by the Conservative government in 1981. The extent of the cuts was debated at length in the Commons and ultimately reduced by half; but three foreign-language programs were eliminated (Langdon 1981).

While the BBC maintains its totally noncommercial character even to the point of banning visual advertising in backgrounds (Wareham, 1976), the British have had advertising on television—

though they are careful not to call it commercial television—since 1954 when the Independent Broadcasting Authority (IBA) was created. A 1972 act created Independent Local Radio, ultimately 26 stations with another 44 approved, some of these competing directly with the BBC's 20 local outlets created in 1968.

IBA is a central body appointed by the Home Secretary, who appoints the fifteen regional program companies. IBA supervises programming and transmits the signal. The program companies themselves are financed entirely by advertising; they remit a portion of the proceeds back to IBA to cover its costs. In addition, IBA controls the amount and placement of advertising—on television six minutes an hour averaged over the broadcast day, and nine minutes an hour on radio (Schiller 1980).

An IBA restructuring in 1980 left some critics unsatisfied, one arguing, for example, that it might have produced one large station in each region together with a network of smaller stations that could precisely hone in on local audiences (Marerison 1981). IBA did issue a mandate for broader public participation in ownership of the companies, to give preference to local people and companies and with special consideration to be given to unsuccessful bidders for the franchise (*Economist*, January 1981).

A fourth channel, recommended by Annan, was to start in the fall of 1982, complementary to the existing program companies. Programs were to be provided by independent producers as well as the companies themselves, predominantly the Big Five companies responsible for most of the IBA production.

In Sweden, a monopoly is granted to Sveriges Radio, a joint non-profit stock company owned 60 percent by popular movements, including labor; 20 percent by the press; and 20 percent by business. As in the case of the BBC, the system is financed by receiver fees. The separate radio fee was abolished in 1978. Operating costs for school radio and TV programs are carried by the national budget rather than fees. There is still some agitation in Sweden for limited spot commercials, but no political party supports the idea (Radio and Television 1977).

Norway and Denmark, which are greatly influenced by Sweden, also have rejected advertising; Iceland permits some ads on the grounds that the population is too small to support a system by fees alone. In Finland, about 20 percent of the costs of the monopoly Finnish Broadcasting Company (YLE) are financed by ads. For TV broadcasts, YLE is assisted by Oy Maino-TV Reklama Ab, a joint stock company that broadcasts 880 hours of commercials and programs annually on the three television networks. Mainos TV pays for broadcasting time and technical services (*YLE Radio, 1977–78*).

The Netherlands parliament debated fourteen years before deciding in 1965, after a government crisis, to allow advertising on the air. The first ads were aired on television in 1967 and on radio in 1968. They have since become important to the system's support, with profits tripling in the first decade. The broadcasting "clubs" that receive a share of time on radio and television also share in the receiver fees and in profits from advertising according to their share of broadcast time. Since time allocated is based on number of membership fees, the system has been criticized as drifting to a market orientation, with viewing figures as a goal in themselves rather than to provide access for different viewpoints, the basis on which the structure rests. A block of time—180 minutes a week on the two TV channels and 234 on the three radio frequencies—is sold by the broadcast authority's Advertising Foundation (STER). Ad rates are approved by a board, known as the Advertising Council, appointed by the government, which also monitors ad acceptability (*Advertising on Radio and Television in Holland*).

France presents still another approach—a mixture of fees, government grants, and advertisements supporting three television companies and the separate national radio system. Two of the TV program companies that came into being when the monolithic ORTF was split up in 1974 are supported partly by advertising, which is not to exceed 18 minutes a day. Ads are sold by a government organization that works on commission. The third channel, France-Régions 3, is the public access or "free thinking" station serving the regions and carries no advertising.

All radio broadcasting, except FR 3's regional broadcasts, is centered in Paris under Radio France and also is supported by fees. Fees are set by parliament during the vote on the national budget and distributed to the program companies on a formula after evaluation of how well they have met their obligations under the broadcast regulations, of the "quality" and "cultural value" of the programs, and on total listenership judged by government listener surveys (*Cahiers des Charges*). Three support societies that transmit programs and provide production and auxiliary services are supported by fees or assessment against the program companies. Revenue from advertising is limited to a third of the total allocated from listener fees, but about half the budgets of the two channels that accept advertising comes from commercials—altogether about $500 million a year (Hollstein 1978c).

Germany has two broadcasting systems: the ARD, a network of the nine independent state broadcasting systems, and ZDF, the second channel, which broadcasts nationwide (Williams 1976). Two of the state systems, NDR in Hamburg and WDR in Cologne, carry no radio commercials. TV advertising on both ARD and ZDF is limited to

20 minutes a day in blocks of 5 to 7 minutes each between 6 and 8 p.m. and never on Sunday. Some of the state companies depend greatly on ad income, but in none is the advertising revenue more than half the budget. In the largest state system, WDR, advertising accounts for only about 12.5 percent at ZDF, about 40.0 percent. Because it offers the only nationwide electronic advertising, ZDF's time is fully booked years ahead and can command a substantially higher rate than any of the state companies.

Broadcast ads in Britain and Holland were allowed at least in part because of competition from pirate radio stations that broadcast in the 1960s from ships or abandoned drilling rigs off the coasts. The last of them had to be silenced by Dutch police and marines, who raided a rig. But pirate stations still bedevil broadcasting monopolies in several countries, notably Italy, Holland, and France.

Nowhere have demands for private commercial broadcasting been met in such a bizarre way as in Italy. Until 1976, broadcasting there was a monopoly guaranteed to RAI, a joint stock company. Radio stations carried no ads, and advertising on TV was limited to 12.5 minutes a day. In 1976 the Italian Constitutional Court ruled that UHF and cable offered a way for private ownership of local stations while upholding the RAI monopoly as a national carrier (Santoro 1977). The result has been an enormous mushrooming of stations, more than 400 in television and 3,000 in radio, supported by advertising and aiming for large viewership through programming of old movies, quizzes, horoscopes, sports events, and pornography (Cleverly 1976). One poll found that most stations were middle-of-the-road in political inclination, with only 5 percent Communist and another 5 percent on the far right; 11 percent had no ideology except to make a profit (Schiller 1980). The court laid down some guidelines, including a suggestion that the RAI advertising limitations apply to the upstart stations (Reed 1979), but by late 1981 the parliament was still struggling with the regulation problem.

Before the 1980 national elections in France, at least 180 pirate radio stations went on the air in anticipation of a socialist victory that would lead to a revision of the broadcasting monopoly (*Economist*, 1981), which has always been an object of complaint from the left. François Mitterand, who swept to the presidency in those elections, operated one of those stations and himself briefly faced the threat of prosecution. His government has recognized the right of the new stations to broadcast but has banned advertising on them, an action that made it appear not many will survive (Levy 1981).

In Holland, nearly a hundred television pirates are broadcasting on the cable system. The companies beam a signal to a company's antenna on the roof of an Amsterdam hotel after the station goes off the air. Threats, confiscations of equipment, and fines have not silenced the pirates because small shopkeepers have welcomed the opportunity to advertise on the stations at modest cost (*Economist*, 1981).

Television advertising undoubtedly has had some adverse effect on newspapers and magazines, especially in countries like Ireland and Italy, which have never had a strong newspaper press. In Ireland, broadcast advertising has been allowed since 1926 because the economy has been unable to support a system entirely financed by license fees. By 1976 television was attracting more than 40 percent of all ads, and in 1978 a second TV service accepting ads went on the air (Ashdown 1981).

The introduction of commercials on the air has often meant some concessions to publishers. The Dutch allocated 40 percent of TV ad profits to the Dutch daily press to compensate it for the presumed loss of advertising the first five years. Since then, the daily press has received a flat sum yearly out of STER profits. In Germany, publishers have pushed for many years for a commercial system in which they would have an ownership stake. In 1958 several participated with other industrialists in founding a company—Free Television. They actually obtained federal loan guarantees before the government broke off an alliance with the company in favor of a federal-state TV company, which ultimately became ZDF. TV inroads seem not to have a great impact on print media, however. Germany still has a strong periodical press, dominated by the great illustrated magazines, and newspaper circulation has remained at a constant 21 million copies a day for the past decade, despite the printers' strike and the recession. Nevertheless, German associations of newspaper and magazine publishers have agreed to join a new company being formed to start transmitting programs by satellite (Lux-Sat) in 1985. They have agreed that the program for Germany will limit ads to 20 minutes a day (*IPI Report* 1980).

Radio-Television Luxembourg is an aggressive commercial company that broadcasts five radio programs in five languages and two TV programs from ten transmitters in the grand duchy. The radio service covers the whole of Germany. RTL's influence is strongest in Belgium and France (it is owned by investors from those countries), and its French program is on the air 22 hours a day.

Some experts think satellite transmission will pose extraordinary difficulties. It will be expensive, so as to require a mass market, and Europe is still far from homogeneous or unilingual (Bell 1981). And so far, interest in foreign programs has been low in many countries. Holland's NOS insists that research done there shows nearly half the Dutch can receive one or more foreign stations but fewer than 10 percent watch (Kooyman 1981).

Publishers are losing the battle everywhere in Europe for a share of Teletext, a system originated by the BBC that allows "pages" of information to be called up on the TV screen by a press of the keypad. Teletext systems are in various stages of development in at least eighteen countries and are becoming important in Britain and France.

On-air advertising seems to promise the best of all worlds—steady income plus freedom from government appropriations and control. Nevertheless, it already has led to numerous complaints that broadcasting on the U.S. model leads to a furious quest for viewer numbers and a debasement of programs to reach the lowest intellectual demand. Critics have long deplored American television and the exportation of its programs to Europe. They see commercial broadcasting as the preparation of the viewer for the consumption of largely American products. They also argue that it introduces millions to an unreal and frivolous standard of living that urges people to buy goods of secondary importance or encourages excessive installment buying.

Tightened budgets have not necessarily led to more importation of American series in most countries, largely because the government-sponsored systems aim to protect national cultural values and are obligated to air a fixed percentage of nationally originated programs. In France, it is said that presidents of program companies dream of releasing plenty of American imports because they cost so little—the dubbing costs alone—but 60 percent of the programs must be French. In Germany, tight budgets have led to more and more discussion programs, which are relatively cheap. But the trend toward cheap foreign programs—about one-fifth are imported—is down simply because they are becoming less and less palatable to the German viewer. ZDF mounts some co-productions with England, Switzerland, France, Italy, and Sweden because European countries cannot produce many big and expensive shows alone any longer, though Annan (1977) looked with distaste at co-productions as a means for additional BBC revenue and urged that they be regarded only as a supplement "which may come the way of programs that merit it."

REFERENCES

Advertising on Radio and Television in Holland. Hilversum: Netherlands Broadcasting Foundation, (n.d.).

Annan, Lord. *Report of the Committee on the Future of Broadcasting.* Cmnd. 6753. London: Her Majesty's Stationery Office, 1977.

"Arms Group Swallows French Press Group." *IPI Report,* February 1981, p. 4.

Ashdown, Paul G. "Ireland's Troubled Press." *Nieman Reports* 35, no. 4 (Winter 1981): 25.

BBC Annual Report and Handbook 1981. London: British Broadcasting Corp., 1981.

"BBC's Brave New World." *Economist*, November 7, 1981, p. 18.

Bell, David. "Out of Thin Air." *Europe*, December 1981, p. 28.

Bernstein, Harry. "British Unions Seek Instant Industrial Democracy. *Los Angeles Times*, March 19, 1978, sec. 6, p. 6.

"British Publisher Defeats Closed Shop Attempt." *Editor and Publisher*, March 18, 1978, p. 15.

Cahiers des Charges. Paris: Sociétés Nationales de Télévision et de Radiodiffusion, Secretary of State, n.d.

Cleverly, Graham. *The Fleet Street Disaster: British National Newspapers as a Case Study in Mismanagement.* London: Constable, 1976.

Ejbye-Ernest, Arne. *Fact Sheet: Denmark, Mass Communications, the Press.* Copenhagen: Ministry of Foreign Affairs, Press and Cultural Relations Department, 1979.

"Europe's Economic Malaise: Widening the Split With the U.S." *Business Week*, December 7, 1981, p. 74.

Fleming, Louis D. "Newsstands in Italy: Colorful Bottlenecks." *Los Angeles Times*, December 27, 1971, p. 1.

"Free (Socialist) News." *Economist*, October 10, 1981, p. 6.

"Germany Prepares for Satellite TV War." *IPI Report*, May 1980, p. 1.

Gorostiaga, Eduardo. "Twenty Years of Television in Spain." *EBU Review*, January 1977, p. 17.

Hardastle, Sally. "Revolution at the Mirror." *Listener*, January 26, 1978, p. 98.

Hollstein, Milton. "Joint Operation Bolsters Two Dailies in Amsterdam." *Editor and Publisher*, September 29, 1973, p. 70.

———. "Portugal's Press at a Crossroads." *Nieman Reports*, Summer/Autumn 1977, p. 55.

———. "Apricot Colored Success." *Grassroots Editor*, Spring 1978a, p. 7.

———. "The Changing Press of Paris." *Journalism Quarterly* 55 (Autumn 1978b): 438–44.

———. "French Broadcasting After the Split." *Public Telecommunications Review*, January/February 1978c, p. 14.

———. "Government and the Press: The Question of Subsidies." *Journal of Communication* 28, no. 4 (Autumn 1978d).

———. "Portuguese TV: Weathering the Storm." *Public Telecommunications Review*, January/February 1978e, p. 38.

"Italy Unveils Press Plans." *IPI Report*, August 1981, p. 1.

Jacobs, Eric. *European Trade Unionism.* New York: Holmes and Meier, 1973.

Jenkins, Simon. "Why the *Times* and *Sunday Times* Vanished." *Encounter*, August 1979, p. 59.

Kooyman, A. "The New Television Culture." *EBU Review*, January 1981, p. 31.

Langdon, Julia. "Threat of Revolt of Reprieves BBC Services." *Guardian*, October 17, 1981, p. 1.

"Last Hurrah for Regional Television." *Economist*, January 3, 1981, p. 13.

"Late Night Pirate Show." *Economist*, October 11, 1981, p. 52.

Levy, Beata. "Mitterand Moves to License the Pirates." *IPI Report*, July 1981, p. 6.

Livre Blanc: La Bataille de la Liberté 1974–76. Paris: Le Parisien Libéré, 1976.

Long, Gerald. "The Times Dispute, Not Just Another Fleet Street Squabble." *IPI Report*, October 1981, p. 5.

"Lords' Debate Rages Over the Newspaper Industry." *U.K. Press Gazette*, May 4, 1981.

"Many Newspapers in Europe on Verge of Going Bankrupt." *Editor and Publisher*, July 13, 1974, p. 18.

Marerison, Tom. "How ITV Could and Should Have Been Restructured." *Listener*, January 8, 1981, p. 44.

Menier, Andre. Press Officer, Belgian Embassy, Washington, D.C. Interview, December 1981.

Motta, Mario. "The Radio Situation in Italy." *EBU Review*, September 1979, p. 18.

"Morning Circulation Tops P.M. Total for 155 Groups." *Editor and Publisher*, October 3, 1981, p. 12.

Nixon, Raymond. "Factors Relating to Press Freedom." *Journalism Quarterly* 37 (Winter, 1960): 13.

"The Propaganda Habit." *Economist*, April 15, 1978, p. 65.

"Questions Relating to Information." *UNESCO Report Transmitted by the United Nations Secretary-General to the General Assembly.* 33rd Session. Agenda item 77u(a) (October 6, 1978).

"Radio and Television License Fees 1980." *EBU Review*, May 1980, p. 46.

Radio and Television 1978–85, Proposals of the Swedish Broadcasting Commission. Stockholm: Ministry of Education and Cultural Affairs, 1977.

Rattner, Steven. "Bad News at the *Financial Times.*" *New York Times*, November 8, 1981, p. 8F.

Reed, David. "Putting Back the Pieces of the 'Lisbon Jigsaw.'" *IPI Report*, March 1979, p. 6.

Royal Commission on the Press 1947–49, Report. Cmnd. 7700. London: His Majesty's Stationery Office, June 1949.

Royal Commission on the Press 1961–62, Report. Cmnd. 1811. London: Her Majesty's Stationery Office, September 1962.

Royal Commission on the Press, Final Report. Cmnd. 6810. London: Her Majesty's Stationery Office, July 1977.

Santoro, Emanuelle. "Judgment of the Italian Court on the Monopoly of RAI Radiotelevisione Italia." *EBU Review*, January 1977, p. 28.

Schiller, Joachim. "Television, Italian Style." *World Press Review*, February 1980.

Schlottz-Christensen, Alf. "How European Organizations Are Coping with Technology." *Editor and Publisher*, June 3, 1978, p. 46.

Serna, V. De la. "Public Looks in Vain for More News Coverage." *IPI Report*, January/February 1980.

Snijers, Max. "Charter Defines Dutch Editors' Status." *IPI Report*, September 1976, p. 1.

"Springer May Sell Papers to Rival." *IPI Report*, July 1981, p. 3.

Taylor, Robert. *The Fifth Estate, Britain's Labor Unions in the 70s*. London: Routledge and Kegan Paul, 1978.

Television and Radio 1981. London: Independent Broadcasting Authority, November 1980.

Thorndahl, Bent. "No Winners in Denmark's Long Printing War." *IPI Report*, July 1981, p. 7.

———. Copenhagen. Interview, August 6, 1979.

Wareham, Neville. "The BBC and Advertising." *EBU Review*, July 1976, p. 21.

"Who Will Control the Media?" *Economist*, May 23, 1981, p. 48.

Williams, Arthur. *Broadcasting and Democracy in West Germany*. Philadelphia: Temple University Press, 1976.

Williams, Raymond. *Communications*. Middlesex, England: Penguin Books, 1962.

YLE Radio 1977–78. Helsinki: Finnish Broadcasting Co.

15. MEDIA ECONOMICS IN THE THIRD WORLD

FRANCISCO J. VASQUEZ

The study of media economics in the Third World has been a long-standing concern among mass communication scholars. Evidence of this concern is generally found within larger research efforts examining the factors related to press freedom in various countries. Lowenstein (1967), for example, measured press freedom in the world using 23 indicators, of which at least 12 were directly or indirectly related to economic variables of the mass media. Most of the studies concentrating on variables such as "media ownership," "control of newsprint," "taxation of media profits," or "media subsidies" share the underlying assumption that whoever provides the financial support for the media, or has the power to constrain their operations through economic measures, will be likely to dominate that particular media system. This assumption is not challenged here, but a case is made for the examination of structural factors that may provide a broader explanatory framework for the study of this theoretical relationship.

This chapter presents a structural perspective that focuses on the functions and consequences of mass communication in developing societies. These functions and consequences, in turn, are seen as determining various kinds of economic structures of the mass media, including the kind and amount of financial support they receive from the government or private groups, the development of distinct patterns of ownership and control of these media, as well as the nature and characteristics of the institutional frameworks that regulate and oversee media operations.

A REEXAMINATION OF DOMINANT ASSUMPTIONS

The study of the relationship between media economic structures and the extent of press freedom that exists in any given country has been a problematic one. Researchers investigating this relationship often encounter serious difficulties in gathering relevant data. The problem is especially acute in developing countries where the lack of reliable and timely statistical data on media-related variables makes it almost impossible to conduct comparative inquiries that could shed some light on this relationship. As a result, social researchers limit themselves to conducting case studies and isolated investigations, which, although valuable, are likely to generate additional questions and increase the uncertainty about this relationship. Undoubtedly, the limited access to the appropriate body of data has also contributed to a slowdown of theory-construction efforts. In fact, this particular area of research has been severely afflicted by a lack of a theoretical framework that could help organize isolated findings in a more comprehensive way.

What we have learned from previous studies is that there is a multiplicity of factors that could potentially affect the quantity and the quality of media messages disseminated across a social system. But these factors, which are often examined in a linear fashion, have not produced findings that could be generalized to other social systems. This is not to say that the only acceptable propositions are those that are "universal" and fit every social system, but a reasonable level of generality should be expected from a discipline that claims to be "scientific." In particular, what stands out is our inability to (1) reach conceptual agreement on the definition of variables that could have an effect on this relationship; (2) find the appropriate operational definitions for these variables; and (3) isolate with greater precision the effects of a variety of extraneous, interacting variables that generally confound our results. This situation not only has compromised the development of a parsimonious theoretical model but it has blurred the interpretation of findings from various studies, which at times seem to yield contradictory results or reach conclusions that do not fall within the predicted "theoretical" pattern.

For example, few people doubt the proposition that government subsidies are detrimental to freedom of expression. But based on what we know about this particular relationship, we would have to recognize that we are not ready to make such a generalization. For instance, how could a model that starts with that assumption explain the fact that Swedish newspapers are heavily subsidized by the government, yet Sweden can still be categorized among those nations with a relatively free press? This example is chosen intentionally, because the reader may already be thinking that Sweden presents a series of characteristics that make it substantially different from other nations. But what are these differences? One might suggest that these differences are related to the structural characteristics of Sweden or, one might say, to those of all developed nations, which are very distinct from those of developing nations. Does it mean, then, that we have to look at propositions that fit the industrialized world as compared with those that fit the developing world? Unfortunately, using the dichotomy of industrialized versus developing nations will not solve our problems because contradictions are found even among nations that exhibit similar levels of economic development.

Another widely held assumption among students of communication is that government ownership or direct financial support of mass media leads to centralized government control (Lent 1974, Hachten 1975). This notion is based on the belief that economic control of media is indistinguishable from political control, and that there is a one-to-one correspondence between the two. Data compiled by UNESCO (1975) seem to provide support for this view, especially when we examine the situation in developing countries where a high degree of concentration of the mass media in the hands of government or its agencies seems to correlate almost perfectly with the degree of independence these media enjoy. However, this is not necessarily the case in every nation. As some writers have noted, political and economic pressures on mass media do not necessarily run side by side, and may even be considered as conceptually different (Mond 1974). It has been suggested, specifically, that concentration of ownership of media outlets is not identical to centralization of government control of the mass media messages (Kent 1975). An example is Colombia, where control is highly centralized, but the two largest newspapers in the country are in the hands of the leaders of competing political parties. Therefore, regardless of who is in power at any given time, there is always the possibility—theoretically, at least—that a strong voice may remain in the opposition (Merrill, Bryan, and Alisky 1970).

Another source of contradictions stems from the hypothesis that press systems owned and controlled by foreign interests are more likely to be politically independent. This proposition has been advanced in various theoretical papers, but it does not fit the findings reported by Hachten (1971) from a study of the press in Kenya, where in spite of the fact that most of its financial support was coming from outside the country, the local press was extremely controlled, not directly, but local editors were very sensitive to the government's wishes and exercised a great deal of self-control.

A STRUCTURAL VIEW OF MASS COMMUNICATION

The examples discussed above make it clear that the question of why some national press systems are more or less controlled cannot be explained by looking exclusively at financial structures of mass media. It is necessary to examine system-level variables that determine the various functions that these media perform in different social contexts. In this perspective, the factors that prompt national governments to permit or restrict the free flow of ideas, to exercise direct or indirect control on the press, or to provide more or less financial support to some media outlets are seen as *reflections* of the kind of social structures in which these media operate.

The so-called reflection hypothesis is broadly based and has yielded various theoretical interpretations among social scientists. Some theorists contend that the *structure* of mass media reflects the social structure in terms of size, organizational complexity, and degree of differentiation among actor roles (Riley and Riley 1965). Others have proposed that the *content* of mass media reflects the values, goals, ideologies, and aspirations that prevail in society (Tuchman 1974). Both interpretations are similar in the sense that they describe the role of mass media in terms of structural processes that take place in every social system. These interpretations also share the underlying assumption that mass media represent a subsystem that is constantly interacting with other subsystems in society.

Structural processes can be conceptualized as occurring at different levels of analysis (Dobriner 1969). For example, from a macroscopic perspective, the social structure can be seen as shaping the overall organizational characteristics of the mass media system, including the patterns of media ownership. This view is inherent in the work of Siebert, Peterson, and Schramm (1956) when they attempt to describe how different media systems operate in the world. In their formulation of a fourfold typology of "theories of the press," the authors suggest that the structural characteristics of the social system (e.g., kind of political structure) play a determinant role in shaping patterns of control and press performance.

At a lower level of analysis, the social structure can be seen as determining the interaction between mass media and other subsystems. The nature of this interaction not only has important consequences for the way in which information will be used, distributed, and controlled within a social system but it also determines how financial resources for mass media will be allocated. The De Fleur and Ball-Rokeach (1975) "dependency model" of media effects focuses on the interactive nature of different subsystems in society when they propose, specifically, that the basis of media influence lies in the relationship between the larger system, media's role in that system, and the audience relationship to media. The main assumption, similar to what Siebert, Peterson, and Schramm had suggested earlier, is that the societal system, through its normative structure, sets certain limitations on the media system. In both analyses, it is implicit that the social structure affects media's organizational characteristics and modes of operation, creates differential systemic needs for information, and determines the way in which information is valued within a particular social system.

At a still lower level of analysis, the social structure can be seen as having an impact on the performance of groups and actor roles within mass media or a specific media organization. This approach is apparent in Breed's (1955) examination of social control processes in the newsroom and in Matejko's (1970) analysis of newspaper staffs in Poland. Both approaches conceptualize the newspaper as a discrete social system that can be analyzed in its relation to other system components in society.

A structural approach to the study of mass media systems also assumes that societal constraints on mass media may be direct or indirect, and may come from a variety of institutional and noninstitutional sources. The legal system, for example, representing a formalized aspect of the normative structure of a society, defines the rights and obligations of media institutions through the establishment of laws and regulations that may directly affect media operations (e.g., libel, privacy, or obscenity laws; licensing procedures and regulation of broadcasting; provisions guaranteeing or limiting access to information). The economic sector of society also constitutes an important source of control for mass media, but it represents only one aspect of the control mechanisms. Economic control may come from private and governmental groups and is generally regarded as an indirect source of control. Controlling the flow of advertising revenues, fixing tax rates for media profits, or establishing special taxes on newsprint or media technology imports are all manifestations of the degree of importance that any given social system attaches to the communication sector. Whether or not a government or dominant power group in a country decides to exert any or all economic controls on mass media depends on the functions that these media may have in any particular social system.

SOCIAL STRUCTURE AND MEDIA FUNCTIONS

Two aspects of the relationship between social structure and mass media are relevant in this kind of analysis. One is the consideration of system-maintenance functions of media systems. Of particular interest here is the consideration of the mass media system as a vehicle of social control, which is intended to control internal conflict and ensure the equilibrium of the total system. Another aspect relates to the integrative function of mass media, which aims at the achievement of political, ideological, cultural, or religious integration within any particular system. The major premise in this theoretical perspective is that these functions determine the major economic decisions affecting mass media.

System-Maintenance Function

A structural perspective assumes that information control is part of a larger process of social control that exists in every social system. No matter how "democratic" or "authoritarian" a political regime may be, there are always various information control mechanisms intended to ensure the survival of the social system. These mechanisms may not necessarily take the form of direct constraints on the press, but they may be shaped in terms of official policies that have a more indirect effect. In developing countries, however, direct control of the press seems to be more frequent, as the presence of authoritarian regimes also appears to be the norm rather than the exception.

When an authoritarian government engages in information control activities, these are generally intended to silence opposition groups and suppress ideas that could disrupt system equilibrium. Information control may be part of the official policies of a government and may emanate directly from the political structure of the social system. India is a case in point. The Maintenance of Internal Security Act (MISA), which was intended to regulate political activities, has had a profound effect on the press and has become one of the most serious threats to press freedom. But, while the political structure defines explicitly the sanctions associated with violations of MISA, it also establishes a system of rewards for compliance with officialdom. India publishes the largest number of daily newspapers among Asian nations, but financial problems make the existence of smaller papers very difficult. Many cease publication every year, only to be replaced by new ones. Ownership is predominantly private and newspapers are operated by common-ownership groups, which account for more than 60 percent of the total circulation. But the precarious situation of smaller publications makes them extremely vulnerable to economic measures dictated by the government. One of the most serious problems is associated with the shortage of newsprint. Because internal production accounts for only 20 percent of total needs, India must import the rest at the expense of foreign-currency reserves. Thus the government has an official newsprint allocation policy, which in theory is intended to ensure a fair share of this crucial resource. In practice, however, some newspapers—especially those that comply with government regulation—seem to be granted larger imported newsprint quotas and are more frequently exempted from posting import license fees.

The Indian press has also been very sensitive to government pressures exerted through the Directorate of Audio-Visual Publicity (DAVP), an agency that controls the placement of all central and municipal government advertising, which accounts for almost half of all advertising in India. The government has repeatedly used this agency to discipline newspapers that criticize or oppose official policy. Depriving the press of advertising revenue has been traditionally one of the most effective means of enforcing conformity, but this practice became especially prevalent during the period that followed the declaration of a state of emergency in June 1975 (Verghese 1978).

At that time, several newspapers were targeted for government action, including some of the larger and more influential publications. The *Statesman*, published in Calcutta and Delhi, was investigated on charges of misuse of newsprint and later was cut off from all government advertising. The newspaper stood firm to these pressures, but the government counterattacked and tried to gain control of the newspaper by buying out shares owned by various private Indian companies. This attempt was unsuccessful. In the case of another newspaper, the *Indian Express*, the government tried to influence the newspaper's editorial policies through gaining a majority representation on its board of directors. Other tactics included direct threats against the owner and his family, cutting off advertising, instructing banks to deny credits to the *Express*, charging the newspaper with not paying property taxes, and exercising precensorship. In spite of all these pressures, the *Express* held out until the end of the emergency period in 1977 when elections resulted in a victory for the opposition party.

System-maintenance objectives may also be manifested through governmental policies that may appear to give the press relative freedom to operate. Even in the more authoritarian countries there may be times in which some concessions may be given to the press to function with a certain degree of autonomy. In most cases, however, these gestures are token demonstrations of freedom and may be more properly seen as necessary measures for the system to survive external criticism and maintain a minimum of internal stability by projecting an image of tranquility and normality.

An example is Chile, where the military government has banned all publications that were supportive of the government of Salvador Allende, yet they have allowed the publication of *HOY*, a magazine that since its inception in 1977 has been very critical of the current government and has become the most important voice of the opposition. The magazine now enjoys the highest circulation in the country, but it has had its share of financial difficulties. In particular, it has had to endure tough competition from other publications for advertising revenue. Clearly, *HOY*'s share of government advertising has been kept to a minimum, thus the publishers have been forced to seek financial resources from other sectors. Although it has never been confirmed, it has been rumored that the magazine receives considerable support from private foundations operating outside Chile. From a structural perspective, however, the survival of *HOY* probably may not depend so much on its ability to secure continuous funding, but on the military government's perception that allowing its publication may be beneficial to the image they project on international circles.

The system-maintenance function of the press is a feature of all social systems, including those that could be labeled as democratic. One could advance the proposition that all governments have an ultimate interest in maintaining the status quo; what varies is the way in which stability is achieved and maintained. In some cases, system-maintenance objectives may take the form of a series of measures that may be seen as beneficial for the press and its freedom to operate. It was suggested above that government subsidies may not necessarily be a negative influence on the press because they are not always intended to muzzle the press. Returning to the example of Sweden, it can be observed that the Swedish government has had a great interest in alleviating the financial difficulties of some smaller publications. Such government behavior is generally seen as benign, but analysis of these practices generally underscores the importance of system-stability objectives. In the case of Sweden, when subsidies are given to failing newspapers the overall interest of the government is to keep the balance of power among competing political groups, as a means of facilitating the achievement of societal goals. The main objective of the control structure is to limit the power of any one group with respect to media ownership and control. Thus the system ensures the continuation of a pluralistic system, under the assumption that formalized means of communication are necessary to manage internal conflict and maintain the parts of society as an integrated whole.

The Integrative Function of Mass Media

It has frequently been noted that mass media serve an integrative function in society. This assertion is generally associated with systemic views of mass media, which assume that the entities or units that constitute the system interact in a patterned way to maintain and integrate the structure of which they are a part. Interactive processes not only occur between individual members of the social system but also between groups, institutions, communities, or larger systems. This interaction, which is crucial for the survival of the system, is sometimes conceptualized in terms of "systemic linkages" (Loomis 1960), or in terms of "inputs" and "outputs" that flow between various systems or subsystems (Warren 1963). Nevertheless, despite the high degree of interrelatedness that exists between the units of a system, each one of these units still engages in boundary-maintaining activities, which are intended to (1) establish them as separate entities; and (2) develop solidarity mechanisms that will ensure internal cohesion, identification, and loyalty.

Mass media are generally seen as performing a crucial role in the functional and normative integration of social systems (Allen 1977). But while mass communication is regarded as a necessary condition for systemic integration, it represents only one aspect of a larger process that includes other institutional sectors of the system.

The normative integration hypothesis conceives mass media as providing symbols and messages that reinforce social norms and values. Thus, the content of mass media is seen as promoting the cohesion, solidarity, and degree of consensus necessary to sustain an integrated social system. If mass media are to generate and maintain value consensus and promote identification with the larger community or nation, there will be an interest in controlling the kind and amount of messages disseminated by these media.

System-maintenance and integrative functions of mass media are conceptually related in the sense that both functions generate various patterns of information control. But while system-maintenance function involves the control of information structured in the form of news processes, the integrative function includes both information and entertainment aspects of mass communication.

Information control processes intended to achieve or maintain systemic integration are likely to affect the economic structure of mass media in several ways. Of particular importance here is the extent to which this process affects the (1) allocation of financial resources for the production of media content, (2) governmental policies regarding the import of foreign media content, and (3) the guidelines and prescriptions that regulate the introduction and utilization of new media technology.

The use of mass media as a vehicle of systemic integration involves the control of information that flows within the social system as well as the information that enters and exits that particular system.

Systemic integration touches on various aspects of the cultural, ideological, religious, and political realms of the social system; therefore, patterns of control may be present at various entry points of the system. For example, systemic integration may be oriented toward the preservation of the cultural heritage and the reaffirmation of deeply ingrained values within the system. In this case, the control process may include the filtering of the incoming flow of communication from other social systems, which may be seen as leading to cultural invasion and the weakening of the host culture.

This seems to be the underlying assumption when Third World nations voice their complaints about the one-way flow of communication that exists between industrialized and developing nations. The specific claim has been that the influx of foreign communication in the form of news television programs, music, movies, and advertising tends to promote foreign values, attitudes, and life styles. The proposed solutions for this particular situation include the establishment of national and/or regional news agencies, an increase in locally produced television programming and films, and the utilization of advertising messages and formats more suited to the national culture. Undoubtedly, a big problem in implementing these solutions is of an economic nature. For if a country rejects the use of foreign media content and sets limitations on foreign ownership and patronage of its media outlets (Lent 1980), it is questionable that it could readily develop the infrastructure to produce its own content or have the financial resources to run its media system. There are exceptions, of course. Oil-rich nations, especially, have unlimited economic resources to acquire both the hardware and the software necessary for a sophisticated media system; but this has not occurred on the scale that one would imagine. In fact, as discussed later, these nations present distinct structural characteristics that tend to limit the introduction of communications technology and the development of a modern media system.

A general trend that can be observed in developing countries is the overt attempt by national governments to gain control of mass media. This is accomplished through direct government ownership or through the establishment of mixed-ownership systems in which the government shares with private interests the responsibility for media operations.

Government-owned media seem to be the dominant pattern in countries where ideological or political integration are primary concerns. In some nations, mass media are utilized as instruments of the "revolution," to promote "nationalistic ideologies," or to reaffirm national goals. When the role of mass media is defined in these terms, the government not only has justification for owning media but also confers upon itself the power to control messages disseminated by media.

Examples to illustrate this point are abundant in the Third World. When in the 1950s and '60s the outcome of various revolutionary movements in Africa, Asia, and Latin America forced government changes, the new regimes saw clearly that mass media could be instrumental in the process of ideological integration of vast sectors of the population (Lent 1971, Barton 1979, Pierce 1979). The paradox is that while these countries were achieving political independence from the colonizing or dominant powers, press freedom was gradually eroding or disappearing. For example, when Fidel Castro ascended to power in Cuba, control of mass media became a top priority of the revolutionary government. The new administration regarded mass media as a vehicle for the socialization of individuals, the achievement of national consensus, and the acceleration of the process of social change. Thus, the government saw the necessity of assuming control of mass media both in terms of ownership and through the definition of official policies and guidelines which emphasized that the content of media should foster the realization of revolutionary goals (Nichols 1979).

A similar situation occurred in Peru when the Revolutionary Government of Juan Velasco Alvarado came to power in 1968. The new military regime inherited a media system that was largely in private hands, but this system was not seen as suitable for the fulfillment of the new social programs that were about to be launched. In terms of ownership, a large proportion of mass media was in the hands of family monopolies. For example, five families controlled between them 13 of the 19 television stations and 44 of the 222 radio stations in the country (De Sagasti-Perrett 1977). In addition, the larger communication enterprises were dominated by foreign interests through interlocking directorates in banking, industrial, commercial, or agricultural activities. A major concern of the new Peruvian government was the high proportion of foreign content in mass media, which was accompanied by an overload of advertising promoting foreign economic interests. Government actions to correct this situation included the establishment of a state monopoly of newspaper importation and the General Law of Telecommunication, which set strict guidelines for radio and television operations regarding programming and publicity.

In the Peruvian example, the concerns about the role of mass media in promoting national goals and achieving systemic integration were reflected in restrictions against foreign ownership of media and, more important, in the continuous encouragement to produce locally the media content that could mirror the social values and ideologies advocated by the government. But, unlike the experience in Cuba, the effort to change the structure and content of media in Peru was a slow process that lasted more than five years. In this process the government worked within the institutional framework to bring about the desired changes. An example is the General Law of Telecommunication, which evolved from a purely theoretical and abstract set of norms and regulations to the implementation of concrete programs such as the creation of the Associated State Enterprise of Audio Visual Production of Peru (TELECENTRO). This organization was born as a mixed enterprise with private interests, but the government owned 66 percent of the shares. The main objective of TELECENTRO was to increase state control of television programming, which would facilitate the realization of more specific goals, such as having a larger proportion of national programming, increasing the emphasis on education and information in television, and promoting a more nationalistic orientation.

Another measure that had significant impact on mass media was the Law of Promotion of the Cinematographic Industry, which was intended to develop a national film industry that could compete with foreign films. Thus, the government established financial incentives for the production and distribution of films that preserved cultural values and had a national orientation.

Similar patterns of government media control have been observed in other countries, where nonrevolutionary changes in the political structure have required various processes of social adjustment and integration including identification with the new regime and acceptance of programs proposed by the government. This has been especially evident in some Caribbean nations where government control of mass communication channels has been justified on the grounds that mass media should promote and support developmental efforts (Lent 1980). Since the mid-1970s, various governments in the area have stated explicitly that the development process cannot be achieved without the support of mass media.

In Guyana, the government has followed this directive to the letter and has been successful in gaining control of media and establishing a virtual state monopoly. Since 1979, there has been only one newspaper, *The Mirror*, that has remained a privately owned enterprise. Similarly, in Jamaica, the Manley government has defined press freedom as a matter relating to the "social responsibility" of the press, which means that the press must be "socially responsible" in understanding that the national interest and the achievement of national goals are overriding concerns. In Jamaica even the two daily newspapers owned by private interests have not been able to escape completely from the government's influence and control.

The use of mass media for systemic integration can give rise to different patterns of control. In the Middle East, for example, control exists not only in terms of the ownership and content of the media but there are also institutional controls that severely limit the growth and development of media systems. A study by Ruggels, Pyszka, and Hall (1976) in Saudi Arabia has looked specifically at factors that limit the introduction of modern communication technology. Saudi Arabia, like many oil-producing Middle-Eastern nations, presents a series of interesting structural characteristics. It has unlimited financial resources, thus it has surpassed the economic barriers to develop an effective communications network, but the use of these resources in the communication sector is constrained by institutional limitations. The most important one is the predominance of a religious system that has been systematically opposed to the use of mass communication.

The introduction of radio was strongly opposed by religious leaders, and even when radio was eventually accepted as a mass medium in the Arabian Peninsula (because of its ability to disseminate religious information), there were strict regulations of broadcast content. The introduction of television went through the same process, and its acceptance was even more difficult on religious grounds. Most prominent is the Koran's prohibition of the pagan worship of images, which especially affects the visual media. In fact, most of the traditional Moslem literature criticizes the use of the human figure and the portrayal of living creatures in art forms. Television was eventually tolerated in the Islamic world; but most Islamic countries still impose severe restrictions on content that makes any reference to alcohol, promiscuity, gambling, violence, intimacy between the sexes, and non-Islamic religions.

In the Islamic nations, the assimilation of film as a mass medium has varied across nations. While Saudi Arabia does not produce motion pictures and discourages the showing of entertainment films, Lebanon (which, of course, has a large Christian population) has an active film industry with five film studios producing features under the supervision of the National Center for Film and Television. In addition, Lebanon imports foreign films from the United States, the

Soviet Union, and European countries, and cinema attendance per capita is one of the highest among Third World nations.

The use of the film medium as a means of systemic integration has been especially evident in India where film represents perhaps the major medium of communication. Film is regarded as the largest single factor responsible for breaking down the regional and cultural barriers between people of different states (Barnouw and Krishnaswamy 1980). India now produces almost 750 feature films a year in about 15 major Indian languages. The film industry employs more than 200,000 people and works with a budget of $150 million, which produces revenue of more than $500 million.

The Indian film industry is a phenomenon of puzzling complexity. It started under a clearly religious influence. But since religion and social values are inextricably intertwined, the film industry has articulated and catalyzed change and can be regarded as the most powerful modernizing influence in India. However, the hopes for the film medium to become a major force in the process of development seem obscured by the limited reach of this medium. Despite their popularity, films are confined for the most part to urban and semi-urban centers. Most of India's rural people, more than 80 percent of the total population, may have never seen a film in their lives.

Nevertheless, the Indian government has played an important role in film development by providing the financial resources through the National Film Development Corporation. Undoubtedly, the decision to support the film industry is related to the perceived advantages of preserving the cultural heritage and shaping a new generation of Indians with a high regard for tradition. Controls over the Indian film industry exist in the form of direct censorship and in the form of indirect pressures on the selection of topics examined in features and documentaries. The government has produced or sponsored important films on development and on the national heritage of India, but the social problems that afflict vast sectors of the Indian population are seldom portrayed in these films. This, of course, is another manifestation of an effective information control mechanism that exists at the level of the total system.

CONCLUSION

The preceding analysis should call attention to the importance of social structure and media functions in the examination of the relationship between media economic structures and the extent of autonomy that these media may enjoy.

The advantage of a structural perspective lies in the fact that the identification of some key characteristics of social systems could improve predictions about how and to what extent certain media structures are related to specific patterns of information control. The identification of system-maintenance and integrative functions of mass media in any social system should help in the specification of a theoretical model in which structural characteristics may be treated as antecedent variables affecting the allocation of economic resources for mass media and determining patterns of media ownership. The resulting media structures, which are seen as interacting with other structures or institutional sectors in the system, define the way in which information will be used, distributed, and controlled within a particular system.

REFERENCES

Allen, I. L. "Social Integration as an Organizing Principle?" In G. Gerbner, ed., *Mass Media Policies in Changing Cultures*. New York: Wiley, 1977.

Barnouw, E., and S. Krishnaswamy. *Indian Film*. New York: Oxford University Press, 1980.

Barton, F. *The Press of Africa*. New York: Africana Publishing, 1979.

Breed, W. "Social Control in the Newsroom." *Social Forces* 33 (1955): 326–35.

De Fleur, M., and S. Ball-Rokeach. *Theories of Mass Communication*. New York: David McKay Co., 1975.

De Sagasti-Perrett, H. "Mass Media Revolution in Peru." In G. Gerbner, ed., *Mass Media Policies in Changing Cultures*. New York: Wiley, 1977.

Dobriner, W. *Social Structures and Systems: A Sociological Overview*. Pacific Palisades, Calif.: Goodyear Publishing, 1969.

Hachten, W. "Ghana's Press under the NRC: An Authoritarian Model for Africa." *Journalism Quarterly* 52, no. 3 (Autumn 1975): 458–64, 538.

———. *Muffled Drums: The Mass Media in Africa*. Ames: Iowa State University Press, 1971.

Kent, K. "Mass Communication, Information Control and Development: A General System Theory Analysis." Ph. D. dissertation, University of Minnesota, Minneapolis, 1975.

Lent, J. "Mass Media in Laos," *Gazette* 20 (1979): 171–79.

———. "National Development and Mass Media in the Commonwealth Caribbean." Paper presented at the Fifth Annual Meeting of the Caribbean Studies Association, Curacao, May 8, 1980.

———. *The Asian Newspapers Reluctant Revolution*. Ames: Iowa State University Press, 1971.

Loomis, C. *Social Systems: Essays on their Persistence and Change*. Princeton, N.J.: Van Nostrand, 1960.

Lowenstein, Ralph. *World Press Freedom, 1966*. Columbia, Missouri: Freedom of Information Center, Publication no. 181, May 1967.

Matejko, A. "Newspaper Staff as a Social System." In J. Tunstall, ed., *Media Sociology*. Urbana: University of Illinois Press, 1967.

Merrill, J., C. Bryan, and M. Alisky. *The Foreign Press: A Survey of the*

World's Journalism. Baton Rouge: Louisiana State University Press, 1970.

Mond, G. "Press Concentration in Socialist Countries." *Gazette* 21, no. 3 (1974): 145–61.

Nichols, J. S. "Cuba: Right Arm of Revolution." In Robert N. Pierce *Keeping the Flame: Media and Government in Latin America.* New York: Hastings House, 1979.

Riley, John, and Matilda Riley. "Mass Communication and the Social System." In Robert Merton, *Sociology Today.* New York: Harper & Row,

Ruggels, W. L., R. Pyszka, and D. Hall. "Institutional Limits on the Introduction of Communication Technology." In G. Chu, S. Rahim, and D. L. Kincaid, eds., *Institutional Explorations in Communication Technology.* Communication Monographs No. 4. Honolulu, Hawaii: East-West Center, East-West Communication Institute, 1976.

Siebert, F., T. Peterson, and W. Schramm. *Four Theories of the Press.* Urbana: University of Illinois Press, 1956.

Tuchman, G. *The TV Establishment: Programming for Power and Profit.* Englewood Cliffs, N.J.: Prentice-Hall, 1974.

Verghese, George. "Press Censorship under Indira Gandhi." In Philip C. Horton, ed., *The Third World and Press Freedom.* New York: Praeger, 1978.

Warren, R. *The Community in America.* Chicago: Rand McNally, 1978.

16. MEDIA ECONOMICS IN THE COMMUNIST WORLD

MARK HOPKINS

Start with the adage "He who pays the piper calls the tune." A Marxist-Leninist would say that he who owns the means of production decides the manufacture. The avowedly materialistic theme running through both these thoughts describes rather accurately economic arrangements of mass media in the Soviet Union and in East European Communist systems modeled after the Soviet Union.

In brief, a Communist party bureaucracy controls the media content in the Soviet and similar systems because the party operates the levers of economic machinery. Put it another way: Since there is no unregimented economic marketplace in a centrally planned economic society, mass media respond *primarily* to other than the financial forces of advertising revenue, subscription rates, distribution costs, payrolls, and capital expenditures—the litany that describes the familiar world of publishing and broadcasting in, among others, Western societies.

THE SYSTEM

Take the Soviet Union as the archetype. There are variations in East European countries, in the People's Republic of China, in Cuba or Vietnam. But for general discussion, the Soviet system is the key to glimpsing the economic relations between the society at large and mass media in Communist systems.

Virtually everything in the Soviet Union is state owned. Not just the land and factories but, as far as mass media are specifically concerned, the broadcasting transmitters, printing presses, television and radio set factories, and the entire distribution system for newspapers and magazines.

The genesis goes back to the Bolshevik Revolution in November 1917 and the immediate weeks thereafter. The Russian revolutionary Vladimir Lenin, making the Marxist argument, contended that the press served the ruling economic class. It followed logically that Lenin's Bolsheviks moved quickly to acquire physical and financial control of the press after they seized power. In February 1918, for example, the young Bolshevik regime tried to nationalize printing plants (*Dekrety* 1957). Never mind that it took some years before reality matched ambition. Ultimately, the entire means of issuing the press (and most other productive capacity) were taken over by the Bolshevik state.

There is a lineal progression from Lenin's particular Marxist interpretation of the press and the huge Soviet mass media system of today. Since the Soviet Communist party/government bureaucracy in effect owns the means of producing mass media, it is obvious that it has final authority over the printed and broadcast word. The arrangement is so thorough that *only* Soviet state organizations can legally operate printing presses or broadcasting stations. Even duplicating machines and typewriters are supposed to be registered in the Soviet Union.

State ownership of the means of producing mass media is the beginning. Additional political devices in the Soviet Union assure the Communist party's direction of the media. But without the first—the economic arrangement—the second would be more difficult.

THE DAILY OPERATION

The Soviet media establishment keeps two sets of books, as it were. One set would be familiar to an American or West European accountant or a publishing empire. Necessary entries, in rubles and kopecks in the Soviet case, are made for income, costs, disbursements, transfers, and the like. There is, after all, a money economy operating in the Soviet Union, even if the value of the ruble is artificially set and bears no true relation to its worth outside the country. Printers, secretaries, editors, announcers, writers, cameramen, studio technicians, and senior managers are all paid in rubles. *Pravda*, the Soviet Communist party's well-known first-rank newspaper, has a budget of sorts. The local, much smaller Soviet provincial newspaper has a much stricter budget. The State Committee for Radio, Television and Broadcasting must work its plans for expansion into government spending limits. Newspapers in the Soviet Union generally run four to eight pages because newsprint shortages impose constraints, although political leaders may well desire larger newspapers.

This is to say that within the secretive bureaucracies that run the Soviet Union, there are fights over allocations of economic resources. The media get their share, and in a sense, then, a financial system influences the size and shape of mass media. But these running battles for scarce capital are not what decide whether ultimately a particular newspaper will publish or a television station will broadcast—nor, it should be stressed, the content. These decisions are made in the first instance in Soviet political centers, and only then are they relegated to economic planners and accountants.

For domestic accounting purposes, the Soviet mass media operate on the system of *khozraschet* (Hopkins 1970), or economic accountability. They are supposed, then, to be financially self-sufficient, even to make a profit, within the price structure decided on by other state agencies. Since this price structure, from wages to newsprint costs to transmitters, is created outside of the newspaper or periodical management and the television and broadcasting hierarchy, the Soviet mass media system as an institution really has little to do with the functioning of *khozraschet* except to stay within budgets.

We do not know precise annual budgets for *Pravda*, for Moscow Television, or generally for the huge Soviet media network that includes 8,019 daily and weekly newspapers and 5,265 periodicals plus a central television that broadcasts 85 hours of programming daily on a national network and a central radio transmitting 160 hours of programming (*Zhurnalist* 1981, *Rasprostraneniye*, 1981, *Ezhegodnik*). Simple arithmetic—the cost of an issue of *Pravda* multiplied by its reported press run—reveals a theoretical annual *Pravda* income of about $100 million. But that figure is misleading. Not all copies of *Pravda* are sold for cash. The central press distribution agency Soyuzpechat handles subscription copies for the entire Soviet newspaper and periodical press and charges a fee for its services (Hopkins 1970). Even if we did know *Pravda's* net income, we have little idea of its total costs. Soviet journalists are well paid; they receive monthly salaries two or three times higher than an average industrial worker plus income from freelance writing. But we do not know *Pravda's* payroll for the editorial staff, let alone for administrative and production elements. It is known that ultimately *Pravda* and the Communist party press empire not only pay their way but produce a handsome profit.[1] Its income rose, for example, by 46 percent between 1975 and 1980 (*Pravda*, 1981).

The Soviet radio and television broadcasting system receives revenue, indirectly, from fees that listeners and viewers pay for their receivers, the common European arrangement. The state news agency TASS sells its product to both Soviet and foreign subscribers, as does Novosti, the information agency.

At the other end of the scale, small newspapers and local periodicals only recently were prodded along the path of financial self-sufficiency, encouraged to sell local advertising to reduce dependence on state subsidies. *Pravda*, on September 15, published a party Central Committee decree directing editors of *radio* (i.e. district) newspapers to look to advertising revenue as a main source of income, replacing state subsidies. More recently, in an interesting cost-cutting move, Soviet management of periodicals was directed to reduce numbers of issues as a means of saving printing paper. The resultant savings were to be allotted to publications with high consumer demand, such as cultural and children's periodicals, which would show better retail sales (see *Zhurnalist*, September 1981).

New publications, such as local weekly newspapers, are created regularly and announced routinely in *Zhurnalist*, the Soviet periodical dealing with media developments. A study of these listings suggests that new publications come automatically with new factories, or collective farms, or small population centers, somewhat like standard equipment.

The element of financial gain or loss is then an issue within the Soviet media system, but not on the larger scale of Soviet society.

"CALLING THE TUNE"

There is another set of books for the Soviet media establishment. The one just described is figured in rubles, the accounts showing some profits, some losses. Other ledgers deal with what Soviet mass media print, say, and show. This "accounting" of Soviet media is most closely analogous to economic influences on, say, the American television industry. Network television in the United States daily broadcasts hours of programs chiefly created for financial profit. That is, soap operas, game shows, and situation comedies are broadcast mainly to attract huge viewing audiences, thereby drawing revenue of advertisers. In this system the American television media staffs of writers, producers, managers, and the like are ultimately beholden to commercial sponsors.

In the Soviet system the sponsors are political centers, not manufacturing or service industries. Soviet writers, producers, editors, and managers are linked to Soviet offices that decide budgets and allocate resources. In practice, these are the administrative divisions of the Communist party Central Committee and, of course, ultimately, the policy-making party Politburo. Government agencies, first and foremost the Ministry of Finance and Gosplan, the state economic planning organization, are also intricately involved in the budgetary and resource distribution process affecting mass media.

The arrangement is even more complex. Through a historically entrenched Soviet political practice, the chief management and editorial staff in Soviet media are named with the approval of the central party apparatus, according to what is called the *nomenklatura* (Hough and Fainsod 1979). This is a list of positions not only in the Soviet media but in Soviet industrial, academic, government, and military organizations that are filled by the party. This arrangement results in an interlocking management. Indeed, senior mass media management and editorial figures are also members of the Communist party Central Committee, and they are promoted to that prestigious rank purposely to cement a bond (see *Zhurnalist*, April 1981).

In financial or economic terms, this Soviet arrangement at the crassest level means that all Soviet press, radio, and television executives and editors are on the company payroll. Their very salaries are drawn from a system in which they are one and the same with—to return to the American analogy—the product sponsors.

But this is to reduce the relationship to its crudest comparison. It is more refined, for men (and a few women) who succeed in the Soviet mass media establishment are first of all politically in harmony with the system. That this harmony of personal views and state or party policy also brings good salaries and, more important, the things money cannot buy in the Soviet Union, such as foreign travel, access to imported consumer goods, special preference for housing or automobiles—these rewards may motivate some and may be only marginal to others. They are, in any case, not the prime movers for the most successful in the Soviet media machinery—or at least as far as one can assess from the evidence.

Central in this arrangement, however, is the financial dependence of Soviet mass media management on the Communist party, simplistically put. Therefore, Soviet media respond by one accounting system quite readily to economic forces. The analogy (with the American sponsor/programming relationship) recognizes that in a centrally planned economy like that of the Soviets, the government and productive centers are virtually one and the same. Once this convergence is clear, the financial reliance and control of Soviet mass media is equally apparent.

What one ends up with in the Soviet system, then, is something like the corporation house organ in the United States. At the risk of belaboring a point, the economic arrangement of the company publication assures that its content harmonizes with management's aspirations, no less than the publication of any special interest group, whether it be a labor union or religious organization, that financially supports a press or broadcasting operation. For precisely the same reason, the Soviet media reflect and support the policies of the Communist party/government hierarchy.

BEYOND MOSCOW

The Soviet system was impressed on what we now call Eastern Europe during a few years at the end of and immediately after World War II. More than a generation later, individual histories of Poland, Czechoslovakia, Hungary, Romania, Bulgaria, and East Germany are revealed in mass media that also reflect the Soviet organization.

As a general rule, the press, radio, and television in Eastern Europe are financed as they are in the Soviet Union. Major daily newspapers are voices of and beholden to Communist parties. Television and radio networks are intricately linked to political establishments and assured of economic support, not because they will yield money profits, but first for political gain (Paulu 1974). Thus, the state information agency PAP of Poland, or Ceteka of Czechoslovakia, or BTA of Bulgaria dutifully issue what amount to public relations releases because, in the end, that is what their staffs are hired and paid to do.

But traditions and cultures run deep. Polish mass media under Communist party direction differ in tone and style from Hungarian mass media, also under Communist party direction. East German media, competing against television broadcasts from West Berlin, show a different character than does the isolated Bulgarian press.

In free market economies, where mass media survive and flourish only when they satisfy consumers, national traditions and mores mark the press precisely because of economic influences operating on editorial management. To suggest an extreme example, a newspaper written in the style of, say, the German intellectual press would not likely last long in an American setting. In entrepreneurial economies, there is a delicate righting effect of finances on the content of mass media.

Not so in Eastern Europe, although individual publications differ markedly from country to country. Indeed, were marketplace economics to have full sway in Poland, for example, the religious press would be far more prevalent than it is today. It is noteworthy that until martial law was declared in Poland on December 13, 1981, the mass media were undergoing radical change partly because the financing was different. The mass union organization, Solidarity, was subsidizing its own newspapers. Not only was their content different in tone and substance from that of the previous, Communist party dominated trade union press, but the standard Polish mass press was reflecting different points of view as it moved to take advantage of the political moment and compete effectively with the Solidarity media.

The latest Polish attempt at political reform produced an unusual press. The norm in Eastern Europe is the politically subsidized mass media sharing the standard Marxist-Leninist vocabulary in matters of state economic planning, the role of the Communist party, and the onward march of communism, mixed with individual national flavor in matters of manners and morals. But none of this content has predominantly to do with economics. Indeed, the standard criticism of populations in Eastern Europe is that their mass media are dull and untrustworthy. But since media in these countries enjoy a virtual monopoly in the controlled market, there is nowhere else to get information (save for foreign radio broadcasts and occasional foreign press). And the consumer therefore takes what he can find.

THE YUGOSLAV CASE

Yugoslavia has almost all the trappings of the one-party state that exist in neighboring Hungary or Romania; The League of Communists—the Communist party—brooks no serious opposition. The secret police and the army are in the final analysis the guarantors of the League's authority. More than private grumbling about the leadership or Yugoslav foreign policy or internal nationalities' rights is given short shrift.

At the same time, Yugoslavia enjoys open frontiers. Yugoslav citizens are free to travel abroad and return. Tens of thousands of them work in Western Europe. State planning functions alongside an industry under worker management and an economy laced with private agriculture and retail trade.

In these circumstances, the Yugoslav mass media are remarkably different from what one finds in Eastern Europe. Belgrade Television relies not only on monthly taxes on television sets for income but on advertising revenue. This fact presses Belgrade TV program managers to broadcast at least some material that will have broad appeal. Two of Belgrade's leading daily newspapers are tabloids that run heavily toward human interest, sensational news. The circulations of *Vecernje Novosti* and *Politika Ekspres* far exceed the serious, respected *Politika*. Meanwhile, *Borba*, the official newspaper of the League of Communists, survives only with financial subsidy of the party. The press in Zagreb, capital of Yugoslavia's Republic of Croatia, and in Ljubljana, the Slovene Republic capital, reflect the same characteristics as the press in Belgrade.

Yugoslavia is thus a compelling model of a press system functioning in a one-party state and a mixed economy, and clearly exhibiting the influences of both.

SUMMING UP

The history of Soviet mass media, as Bolshevik revolutionaries grafted it to the Russian press and then nurtured it into the communication system of today, suggests that the form of economic ownership of mass media is one important control, but only one. Independent financial support of media does not guarantee their editorial independence. Nor does a single source of economic backing necessarily translate into a mouthpiece press. The press in Nazi Germany remained in private business hands. It was intimidated by political terror. The American Armed Forces Radio and Television network is entirely funded by the Department of Defense, yet it broadcasts an array of opinion, some critical of the military. The Yugoslav mass media are substantially independent in their financing, but they operate within recognized political limits.

When one looks more closely at media systems like that of the Soviets, to find arrangements by which content is shaped and directed, what one finds is the merger of political and economic power in the same hands. It is this that assures the ruling Soviet Politburo that no seriously dissenting voices will gain stature among the mass media. A monopoly of economic power alone in any society most assuredly will also guarantee the same result. But that very monopoly seems possible only when political and economic establishments join forces.

By contrast, in Communist countries where political authority over the economy is not complete, mass media respond to other power factions. The relatively small press of the Catholic church in Poland is one example. The daily tabloids in Yugoslavia are another. In both instances, someone besides the party/government finances the newspapers.

The role of the mass media is sometimes a separate matter from their economic ownership. The privately owned American press may not openly advocate nationalization of production, to prove its autonomy, but it is clearly a consistent critic of American business. The true Marxist-Leninist might dismiss this criticism as so much fine-tuning of the instrument. Yet, the American press on the whole seems more the adversary than the apologist for private enterprise. In the Soviet system, the state-owned press is unmistakably enlisted to help achieve state set goals. This fact, however, seems to go back to Lenin's particular interpretation of the role of a press in a society. It is just as conceivable today in the Soviet Union that mass media could be far less secretive than they are, although remaining under state ownership. One has only to compare the Bulgarian and the Hungarian media to document that in the Communist social model, the content can vary markedly. It depends, it seems, on which leadership is calling the tune.

NOTES

1. *Soyuzpechat* reported a 71 percent greater profit in 1980 than five years earlier. Its trade turnover, on which its fees were based, was nearly 32 percent greater.

REFERENCES

Dekrety sovetskoi vlasti. Moscow: 1957.

Ezhegodnik Bolshoi Sovetskoi Entsiklopedii.

Hopkins, Mark W. *Mass Media in the Soviet Union*. New York: Pegasus, 1970.

Hough, Jerry, and Merle Fainsod. *How the Soviet Union Is Governed*. Cambridge: Harvard University Press, 1979.

Lenin o pechati. Moscow: 1959.

Paulu, Burton. *Radio and Television Broadcasting in Eastern Europe*. Minneapolis: University of Minnesota Press, 1974.

Pravda. September 15, 1968; February 24, 1981.

Rasprostraneniye pechati, no. 4 (April 1981); no. 10 (October 1981).

Zhurnalist, no. 4 (April 1981); no. 5 (May 1981); no. 9 (September 1981).

THE CONCEPT AND PRACTICE OF PRESS FREEDOM

17. PRESS FREEDOM IN WESTERN SOCIETIES

HANNO HARDT

The idea of freedom is a legacy of antiquity. As a physical and spiritual condition, freedom is inevitably linked to human activity, to the relationship among individuals, and among individuals and material objects in the establishment of economic and political systems of survival.

The ideas of freedom of expression and freedom of the press have grown out of an awareness of communication as a basic element in the formation of human relationships. The notions of intellectual freedom and the concerns for liberty of thought have stimulated the growth of Western culture and have become the foundation for democratic societies.

This chapter traces the development of communication, providing the historical context necessary for understanding the nature of freedom of expression and the press as it exists in contemporary Western societies. In addition, the chapter focuses on the effects of mass society and the institutionalization of the press as the producer of economic and political realities at the expense of the individual, who remains uprooted from his community and from an environment of true participation in the affairs of society.

291

The historical study of oral communication, mass communication, and freedom of the press becomes part of an inquiry into the social and cultural history of people, whose curiosity to explore the unknown and whose urge to share their observations with others helped form a basis for the establishment of a mass communication system. The study of human communication in a historical framework should not only provide insights into the growth of individual and social consciousness but should also suggest a *necessary* approach to an understanding of the human condition, since individuals are present in the history of their communication. In the past, "histories" of communication and freedom of expression and the press, in particular, have emphasized the development of style, content, and form per se. These histories often have consisted of sets of chronologies, which have yielded limited, if not inadequate, explanations and insufficient prerequisites for an inquiry into the story of human communication. Thus, Gutenberg's invention and the birth of the printed word in Europe, important as they were for their time and with respect to subsequent developments, must be viewed in the larger and more general context of Western civilization, when, with the growth of knowledge and the increasing restlessness of people through economic and political conquests and religious and scientific revolutions, geographical and psychological confinements became unbearable for the individual.

The struggle for freedom of expression is an age-old struggle of groups and individuals against their political environments. The Greeks in their experience of the *polis* elevated speech, not action, to a measure of success in the political arena, and rhetoric was a major subject of education. Plato, in his *Apology for Socrates*, offered one of the earliest and most powerful arguments for liberty of thought and public discourse when he said, "In me you have a stimulating critic, persistently urging you on with persuasion and reproaches, persistently testing your opinions and trying to show you that you are really ignorant of what you suppose to know. Daily discussion of the matters about which you hear me conversing is the highest good for man. Life that is not tested by such discussion is not worth living" (Bury 1975, p. 23).

The demands of the *polis* created conditions under which speech and thought became central elements of life in the public sphere. The Greeks in their social and political concerns for the individual as a member of the *polis* provided not only excellent language training for ambitious and talented politicians and educators but as a community were also highly conscious of the importance of various modes of communication. Their involvement in social communication, defined here as *participation* in the process of social communication, was almost complete; it was voluntary and extremely popular among all sections of Greek society, if one considers for a moment the development of oral communication in the realm of the ancient theater, literature, philosophy, and politics. On stage, at private gatherings, and in the political arena words became effective tools in the social and political struggle for power and prestige; intellectual strength, as well as rhetorical abilities, became major prerequisites for success in the public eye. An awareness of language as a political and social weapon and thus as a facilitator of political and social control transcended Greek civilization. The oral tradition also furnished vital links of continuity, not only throughout the Mediterranean area, but also over time into and beyond the era of the Roman Empire.[1] Thus communication became the binding force in the cultural and political development of the state.

At the same time, all modes of communication reflected the emphasis of Greek thinking upon man as the center of the universe and thus the subject of writers and their social concerns and philosophical studies. Specifically, the discussion of communication since the beginnings of Western civilization and through its Greek heritage has had its roots in ethics, a subject of significant interest to Greek philosophers. Aristotle's efforts to explain the secrets of communication in his *Rhetoric* and, more generally, the importance of rhetoric in Greek, Roman, and medieval history suggests a basic and longlasting interest in the understanding of man as a communicator and ethical being. Recognizing that the process notion of communication involves not only the communicator and his message but the audience as well, Aristotle demanded a special knowledge of "ethics and politics" as prerequisites for successful communication, since "they have to do with the conduct of men as individuals, and with men in groups" (Cooper 1932, p. 9). Implicit in early definitions of communication is the idea that in its dialectical and rhetorical aspects, language established the basis for a human dialogue not only through the commonality of words or symbols, but also through involvement or participation of all as individuals or groups in the communication process and, therefore, by its very nature, in a confrontation over the question of control.

Public speaking, or mass communication in its earliest form, was encouraged and developed more systematically by the Sophists, who turned rhetoric into one of the most important features of Greek education, which influenced major sections of public life. The struggle for political leadership frequently took place in the public realm where the search for truth was to permeate fanciful rhetorical trickery and straightforward verbal confrontations. The art of government rested greatly upon the communication skills of politicians, who were keenly aware of the importance of language and effective communication. Alexander the Great, for example, was not only a superb soldier and field marshal but also a shrewd manipulator of public opinion and an image builder for his own cause.

Among the numerous incidents of Alexander's persuasive powers is a speech delivered to his soldiers who threatened to desert him after a long campaign in Asia. Pleading with his disillusioned soldiers he said, "My victories are yours. Asia Minor, Syria, Egypt, Mesopotamia, Persia I offered you for enjoyment, they belong to you.... I have nothing, I am guarding you, so you may sleep...show your wounds and I will show you mine" (Burckhardt 1898–1902, p. 432). In the publicness of court procedures, as the trial of Socrates indicates, accuser and accused argued vehemently and with great skill, trusting that their reasoning would convince the tribunal and lead to a just verdict. Festive events, funerals, and numerous special occasions, finally, provided additional opportunities for more public oratory; while stage performances created a medium for the dissemination of social and political criticism as well as for participation in common emotional experiences. Although confined to the immediate physical surroundings and defined in terms of a specific instance of a "live" performance, the effects of Greek rhetoric on society, and especially in its competition with scholarship and teaching, allowed a first glimpse at the nature of mass communication with all its implications for larger and more heterogeneous audiences in centuries to come (Bauer 1930, Blass 1887–98, Burke 1950, Clark 1957, Damaschke 1921, Kennedy 1963, Lausberg 1960, Nestle 1942, Riepl 1913, Zimmern 1922).

Underlying this development of social and political communication, philosophical discourse, and scientific speculation was the more general development of language, in particular the Greek language, which became the vehicle for the rise of scientific thinking and the growth of a scientific mentality that affected subsequent periods of European history. As Bruno Snell (1960) remarks, "Greek is the only language which allows us to trace the true relation between speech and the rise of science; for in no other tongue did the concepts of science grow straight from the body of the language" (p. 227). Proclaiming a rational order of the universe and the existence of a rational principle governing the physical as well as the moral order of the world, Greek civilization became a powerful cultural and political force, advocating a belief in human reason and setting the stage for the development of European thought. The ultimate success of Greek ideas, however, was due to the invention of writing and, earlier, the adoption of the phonetic alphabet. As a unique system of separating sound and sight from semantic and verbal content, it furnished the necessary technique for the translation of other cultures and stood in contrast to the pictographic or idiographic writings of Eastern civilizations. Marshall McLuhan pointed out that the phonetic alphabet makes a distinctive break between visual and auditory experiences of man, giving the user an eye for an ear and freeing him from the tribal trance of resonating word magic (McLuhan 1964).

Language as a particular social and cultural characteristic of human beings can be defined as a system of symbols used in a particular geographical region and subject to frequent and often radical changes under the influences of foreign thought and behavior. In this sense, one should perceive a national culture in terms of a process of acculturation involving external as well as internal social, cultural, or political forces operating on a continuum and effecting changes in the modes and systems of communication. Moreover, if one sees in language not only a vehicle of technical and cultural development of the individual and society but also an index of social thought and a way of thinking and being, comparative studies may yield valuable information about processes of conceptualization and creation of world views that may lead to a better understanding of "foreign" ideas and political behavior among nations.

A closer look at the language communities of Europe reveals different languages spoken within each of them, one frequently functioning as a common language used for communication within political or regional units. Generally, a common language is based on one dialect spoken in an area. Its selection and rise to a national language has often been the result of the political leadership or cultural status of a particular community. This was true for Latin (Rome) and Greek (Athens) and was equally important for the growth of the major European languages; the dialect of Paris was as important for the development of common French as the dialect of London was for English. In areas with a tradition of political divisions or rivalries, however, the process was complicated and often longer-lasting than in rather isolated or politically united countries. Germany and Italy, for example, had similar problems; based on the cultural achievements of Florence, its dialect emerged as the national language of Italy; the ruling landowners of Eastern Germany supplied the basis for a common German tongue. Generally speaking, the rise of common languages in these countries was a necessary condition for the following social and political events that led, ultimately, to the establishment of democratic forms of government and the recognition of individual liberties within a political system.

Literature played an important part in this development. While the earlier presentations of poets and *minnesingers* were rendered in local or regional dialects, most of the medieval essayists and philosophers preferred Latin, perhaps as a sign of education and status or recognition by the church, perhaps as a deliberate selection of their audiences and a sign of contempt for the uneducated masses. Concurrently, however, a body of mostly political and social communication grew and prospered in the profane literature of the times, frequently in satirical plays, songs, and ballads performed among peasants and artisans and often in protest and defiance of secular or church rulers (Bauer 1930). It was Dante, among the more prominent writers, whose *Divine Comedy* broke with the medieval tradition by introducing a personal element of criticism to the work aimed at secular and ecclesiastical authorities with its publication of social and political conditions in Italy. In the context of Dante's life and time, the *Divine Comedy* was a highly critical essay, written in the dialect of Florence instead of Latin and aimed at a mass audience rather than at the small class of educated and privileged citizens.

Dante's work, marking the beginning of humanism in Europe, established a trend of national literature that consciously escaped the restrictions of Latin as a foreign language, emerging in a natural form that promised not only artistic freedom but also an era of social and cultural expansion beyond the influence of the church in Rome (Bauer 1930, Burke 1950, Schopenhauer 1926). Poets and writers in increasing numbers helped create national languages by making use of dialects and performing in styles comprehensible to the common people. Thus the languages of Luther and Sachs in Germany, Rabelais and Montaigne in France, and Chaucer and More in England influenced others, liberated their thoughts, and helped realize national identities. In the spirit of the rhetorical tradition, humanism again emphasized the importance of language; in particular it stressed its renovation, attacking dead or deadly forms of language and underlining the relationship of language and life or action (a notion that was to be revived by logical positivism). These concerns permeated folk literature, philosophical treatises, and perhaps most significantly, the propagandistic writings of Luther, including his translation of the Bible.

But the notion of tolerance that underlay the idea of freedom of expression in the Greek tradition, the presence of different ideas and of dissent, gradually disappeared. The rise of high culture was accompanied not only by a division of labor, the accumulation of property, and monopolies of learning but also by authoritarian rule. Even the rise of common languages in Western societies resulted in the suppression of other languages or dialects within national boundaries, leading to cultural oppression of minorities. Freedom was defined by those in power: kings, feudal lords, and the church. And the idea of democracy as a cultural system, which gave individuals or groups in primitive societies opportunity for expression and action, gave way to authoritarian forms of control over speech and thought and human activities.

The rise of humanism created an atmosphere of change between the fourteenth and sixteenth centuries that was based on significant developments in human understanding of the social and material world. The scientific revolution that followed, between the sixteenth and eighteenth centuries, was not merely a triumph of Copernicus, Kepler, and Galileo over Aristotle and Ptolemy but an intellectual revolution that suggested a new way of thinking about the world. Science and not religion became the language to decipher the mysteries of nature; the break ended the domination of the Scriptures as an authoritative source of knowledge about the world and established the genius of science as the locus of understanding the universe.

Europe celebrated the return to Greece and Rome, emphasizing pagan culture by imitating its forms and styles of architecture and literature, and Italy's city-states led the way to a cultural and political Renaissance. The writings of Erasmus, More, Rabelais, Machiavelli, Montaigne, and others were widely circulated in Europe, whose intellectual elite merged their ideas with various attempts to cope with the philosophical and political dogmas of the day. In addition, there were the religious reform movements, which turned into social and political campaigns when Renaissance thinking and the widespread secularization of Europe prepared the way for men like Luther. He emerged not only as a religious reformer but also as a champion of the people, in whose language he addressed himself to the problems of the church.

The Reformation, as a challenge to the authority of the Pope and as a reaction against the abuses by the church, also rested in social and political ideas in Germany. The Peasants' Revolt, in particular, as an uprising against the extortion by the landed nobility, has been called a turning point in modern history. Karl Mannheim (1936) argued that politics in the modern sense began at this time, "if we here understand by politics a more or less conscious participation of all strata of society in the achievement of some mundane purpose, as contrasted with a fatalistic acceptance of events as they are, or of control from 'above'" (p. 212).

Luther's appeal to common people was an appropriate strategy also in the light of the new printing technology that enabled him to disseminate his messages rapidly to large numbers of individuals, who recognized in his writings their own experiences, the joys and frustrations of their simple and hard lives as recorded by Luther in

simple, unpretentious language. Above all, Luther was a good observer of common people; he also understood their language and used it
accordingly.

Prior to this time, the idea of Christendom had transcended the
Western mind; for centuries, the papacy had struggled against secular authorities by using rhetorical devices reminiscent of the earlier
Graeco-Roman period to arouse the masses against rising pagan influences and disobedient clergy. But the church could not prevent the
loss of its strongest supporter: the feudal aristocracy. Trade and industry developed strong alliances with central governments and
established a new social force—the middle class—which sought protection of its business interests from governments in exchange for
financial advantages. Economic and military strength proved more
powerful than previous alliances with the church, whose domination
in social and political matters had been one of the characteristics of
medieval Europe.

The results of the Reformation were discouraging for those who
had expected liberty and freedom for all. The alliance of church and
state became strong; and whereas spiritual liberty was acknowledged,
the physical existence of individuals was placed under state control.
Censorship became an effective mechanism to control the flow of
ideas through books and pamphlets. Lutheranism, Calvinism, and the
French Huguenots contributed to the rise of modern man, but the
separation of civic or public activities from the inner life of individuals has resulted in a dualism that has left its mark on Western
civilization by freeing political and economic activities from ethical
and religious constraints.

At the same time, the world grew larger with the discovery of
America (Christopher Columbus, 1942) and new sea routes around
Africa (Vasco da Gama, 1497) and South America (Ferdinand Magel-
lan, 1519), and with the extensions into outer space (Nicolaus Copernicus, Johannes Kepler, Galileo Galilei), introducing the age of
science and empiricism and further diminishing the role of the church
in Europe. The gradual emancipation from church authority led to
the growth of individualism and resulted in a new social structure of
European society. Man became the master of his own destiny, aided
by the invention of movable type, which allowed him to conquer the
reality of life, share his social and political ideas, and create a new
community in which the anonymity of the communicator became an
acceptable replacement for the personal communicator-audience relationship of earlier years. It was now the message, not the "messenger," that created the reality of the communication experience and
led to a crucial change in the relationship between communicator and
audience.

Throughout the fourteenth and fifteenth centuries, criticism of the church and feudal rulers increased in pictorial presentations, songs, and pamphlets. The manuscript age was coming to an end, typographical man was born, and the process of secularization opened a new era of mass communication. The growth of the middle class, its interest in the affairs of the state as they affected its economic conerns, as well as a growing rate of literacy helped create greater demands for news, expanded the size of audiences, and crossed geographical and social boundaries. Earlier, reading had been a privilege of the clergy and a few members of the nobility; libraries frequently had been church property and the flow of information had been controlled by the interests of the church with its emphasis on the dissemination of knowledge favorable to established church doctrine.

Now, correspondence networks of merchants like the Fugger family of Augsburg, Germany, increased in size and volume and led to the establishment of postal routes from Italy to the Netherlands. As early as 1489, the House of Taxis received postal privileges from Maximilian I that led to an elaborate system of postal routes and to the organization of major news-gathering centers under the direction of local postmasters in cities like Nuremberg, Augsburg, and Frankfurt. This development was accompanied by a rapid distribution of printing companies, which spread from Mainz, Germany, along the Rhine valley to Italy (1464), Switzerland (1465), France and Holland (1470), Spain and Hungary (1473), England (1476), and Sweden (1483). With the exception of Russia (1553), Europe had over 1,700 printing presses located in almost 300 towns and cities across the continent by the year 1500; they supplied a growing reading public with pamphlets and books by the great humanists, philosophers, and religious reformers of the age. While most of the works were of religious or legal character, some printers published a variety of books. The Englishman William Caxton, for instance, printed almost all works written in his native tongue up to his time before he died in 1491, and his accomplishment suggests the zeal and imaginative productivity found among contemporary printers all over Europe (Febvre and Martin 1976, Isaacs 1931, Eisenstein 1979, Chappell 1970).

The transition from the manuscript age to the age of the printing press was governed by the specific demands of the public and the political necessities of the time. Thus, religious materials, Bible translations and religious tracts in particular, dominated the marketplace for several years; letter writing also continued to increase. For this reason, newspapers did not appear in Europe until the time when letters, posters, occasional publications, and books no longer fulfilled the requirements of society, when the flow of ideas was overwhelming and the demands of the people for news and information were too great to be satisfied by "conventional" methods. In addition, church and secular rulers, recognizing the advantages of the new media for the faster and more expedient dissemination of their own doctrines, as well as their disadvantages of posing potential threats to authoritarian rule, were quite efficient in erecting effective barriers against subversive and unauthorized publications of ideas.

The flow of ideas and the discovery of the power of the word through books, pamphlets, and, some time later, newspapers, became a political concern of church and state. In an effort to control the knowledge of society, to strengthen the position of authority, and to define the limits of free expression in society, censorship and privilege became major weapons. When the Archbishop of Mainz first implemented a licensing system, it was soon supported by Pope Alexander VI (1492–1503), who extended it to all "Christendom" before the appearance of a book index. Shortly after the Council of Trent (1545– 63) the Catholic church issued an official index of prohibited books, and by 1564 church censorship was a centralized institution, which ordered books to be burned and individuals violating church orders to be excommunicated. But the problem of thought control was also an important political issue for national states, since revolutionary theories were a constant threat to central governments in Europe.

Afraid of the consequences of a free flow of political thought, France developed a rigid form of censorship that extended even to private correspondence. The death penalty was introduced in 1557 for individuals importing forbidden books; earlier, a decree regulating the book trade in Paris had announced that "experience has shown the kings of France how prejudicial to the state is the liberty of the press." Newspapers developed in France in the early seventeenth century and were subjected to a licensing system; during some periods, only official newspapers were allowed to be published. This situation remained basically unchanged until the French Revolution, when the number of newspapers and periodical publications increased from 41 (1779) to about 1,400 (1789), only to be curtailed by a new wave of governmental restrictions under Napoleon I, who said in 1800, "If I let the press do what it would like to do, I would be out of office in three months" (Avenel 1900, Cunow 1912, Hatin 1859–61, Mitton 1954, Manévy 1968).

In England, the Tudor policy of strict control over the press was maintained throughout the sixteenth century in the form of royal privileges and licensing systems and was formalized by the Star Chamber decree of 1586, which limited the number of printers and presses, confirmed the Stationers' Company powers of search and seizure, and provided for a joint administration with ecclesiastical officials. News-books appeared in 1622 and were slowly replaced by weekly news-papers starting in the latter part of the seventeenth century, always under direct government control until the expiration of the Regula-tion of Printing Act in 1694, which was replaced by more subtle con-trols through taxation and subsidies and criminal and parliamentary prosecution (Cranfield 1962, Grünbeck 1936, Herd 1952, Frank 1961, Siebert 1952).

The situation in Germany was similar and yet different from the French or British example because of the peculiar, fragmented polit-ical situation. Some states (Bavaria, Saxony, Prussia) offered licenses to postmasters for the printing of newspapers; others (Ham-burg, Augsburg) provided asylum for editors whose ideas of press freedom did not coincide with the official concepts of free expression in their states. In other parts of Germany, rulers published official newspapers for the "education" and "welfare" of their subjects, and for propaganda purposes and reasons of financial gains through advertising, thereby limiting the field for privately owned news-papers (Groth 1928–30, Koszyk 1960, Lindemann 1969, Salomon 1900–6).

The licensing systems and censorship in most parts of Europe forced editors to remain within the limits of officially sanctioned opinions and led the crusading and revolutionary individuals among them to different outlets for their ideas. Pamphlets became the medium for philosophical debates (Locke, Montesquieu, Milton), and the arts provided a forum for the criticism of political and social sys-tems. Letters, memoirs, educational novels, and newspapers—as well as plays, poems, and songs—comprised the literature of dissent dur-ing the seventeenth and eighteenth centuries. These forms were largely ignored by censors because of their assumed nonpolitical con-tent, according to contemporary standards, but still they reached a large number of people. The book became one of the most important communication media during these years, linking theological and philosophical dialogues that involved Europe's intellectual elite and its influence on the political forces that were responsible for the fol-lowing revolutionary developments in various parts of the continent.

The curiosity of individuals about their environment turned into a challenge to the authority of the Bible and of the Sword, and the issue of intellectual freedom emerged as the first chapter in the his-tory of freedom of expression. The growth of reason, the decline of Christian mythology, and the triumph of science provided the back-ground for the birth of the modern world. The concurrent develop-ment of technology as a means of territorial expansion and the more efficient accumulation of wealth also provided opportunities for change. But opposition to authority and demands for liberty turned into a struggle over the control of technology. The Industrial Revolution with its origins in England, the emergence of the United States as a political and economic force in the Western world with the success of the American Revolution, and the move toward democratic elected governments since the French Revolution provide the parameter for the discussion of freedom of expression and freedom of the press in the modern age of Western societies. Underlying these political developments, however, was the status of the individual in society, the meaning of individualism, and the consequences for the liberty of man as the supreme democratic doctrine.

The emergence of the individual from the restrictive powers of church and state is one result of the rise of the bourgeoisie, whose confidence in the individual was expressed not only through economic accomplishments but also through other means. Books and other printed matter in the vernacular, autobiographical writings, and the artistic expressions of personal identities (as in painting) were among the material cultural products that supported the notion of individualism as a social and cultural force. The idea of freedom as a topic of philosophical debates and its application to the political reality of the city-states in Italy, the monarchy in England, and the aristocratic rulers of German-speaking countries was not only an expression of independence from the restraints of feudal and ecclesiastical power but also a recognition of individualism as a major political and social concept. This intellectual trend, however, collided with the reality of industrialism and its need for collective action, when economic and political power was concentrated in the bourgeoisie.

In the aftermath of revolutions in America and France, as well as in other European countries between 1776 and 1848, a new ruling class emerged to help shape the reconstruction of the social order. The problems of class and economic position were a result of the Industrial Revolution in Europe. With the decline of the aristrocracy, the bourgeoisie became a major force in a society based upon industrial capitalism. Laissez-faire private enterprise and the law of supply and demand became the philosophical foundations of capitalism. It was also an age in which economic interests were considered primary by conservatives, who saw them as a liberating force for mankind, and by radicals, who defined them as a source of alienation and inhumanity. Capitalism at this stage had outgrown its beginnings of individual activity and material well-being to become a widespread, organized effort to direct industrial and mercantile power to control an increasingly urban society in which the machine displaced artisans and craftsmen. The idea of laissez-faire became synonymous with freedom and democracy.

The writings of major European and American thinkers, among them Locke, Jefferson, and Rousseau, provided the rationale for the enunciation of certain universally normative rights of individuals. They included protection against the power of the state and support for the right to vote and the right to expression. But the formulation of these rights was more than the protection of individuals; it must also be understood in the context of a desire to maintain and strengthen the community. Thus individualism can be understood properly only as an aspect of a collective activity that finds expression in the community of men and women. Aristotle expressed this notion of community when he said,

> We thus see that the polis exists by nature and that it is prior to the individual. (The proof of both propositions is the fact that the polis is a whole, and the individuals are simply its parts). Not being self-sufficient when they are isolated, all individuals are so many parts all equally depending on the whole (which alone can bring about self-sufficiency). The man who is isolated ... is no part of the polis ... (Man is thus intended by nature to be a part of a political whole, and) there is therefore an imminent impulse in all men towards an association of this order. (Minar and Greer 1969, p. 192)

In addition, Aristotle suggested that language as a medium of expression and as a weapon against injustice and immorality forms a common bond among individuals. Thus, the protection of speech as a prerequisite to the idea of community becomes a major issue as a political demand in the development of democratic governments. It also is a social and cultural issue because expression of creative, emotional, and spiritual aspects of human existence are vital for an understanding of the world. Thus freedom of expression becomes a necessary condition for the attainment of community, as the essence of *polis*, and it resurfaces in modern times as freedom of the press and as a political issue when the establishment of democracies may be seen as an attempt to establish an equilibrium of power that had not existed during aristocratic rule. While theoretically based on choice and social contract, in Lockean terms, the practice of bourgeois reconstruction of societies moved beyond the creation of just or human conditions; instead, economic power was used to manipulate the state (e.g. the representatives of sovereign rule by the people) to the disadvantage of industrial workers. In that instance, the state became a class instrument of oppression.

The achievement of community remained a utopian vision, however, even at a later stage of the social and political development when collective organization among workers established their political presence. The need for justice, which is a basic substance of the community, may have been felt widely, but the disequilibrium of power created by the Industrial Revolution could not be changed effectively.

Although in possession of their political franchise, large segments of the population in Western societies were excluded by defining them in economic terms. Thus sovereign power, that is, the authority to act in the name of society, remained with the middle class. As a result, the modern state emerged as a supreme allegiance of men and as a symbol of power and unity of the governing interests. Walter Lippmann (1974) expressed this development when he said,

> It is of no importance in this connection whether the absolute power of the state is exercised by a king, a landed aristocracy, bankers and manufacturers, professional politicians, soldiers, or a random majority of voters. It does not matter whether the right to govern is hereditary or obtained with the consent of the governed. A state is absolute in the sense which I have in mind when it claims the right to a monopoly of all the force within the community, to make war, to make peace, to conscript life, to tax, to establish or disestablish property, to define crime, to punish disobedience, to control education, to supervise the family, to regulate personal habits, and to censor opinions. The modern state claims all these powers, and in the matter of theory there is no real difference between communists, fascists, and democrats. There are lingering traces in the American constitutional system of the older theory that there are inalienable rights which government may not absorb. But these rights are really not inalienable because they can be taken away by constitutional amendment. There is no theoretical limit upon the power of the ultimate majorities which create civil government. There are only practical limits. They are restrained by inertia, and by prudence, even by good will. But ultimately and theoretically they claim absolute authority as against all foreign states, as against all churches, associations, and persons within their jurisdiction. (pp. 74–75)

During the eighteenth and nineteenth centuries newspapers gained importance as vehicles of political thought. With the quickening of the political pace during the democratic era, government officials needed a new medium, one designed to deal adequately with the increasing flow of information and the demand for an instant forum for political debate. Aided by technological advancements, newspapers became a socially and politically strong and important platform, taking over the role of books and periodicals of earlier years. Politics had become a matter of public interest and concern. Europe witnessed the emergence of the party press, which participated actively in the political process, and of the general interest newspaper, designed to serve mass audiences at a cheaper and faster rate than any other medium of communication.

During this period, advertising developed as a major source of newspaper revenue, replacing, in a way, party affiliation or direct sponsorship by commercial or industrial interests. Increasing competition among the press and the emerging electronic media, which were often protected through affiliation with the government or through a public interest status supported with licence fees (with the exception of the United States, where a commercial broadcasting system existed from the beginning), led to media monopolies and threats to the diversity of opinions in Western Europe and the United States.

Throughout these years, and especially after World War II, the press in Western democracies has been operating under the protection of laws regulating freedom of expression and the press. Based upon natural law concepts of man developed earlier in European history, the interpretation of articles of the constitutions or administrative laws in these countries have yet to address the modern dilemma, that one's right to expression has been fundamentally transformed to the extent that it is often reduced to a right to consume available information. The inadequacy of information available through traditional media coverage has been illuminated by the development of an underground press during the 1960s in the United States and, most recently, by the establishment of neighborhood and community newspapers by citizen action groups in Western Europe. Addressing specific local problems and national political issues ignored by traditional media, these publications have represented the voices of dissent and opposition to official policies. They are evidence of the existence of groups whose views are not reflected in the established media. They are also perhaps the most promising sign that people continue to seek new ways of exercising their right of expression.

In summary, the importance of communication in society has been demonstrated over many centuries, from the oral tradition of primitive cultures to the age of technology in highly developed societies. The power of the word, its extension through writing and printing, have played a major role in the establishment of empires. From Alexander the Great and his territorial conquests to religion and ideology and their conquests of the mind, communication has remained a medium of control.

The question of freedom of the press must not only be viewed as an aspect of freedom of expression but also as a need to protect an institution that has an important function to provide economic and political images that support the status quo or point in the direction of desired change.

Early newspapers were established for economic and political reasons. They served the need for specific information about the human environment; the gathering and dissemination of information remains a prerequisite for the organization of human activities. Freedom of the press, under these conditions, developed as a right that gave special interests in society the power to communicate efficiently and effectively to large numbers of individuals. The press as an information broker and as a potentially vital link to society gained a privileged position among other societal institutions, a fact that has not significantly changed since the eighteenth century. Freedom of expression, on the other hand, has most frequently been defined as an individual right. Its meaning has been clarified through episodes of dissent and opposition throughout history. In those instances, in which the press became a vehicle for the dissemination of seditious ideas, censorship or suppression were used by authorities to secure the stability of the political system. In neither case—of the press or of the individual—has freedom been absolute. The state (or the authority) reserved the right to protect itself. Freedom of expression and freedom of the press have always been limited by the threat they pose to the established order.

Thus the history of the press in Western democracies is also a history of the suppression of unpopular ideas. The state as the ultimate authority on social, economic, or political truths has more than once acted on its own behalf to safeguard its existence. The development of Western democracies has from its beginnings relied on communication systems; the growth of the newspaper and magazine industry, followed by the electronic media, was a necessary condition for the success of democratic governments, which needed access to and feedback from their constituencies. In this process, however, special interests rather than individual needs provided information through the press. The individual who had been de-tribalized and removed from his community identified with the mass society. The public sphere of the community was effectively destroyed; it was replaced by a marketplace of ideas that stressed consumption as participation in the democratic system.

NOTES

1. For an understanding of the influence of Greek civilization on the formation of Western culture, see Cornford 1952, Dodds 1951, Havelock 1963, Innis 1951, Lord 1960, Nestle 1923–24, Popper 1962, and Snell 1953.

REFERENCES

Avenel, Henri. *Histoire de la Presse Française*. Paris: 1900.

Bauer, Wilhelm. *Öffentliche Meinung in der Weltgeschichte*. Potsdam: 1930.

Blass, Friedrich. *Die attische Beredsamkeit*. Leipzig: 1887–98.

Burckhardt, James. *Griechische Kulturgeschichte*. Vol. 4. Berlin: Speman, 1898–1902.

Burke, Kenneth. *A Rhetoric of Motives*. New York: 1950.

Bury, John B. *A History of Freedom of Thought*. Westport, Conn.: Greenwood Press, 1975.

Chappell, Warren. *A Short History of the Printed Word*. New York: 1970.

Clark, Donald. *Rhetoric in Graeco-Roman Education*. New York: 1959.

Cooper, Lane. *The Rhetoric of Aristotle*. New York: Appleton-Century-Croft, 1932.

Cornford, Francis P. *Principium Sapientiae*. Cambridge: 1952.

Cranfield, G. A. *Development of Provincial Newspapers*. London: 1962.

Cunow, Heinrich. *Die Parteien der grossen Französischen Revolution und ihre Presse*. Berlin: 1912.

Damaschke, Adolf. *Geschichte der Redekunst*. Jena: 1921.

Dodds, E. R. *The Greeks and the Irrational*. Berkeley: 1951.

Eisenstein, Elizabeth. *The Printing Press as an Agent of Change*. 2 vols. Cambridge: 1979.

Febvre, Lucien and Henri-Jean Martin. *The Coming of the Book*. London: 1976.

Frank, Joseph. *Beginnings of English Newspapers*. Boston: 1961.

Groth, Otto. *Die Zeitung*. 4 vols. Mannheim: 1928–30.

Grünbeck, Max. *Die Presse Grossbritaniens*. 2 vols. Leipzig: 1936.

Hatin, Eugene. *Histoire et litteraire de la presse en France*. 8 vols. Paris: 1859–61.

Havelock, Eric A. *Preface to Plato*. Cambridge, Mass: 1963.

———. *Preface to Plato*. Universal Library ed. New York: Grosset & Dunlap, 1963.

Herd, Harold. *The March of Journalism*. London: 1952.

Innis, Harold. *The Bias of Communication*. Toronto: University of Toronto Press, 1951.

Isaacs, George A. *The Story of the Newspaper Printing Press*. London: 1931.

Kennedy, George. *The Art of Persuasion in Greece*. Princeton, N. J.: 1963.

Koszyk, Kurt. *Deutsche Presse im 19. Jahrhundert*. Berlin: 1960.

Lausberg, Heinrich. *Handbuch der Literarischen Rhetorik*. München: 1960.

Lindemann, Margot. *Deutsche Presse bis 1815*. Berlin: 1969.

Lippmann, Walter. *A Preface to Morals*. New York: Time Books, 1974.

Lord, Albert B. *The Singer of Tales*. Cambridge, Mass.: 1960.

McLuhan, Marshall. *Understanding Media: The Extensions of Man*. New York: McGraw-Hill, 1964.

Manévy, Raymond. *La presse française de Renaudot à Rochefort*. Paris: 1968.

Mannheim, Karl. *Ideology and Utopia*. New York: Harvest Books, 1936.

Mergenthaler Co. *Ottmar Mergenthaler and the Printing Revolution*. Brooklyn: 1954.

Minar, David W. and Scott Greer, eds. *The Concept of Community*. Chicago: Aldine-Atherton, 1969.

Mitton, Fernand. *La presse française*. 2 vols. Paris: 1954.

Nestle, Wilhelm. *Geschichte der Griechischen Literatur*. 2 vols. Berlin: 1923–24.

———· *Vom Mythos zum Logos*. 2nd ed. Stuttgart: 1942.

Popper, Karl R. *The Open Society and Its Enemies*. London: 1962.

Riepl, Wolfgang. *Das Nachrichtenwesen des Altertums*. Leipzig: 1913.

Salomon, Ludwig. *Geschichte des Deutschen Zeitungswesens von der ersten Anfängen bis zur Wiederaufrichtung des Deutschen Reiches*. 3 vols. Oldenburg: 1900–06.

Schopenhauer, Arthur. *The Art of Literature*. London: Allen & Unwin, 1926.

Siebert, Frederick S. *Freedom of the Press in England, 1476–1776*. Urbana: 1952.

Silver, Rollo G. *The American Printer, 1787–1825*. Charlottesville: 1967.

Snell, Bruno. *The Discovery of the Mind*. Cambridge, Mass.: 1953.

———. *The Discovery of the Mind*. New York: Harper & Row, 1960.

Wroth, Lawrence C. *The Colonial Printer*. New York: 1964.

Zimmern, Alfred. *The Greek Commonwealth*. Oxford: 1922.

18. PRESS FREEDOM IN THE THIRD WORLD

SUNWOO NAM

The unfinished political revolution in Latin America in the nineteenth century and the political independence that swept Africa and Asia after World War II have put democratic ideals in the minds of most people living in the vast area of the world euphemistically called the Third World.[1] High among the democratic ideals for which many sacrificed their lives is the concept of universal human rights, or civil liberties. They include freedom of expression, best expressed through the vehicle of the press. Without freedom of speech and of the press, popular sovereignty is not tenable; hence, press freedom, as the sine qua non of democratic civil and political rights, has a universal appeal. It is no wonder that practically all the world's constitutions pay at least lip service to the ideals of free speech and press freedom, as well as to the free exercise of religion, contradictory practices notwithstanding.

For ideals in constitutions are one thing, and practices are another. In the stable democratic nations of Western Europe and the United States, the discrepancy between the ideal and the practice of free press is not all that great and is not subject to wide variations;

in the Third World, the discrepancy is often great and fluctuates randomly. Such is the case if we apply the Western definition of free press that includes the following principles:

1. The prohibition of government interference with the press in the form of censorship and similar previous restraints
2. The principle that any restrictions on press freedom must be applied or subject to review by the courts, and that courts alone have the right to impose penalties. (Michael Ta Kung Wei 1970, p. 92)

The question, however, is whether Third World nations use the Western definition of freedom of the press or whether they have their own definitions. How is press freedom defined in the Third World? We have to remember that most Third World nations represent a "no man's land where social institutions are still being shaped, where democracy is in the balance and one-party states are developing, and where the relations between press and government are ill-defined. The press is caught up in an ideological whirlpool and there is little ground for optimism that the Western concept of a free press will survive" (Sommerlad 1962, p. 142).

With Sommerlad's words as a backdrop, let us look at some of the constitutional guarantees (verbal definitions) of freedom of the press in several countries. There are two varieties of constitutional clauses: Some simply state that the right of free speech and a free press is guaranteed to all; others say that it is guaranteed with certain exceptions. Jamaica, a member of the British Commonwealth, provides an example of the latter; Article 22 of the Jamaica Order in Council (constitution) provides:

(1) Except with his own consent, no person shall be hindered in the enjoyment of his freedom of expression, and for the purposes of this section the said freedom includes the freedom to hold opinions and to receive and impart ideas and information without interference, and freedom from interference with his correspondence and other means of communication. (2) Nothing contained in or done under the authority of any law shall be held to be inconsistent with or in contravention of this section to the extent that the law in question makes provisions—(a) which is reasonably required—(i) in the interests of defence, public safety, public order, public morality or public health; or (ii) for the purpose of protecting the reputations, rights and freedoms of other persons, or the private lives of persons concerned in legal proceedings, preventing the disclosure of information received in confidence, maintaining the authority and

independence of the courts, or regulating telephone, telegraphy, posts, wireless broadcasting, television or other means of communication, public exhibitions or public entertainment; or (*b*) which imposes restrictions upon public officers, police officers or upon members of a defence force.

Constitutional guarantees with no strings attached can be found in the constitution of Botswana; it contains what is in effect a bill of rights providing for the "protection of fundamental rights and freedoms of the individual" in the areas of speech, religion, press, and assembly. Of course, freedom of the press is never meant to be absolute and unqualified in Third World nations. Even in libertarian countries, under carefully limited circumstances, prior restraints are justified. What distinguishes Third World nations from the more or less libertarian Western world is, among other things, a rather elaborate set of restrictive (press) laws that spell out the duties of the press rather severely. A case in point is "Act No. 11 of 1966 on the Basic Principles of the Press with the Blessings of God Almighty" issued by the President of Indonesia.

Function, Duties and Rights of the Press
Article 2
(1) The National Press is an instrument of the revolution constituting an active, dynamic, creative, educative, informative mass medium with the social function of stimulating and encouraging in progressive thinking, covering all manifestations of the life of the Indonesian society.
(2) The National Press is obliged to:
    a. safeguard, defend, uphold and implement Pancasila [five principles] and the 1945 Constitution consistently and in all its purity;
    b. fight for the implementation of the Message of the Sufferings of the People based on Pancasila Democracy;
    c. fight for truth and justice based on the freedom of the press;
    d. foster the unity of progressive-revolutionary forces in the struggle opposing imperialism, colonialism, neo-colonialism, feudalism, liberalism, communism and fascist-dictatorship;
    e. become the channel of constructive, progressive and revolutionary public opinion.

The same law provides for a Press Council, the chairman of which is the Minister of Information, and for the reserved right of the government to establish a news agency as well as a daily newspaper at its discretion. Article 11 stipulates: "Press publications contrary to Pancasila as is the case with those based on the ideology of Communism/Marxism-Leninism are prohibited." The Third World, located between the Western world and the Communist world, has at one extreme some of its countries copying the Western libertarian concept of the press and at the other extreme some countries that consciously model themselves after the Marxist-Leninist concept of the press. And there are countries that fall in between the two extremes, most of which try desperately to develop their countries as fast as possible to keep up with "the revolution of rising expectations," if not to forestall "the revolution of rising frustrations." Countries that opt for the Western model, particularly those with a British colonial legacy, generally provide a great deal of press freedom under normal circumstances and resort to emergency powers only if the leadership feels threatened by external or internal foes. In countries such as Nigeria, India, and Jamaica, newspapers are typically privately owned, whereas broadcast media are either exclusively government owned or controlled or are under a dual system of public and private ownership.

Countries with a Communist/socialist orientation, such as Ethiopia, Afghanistan, and Angola, proscribe a free and independent press. In these countries, practically all media are government or party owned and controlled, which means the Western concept of a free press is not allowed. For instance, *Country Reports on Human Rights Practices* (1981) by the U.S. State Department says about Angola:

> The constitution guarantees freedom of expression,
> assembly, conscience, and belief, as well as separation of
> church and state, but qualifies the exercise of these freedoms
> by requirements that activities must fall within "the area of
> realizing the fundamental objectives of the People's Republic
> of Angola," that they must be "in the national interest," or
> that they "conform to public order." Freedom of Assembly is
> denied to any other political movement by the MPLA (the
> Popular Movement for the Liberation of Angola)
> government . . . there are numerous reports of arrests of
> people who voice support of an opposition movement or
> alternative political systems. Censorship of political
> expression exists, and the circulation of Western journals
> and periodicals is tightly restricted. The government
> controls or owns the media. (pp. 12, 13)

Regardless of the ideology of a Third World nation, strong developmental efforts by ruling elites in Third World nations do not leave much room for a free and independent press in the Western tradition. One leader of a developing country was reported to have said that the freedom of the press (given the possibility that excesses of a free press may wreck the government's plan for rapid develop-

ment) is obscene when people are starving to death. Also, Singapore's
Prime Minister Lee Kuan Yew stated in 1971: "In such a situation
[divisive ethnic differences and the lack of education among his peo-
ple], freedom of the press, freedom of the news media should be subordinated to the overriding needs of the integrity of Singapore, and
the primary purpose of elected government (development)" (USICA
1979, p. 65). Rapid development of the economy denotes planning that
is centrally conceived and executed with speed in implementation at
a premium. Most leaders of developing countries would readily have
agreed with Indira Gandhi when she said in a statement to parliament in July 1975: "When there are no papers, there is no agitation. . . .
That is why we imposed censorship. . . . Newspapers were spreading
rumors, allegations, and inciting people into agitations."

Ferdinand Marcos employed similar apologia on clamping tight
control in 1972 on the once robust Philippine newspapers. Licentious-
ness of the press had bred a climate of subversion in the country. If
the papers had been let alone, he said, they could have dwelled on the
shortcomings and excesses of the movement to create "a new society,"
and criticism of the movement would have engendered cynicism among
the citizens, finally wrecking the goals of the government for rapid
development. Therefore, the activities and the content of the papers
were controlled. So the argument can run in the minds of ruling
elites. In this context, political leaders can hardly tolerate critics and
intellectual gadflies regarded as impediments interfering with development. If anything, they want to see media operate to aid the developmental process as teachers, inspirers, and propagandizers of the
masses, almost as Lenin conceptualized the role of the press in a Communist society.

As Nam and Oh (1973) concluded in their study of press freedom
in the world:

> In short, when development is apotheosized, there can be
> little room for freedom of the press, which is the antithesis to
> the planned nature of the developmental efforts. In fact,
> developmental politics seems to be an antithesis of
> democracy, of deliberation and long-winded decision-making
> process [typical of the Western democracies]. (p. 745)

Lord Roy Thomson was quoted by Sommerlad (1966) as saying
the following with regard to potential excesses of the press, which
might compromise the stability of the government or the ruling elite:

> From my own experience, I am convinced that in some of the
> new nations of the world, criticism of Governments may
> legitimately be subject to some degree of restriction. Some of
> the journalists in these developing countries do not have

sufficient background of knowledge, experience and
judgment to enable them to restrain themselves from
destructive or inflammatory criticism which, exposed to
populations which have not yet learned the art of political
stability, could lead to serious unrest and even
revolutionary activity. (p. 143)

It can be said in behalf of the press that political leaders do not
have a monopoly on love for the people or on what is best for the country. As journalists see it, unless the press is given the role of what
Lucian Pye called "inspector-general," allowing it a great deal of
latitude, the developmental programs of ruling elites may end up
enriching a relatively few individuals because of the inherent temptation to be corrupt in any power situation. Journalists believe what
Lord Acton aptly said: "Power corrupts and absolute power corrupts
absolutely." The tendency of journalists to be critical of government
for the most part stems from a genuine desire to see their country-
men's lives improved rather than to cause disruption or unrest.

Also, it is increasingly a question of legitimacy that aggravates
the relationship between government and media in Third World nations. In the giddy first years of independence, the most prominent or
most charismatic leaders of liberation movements became the ruling
elite, with no questions of legitimacy raised. And leaders of the press,
more often than not, were fighters who had struggled for independence. Among them, some in government and others in media, differences of opinion as to the best direction for the nation could and were
manifested to a degree; but the immediate task of state and nation
building submerged those differences for a time amid the attribution
of legitimacy to the leadership by media and the population in
general.

Nevertheless, when the fruits of independence are not forthcoming fast enough to satisfy rising expectations, fed in part by grand
promises by the leadership and in part by mass media's portrayal of
how the developed world lives, disillusionment sets in. Media then
lead the way in this disillusionment by exposing the gap between
promises and delivery, and corruption is often given as the reason for
espousing a change in leadership. By this time, the leadership has become entrenched, especially "the father of the country" or charismatic
leader, such as Sukarno, Nkrumah, and Syngman Rhee. These then
often develop a kind of messianic complex, thinking that they alone
can rule the country for the good of the people. This in turn leads to
tinkering with the constitution to allow the leader to be elected time
and again, or to rely on the military and the secret police to perpetu-
ate his rule and his party.

This process is easily detected by the press, which begins to raise questions about the legitimacy of the leadership, which in turn does not see much choice except to control the press so that any opposition to the continued success of the regime can be dealt with. By this time, any opposition is defined by the leadership not only as antiregime but also as antistate.

If the president is very old, then his lieutenants wield real power, further weakening the leadership's claim to legitimacy. If the country is beset with economic troubles, as most Third World nations are, and is troubled in its relations with neighboring countries, the military becomes the prime candidate for power. Since the military represents a relatively young generation, compared to the media principals who cut their teeth in the anticolonial struggle, the question of legitimacy becomes exacerbated with the new military "supreme council for national redemption" demanding that the media play the role of legitimizer and that media owners deplore the upstarts. That explains why mass media become one of the first targets of a military coup. Once the military has tasted power, it becomes enormously difficult to keep it out of the political process, even after a nominal return to civilian rule. Legitimacy then belongs to anybody who can wield enough power over the populace and over the mass media. In short, might makes right, with the coerced mass media being nothing more than handmaidens to the powers that be.

As mentioned, most nations of the Third World pay lip service to press freedom in their constitutions. However, those guarantees can suddenly turn into empty words. Even India, the much-vaunted example of the world's largest democracy, had a dark period of emergency rule that lasted for twenty months from June 1975 to the 1977 election in which Indira Gandhi was defeated. "Even before the emergency was declared late at night on June 25, the government had imposed a form of censorship earlier that night by cutting off the electricity supply to the newspapers in Delhi and by raiding newspaper offices in a number of cities to prevent the country from learning the next day what had happened that night in terms of the mass arrests of political leaders and so on" (Verghese 1978, pp. 221–22). Verghese, the former editor of the *Hindustan Times*, quotes from the official guidelines: "The purpose of precensorship is to ensure that no news is published in a manner that contributes to demoralization about the general situation or the public interest in all aspects as determined by the central government." Among the prohibited things in newspaper coverage was anything that "will contribute even in a remote way to affect or worsen the law and order situation," "any action or statement or event likely to cause disaffection between the government and the people," and any report "denigrating the institution of the Prime Minister." Then Verghese adds: "These prohibitions were so broadly stated to cover anything and everything. Further, there was a total ban on the publication of the proceedings of Parliament and the state legislatures, without clearance by the censor, and also a ban—that is, a pre-censorship ban—on publication of the proceedings of the courts and court judgments."

The Gandhi government took several steps to institutionalize control of the press, including prior restraints. The first step was the enactment of a Prevention of Publication of Objectionable Matters Act. Then came the repeal of an act legislated in 1956 that gave newspapers immunity in reporting the proceedings of parliament. A third move was the abolition of the Press Council, the self-regulating body of the press serving as a buffer in the relationship between press and government. Also, four news agencies were merged into one with an eye toward positive news management in addition to making them a sort of censorial gatekeeper. Other attempts were made to hassle the press, such as takeover bids of large papers and threats to cut off government advertisements to recalcitrant newspapers.

During this period of unprecedented tribulations for the Indian press, a number of large papers that own other industrial interests docilely accepted the yoke imposed by the government, whereas a number of small Indian papers fought the issues in court and obtained favorable decisions. "The courts were a major source of support and, throughout the emergency, the judiciary played a notable role in upholding freedom" (ibid., p. 226). Only Mrs. Gandhi's expectation that the media would remain cowed led to a relaxation of controls during the election campaign in 1977 that resulted in the victory of the Janata party and the restoration of press freedom.

What happened once in India can happen there again—and can happen elsewhere. Indeed, elsewhere things are already either as bad or worse. An example of a worse situation occurred in Korea in 1980. The U.S. State Department observed that "advance censorship [prior restraint] by military censors of all periodicals, in effect since President Park's assassination in October 1979, became tighter after Emergency Martial Law was imposed on May 17, and has been enforced assiduously. Editors are said to be pressured to give space to government-furnished articles extolling the 'new era.' Criticism of the government and its leadership and other expressions of dissent have disappeared from the press and electronic media."

The State Department's *Country Reports on Human Rights Practices* (1981) continues in its section on South Korea:

In August 1980, the press was subjected to a "purification" process in which one hundred seventy-two publications were shut down and hundreds of journalists were fired. The publications closed included many which the martial law

authorities judged to be of no social value, but some others
had a history of dissident or independent political views.
While many of the 400 journalists who lost their jobs held
political views unacceptable to the government, many others
were dismissed for alleged corruption. Nine journalists,
including the president and other officers of the Korean
Journalists Association, were arrested. . . . The content of
television shows has also been affected by the government
purification program.

As of January 5, 1981, the government has merged
Korea's two privately owned news services into one
government-controlled agency. Some pro-government and
independent newspapers and broadcasting stations have
recently been merged, ostensibly for reasons of cost and
efficiency but these mergers also allow closer government
supervision. Retired military officers have been installed by
the government in all newspapers and broadcasting stations
as building and safety inspectors but are generally believed
to be there to monitor news content.

Of course, the Korean government stressed that all these developments were strictly voluntary, instituted by the mass media
themselves. But there were enough scraps of evidence to contradict
this. First was the speed with which this major reformation was
achieved. The whole process took place within a matter of two to
three weeks, with the exception of the amalgamation of the news services into a single agency, which took a couple of months. Second,
such a major deprivation of property rights—for example, the Sam-
sung Industrial Group had to give up its Dongyang Broadcasting Corporation TV-radio network—just does not happen spontaneously. In
fact, according to an account in the *New York Times*, the newspaper
and broadcasting station owners were called to a meeting one day by
the dreaded Capital Garrison Command, and a colonel handed them
papers signing over their properties.

Even in the strictly controlled news columns, there were hints
that media permutations were anything but voluntary. One short
item in the once independent *Dong-A Ilbo* mentioned "the somber and
depressed mood" of the Korean Newspaper Association meeting that
"decided on such measures of restructuring." The *Dong-A Ilbo*, in an
editorial reviewing the nineteen-year history of its sister station,
which was also gobbled up by the official network, said obliquely that
"ten thousand emotions criss-crossed" on the occasion of its closing.
The government itself may have tipped off its heavy-handed involvement when it offered tax breaks to the affected newspapers.

Control of the Korean press has been achieved through various
other means. The newly passed press law stipulates that a news-

paper's registration (license) can be revoked if, among other reasons, it is found to "encourage or praise violence or other illegal acts disrupting public (social) order" repeatedly. Of course newspaper owners want to protect their properties and exercise self-censorship, which prevents publication of any items that are likely to run afoul of such a vague provision. Also, only "trustworthy" owners are in positions of power in mass media. For instance, the president of the newly merged wire service is Kim Sung-jin, a minister of public information under Park Chung-hee, and under Kim's leadership no reporting out of line with government thinking can be expected.

The government was shrewd enough to stop even indirect means of getting around the censorship. This was practiced in the 1970s by a few courageous newspapers. For example, they would print a series of "historical" articles on the NKVD's atrocities under Beria. Reading between the lines would inform the discerning reader about the brutalities perpetrated by the Korean CIA. How did the government handle that? By coopting bright and ambitious journalists from erstwhile "opposition" publications, who could deal with such passive resistance. A case in point is a former managing editor of *Dong-A Ilbo*, Lee Eung-hee, who is now the presidential press secretary. As a close friend of the current editor in chief of the paper, Lee sees to it that no unfavorable reporting on the Chun government ever gets printed.

Another method of control is to bind publishers and editors of private newspapers in a web of indebtedness to the government by giving their papers special loans from semiofficial banks and the media leaders honorary positions in quasi-official organizations. One of the foremost critics of the Park dictatorship, Cheon Kwan-woo, who had been persecuted for a long time, has recently been wooed into the chairmanship of the "central consultative committee of the national movement of reunification."

There are even worse places for the press than Korea, and one such place is Argentina. Over the past twenty-five years, Argentina has experienced cyclical changes between civilian and military governments. Since 1955 there have been six civilian and six military presidents. Beginning in 1969, violence mounted steadily, first from the left and then from the right, as groups with widely divergent political objectives struggled for dominance. To quote a 1981 State Department report:

> At the time the military took control of the state in 1976, the
> situation in Argentina had deteriorated sharply, courts and
> political leaders were intimidated, inflation approached 800
> percent, and many essential public services were disrupted.
> Terrorism had taken on broad dimension: bombings,
> robberies, kidnappings and assassinations for political
> reasons were common occurrences. Organized terrorist

groups on both sides of the political spectrum numbered
some 5,000–6,000 persons.... Maintaining the state of siege
imposed in 1974 by President Maria Estela Peron, the armed
forces closed congress, deposed the president, and replaced
all members of the supreme court. Elected state and local
government officials were replaced by military officers, and
political party activities, including the right of assembly,
were prohibited.... The security forces embarked on a
widespread campaign of violence aimed at terrorists as well
as those elements of society they considered subversive.
Many known or suspected terrorists, as well as many persons
with no subversive record, disappeared. Many others were
detained by the executive without any specific charge under
the state of siege powers of the constitution. In 1978
spokesmen for the government announced that the war on
terrorism had been won....

It is axiomatic that the press as a subsystem of the overall political system of a country either suffers or prospers with the larger unit.
It is to be expected that freedom of speech, the press, religion, and
assembly all have been severely circumscribed in Argentina since the
imposition of the state of siege in 1974. What was the situation of the
Argentine press in 1980? In that year, according to the 1981 State Department report, exercise of freedom of speech and assembly expanded, although political leaders still risk arrest if they overstep
"the uncertain and undefined bounds of permitted political activity
and statement."

The press is not legally subject to prior official censorship
except for moral content. However, the government-imposed
guidelines result in self-censorship. The Argentine
Publishers' Association, after its annual meeting in 1980,
issued a statement that "it is impossible to state that press
freedom exists in Argentina." In the past, journalists have
been among the Argentines who disappeared. Some are
currently under detention. The government has intervened
or confiscated a number of newspapers, notably *La Opinion.*
Nevertheless, newspapers actively criticize the government
in many areas and report the remarks of opposition
politicians. Coverage of such issues as human rights and the
disappearances increased during 1980. In August a
declaration signed by 180 prominent Argentines calling for
clarification of the whereabouts of disappeared persons was
published in a prominent daily newspaper. Most foreign
publications enter Argentina without censorship.

What about Third World countries on the left of the political
spectrum? Three examples will suffice. In Ethiopia, the Provisional
Military Government of Socialist Ethiopia, having taken power in

1974 by deposing Emperor Haile Selassie, has extended its control over nearly all elements of the society. According to the 1981 State Department report:

> Serious violations of individual rights and civil and political liberties continue to occur within Ethiopia.... The human rights situation was at its worst in 1977 and 1978, as the government killed perhaps 10,000 men, women and children, and imprisoned tens of thousands of others in the Red Terror, a campaign to eliminate urban opposition to the regime. Because the government has since consolidated its control over the urban centers of the country, the level of human rights abuses is now lower, although there is no legal protection against abuses.

The Ethiopian government's control over speech, media, nonreligious assemblies, trade unions, and other forms of expression is described by the State Department's report as "absolute and firmly enforced." The same report adds: "Political control is apparent in all forms of the media. Many journalists have been arrested for political reasons over the past several years. Some issues of foreign news magazines are banned. Books, both domestic and foreign, are censored.... In sum, no criticism of the government is allowed in any form, in any forum."

In Colonel Muammar Qaddafi's Socialist People's Libyan Arab Jamahiriya, press freedom exists in name only. According to the State Department's report, which in this case is based heavily on unofficial sources because of the absence of a U.S. mission in Libya, the government restricted basic civil and political freedoms during 1980. "Libyans are most circumspect about uttering dissident views toward the regime's policies.... The media are controlled rigorously, and newspapers do not print editorials."

A quarter of the globe away, Afghanistan has been torn by dissension and civil unrest since the April 1978 coup, which provided a pretext for the massive Soviet intervention by way of an occupation army in late December 1979. The Soviets then overthrew the existing government and installed a regime headed by Babrak Karmal. To return once more to the State Department's report:

> All Afghan media are controlled by the regime and its Soviet patrons, who exert tight control over content. The press, radio and television are used solely to convey and reflect official policy. No criticism is allowed. On the other hand, in Kabul and other cities shabnamas, or "night letters," circulate surreptitiously. The regime considers circulation of such night letters to be criminal acts subject to severe sanctions.

Is it possible to group Third World countries according to their degree of press freedom? Raymond D. Gastil's *Freedom in the World: Political Rights and Civil Liberties, 1979* provides a handy measure for that purpose. Table 18.1 is a modification of Gastil's "Ranking of Nations by Civil Liberties"; in our table, countries not belonging to the Third World and not independent are eliminated.[2] Civil liberties "include freedom of the press, the openness of public discussion, the existence of organizations separate from the government, an independent judiciary, and the absence of political imprisonment. Everything is in comparative terms. All nations fall short of perfection; on the other hand, perfect despotism would be hard to create or maintain. The sense of *degrees* of freedom that this approach produces is an important lesson in itself" (Gastil 1979, p. 5). A rating of (1) is most free and a rating of (7) is least free. "Instead of using absolute standards, standards are comparative—that is, most observers would be likely to judge states rated as (1) as freer than those rated (2), and so on" (ibid., p. 15). In order to bring the table up to date, an attempt was made to compare the table with the State Department's human rights report to the extent that this was possible.

A few observations on the table are in order. First, one is struck with the preponderance of Third World countries in scales 5 to 7, which indicates the lack of press as well as other freedoms. Seventy-one countries are in scales 5 to 7, whereas only 24 countries are in scales 1 to 3, and 18 countries are at the midpoint of 4. It should be pointed out that the table is not a sensitive enough instrument for differentiating fine degrees of the scope of freedom, say, between South Korea and Argentina, both of which fall in scale 5; as the earlier discussion in this chapter indicated, the South Korean press may be a little less constrained than the Argentine press. Generally speaking, Third World countries with a British colonial legacy, such as Barbados, India, Botswana, and Nigeria, seem to enjoy more press freedom than other countries. As footnotes to some countries show, the political situation in many Third World countries is so unstable that in the course of a year, a major redirection may happen on the political scene by way of coups and other political developments. Needless to say, political instability is not conducive to the flowering of press freedom.

As was shown in the earlier discussion of press freedom in several countries, there are many overt and subtle press restrictions. The following summary of restrictions or pressures, many of which are used consistently or intermittently by governments of Third World nations, is culled from a section of Merrill, Bryan, and Alisky's 1970 pioneering book on international communication and is elaborated to some extent.

TABLE 18.1
Ranking of Nations by Civil Liberties as of 1980

Most Free						Least Free
1	2	3	4	5	6	7
Barbados	Bahamas	Botswana	Bahrain	Argentina	Algeria	Afghanistan
Costa Rica	Dominican Republic	Colombia	Bangladesh	Bhutan	Burma	Angola
	Fiji	Dominica	Brazil	Bolivia[3]	Cameroon	Benin
	Gambia	Jamaica	Comoro Is.	Central African Republic[4]	Cape Verde Island	Burundi
	Honduras[1]	Nigeria	Cyprus	Chile	Chad	Congo
	India	Senegal	Djibouti	China (Taiwan)	Gabon	Equatorial Guinea
	Papua New Guinea	Sri Lanka	Ecuador	Egypt	Guinea-Bissau	Ethiopia
	Solomon Islands	Tonga	Ghana	El Salvador[5]	Haiti	Guinea
	Trinidad & Tobago	Turkey	Guyana	Grenada	Iraq	Iran[8]
	Venezuela	Upper Volta	Kenya	Indonesia	Jordan	Laos
	Western Samoa	Zimbabwe[2]	Kuwait	Ivory Coast	Libya	Malawi
			Lebanon	Korea (South)	Madagascar	Mozambique
			Malaysia	Lesotho	Mali	Somalia
			Mauritius	Liberia	Mauritania	Yemen (South)
			Mexico	Maldives	Niger	
			Morocco	Nepal	Oman	
			Peru	Nicaragua	Rwanda	
			Thailand	Pakistan	Sao Tome & Principe	
				Panama		

Paraguay
Philippines
Qatar
Seychelles
Sierra Leone
Singapore
Sudan
Surinam[6]
Swaziland
Tunisia
Uganda[7]
United Arab Emirates
Yemen (North)
Zambia

South Africa
Syria
Tanzania
Togo
Uruguay
Zaire

[1] Honduras, which was in scale 3 in 1979, has been moved up to scale 2 because of the end to military rule in 1980.

[2] Rhodesia, which was in scale 5 in 1979, has been moved up to scale 3 because of the improved political situation of the new country, Zimbabwe.

[3] Bolivia, which was in scale 3 in 1979, has been moved down to scale 5 because of a military coup in 1980.

[4] Central African Empire, which was in scale 7 in 1979, has been moved up to scale 5 because of the overthrow of Emperor Bokassa and the resulting improvement in civil liberties since September 1979.

[5] Grenada, which was in scale 3 in 1979, has been moved down to scale 5 because of a coup in March 1979.

[6] Surinam, which was in scale 2 in 1979, has been moved down to scale 5 because of a military coup in 1980.

[7] Uganda, which was in scale 7 in 1979, has been moved up to scale 5 because of the overthrow of Idi Amin and the resulting improvement in civil liberties since mid-1979.

[8] Iran, which was in scale 5 in 1979, has been moved down to scale 7 because of Islamic revolutionary excesses.

1. Legal pressures
   a. Constitutional provisions—e.g., Brazilian constitution
   b. Security laws—e.g., anti-Communist law of Korea
   c. Press laws—e.g., press law of Indonesia.
   d. Penal laws—e.g., criminal codes on libel, contempt of court
2. Economic and political pressures
   a. Bribes, subsidies, and special favors
   b. Control of newsprint
   c. Leverage of official advertising
   d. Control of bank loans
3. Secrecy
   a. Denial of access to government information—e.g., the Argentine press's inability to get a list of "disappeared persons"
   b. Ubiquity of press spokesmen as a means of news management
4. Direct pressures: prior restraints and force
   a. Licensing/registration
   b. Certification of bona-fide journalists
   c. Self-censorship based on broad guidelines
   d. Telephone system by which government agents tell editors what not to print
   e. Stationing of censors in news organizations
   f. Postpublication reprisals to "teach a lesson"
   g. Getting recalcitrant journalists fired
   h. Arrest, interrogation, and torture, often by "extralegal" security forces
   i. Bombings and other terror activities directed at organs and members of the press.
   j. Forced mergers or closings of media units
   k. Disappearances or killings of journalists by government-instigated goon squads

After this necessarily cursory consideration of freedom of the press in the Third World, comprising at least 113 countries, one is forced to look for explanations for a state of affairs in which most countries suffer from severe control of the press. It seems that politics, broadly speaking, emerges as the key variable. More specifically, different development or modernization models imposed on Third World nations either by their colonial experience or by their conscious adoption of models have different consequences for the press system, and hence for press freedom. Thus we find a relatively free press in British Comonwealth nations. The conscious adoption of the

Communist model by Ethiopia and Angola spells a controlled press system for those countries.

Frederick S. Siebert's (1952) two propositions seem to offer a needed explanation too. The first is: "The extent of the government control of the press depends on the nature of the relationship of the government to those subject to the government" (p. 9). If the relationship is basically an autocratic one (e.g., when one strong man's or one party's rule is perpetuated with everything else in that country subordinate to it), the press is likely to be controlled by the government. If the relationship is more or less democratic with competing parties and personalities vying for power, the press will be more free, reflecting the underlying pluralism of the political system. In other words, the political structure and the subsystem's autonomy, meaning more or less independently functioning judiciary, legislature, press, and other subsystems of a political system, seem to be more important predictors of the extent of press freedom than does the economic development profile.

Siebert's second proposition states: "The area of freedom contracts and the enforcement of restraints of the government increases as the stresses on the stability of the government and of the structure of the society increase." The Arab nations' lack of press freedom may be explained by the perennial state of war between the Arabs and Israel. A similar proposition might be that geographical proximity to a center of threat, actual or perceived, decreases the area of freedom. Since most Third World countries are politically and economically unstable, the press is bound to suffer from much control. Here one can conceptualize the drive for rapid development as a stress situation; the more a country is committed to quick development,[3] the more likely will mass media be used and manipulated by the government. The specter of "the revolution of rising frustration" is a source of constant stress to political systems in the Third World, which tend to turn to the politics of extremism, either communism or its antithesis, right-wing military dictatorships. Neither is conducive to the spirit of press freedom.

If one adds the personal idiosyncracies of some of the rulers of the Third World—the Idi Amins, Bokassas, and Qaddafis—to the already gloomy picture, things indeed look bleak. All the foregoing does not augur well for the future of the Third World as far as political democracy is concerned. It seems that most developing countries will be under developmental totalitarianism of one sort or another, with little room for democracy or the Western concept of a free press. But then, one hastens to add that even Western democracies will not tolerate system-destabilizing press activities when their very existence is threatened.

NOTES

1. In fact, the term Third World in itself represents a concession made to the concept of popular sovereignty that accords dignity to independent nations regardless of the degree of economic development. Various terminologies have been applied to these nations, starting in the nineteenth century with colonies being called the "white man's burden." Later they were called "backward nations." After 1945, for a time the term "underdeveloped nations" was in vogue, concurrently with "less developed nations." This later was dropped in favor of another term—"developing nations"—which in turn gave way to the current usage, the Third World nations.

2. Japan is also excluded, as are well-established Communist countries of the Third World such as Cuba, Vietnam, North Korea, China, Kampuchea, and Mongolia.

3. According to a recent *Washington Post* dispatch, one British adviser to the Ethiopian government said: "Ethiopia is compressing the history of Britain from the Norman conquest to the Industrial Revolution into one generation."

REFERENCES

Gastil, Raymond D. *Freedom in the World.* New York: Freedom House, 1979.

Merrill, John C., Carter R. Bryan, and Marvin Alisky. *The Foreign Press.* Baton Rouge: Louisiana State University Press, 1970.

Nam, Sunwoo, and Inhwan Oh. "Press Freedom: Function of Subsystem Autonomy, Antithesis of Development." *Journalism Quarterly* 53, no. 4 (Winter 1973): 744–50.

Siebert, Fred S. *Freedom of the Press in England, 1476–1776.* Urbana: University of Illinois Press, 1952.

Sommerlad, E. Lloyd. *The Press in Developing Countries.* Sydney, Australia: Sydney University Press, 1966.

Suparto, Ina. "Freedom of the Press in Indonesia during the 1970's." Master's thesis, University of Maryland, 1981.

U.S. State Department. *Country Reports on Human Rights Practices.* Washington, D.C.: 1981.

U.S. International Communication Agency. *The United States and the Debate on the World "Information Order."* Washington, D.C.: 1979.

Verghese, George. "Press Censorship under Indira Gandhi." In Philip C. Horton, ed., *The Third World and Press Freedom.* New York: Praeger, 1978.

Wei, Michael Ta Kung. "Freedom of Information as An International Problem." In Heinz-Dietrich Fischer and John C. Merrill, eds., *International Communication.* New York: Hastings House, 1970.

19. PRESS FREEDOM IN THE COMMUNIST WORLD

DONALD R. SHANOR

The concept of press freedom in the Communist world is part of the overall concept of freedom, which is to say, it is what the government agrees to grant to citizens in order to achieve certain ends. Despite the high-sounding phrases in constitutions from Beijing to East Berlin, freedom of the press, of assembly, and of expression are not rights that citizens enjoy but limited privileges that the regimes sometimes permit to further their own goals.

Nowhere has this been more dramatically demonstrated than in Poland in the closing days of 1981, when the mere decision by Solidarity trade unions to conduct a referendum to determine the degree of public support for the government was met with a military takeover by General Wojciech Jaruzelski.

Jaruzelski's government had clearly decided that getting citizen's opinions on its performance was contrary to its interests. But a few hundred miles away, in Hungary, another Communist government regularly commissions public opinion surveys and considers their results a valuable tool in guiding policy. To be sure, it does not encourage questions of the boldness of Solidarity's, and it suppresses findings that go beyond what it considers acceptable limits of criticism. But the Hungarian government's tolerance in this and other areas of public expression means that Hungarians enjoy the greatest access to free information of any people in the Communist world.

The Polish and Hungarian situations show that freedom of the press in the Communist world is determined by regimes, not by the press or its readers. They also show that there are wide variations throughout Communist-ruled countries on the freedoms permitted, and as Poles found after December 13, when Jaruzelski proclaimed his state of emergency, there are wide variations within a single country, depending on circumstances.

The usual pattern is to go from too much suppression, not only in liberties but in the political and economic fields, to what the regimes eventually consider too much freedom, which is then followed by further suppression. Sometimes there is a further period of officially tolerated and regulated freedom; Hungary is the best example. Sometimes, as in Czechoslovakia, the suppression seems to be permanent; and sometimes, as in the Soviet Union, there is yet to be a genuine period of liberalization. Poland had the freest press in the Communist world between August 1980, when Solidarity was born, and December 1981, when the military took over. Within hours, it had the most heavily censored and restricted: All but two newspapers were closed, telephone and other transmission lines were blocked, thousands of journalists were dismissed and hundreds were arrested, and television announcers were told to appear in military uniforms when reading the carefully censored government announcements that passed for news.

Poland had thus gone from the top of the press freedom scale to the bottom, overnight—as did Czechoslovakia thirteen years earlier, when they had a few weeks' interim of underground newspapers. In 1982, both nations shared the bottom position with countries like Albania and Romania, which never permitted press freedom; Cambodia and Laos, which lost it under Communist rule; and the Soviet Union, which experienced a literary thaw in the late 1950s but stopped it before it had much chance of influencing the nation's journalists. Hungary stood at the top of the scale—that is, apart from Yugoslavia, which in this chapter is not considered to be a member of the Communist system—and in between were nations like Cuba, East Germany, and China, where some flexibility was tolerated by the regimes from time to time and then usually taken back.

It could be said that a Western writer's bottom of the scale might be a Communist official's top. At crisis times, such as Poland's under the military regime, this view is doubtless true. But when regimes are not pressed back against the wall by economic or political problems, they tend to lift restrictions on the press, knowing that it can be a friend to authoritarian governments when properly handled. They know this from experience; they also believe it because it is contained in the ideology that all nations of the Communist system subscribe to—Marxism-Leninism.

Vladimir Ilyich Lenin understood the power of the press better than any other political leader of his era. He saw its power as an instrument of organizing a radical opposition under Czarist rule and as a tool for organizing an entire society under his own rule. Lenin's formula was simple: press freedom for our side as long as our enemies are in control; once *we* are in control, no press freedom for them. Lenin's successors took the formula one step further by abolishing freedom of the Communist press in a Communist society.

Lenin also saw the press as a positive force. "The principal thing, of course, is *propaganda* and *agitation* among all strata of the people," he wrote in 1902 in his treatise *What Is to Be Done?* in describing the need for a party newspaper. Propaganda and agitation, in the first stage, was against the regime, he wrote: "The press has long ago become a power in our country, otherwise the government would not spend tens of thousands of rubles to bribe it . . . [but] it is no novelty in autocratic Russia for the underground press to break through the wall of censorship and compel the legal and conservative press to speak openly of it." Only after the October revolution did the press turn into an instrument for stressing the positive. First, the opposing voices had to be eliminated, whether they were from the ranks of the bourgeoisie or radicals who differed with Lenin.

In his biography of Lenin, Leon Trotsky (1925), Lenin's closest lieutenant, described with approval how Lenin dealt with the press of the moderate wing of his party, the Mensheviks:

> He reveals the situation unmercifully exactly where they had expected that he would veil it. The Mensheviki had that experience more than once in the early periods of the revolution when the accusations of the harm to democracy had all their freshness. "Our newspapers are shut down." "Naturally! But unfortunately not yet all. Soon they will be shut down entirely." (*Stormy applause.*) "The dictatorship of the proletariat will put a complete end to this disgraceful sale of bourgeois opium." (*Stormy applause.*)

There probably was more stormy applause when Lenin moved against the entire nonsocialist press in a decree issued two days after the revolution in 1917. The measure, his government said, was only temporary and would be repealed "as soon as the new regime takes firm root." Under the decree, not only newspapers antagonistic to the

Bolsheviks but those differing only slightly on tactics or doctrine were shut down, including the ones published by Lenin's former collaborator, Georgi Plekhanov, and by Maxim Gorky, the writer now much honored in the Soviet Union. David Shub (1966) wrote in *Lenin: A Biography*: "Since that time, there have been no independent newspapers in Russia." The limited rights the liberals and socialists had enjoyed under the czars, he wrote, were denied to all by Lenin. The Bolsheviks' system of press monopoly and censorship eliminated not only the daily political press but those venerable organs of culture, literature, and ideas that had nurtured generations of Russian rebels. Their contributors had included Tolstoy, Dostoevsky, Turgenev, and many others in a line that went directly back to the Decembrists, the early-nineteenth-century counterparts of today's Soviet dissidents. "The freedom of speech for which generations of Russian revolutionaries had fought was completely destroyed within a matter of months," Shub wrote.

Soviet writers have long since dismissed both the Trotsky and Shub biographies of Lenin, but they do not dispute the central theme of Lenin's view of the press. To the Communist, it is the most natural thing in the world to ban the opposition press and censor faithful party organs, and they insist that actions such as these require no apology. This is so because press controls are based on principles of scientific socialism, not the mere caprice of authoritarian minds. Opposing views are not wanted; the party already has all the answers. The concept of the press acting as a forum for a range of ideas and policy suggestions that could be considered by the government is anathema. What is called pluralism in the West and is tolerated, if not always welcomed, by the government in power is called counterrevolution in the East and is punished.

Such views—and they have been expressed to the author over the years in dozens of interviews with Communist journalists and professors—are based firmly on Leninism, as their proponents usually stress.

But are the tactics for seizing power from the czars at the turn of the century the proper ones for trying to guide a nation and an international political system as they approach the year 2000? In *What Is to Be Done?* Lenin is writing about a strictly controlled party press system as "a most practical plan for immediate and all-around preparations for the uprising" he was planning. In other nations in the 1980s, media specialists, schools of journalism, and editors are concerned with a different kind of revolution: that of microchips and satellite communications. In the Soviet Union and its dependencies, students are still studying *What Is to Be Done?* and moving on to jobs as censors or journalists whose careers will be spent praising the system, at worst, or becoming frustrated trying to draw attention to its shortcomings, at best.

Sometimes, however, things get so bad in a Communist country that Leninism has to be forgotten for a time and the press freed of some of its shackles. China's Democracy Wall, Poland's sixteen months of Solidarity, and Czechoslovakia's 1968 Prague Spring were examples of such relaxations. How does it happen that a regime departs from the standard diet of headlines that praise and uplift, pictures that show workers and farmers producing record quotas, editorials that seldom admit a mistake?

Eduard Goldstuecker, one of the leaders of the 1968 reform movement in Czechoslovakia, once said that what got the press moving in his nation was the fact that the economy had ceased to move. Production was stagnating; there were shortages in the shops and unsold goods that nobody wanted in the warehouses. And yet the party and government refused to alter their orthodox plan. Popular discontent made it possible to relax censorship and let the journalists take the lead in pushing for economic reform. "To outsiders, it may seem that the whole [Prague Spring] movement was a result of ferment among the intellectuals," Goldstuecker said.

> This, however, is an optical illusion. They did play a big role.
> But objectively, it was only a secondary role, a catalyst to
> speed up the process. The great economic reforms simply
> couldn't be carried out without far-reaching democratization.
> This was the pressure of necessity. On top of this came the
> pressure of the intellectuals, who understandably wanted
> more freedom. (Shanor 1975)

As had happened in Poland in 1956 (and was to happen again in 1980), the Czech and Slovak censors simply decided not to do their work anymore, and to let journalists and editors test the limits of what they could write. In both the Polish and Czechoslovak cases, and in post-Mao China at the time of the Democracy Wall, press freedom was viewed as a lesser evil to the political or economic chaos it might be able to alleviate.

In Czechoslovakia, a liberal parliament followed up the de facto abolition of censorship with an amendment to the censorship law that abolished all prior "action taken by state agencies against freedom of speech and pictorial representation." In keeping with European legal traditions, as opposed to American First Amendment guarantees, however, even this most liberal of Communist censorship laws did not do away with the right of government to intervene *after* publication. The law made clear that the abolition of censorship "does not affect the powers of the state prosecutor and of the courts" to step in if necessary (Radio Free Europe Research 1968).

As it turned out, the intervention was carried out by the Soviet Union and Warsaw Pact armies less than two months after the June 28, 1968, passage of the censorship law. To say that the free press in Czechoslovakia caused the Soviet intervention, as some critics of the journalists' reform movement have, seems to be ignoring the many other factors that motivated the Soviet leadership, including the decline of party influence and concern about the border with West Germany. But it certainly was among the main causes. For this we have no less an authority than Gustav Husak, the Czechoslovak party leader and head of state.

Husak understood the power of the press, as Lenin did, from both the standpoint of the outsider trying to gain power and the insider trying to maintain it. In the 1950s, he had been imprisoned for "bourgeois nationalism," and as the Prague Spring approached, he had used the growing press freedom to demand his own rehabilitation and that of others unjustly convicted.

But, after the Soviet invasion, Husak became the leader of the "realists" chosen by the Russians to crack down on the press and other liberalized institutions. A month after being named party leader, in May 1969, Husak provided an unusually frank description of the dangers, from the Communist view, of press freedom, and of what could be done to curtail it. In 1968, he said, "Room was opened for the entrance into political life of anti-socialist forces ... [which] succeeded in seizing many important power-political instruments such as decisive influence in the press, radio and television, in some links of the Party, in mass organizations, and the like."

Husak was quite open about the effects of the decision by party liberals to abolish censorship in February 1968. He said that with the censors gone, it was possible for liberals in the mass communication media to exert their influence on the party, the government, and society. Husak indicated that some way might have been found to eliminate the censors and still retain control, a reference to imposing stricter party discipline on journalists and editors, almost all of whom were party members. But because of divisions in the leadership, these controls were not imposed, and the result was a current of what Husak called anti-Soviet, anti-Marxist, and liberalist views—and what the West called the re-creation of a free press.

Husak went through the ritual, blaming Western subversion and prewar bourgeois ideas for part of the situation, but admitted that most of the trouble was caused by good party members. He said these liberal forces operated legally, within party bodies, and occupied positions right up to the top. They were particularly influential in mass media, he said, and he accused them of manipulating audiences through the misuse of the concepts of freedom, democracy, and humanism. The result was disorientation of even loyal party members, a weakening of all the basic ideas of a socialist society—a revealing admission of how a leading Communist views the power of media. The liberals moved from this position of influence to an attempt to seize power, according to Husak, and it was at this point that the Soviet Union and neighboring Communist countries decided to invade, ending press freedom.

Husak, in assessing ways to overcome the political crisis that continued after the Soviet invasion, put stiffer controls on media in first place, just as he had given first place to media in his analysis of what had gone wrong in the country in the months before the invasion. He said the new party leadership had been able to take firmer control because it restored the party presence to the press, radio, and television, weeding out the liberals in the process. This meant the return of ideology rather than news or political values to decisions on what to print or broadcast.

Those journalists and editors willing to submit to this new form of censorship were able to keep their jobs, at least for a time. Those too strongly identified with the reform movement, or too resistant to party directives, were dismissed from their jobs and often lost their party membership at the same time.

Husak made it clear that these purges and controls were going to be a permanent feature of Czechoslovak political life, that the press and broadcast media were not going to be permitted to take their own course. Party officials and censors sent into every editorial room made sure of that. The media, Husak said, would be prevented from ever again working against the interests of the people and the state. He made it clear that the leadership would define those interests, and that journalists would return to the party's idea of their proper role— "our convinced assistants in responsible work."

It is unusual for Communist leaders to speak so directly of party weakness and the need to impose controls and fire journalists, whether or not the people like or understand it. Such frankness is brought out most often, as it was in Husak's case, by a crisis so grave that normal bureaucratic obfuscation simply will not suffice. Since that time, what both Soviet and Czechoslovak officials call "normalization" has proceeded to the point where it is no longer necessary to be as open as Husak was about the system of controls that keeps the press from telling the truth. But word of the system, in Czechoslovakia and other countries, gets out in other ways. One of the most important disclosures came about through the defection of a Polish censor in 1976, which made available to Western analysts detailed documents describing the Polish system of press controls.

The Polish documents, the first such complete account of censorship rules and processes to reach the West since the Smolensk archive of Soviet materials became available in 1945, were used by two Rand Corporation researchers, Jane Leftwich Curry and A. Ross Johnson (1980), as part of their study of the Polish media system.

They found that censorship was only one facet of an integrated system of control over what Polish citizens could read, view, or listen to, a system that began with personnel selection for media and included such details as the requirement that censors approve the text of a name card before it was legal to print it. The supervisory organ is the Central Committee Press Department, whose top official, a Central Committee secretary, reports to two Politburo members—one responsible for propaganda and ideology, the other for adjudicating appeals from censorship decisions.

The Party daily, *Trybuna Ludu*, the television evening news, and the Party theoretical journal, *Nowe Drogi*, are under the direct control of the Press Department. In addition, the department selects most key journalists for chief and departmental editorships in the leading papers and publishing houses and for management positions in the censorship office, even though the latter is nominally an organ of the government, not the party.

The authors stress that the Press Department is continually involved in directing media operating through officials, called "instructors," who are assigned to a group of media institutions dealing with the same subject or having similar political importance. The instructors work closely with editors and censors in these journals. They read and critique journals regularly, review censors' decisions, tell editors what topics ought to be covered, and rule on any proposed changes for journals. Press Department instructors are considered quite critical of the journals by the leading editors interviewed by Curry and Johnson.

The Press Department also supervises the censorship office in its responsibilities of passing on everything printed, broadcast, filmed, or performed in Poland. The censors work under two kinds of written guidance: directives covering general issues and "instruction notes" that are kept up-to-date as political developments change. In addition, they meet with supervisory personnel. They also trust their own judgment—judgment that is helped along with frequent refresher courses and a steady supply of evaluation materials.

Censors are assigned to editorial offices in teams of two or three, and are rotated periodically to minimize personal contact with editors. They read galleys of newspapers and magazines before the regular printing run begins, and if changes or deletions are called for, they meet with the editors to discuss them. Editors can appeal decisions, but for daily newspapers and the evening news, time pressures often dictate the elimination of the material pending a ruling.

Curry and Johnson conclude that censorship in Poland is neither uniform nor consistent. Individual censors often make independent judgments on nuances, and the strictness of censorship is normally inversely proportional to the size of the audience of a journal. Censorship practices for one journal may not be considered appropriate for another. Journalists and writers who have undergone strict censorship in the past are more carefully scrutinized than those who have been more cautious in following the party line. Having a high-ranking chief editor is no protection for journalists against censorship, since such editors are more likely to take risks and to submit more controversial articles. Mieczyslaw Rakowski (later Deputy Premier), chief editor of *Polityka*, a weekly intended for the intelligentsia, is the best example of the controversial editor who focuses censors' attention on his staff.

The press can also serve as a safety gate for controversial plays, films, and books. Censors may permit their production as evidence of cultural liberalism, but then allow only negative reviews to appear in the press, as in the case of Andrzej Wajda's film *Man of Marble*.

All of the cumbersome apparatus described by Curry and Johnson could not stop the momentum of a free press in Poland after August 1980. But with the imposition of military rule in December 1981, an even more severe system was instituted. As with Czechoslovakia, it will long be disputed how much of a role the outspoken Polish press had in precipitating the crackdown. But it is clear that its criticisms of both the Polish regime and Poland's relationship to the Soviet Union were causing deep concern in Warsaw and Moscow.

The Soviet Union was able to show the world once again that military might is the ultimate censor in its sphere of influence. But even its power is limited; it may extend into Poland, but it does not reach across its southern and eastern borders, those with China. And China, oblivious to Soviet objections, has been carrying out a media policy at variance with Soviet wishes for two decades—since the beginnings of the Sino-Soviet split. Under Mao Zedong, it reflected the turbulence of the Cultural Revolution and the Chinese campaigns for Third World allegiance. Since the death of Mao and the defeat of the "Gang of Four," it has undergone what one Chinese editor has described as "the first and the greatest liberation in journalism in more than 30 years" (Yu 1981). Both radical and liberal phases have been criticized by Moscow; and in both cases, the criticisms have been repudiated or ignored.

The Chinese have not eliminated party control or censorship, and as crackdowns on both domestic journalists and foreign correspondents showed in 1981, they have not instituted a consistent policy toward what may be printed and broadcast. In one case at the end of 1981, the party's main organ, the *People's Daily*, refused to reprint an attack on a film writer that had been carried by the military newspaper, the *Liberation Army Daily*. The party paper argued that writers should be encouraged instead of punished. The writer, Bai Hua, had written a script criticizing the party's role in permitting the tragedies of the Cultural Revolution. This in turn was attacked by party conservatives, using the more conservative military daily. The dispute between the two party papers was finally resolved when the writer criticized himself on the pages of the *Liberation Army Daily* (Lendvai 1981).

A description of the Chinese media system sounds very similar to that of the Polish; indeed, both are based on Leninist rules of strict control and service as propagandist of party policies. The Chinese Central Committee Department of Propaganda guides the media, and the *People's Daily* and the Xinhua News Agency are the official bearers of policy. Since the eclipse of the "Gang of Four," there is more regional autonomy in how the centrally directed news is used and interpreted, but the final arbiter remains the Department of Propaganda and the newspaper and news service directly under it.

Another change since the advent of the pragmatism of Deng Xiaoping has been more news in the papers, with shorter stories and livelier writing. Papers closed down by the "Gang of Four" have been reopened, and journalists are permitted to go a little beyond the official news releases in their search for information. "Both radio and television have been liberalized, although the liberalization is perhaps more evident in cultural than informational programs," F.T.C. Yu (1980) wrote in a study of Chinese media. "The strain of conformity upon those in the broadcast media, once unspeakably great, has been greatly eased." Writing about both print and broadcast journalists at the conclusion of an interview project in China that included 151 journalists, Yu said: "China, very definitely, is on the verge of making a breakthrough into a new journalistic epoch."

Yu found that the world "liberation" came up frequently in his interviews, and as a part of official policy, not merely a popular expression. The National Conference on Journalistic Work in 1979 had two items on its agenda: first, to review and draw conclusions on experience and liberate the thinking, and second, to shift the focus of propaganda and journalism to socialist economic reconstruction.

Yu heard a great deal of talk about "practice being the only criterion in attesting to the truth," about "truth in journalism," and about "the importance of reporting facts." But he warned against leaping to the conclusion that all Chinese journalists have become believers in objective reporting. Now as before, he wrote, news to the Chinese journalists means mainly the process of developing socialism and eventually communism, and it is in this context that they use news to aid the development of the country (Yu 1980).

It is clear that the Chinese have not abolished censorship and that the moves permitted by the party toward more liberal interpretations of what may be printed or broadcast are mild indeed by Western standards. But in one part of the media system the Chinese are far ahead of any other Communist nation in the important task of informing functionaries of party and government about what is going on in the world outside their nation, and what other nations' media are writing and broadcasting about them.

This task is carried out in every Communist system through information bulletins that are not circulated to the general public, as party newspapers are. The models are the different-colored TASS bulletins produced by the Soviet news agency since the 1930s, with the color indicating the degree of sensitivity and hence the restricted nature of its circulation. Green and blue TASS reports contain foreign news of general interest, without items considered anti-Soviet, and get relatively wide circulation, although exact figures are not known. The white TASS is more complete, and includes accounts of difficulties in Communist countries. The highly sensitive red TASS is limited to editors in chief, ministers and deputies, and high party, army, and security officials.

There is an even more select report about which little is known in the West, according to Paul Lendvai (1981), a specialist on Communist media. Lendvai writes that the compilation of special bulletins, containing full and unbiased information on world events, is possibly the most important task of the central news agencies in Communist countries. There is a special department, with its own editorial staff, solely for the production of various editions of the bulletins. It relies on news from Western news agencies, broadcasts, and the press. He notes that this is precisely the material that Communist news agencies seldom carry on their general news wires.

Lendvai says that Communist correspondents abroad also contribute to the special bulletins, filing reports with a degree of frankness not permitted in their usual work for party media. "Many people wonder what the numerous TASS and Novosti correspondents in the various Western capitals actually do when the Soviet press carries only sparse information about the countries concerned," he continues. "[They] work primarily for the confidential bulletins. They transmit not just news reports, but also summaries of important articles from the local press, often with a brief evaluation. At important press conferences with premiers or ministers, Soviet correspondents busily take notes or tape the entire session for the confidential bulletins."

Chinese reporting for the special bulletins is similar to that of Soviet and other East European journalists, but the circulation policy is dramatically different. Eleven million copies of Xinhua's *Reference News* are printed and circulated every day—"nearly twice as large as the circulation of the *People's Daily* and more than five times as large as the *New York Daily News*, the largest daily in the United States," Yu (1980) notes. "But this is an 'internal publication'; it's classified."

In five sample issues of *Reference News* and eight of the *People's Daily* examined in November 1979, Yu found that 39 percent of the news items in the restricted bulletin were about the United States, while only about 16 percent of the *People's Daily* foreign news stories concerned the United States.

Was this an indication that Chinese authorities are interested in getting information about the United States to higher cadres and not necessarily ordinary readers of *People's Daily*? Yu concludes: "I came away with the feeling that the main concern of those journalists who manage or handle the flow of information from or about the United States is not to raise the level of Chinese interest in the United States or to promote better understanding but to provide the population with sufficient and appropriate information that would be helpful in the advance of the policy of Four Modernizations and the development of the country."

Despite its liberalization program and its independence from Soviet control, then, China falls under Lendvai's definition of the media systems in Eastern Europe: institutions where "information is regarded as a privilege and access to uncensored news depends on rank and connections."

But, as Lendvai and others have suggested, there is one way in which the average citizen of a Communist country can obtain information of a quality equal to that of the highest-ranked foreign news bulletins. They can do this by turning on their radios and listening to the broadcasts of the Voice of America, BBC, Deutsche Welle, Radio Free Europe, Radio Liberty, and dozens of other uncensored organizations. Foreign broadcasts have two immediate effects on Communist media systems. They break the monopoly on what citizens are permitted to know, and they cause the domestic media to be more forthcoming in providing information that officials know their compatriots will acquire in any case from foreign broadcasts.

The benefit for the viewer is even greater—and the problem for the regime more difficult—when television as well as radio can be received. This is the case all around the Western borders of the Soviet Union and Eastern Europe. Estonians, in the north, can receive transmissions of Finnish television, across the Baltic, and since the broadcasts are in a related language, can understand them without too much difficulty. The other Baltic Soviet republics and Poland receive Sweden and Denmark, although here the language affinity is not present. Eighty percent of East Germans can be reached by West German television, and of course have no trouble with the language. German-speaking Czechs, Slovaks, and Hungarians living close enough to the border have a choice of two West German networks or an Austrian one. Romanians and Bulgarians can receive Yugoslav TV, broadcast in a language that is easy for Bulgarians and Romania's Slavic minorities to understand.

To switch the channel selector between East and West during the evening news broadcasts, as millions along the Western edge of the USSR and the Soviet bloc do every day, is a dramatic lesson in news values and censorship. But the difference would be even more noticeable if the Communist authorities were not forced to face the fact that many in their audiences have dual sources of information, and to permit some slight compensation for this fact.

An editor in one of the Soviet Baltic republics discussed this problem of dual sources with me in 1981.[1] The editor readily admitted that everyone with a TV set, himself included, watched Western television for news and entertainment, both of which, he said, were far superior to the Soviet offerings.

"This means that the job of editors in this republic is to recognize this state of affairs and take it into consideration when they put out their papers," he said. "The situation is much the same as that in East Berlin. Part of your job is to be familiar with what the Western stations have said, and then, using the party press from Moscow, write a combined story that explains the events or problems that your readers saw the night before." He explained that "it is a sort of local reply, or Moscow reply, but at the same time it takes cognizance of the outside source."

In these foreign broadcasts, television as well as radio, may lie the key to a more liberal information policy in the Communist-ruled part of the world. It is clear from the examples of the Soviet Union, China, and Poland that the regimes are not going to make information more readily available without outside pressure, unless it is for their own carefully controlled goals.

Yet, while they debate over obscure principles of Leninist control of information, the rest of the world is pushing ahead with the development of new information technology that will pose new threats to this control. Direct Broadcast Satellites, to name only one advance, could broaden the penetration of television signals from a narrow band on the periphery of the Soviet bloc to the entire Soviet—and Chinese—land mass. That is doubtless why Communist countries are so opposed to its unrestricted use.

Perhaps they will shift some of these efforts in time and welcome the flow of information and ideas as a valuable contribution to building their societies. The Chinese, to a limited extent, have already done so.

NOTES

1. Author's interview with an editor who does not wish to be identified.

REFERENCES

Curry, Jane Leftwich, and A. Ross Johnson. *The Media and Intra-Elite Communication in Poland, Summary Report, and the System of Censorship.* Santa Monica: Rand, 1980.

Information Bulletin of the Central Committee of the Communist Party of Czechoslovakia. Prague: June 1969.

Interview with Donald R. Shanor, 1968. Quoted in Shanor, *Soviet Europe.* New York: Harper & Row, 1975.

Lendvai, Paul. *The Bureaucracy of Truth.* London: Burnett, 1981.

Lenin, Vladimir Ilyich. *What Is to be Done?* Moscow: Foreign Languages Publishing, n.d.

New York Times, December 29, 1981.

Radio Free Europe, Research #40, 1968.

Shanor, D. R. *Soviet Europe.* New York: Harper & Row, 1975.

Shub, David. *Lenin: A Biography.* Harmondsworth, England: Penguin, 1966.

Trotsky, Leon. *Lenin.* New York: Blue Ribbon Books, 1925.

Yu, Frederick T. C. *Chinese Knowledge of the United States as Reflected in Mass Communication.* Washington, D.C.: USICA, 1980.

INDEX

ABOUT THE
AUTHORS AND
EDITORS

Donald R. Browne is a professor of speech-communication at the University of Minnesota. His major area of scholarly activity is comparative and international broadcasting, and he has written many articles and book chapters, as well as a monograph and a book, on these subjects. Dr. Browne's research activities have taken him abroad numerous times, and he has had extended residence in West Germany, England, Tunisia, Guinea, and Lebanon.

Anju Grover Chaudhary is an assistant professor in the Department of Journalism at Howard University, Washington, D.C., where she teaches courses in comparative journalism and fundamentals of journalism. She has been a freelance writer and editor, and was an editorial assistant of *Design* magazine in India. She is the author of articles in a number of periodicals in the field of comparative journalism.

Amde-Michael Habte is an associate professor and chairman of the Department of Mass Communications at St. Cloud State University, Minnesota. A native Ethiopian, he holds a Ph.D. degree in mass communication from the University of Minnesota. He has traveled extensively in Africa, Asia, Europe, and Latin America and has represented Ethiopia in several International conferences including the Union of Radio and Television Organizations of Africa and the Frequency Allocation Board of the International Telecommunications Union. He was director of international radio in the Ministry of Information of Ethiopia and was responsible for planning and establishing educational broadcasting in his native country.

Hanno Hardt is John F. Murray professor of journalism at the University of Iowa where he teaches courses in comparative communication, focusing on the history of intellectual and professional traditions. His latest book is *Social Theories of the Press, Early German and American Perspectives*. He has been a reporter and editor in Germany and the United States. He holds M.A. and Ph.D. degrees from Southern Illinois University.

Milton Hollstein has been a professor of journalism and mass communication at the University of Utah for twenty-one years, and for ten of those years chairman of the department. Dr. Hollstein has been a reporter and copyeditor for a number of newspapers including the *Salt Lake Tribune, Deseret News, National Observer, Washington Post, Los Angeles Times,* and the European edition of *Stars and Stripes.* He has researched media in eighteen European countries in recent years and was director of the Northwest Interinstitutional Council on Study Abroad programs in Cologne, Germany, in 1979.

Mark Hopkins is a correspondent for the Voice of America in Peking, China. He has also been security affairs correspondent in Washington, D.C., and bureau chief for VOA in Munich and Belgrade. He has studied at the University of Wisconsin Russian Studies program, the University of Leningrad, and the Belgrade Institute of Journalism. He is author of *Mass Media in the Soviet Union* and *Russia's Underground Press.* He was editor of *Soviet Press in Translation* at the University of Wisconsin.

John J. Karch is a foreign service officer (counselor) with the U.S. Information Agency. While working on this book, Dr. Karch was professor of communication, information and the media, and Eastern Europe at the National War College, Washington, D.C.

Paul Lendvai is editor in chief of *Europaeische Rundschau,* a quarterly publication of politics, economics, and contemporary history. He also does programs for Austrian radio and television. A Hungarian by birth, he was Berlin correspondent for the Hungarian news agency, MTI, until 1956, when he chose to cut his ties with his native country. He is the author of *The Bureaucracy of Truth: How Communist Governments Manage the News.*

L. John Martin is a professor of journalism at the University of Maryland where he teaches courses in international communication, public opinon, and research methods in mass communication. A former newsman and foreign correspondent, he was a research administrator in the U.S. Information Agency during the 1960s. Dr. Martin is the author and editor of books and articles on international propaganda and cross-cultural and political communication, editor of the *International Communication Bulletin,* and associate editor of the *Journalism Quarterly.* He has lived and traveled extensively in Europe, Asia, and Africa.

John C. Merrill is a professor and director of the School of Journalism at Louisiana State University and has taught at the Universities of Maryland and Missouri and in several other American universities. Dr. Merrill has written and edited a dozen books on journalism, about half of them in international communication. He has lectured in some thirty countries and has traveled extensively worldwide.

Rilla Dean Mills is an associate professor of communication at California State University, Fullerton, teaching courses in writing, theory of communication, and the Communist media. He has also taught at the Universities of Mississippi and Illinois. From 1969 to 1972, Dr. Mills was chief of the Moscow bureau of the *Baltimore Sun*. Later, he served as Washington correspondent, covering the State Department and the Supreme Court for the same paper.

Sunwoo Nam is a native Korean who teaches comparative journalism in the College of Journalism at the University of Maryland. Dr. Nam has also taught at the University of Hawaii and at Norfolk State University, Virginia. He worked for *Dong-A Ilbo* (*Oriental Daily News*) in Korea for five years before coming to the United States for graduate degrees in political science and journalism from Stanford and a Ph.D. in mass communication from the University of Wisconsin. He is the author of articles and book chapters on international communication and law of mass communication.

Munir K. Nasser is an assistant professor of journalism and mass communication at the University of the Pacific in Stockton, California. He has also taught at the Universities of Iowa and Birzeit, near Jerusalem. A native of Palestine, he has worked for newspapers and radio stations in Jerusalem, Cairo, and Amman. He is author of *Press, Politics, and Power: Egypt's Heikal and Al-Ahram* and of a number of articles on Third World media. His Ph.D. in journalism is from the University of Missouri.

Kuldip R. Rampal is an assistant professor of journalism at Central Missouri State University where he teaches international communication, news writing and editing. A native of India, he received his Ph.D. from the University of Missouri School of Journalism. Before coming to the United States, he was a reporter for the *Indian Express* in New Delhi. He has also worked for American community newspapers. He is the author of a number of articles on Third World media.

Klaus Schoenbach teaches at the University of Muenster in West Germany. He has also taught at the University of Mannheim, in the Department of Communication at Cleveland State University, and at Indiana University. He received his doctorate at the University of Mainz. He is author of *Trennung von Nachricht und Meinung*

(*Separating News from Opinion*) and specializes in political communication, local news coverage, and content analysis.

Henry F. Schulte is a professor and former dean of the School of Public Communication, Syracuse University. A former reporter and editor, he was UPI correspondent in London and manager of its office in Madrid, Spain. Dr. Schulte teaches international communication, reporting, and communication history.

Donald R. Shanor is a professor and director of the international division at Columbia University's Graduate School of Journalism. Before joining the faculty in 1971, he was a *Chicago Daily News* correspondent in Eastern Europe, Germany, and the Middle East; a UPI deputy foreign editor in New York; and a UPI correspondent in London and Frankfurt, Germany. He is the author of *The Soviet Triangle*.

Paul S. Underwood is a professor of journalism at Ohio State University. He formerly worked for the *Cincinnati Enquirer*, the Associated Press, and the *New York Times*. From 1958 to 1964 he was *New York Times* correspondent in Eastern Europe.

Francisco J. Vasquez is an assistant professor of journalism at Temple University where he teaches international communication, research methodology, and communication theory. Before coming to the United States, he was a television reporter in his native Chile.

Osmo A. Wiio is a professor and chairman of the Department of Communication at the University of Helsinki, Finland. He has also been a professor of economics and director of the Institute of Business Economics. From 1974 to 1977, Dr. Wiio was a member of the board of directors of the International Communication Association. He is author of some thirty books and numerous articles and is a former member of the Finnish parliament.